To Corey
God loves you
Val D. Harvey

Seize the Day
WITH
Yahweh

A Book of 366
DAILY DEVOTIONALS
Based on God's Name

JIM AND VAL HARVEY

WESTBOW
PRESS®
A DIVISION OF THOMAS NELSON
& ZONDERVAN

Copyright © 2015 Jim and Val Harvey.

All rights reserved. No part of this book may be used or reproduced by any means, graphic, electronic, or mechanical, including photocopying, recording, taping or by any information storage retrieval system without the written permission of the author except in the case of brief quotations embodied in critical articles and reviews.

WestBow Press books may be ordered through booksellers or by contacting:

WestBow Press
A Division of Thomas Nelson & Zondervan
1663 Liberty Drive
Bloomington, IN 47403
www.westbowpress.com
1 (866) 928-1240

Because of the dynamic nature of the Internet, any web addresses or links contained in this book may have changed since publication and may no longer be valid. The views expressed in this work are solely those of the author and do not necessarily reflect the views of the publisher, and the publisher hereby disclaims any responsibility for them.

Any people depicted in stock imagery provided by Thinkstock are models, and such images are being used for illustrative purposes only. Certain stock imagery © Thinkstock.

ISBN: 978-1-5127-1628-3 (sc)
ISBN: 978-1-5127-1627-6 (hc)
ISBN: 978-1-5127-1626-9 (e)

Library of Congress Control Number: 2015916998

Print information available on the last page.

WestBow Press rev. date: 10/30/2015

This book is dedicated to all those who taught us the value of beginning every day with a quiet time of Bible study, meditation, and prayer.

Other books by Jim and Val Harvey

What a Difference a Name Makes

Who Changed God's Name?

God's Little Things

Lord, Teach Us to Pray

Helping Christians Discover Their Gifts for Ministry

Study Helps for *Growing Deeper in the Christian Life*
(A five volume study series by Charles Swindoll)

Introduction

Welcome to a year long journey of discovery—one that may transform your way of thinking about God, yourself, and your life experiences.

The term *seize the day* may not be familiar to you, but it expresses a challenge of upmost significance. These three words translate the Latin terms ***carpe diem***, whose meaning is: seize the day, in the sense of making the most of each day. The purpose of these daily devotionals is to enable the reader to gain the utmost value from every day for an entire year. You may well ask how this is possible. The answer is found in the biblical term for God's name—Yahweh.

Yahweh (pronounced YAH-way) is God's preferred name—the sacred name He revealed to His chosen servant Moses in a most unusual encounter—as Moses stood before a burning bush in the desert. God told Moses to lead His people out of their long bondage in Egypt, where they had been enslaved for several hundred years. "Then Moses asked God, 'If I go to the Israelites and say to them: The God of your fathers has sent me to you, and they ask me, "What is His name?" what should I tell them?' God replied to Moses, "I AM WHO I AM. This is what you are to say to the Israelites: I AM has sent me to you." God also said to Moses, "Say to the Israelites: **Yahweh,** the God of your fathers, the God of Abraham, the God of Isaac, and the God of Jacob, has sent me to you. **This is My name forever; this is how I am to be remembered in every generation."** (Read Exodus 3: 1-15.)

Notice again these very important words, **"Yahweh… is My name forever; this is how I am to be remembered in every generation."** Adding to the gravity of this name is the fact that the term ***Yahweh*** is the most frequently occurring noun in the entire Old Testament—some 6,828 times!

But even more noteworthy than the word itself is its meaning. This Hebrew word comes from a root meaning "to be." **Thus *Yahweh*, as God told Moses, means "I AM."** By this special name, God was revealing His very nature to Moses, and to us. As Moses considered the overwhelming task of leading millions of Hebrews out of their bondage to the powerful forces of Pharaoh in Egypt, God was assuring him—I AM whatever you need in order to be all I ask you to be and to do all I send you to accomplish.

Sure enough, in spite of all of Moses' personal inadequacies for such a monumental task, Yahweh proved Himself to be all Moses needed. **Yahweh** is God's covenant name; His name to validate all His promises.

This same all sufficient divine resource is available to every believer today! Yahweh is the same yesterday, today, and forever. He says to each of us, I AM all you need to be and do all I have planned for you.

We can literally seize—make the most of—every day by learning to claim all the strength, guidance, wisdom, and power provided to us by Yahweh.

In these devotionals each day's scripture text comes from the ***Holman Christian Standard Bible***. Other translations may use the term ***LORD*** in place of **Yahweh**, but **Yahweh** is the more accurate translation from the Hebrew and Greek text. While ***Lord*** is an English word meaning "sovereign one," ***Yahweh*** is the Hebrew term which means "I AM."

These devotionals include Scriptures from every book of the Bible.

Format

The format followed for each day's devotional is:

Yahweh in the Word —the actual Scripture text with some helpful explanation.

Yahweh in Your Walk —practical applications through stories and personal experiences.

Yahweh in Your Worship—suggested ways of expressing yourself to Yahweh in prayer.

As you read the New Testament references, you will also need to understand that the name *Jesus* is a Greek form of the Hebrew name *Yeshua* (ya-SHU-ah) meaning "Yahweh is salvation." You may recall that when an angel appeared to Joseph and told him about Mary's condition, he said, "She will give birth to a son, and you are to name Him Jesus (Yeshua), because He will save His people from their sins" (Matthew 1:21).

Now begin the journey with us—a daily adventure of the highest calling and the most life altering experiences—*carpe diem*—seizing every day with Yahweh as your faithful companion, guide, and unfailing resource. This walk will take you to every book of the Bible.

January 1

A New Beginning for Me

Yahweh in the Word

> *"A son was born to Seth also, and he named him Enosh. At that time people began to call on the name of Yahweh" (Genesis 4:26).*

Seth was one of the sons of Adam and Eve, thus Enosh was their grandson. The name Enosh literally means "humanity." In one sense, Enosh's birth meant a new and better beginning for fallen humanity. One indication of this improved era is the fact that people, for the first time, began calling on God by His name Yahweh.

Yahweh in Your Walk

Today marks a new beginning for you—the first day of a new year. We do not know what this period of time will mean for us. However, **we can be assured that if we are serious about earnestly and faithfully calling upon Yahweh as our Savior and Lord, this may well be our best year thus far.**

To "call on the name of Yahweh" means to express ourselves to Him in prayer—in other words, by faith we tell Him our thoughts, either orally or silently. We may call on Him to offer praise or thanksgiving for some special blessing. The call may be in the form of some request for yourself or others. Regardless of the nature of this call, we may be certain that He hears and answers.

Listen to this amazing promise Yahweh made to the prophet Jeremiah: "The LORD who made the earth, the LORD who forms it to establish it, Yahweh is His name, says this: Call to Me and I will answer you and tell you great and incomprehensible things you do not know" (Jeremiah 33:2-3). Although these words were directed to Jeremiah, Yahweh's promise to hear and answer prayer can apply to all who call upon Him sincerely.

Some believers keep a prayer journal in which they record the date of specific requests, and then add the date when the answer appears. Perhaps this would be a good discipline for you as you make a new beginning this new year. **Seize this day by starting a new adventure in prayer.**

Yahweh in Your Worship

Gracious Yahweh, thank You for revealing Yourself to me as the One who is "I AM." Today I worship You and claim a new beginning of learning who You are and all You desire for me. I know You hear and answer me according to what You know is best. My heartfelt prayer is that You will be glorified through me throughout this New Year. I begin this journey by offering myself and all I possess to Your control. My trust is in You for the strength to be a faithful steward every day. Thank You for promising to be with me and to guide me. Use me as Your witness that others may know more about who You are and all You want to be to us. May Your kingdom come and Your will be done through me this year.

January 2

Yahweh Will Provide for Me

Yahweh in the Word

> *"And Abraham named that place, The Lord (Yahweh) Will Provide, so today it is said: "It will be provided on the LORD's mountain" (Genesis 22:14).*

Here is the remarkable account of God telling Abraham to sacrifice Isaac his son as a burnt offering. Abraham revealed his trust in God by preparing an altar for this act of obedience. However, just as this father was about to slay his only son, Yahweh intervened and provided a ram to take Isaac's place. Subsequently, Abraham named that altar "Yahweh Yireh," (pronounced YAH-way YI-rah) meaning "Yahweh will provide." Many years later, this was the same place where Jesus died on the cross—Yahweh's ultimate provision for our sin.

Yahweh in Your Walk

Yahweh Yireh is one of 12 Old Testament terms that reveal to us what Yahweh wants us to discover about Him. (**We will begin each month with a devotional based on one of these twelve Yahweh combinations.**) Abraham learned to trust Yahweh to always provide whatever he needed. We must, by faith, embrace this same amazing truth. All we actually need—all the time—He will provide.

A friend once asked me, "Do you know what single verse in the Bible best summarizes the entire message of the Bible?" When I failed to respond correctly, he quoted these words from the apostle Paul, "My God will supply all your needs according to His riches in glory in Christ Jesus" (Philippians 4:19). Good answer. Yahweh is the ultimate Provider of all we need and He faithfully makes these provisions available to all His people.

Our English word ***provide*** comes from two Latin terms meaning "to see in advance." **Yahweh sees what we need far in advance and makes certain that what we need is there when we need it.** How foolish for us to be anxious about having our needs met. We can safely trust in Him to provide for us. One word of caution: Just because we want something doesn't mean we need it; **there is a basic difference between need and greed.** We must learn to be content with His supply for our needs.

As you begin this new day, refuse to worry about how you will manage to provide for your needs. Rather, make the choice to trust Yahweh Yireh. He is faithful.

Yahweh in Your Worship

Thank you faithful Yahweh Yireh for loving me so much that You promise to meet all my needs out of Your abundant riches in Christ Jesus. I choose to seize this day with the assurance of Your care. When I am tempted to become anxious, remind me of these precious truths. I worship You with sincere praise and gratitude. Help me continue in this spirit of worship throughout this new day.

January 3

Yahweh Provides Forgiveness for Me for the Past

Yahweh in the Word

> *"My soul, praise Yahweh and all that is within me, praise His holy name. My soul, praise the LORD, and do not forget all His benefits. He forgives all your sin" (Psalm 103:1-3a).*

Yesterday we were introduced to Yahweh Yireh, the One who provides all we need. Today let's consider His provision for our past—the need for forgiveness. David probably wrote Psalm 103. He knew from experience the importance of being forgiven. Thus the first provision of Yahweh that David celebrates here is "He forgives all your sin."

Yahweh in Your Walk

We sinners have one need in common—the need for God's forgiveness for our sins. Our past is littered with sinful thoughts and actions. All our sins are expressions of rebellion against God. We have often chosen our way rather than His. And we can never earn Yahweh's forgiveness, no matter how much good we may do—good deeds in the present cannot undo or cover over bad deeds from the past.

Don Harmon was a new convert in our church. His past was one of overt sins. He said to me, "I turned my back on God so often that He must have forgotten what my face looked like!" But when Don turned to Jesus in repentance and faith, his new life was reflected in the glow of his face. He was so relieved of his feelings of guilt. When I assured Don that Jesus paid his sin debt in full, his heart was flooded with peace and joy—the joy of salvation. Several years later Don was diagnosed with terminal cancer. His wife Shirley stayed faithfully by his bedside as he walked through the valley of the shadow of death. However, he never lost his peace with God.

Yahweh has given a simple solution to our need of His forgiveness. Remember this promise: "If we confess our sins, He is faithful and righteous to forgive us our sins and to cleanse us from all unrighteousness" (1 John 1:9). Yahweh can offer this essential provision because the Lord Jesus paid our sin debt when He, who had no sin, died on the cross, taking our place.

Seize this day as a new opportunity to walk with Yahweh by confessing every known sin and claiming the pardon and cleansing He provides. Do not allow Satan to deceive you into thinking your sins are too great and you are too unworthy to be forgiven. **Take God at His Word as you thank Him for His mercy and grace.**

Yahweh in Your Worship

Gracious Yahweh I humble myself before Your throne of grace, confessing that I have sinned against You. Thank You for providing forgiveness for every sin of mine. I believe Your promise of forgiveness and now claim Your strength to resist temptation this day. Use me as an effective witness of Your liberating forgiveness. Help me be a good steward of this good news. I want others to know the peace that passes all understanding—the peace of being forgiven, cleansed and fully restored to fellowship with You.

January 4

Yahweh Provides Me with Help for the Present

Yahweh in the Word

> *"I, Yahweh, am the first, and with the last—I am He… Do not fear for I am with you; do not be afraid, for I am your God. I will strengthen you; I will help you; I will hold on to you with My righteous right hand" (Isaiah 41:4, 10).*

Today we continue learning about Yahweh Yireh ("I AM the One who provides for all you need.") Just as He provides forgiveness for the sins of our past, He promises to provide all the help we need for the present. Notice from this passage the five provisions He makes every day: "I am with you; I am your God; I will strengthen you; I will help you; I will hold on to you with My righteous right hand."

Yahweh in Your Walk

Many years ago, I faced a very challenging opportunity, one that caused me great fear because I felt totally inadequate for the task before me. I prayed earnestly for the Lord to guide me to make the right decision. One morning I simply opened my Bible and began reading. Without any plan in mind, I started with Isaiah 41:1. As I came to verse 10, it seemed as though Yahweh was speaking directly to me. These inspired words brought great comfort and became a personal promise that I have claimed many times since.

Notice the reference to "right hand" (v. 10). I decided to memorize the five promises of this verse by using the five digits of my right hand. An example of the practical benefit of this is that often during the night when I awaken with some feelings of anxiety, I will hold up my hand and affirm these five promises from the fingers and thumb of my right hand: "I am with you… I am your God… I will strengthen you… I will help you… I will hold on to you with My righteous right hand." This simple discipline has often calmed my fears and enabled me to sleep peacefully.

The hand illustration also is an easy way of sharing these promises with others.

Try seizing this day by looking at your right hand as you repeat these five helpful promises. Memorize these words; claim them every time you feel inadequate for any present situation. Ask Yahweh to give you an opportunity to share these truths with others, today and often.

Yahweh in Your Worship

Thank You, Yahweh, that You are the very present help I need for every challenge I will face today. Forgive me when I have doubted Your presence with me. I celebrate the assurance that You are not only present but also working Your will and purpose in me every moment. Help me be more sensitive to Your guidance as I make decisions today. Teach me to trust You more as I seek to walk by faith, not by sight. My desire is to be Your missionary wherever I go today; use me to boldly declare the truth about Your love for all persons, and help me be an example of that love for others.

January 5

Yahweh Provides Me with Hope for the Future

Yahweh in the Word

> This is what Yahweh says, "I know the plans I have for you… plans for your welfare, not for disaster, to give you a future and a hope. You will call to Me and come and pray to Me, and I will listen to you. You will seek Me and find Me when you search for Me with all your heart. I will be found by you" (Jeremiah 29:11-13).

Yahweh Yireh is the One who provides for all our needs in the past, present, and future. These words were first spoken through the prophet Jeremiah to Yahweh's people when they were exiled in Babylon. They were hundreds of miles from their homeland, in bondage to a foreign empire. The Lord offered these wonderful promises to give His people hope for their future. Yahweh's words probably seemed unrealistic to these exiles yet all He promised was done.

Yahweh in Your Walk

My friend was facing the possibility of losing his job. His wife was also threatening to take his children and leave. As I sought to console him, he said, "My future looks rather dark, however, I have claimed God's promise to supply all my needs. There is hope because my future is in His hands." **By exercising faith in Yahweh's plans for us—plans that are good and for our welfare, we can rise above dark clouds of trouble and see a future filled with hope**. Consider these words of confidence in Yahweh Yireh:

> My feeble hope in miracles had waned,
> My faith that He would soon provide was strained,
> Then, prompted by His Spirit, my heart cried,
> **Yahweh Yireh**! My Savior will provide.
> My needs were great but greater than my need
> Was He—**Yahweh Yireh**, so quick to heed
> And help, to hold, to hide me from the storm
> And shelter through the darkest night till morn.   Charles U. Wagner

You may want to copy these comforting words and post them where you can see them often. And why not send another copy to a friend who may need to hear these truths.

Yahweh in Your Worship

Yes, Yahweh Yireh, I do believe that You are providing for my future. I celebrate this blessed hope and praise You that You are faithful to always provide all I need in order for me to become all You want me to be—thank You. Help me remember that the future is always as bright as Your promises. You know all about my future; thank You for being there for me. I rest in the assurance of Your will always being best for me. I ask You to bring someone to me today who needs to hear these precious truths. Enable me to be bold in sharing the words of Jeremiah in today's text with them. How comforting to know that You promise to give us a blessed future.

January 6

Yahweh Is Faithful to Me

Yahweh in the Word

> *"Praise Yahweh, all nations! Glorify Him, all peoples! For His faithful love to us is great; Yahweh's faithfulness endures forever. Hallelujah!" (Psalm 117:1-2).*

Palm 117 is the shortest of all the psalms. And yet these brief words communicate a tremendous truth that will last throughout all the ages of time. Yahweh's faithful love will endure forever. The writer of this chapter responds to this glorious fact in one beautiful word—"Hallelujah!" **Hallel** is the Hebrew word for praise, and **Jah** is a contracted form of Yahweh. Combine them with a connecting letter and we have Hallel-u-jah, meaning "praise Yahweh." Certainly Yahweh deserves all our praise for being forever faithful to His people.

Yahweh in Your Walk

Abraham Lincoln's Gettysburg Address contains fewer than 300 words, which indicates that messages do not have to be long to be impressive and memorable. For example the writer of the 117th Psalm used just 17 Hebrew words to declare a most significant fact: Yahweh loves all persons with a love that will remain unchanged forever!

Think about what this means to you personally as you walk through this and every day. **When the Bible says that Yahweh loves us, it means He is on our side; He is for us.** We know He is for us because He created this good earth and all its wonders and beauties—**for us.** Moreover, He sent His Son, our Lord Jesus, to die on a cross—**for us**. He also raised Him from the dead and seated Him in heaven, where He intercedes—**for us**. Then the Holy Spirit was sent—**for us.** The Lord Jesus is now preparing a place in heaven—**for us**. And some day He will return to this earth—**for us! Is there any doubt that Yahweh loves us and is always for us?**

So, you can walk through this day with the full assurance of Yahweh's faithful love—for you. Regardless of what happens, His love is greater than all your problems, all your shortcomings and failures, all your doubts and fears. Just remember the shortest psalm and its eternal truth.

As a practical application of these truths about love, make certain that other members of your family, friendships, church fellowship, and total strangers know that you are for them—you love them with the unconditional love of Yahweh. Refuse to allow barriers of race, social class, sexual orientation, and religious preference to qualify your love for others. **Be for everyone!**

Yahweh in Your Worship

Faithful Yahweh, I thank You for loving me and all persons with a love that lasts forever, and is unchanging. Today, I choose to seize opportunities to express praise to You. I join the heavenly host in saying: Hallelujah! You alone are worthy of all such praise, honor, and exaltation. Assist me as I attempt to worship You appropriately. Know that my heartfelt desire is to worship You in spirit and in truth—continually. Make me aware of those to whom You would send me with these life-changing truths. Speak to them through me of Your amazing, unchanging love for all.

January 7

Yahweh's Word to Me Remains Forever

Yahweh in the Word

> "The grass withers, the flowers fade when the breath of Yahweh blows on them; indeed, the people are grass. The grass withers, the flowers fade, but the word of our God remains forever" (Isaiah 40:7-8).

These words of comfort came to Yahweh's people as they faced exile to Babylon from their homeland in Palestine. Yahweh compared people (perhaps the Babylonians) to grass and flowers, which are very fragile and temporary. In contrast stands the "word of our God" which endures forever. His words of promise for the future gave them hope beyond their present loss.

Yahweh in Your Walk

An old hymn has these words of prayer to Yahweh, "Change and decay in all around I see. O Thou who changest not abide with me." Surely, in this world of constant change we need a solid, changeless foundation on which we can build our hopes. Yahweh provides such security in His Word that "remains forever."

Hobby Lobby is a popular craft store in our area. The family who began this store is serious about the Bible. They are establishing a Bible museum where rare books and manuscripts concerning this book will be displayed. Steve Green, the president of this company, has said, "We are interested in encouraging people to consider what the Bible has to say. Its incredible story needs to be told."

All of these 366 devotionals focus on some text from the Bible regarding Yahweh, the Bible's author. As you read these sacred, inspired Bible texts each day, you will become better informed about the truth according to Yahweh. In addition you will want to have some planned discipline of daily Bible reading and study. Each time you think on these changeless truths you are laying a solid foundation for your life—now and forever.

The apostle Paul sought to encourage young Timothy when he wrote: "All Scripture is inspired by God and is profitable for teaching, for rebuking, for correcting, for training in righteousness, so that the man of God may be complete, equipped for every good work" (2 Timothy 6:16-17). Thus we know that Yahweh's Word is both permanent and profitable. **As you walk through this day, give time to opening the Book of all books, and growing in the knowledge of timeless truths as you feed on this treasure.**

Yahweh in Your Worship

Gracious Yahweh, thank You for giving me Your precious and everlasting Word. Forgive my neglect of this priceless gift. Be my Teacher and Guide as I seek to learn more about You and Your will for me each day. Help me be more disciplined to open Your Word every day and seek to discover more about You and Your will, and more about myself and how I can worship You in a more acceptable manner. Deliver me from a life that is monotonous and void of Your power.

January 8

Yahweh Calls Me to Be a Builder

Yahweh in the Word

> *"I have built the temple for the name of Yahweh, the God of Israel" (1 Kings 8:20).*

Solomon was chosen by Yahweh to construct His temple in the city of Jerusalem. This chapter records the dedication of that amazing structure. The prayer of Solomon recounts his experience of responding to Yahweh's call to this task.

Yahweh in Your Walk

Do you ever see yourself as a builder? Not of a structure like Solomon's temple, or even a smaller project, but a builder of that which is much more important? Just as surely as Yahweh called Solomon to build a magnificent temple, He calls each of us to be a builder. Here are some examples of the kinds of building we must do:

First, build a life that pleases Yahweh. Hear this command that comes to us from Jude who was the brother of Jesus and wrote the shortest book of the New Testament. "But you, dear friends, as you build yourselves up in your most holy faith and pray in the Holy Spirit, keep yourselves in the love of God, expecting the mercy of our Lord Jesus Christ for eternal life" (Jude 20). Our first and foremost building project is ourselves. We are called to pursue those spiritual disciplines that enable us to become persons who properly reflect the image of Yahweh. Every day should find us adding more to the building up of ourselves in faith and all those virtues that define a child of God.

Next, build relationships that contribute to Yahweh's kingdom on earth. Family relationships come first. Be a builder as a family member—building trust and affection. Ask yourself: Does my family see me as someone who helps build harmony and love in our daily relationships? Give attention and effort toward earning such an important reputation.

Another area of human relationships is our church family. The apostle Paul wrote about this when he said, "For we are God's co-workers. You are God's field, God's building… each one must be careful how he builds on it (the foundation of a church fellowship) (1 Corinthians 3:9-10). Jesus promised that He would build His church, but He uses us to accomplish that building. Think of ways you can be a peacemaker in your church; how you can contribute to its unity in love; how you can participate in reaching out to others with the message of hope in the Gospel. Be a prayer warrior on behalf of the leaders of your church family.

All these suggestions help you fulfil your calling to be a builder for Yahweh.

Yahweh in Your Worship

Yahweh, I know from Your Word that You are building Your kingdom in this world. I want to be available to You for this worthy task. Help me seize every opportunity today to be Your builder—at home, in every relationship, and within myself. Thank You for including me.

January 9

Yeshua (Jesus) Places Me in His Body

Yeshua in the Word

> "Now as we have many parts in one body, and all the parts do not have the same function, in the same way we who are many are one body in Christ and individually members of one another" (Romans 12:4-5).

We owe a large debt to the apostle Paul for giving us the metaphor of the human body being like a local church fellowship. In many of his letters he reminds believers of their role in a local congregation being comparable to that of various human body parts. His point is that Yeshua's plan is for all believers to be a vital part of a local fellowship where they can contribute to the needs of others according to their own giftedness.

Yeshua in Your Walk

We all know of individuals who are physically handicapped through the loss of various body parts. We marvel at their ability to compensate for their loss by use of artificial limbs and other helps. However, nothing artificial is ever as good as the real thing. In a similar fashion every local fellowship of believers needs what each person can contribute, otherwise it remains somewhat handicapped.

As a pastor I have known many professed believers who refused to participate in a local church family. They claimed to be genuine Christians, just not interested in having fellowship with other believers. Often, they were critical of the faults of such groups, pointing out their so called hypocrisies. However, when these lone ranger Christians had need of the service of a pastor or support of fellow believers, none were available.

The psalmist declared, "God sets the solitary in families" (Psalm 68:6 KJV). Yahweh does this because He knows how much we need others to help us in our times of need. Likewise others need our care when they are hurting. **None of us are made to be loners**. We are physically born into a family, and we are spiritually born again having family needs.

What is your testimony at this point? Have you discovered the value of joining with others for worship, learning, serving, and giving mutual support? If Yeshua is your Lord, you will follow Him into the local fellowship where your spiritual gifts and abilities can make that body of Christ better. Even if you are unaware of your need for others, they need what you can contribute to them. You are sent to a local fellowship to be a giver, not one who simply receives what others contribute. What are you seeking to contribute to your church family?

Yeshua in Your Worship

Precious Lord, I offer praise and thanksgiving before Your throne of grace. How merciful of You to include me in Your family of faith. Thank You for all fellow believers have meant to me in my pilgrimage of walking with You. Make me the blessing to others that You have saved me to be.

January 10

Yahweh Provides Strength for Me through His Joy

Yahweh in the Word

> *"Do not sorrow, for the joy of Yahweh is your strength" (Nehemiah 8:10 NKJV).*

The background for this brief but power-filled statement is the celebration over the rebuilding of the wall around the city of Jerusalem. The people gathered in front of the Water Gate where Ezra the scribe stood on a platform and read from God's Word. After the reading, the words of our text were spoken to remind the people of Yahweh's pleasure over the rebuilt wall.

Yahweh in Your Walk

Yahweh's people were returning from years of absence from their homeland, their temple, and all the customs associated with living in the land of promise. When they heard the reading of Yahweh's Word (vv. 1-4), they knew they had returned to the place He had planned for them to live. The "joy of Yahweh" over this restoration brought new strength to His people.

Have you not experienced the renewed strength brought on by joy? Think of some occasion when you received good news, news that was joy-filled, and how that gave you a surge of renewed energy. Let's focus in this brief devotional on some expressions of Yahweh's joy:

1. Zephaniah 3:17 "Yahweh your God is among you... He will rejoice over you with gladness He will delight in you with shouts full of joy."
2. John 15:11 "I have spoken these things to you so that My joy may be in you and your joy may be complete."
3. Hebrews 12:2 "... keeping our eyes on Jesus, the source and perfecter of our faith, who for the joy that lay before Him endured the cross and despised the shame and has sat down at the right hand of God's throne."

When we invite Yahweh to live in us, He brings His joy with Him and this joy of His becomes our joy and our strength. Just the joy of knowing Him and that He is always with us, enables us to overcome the gloom and despair that could be ours due to our depressing circumstances. I once asked a Christian friend, "How are you doing?" He replied, "Pretty good under the circumstances." My response was "What are you doing ***under*** the circumstances; get on top of them by claiming the victory that is yours in Jesus, and stay there!" My words may sound a bit abrupt to you, but they communicate the truth that although we may have no strength of our own to deal with current issues, the joy of Yahweh can become our strength as we rely on Him.

Yahweh in Your Worship

Thank You, Yahweh, for continually strengthening me by Your joy. Help me turn from all that would be depressing as I focus on You and all Your amazing gifts to me. Today I seize these truths by faith and look forward to walking in Your strength and joy.

January 11

Yahweh Gives Me a New Song to Sing

Yahweh in the Word

> "I waited patiently for Yahweh and He turned to me and heard my cry for help. He brought me up from a desolate pit, out of the muddy clay, and set my feet on a rock, making my steps secure. He put a new song in my mouth, a hymn of praise to our God. Many will see and fear and put their trust in Yahweh" (Psalm 40:1-3)

David wrote this song to describe how Yahweh delivered him from trouble. He may have actually been cast into a muddy pit or simply used this as an illustration of being "stuck" in a serious and hopeless situation. Either way, he came out with a new song of praise. One writer says, "David was delivered from the mire to the choir!" And he believed that his testimony would cause others to put their trust in Yahweh also.

Yahweh in Your Walk

This term "new song" appears nine times in the Bible to describe the testimony of those who experience Yahweh's deliverance. This song is one of praise to Him and about His merciful help in times of trouble. Listen to this admonition: "Sing a new song to Yahweh; sing to Yahweh, all the earth. Sing to Yahweh, praise His name; proclaim His salvation from day to day" (Psalm 96:1-2). Also, the apostle John tells of a vision he received while in exile on the Island of Patmos. He saw a slaughtered Lamb surrounded by living creatures who fell down before Him and sang this "new song": "You are worthy to take the scroll and to open its seals, because You were slaughtered and You redeemed people for God by Your blood" (Revelation 5:8-9).

All these references indicate that the nature of this new song is one of praise to Yahweh for His mercy in saving us from our sins by the sacrifice of Yeshua on the cross. At times when I am worshiping alone, I follow this biblical pattern and sing my own new song of praise and gratitude for Yahweh's salvation. Let me encourage you to do this. **Just make up a song (so new it has never been sung, and won't be sung again!) and lift your voice (doesn't have to be a good singing voice) to offer praise to Yahweh in a new way.** This action will seem strange at first, but just know your new song pleases Him.

May we also be willing to participate in congregational worship when new songs are being sung. I favor the old hymns and gospel songs from my younger days, however, many of the newer songs have a better message and need to be included in our experience of worship. **Sometimes we need to "break out of the mold" and worship with new words and unfamiliar music.**

Yahweh in Your Worship

Thank You, Yahweh, for putting a new song in my heart. Help me express this song of praise for Your deliverance of me from the pit of bondage to sin. Use me to seize opportunities to share with others the good news of the salvation only You can provide. I praise You Lord Jesus for what You did for me and all humankind on the cross.

January 12

Yahweh Wants Me to Be Myself

Yahweh in the Word

> *"According to the grace given to us, we have different gifts: If prophecy, use it according to the standard of one's faith; if service, in service; if teaching, in teaching; if exhorting, in exhortation; giving, with generosity, leading, with diligence; showing mercy, with cheerfulness" (Romans 12:6-8).*

The apostle Paul addresses the fact that every Christian has been given some gift (ability) that is needed to make the church (body of Christ) effective. His challenge is to discover our gifts, then use them to serve others and bring glory to Christ.

Yahweh in Your Walk

Have you thought seriously about the fact that Yahweh made you as a unique, one-of-a-kind person? No other person who has ever lived, or will live, is exactly like you. When Yahweh made you, He threw away the mold! This uniqueness not only applies to your outward appearance but also your personality, talents, skills, and—as a believer—spiritual gifts for serving others.

One of the most important personal discoveries is that of finding out who you are. You can never be at your maximum ability until you determine what that ability is, and then work to develop it to the fullest. One writer has said, "One is never stronger than when one is fully oneself." This truth does not deny your need for Yahweh's help, including His mercy and forgiveness for your sins, but allows Him to reveal what He made you to do in serving Him.

How about taking a personal inventory at this point? Ask yourself: What do I most enjoy doing in terms of a vocation? What am I good at doing? If I could choose any way of serving God that actually expresses me as I am, what would that be? Let your answers to these probing questions help you find your place in life. Seek also the counsel of a trusted friend regarding your skills.

Recently, I observed a fine, gifted, Christian leader attempt to serve in a position he was obviously not suited for. After several years, his miss-fit became a problem for him and those he sought to help. As one friend said, "He is like a square peg in a round hole!" Fortunately, Yahweh was merciful and opened a new position for him that fit his skills and gifts. How sad that this servant spent these years seeking to do what he was not gifted to do.

Two words give good advice and can save years of frustration: Be you! **Be who you are when you are at your best.** Be true to your talents, skills, and spiritual gifts. Avoid the mistake of trying to be like someone else—Be you. Trust your Maker to show you why He made you like you are.

Yahweh in Your Worship

Gracious and wise master Builder. Thank You for making me to be a part of Your kingdom on earth. Show me the place where I fit the best. Guide me to reach my full potential, for Your sake.

January 13

Yahweh Wants Me to Live a Disciplined Life

Yahweh in the Word

> *"Apply yourself to discipline and listen to words of knowledge" (Proverbs 23:12).*

The book of Proverbs is known as Wisdom Literature. Listen to the first two verses: "The proverbs of Solomon son of David, king of Israel: For learning what wisdom and discipline are; for understanding insightful sayings;" (1:1-2). The wisdom of disciplining oneself is a major theme throughout these 31 chapters. In our text for today the writer urges his readers to be diligent in applying oneself to discipline.

Yahweh in Your Walk

Today we begin a series of devotionals on what is known as Spiritual Disciplines. We will examine those practices which help produce a Christ-like life. Most of us are not attracted to self-discipline; our old carnal nature rebels against any attempt to force it into practices that restrict freedom to do as one pleases. However, we have all learned that making progress in most areas of human life requires discipline, whether physically, socially, mentally, or spiritually. Tom Landry the legendary coach of the Dallas Cowboys professional football team once said, "The job of a coach is to make players do what they don't want to do in order to achieve what they've always wanted to be." He was speaking about imposing discipline.

Jesus' first followers were known as disciples, a term that means "those who are trained and taught." You can see the close relationship between the words discipline and disciple. He disciplined (taught) these 12 men to obey Him, and thus become like Himself. The purpose for our consideration of these Spiritual Disciplines is to assist us in becoming more like Jesus, which should be every Christian's goal in life. We will begin our study with a look at several disciplines related to our relationship to the Bible—applying ourselves to the discipline of hearing, reading, studying, meditating upon, and memorizing Scripture.

We must be aware of the value of God's word in order to be motivated in these various disciplines regarding it. Listen to these words from the apostle Paul to young Timothy: "All Scripture is inspired by God and is profitable for teaching, for rebuking, for correcting, for training in righteousness, so that the man of God may be complete, equipped for every good work" (2 Timothy 3:16-17). He was reminding Timothy that God's word is profitable for many good reasons. **This is why we need to become more serious about acquiring help from it.**

Yahweh in Your Worship

Gracious Yahweh, thank You for giving me Your word in a language I can understand. Forgive me for taking this blessing for granted and neglecting the study of Your word. I commit myself to becoming more disciplined in pursuing the value I can receive from this amazing resource. I claim Your strength and perseverance as I begin this adventure of spiritual discipline. Help me to thus be better equipped for the work of serving as Your witness and Your disciple.

January 14

Yahweh Wants Me to Be a Disciplined Hearer of His Word

Yahweh in the Word

> *"Those who hear the word of God and keep it are blessed"* (Luke 11:28).

These brief words of Jesus emphasize the importance of hearing biblical truth for the purpose of doing what it teaches.

Yahweh in Your Walk

We begin our look at Spiritual Disciplines with a consideration of the easiest and most basic manner of obtaining truths from the Bible—hearing it. Most of us can testify that our first exposure to God's word was as hearers. Either from parents or Sunday School teachers or by some media, we heard the truths of Scripture. Our Jewish friends are required during childhood to memorize what is known as the "Shema" (the Hebrew word for **hear** or **listen**): "Hear, O Israel: Yahweh our God, Yahweh is One. Love Yahweh your God with all your heart, with all your soul, and with all your strength" (Deuteronomy 6:4-5). What a worthy challenge!

The value of hearing God's word is given in these words: "So faith comes from what is heard, and what is heard comes through the message about Christ" (Romans 10:17). Our decision to have faith in Jesus as our Savior came as the direct result of hearing about Him. And our faith will continue growing as we hear more and more of the truths of Scripture. For example, you may have the faith to overcome the temptation to worry. Such faith will be the direct result of hearing Yahweh's promise to provide for all your needs. A strong faith in other areas comes the same way. **Your faith will grow as your knowledge of Yahweh's faithfulness grows.**

What about developing a better discipline for hearing the truths of the Bible? We have so many opportunities to hear the word—such as various kinds of media, church attendance, using "down time" for listening to reliable Bible teaching on CDs, phones, and videos. When I walk on the treadmill, I listen to a favorite Bible teacher by means of a headset. When you are alone in your car, find a good resource for hearing the Word. You can choose many ways to increase the amount of hearing God's word. One suggestion: Work at being a better **listener.** It is one thing to hear, another to listen. If you attend a church service or Bible study class, seek to improve the art of listening, and always begin by asking Yahweh to help you listen more closely.

We must not fail to remember that Jesus emphasized hearing the truth for the purpose of doing it—"those who hear the word of God and keep it are blessed." As James reminds us, "Be doers of the word and not hearers only, deceiving yourselves" (James 2:22).

Yahweh in Your Worship

Forgive me, Yahweh, for not seeking to hear Your word more often, and for not being a better doer of what I hear. Help me grow in this discipline as I seek to make progress in becoming more like the Lord Jesus. How thankful I am to have Your word in my heart language. And thank You for all Your servants from whom I have had the privilege of hearing Your truths.

January 15

Yahweh Wants Me to Be a Disciplined Reader of His Word

Yahweh in the Word

> *"Blessed is the one who reads the words of this prophecy, and blessed are those who hear it and take to heart what is written in it, because the time is near" (Revelation 1:3 NIV).*

The apostle John introduced his book of Revelation with these words of promise—the person who reads and hears and takes to heart these words will be blessed. That same promise applies to all who read any portion of the Bible with a desire to take it to heart. Books are written to be read and no book is as important and life-altering as this book.

Yahweh in Your Walk

As we continue our consideration of the basic Spiritual Disciplines, we come to the practice of daily Bible reading. The Barna Research Group took a survey of those persons claiming to be "born-again Christians." They discovered that only 18% read the Bible every day! And 23% claimed that they never read the Bible! If you were included in this survey taken several years ago, how often would you have said that you read the Bible? Fortunately, by following this devotional guide you are now among those who read the word of God every day.

Congratulations for being a daily Bible reader. Now, how about becoming more disciplined regarding this worthwhile practice? **Why not move ahead and give more time to reading the most significant book ever written?** Let me suggest some ways this can take place. First, choose a time for each day's reading, preferably early in your day. Perhaps you can begin by reading this devotional guide; then move to some Bible reading plan you have chosen. That will be your second step—deciding on a definite plan for your reading. If you have never read the Bible all the way through, you can easily do this in one year by reading three chapters each day and five on Sundays. Or you may prefer some other plan; the important thing is to discipline yourself to a definite plan for reading the entire Bible.

Since I have read through the Bible many times, I now read from the various sections of the Bible each day—some verses from the Law (first five books), from the prophets, from the Psalms, from the gospels, from Acts, the New Testament letters, and the Revelation. This may sound like too much for you, but I read just a paragraph from each section each day. **Find a plan that works for you and work your plan.** Also choose a translation that you find most easily read. Once you cover the entire Bible, select another translation and repeat your plan. Just "keep your nose" in this book every day.

Yahweh in Your Worship

O Living Word, Lord Jesus, I want to know You better that I may better worship You and serve You. I trust You for the strength to be a serious student of Your precious word. Thank You for sending Your Holy Spirit to be my personal Teacher as I learn from Your Word. I trust You to guide me to the best plan for reading Your sacred truths. I know You alone can keep me faithful.

January 16

Yahweh Wants Me to Be a Disciplined Student of His Word

Yahweh in the Word

> *"Study to show yourself approved unto God, a workman that needs not to be ashamed, rightly dividing the word of truth" (2 Timothy 2:15 KJV).*

Paul, the apostle, wrote these words to encourage young Timothy to be a serious student of the word of truth, by carefully analyzing it and teaching it to others.

Yahweh in Your Walk

Reading this text reminds me of a memorable experience I had as a very young Christian. My mother enrolled me in a Vacation Bible School at our church. Our teacher was a woman named Mrs. McNutt. On the first morning she said us, "Boys and girls our Scripture verse to memorize this week is 2 Timothy 2:15 (which she quoted) and whenever you see me this week, I want your greeting to be '2 Timothy 2:15, Mrs. McNutt.'" All that week we had fun using that means of addressing her. Years later, I came home from college for a spring break. When I saw her again, I gave that special greeting—to her delight. Then many more years later, I had the privilege of writing VBS materials for children and sent her an autographed copy with that same greeting—thanking her for her influence upon me.

Reading the Bible gives us the big picture—a surface view of what this massive book is all about. But **to study the Bible is to go beneath the surface and find hidden treasures**. You need the right tools to do this digging—such as a concordance, Bible dictionary, and commentaries. I suggest you begin collecting these helps if you do not have them. Then decide on the type of study you want to do—word study, character study, doctrine study, book study—choose what interests you. Be prepared with pen and paper—or computer—to record what you discover. Always begin by claiming the enlightenment and guidance of the Holy Spirit as your personal teacher. Jesus promised, "The Counselor, the Holy Spirit—the Father will send Him in My name—will teach you all things and remind you of everything I have told you" (John 14:26).

Also take advantage of opportunities at your church, such as Bible study classes, special conferences, and other offerings to go deeper in study. If you are a member of some Bible class, do your homework with diligence, seeking to learn all you can from each study. Again, there is an unlimited supply of good Bible study materials on video, CDs, and other sources. The real test comes as you discover that authentic Bible study is hard work—do you have what it takes to become a worker who needs not to be ashamed? The proof of your study is in the work you do.

Yahweh in Your Worship

Yahweh, I do want to seize every opportunity to know You and Your will more fully. I ask You to give me the motivation and power to pursue a better understanding of Your word. Help me to seek to study the word for the purpose of doing Your will. Thank You for sending Your Holy Spirit to be my personal Teacher who guides me into all truth.

January 17

Yahweh Wants Me to Be Disciplined to Memorize His Word

Yahweh in the Word

> "How can a young man keep his way pure? By keeping Your word. I have sought You with all my heart; don't let me wander from Your commands. I have treasured Your word in my heart so that I may not sin against You" (Psalm 119:9-11).

The 119th Psalm is the longest chapter in the Bible—176 verses, and all but a few of these verses have some reference to God's word. Memorizing Scripture is one way to treasure it in your heart. Such a discipline has a purifying effect upon us, helping us see ourselves in the light of the word.

Yahweh in Your Walk

During my college days I met a representative of The Navigators, a Christian organization founded by Dawson Trotman in 1933, during his years in the Navy. One practice he advocated was Scripture memory. I became interested when this representative testified to the value of such a discipline to his own spiritual growth. He gave me a small packet of cards, called B-Rations, with Scripture verses printed on them. I began working on memorizing these basic Bible truths and applying them to my life. I can truthfully say that continuing this discipline has impacted my spiritual growth in a very significant manner. Many times I have shared the truths I memorized.

When we have not only heard God's word, and read it, and studied it, but also memorized it, we are placing a powerful tool in the hand of the Holy Spirit to work in and through us. Memorization requires the continual repetition of words until they are fixed in our minds. We have all memorized such things as our address, phone numbers, date of birth, and the names of many people. But few Christians actually pay the price required to memorize Bible verses. You may know John 3:16, and perhaps what is called the Lord's Prayer, and maybe a few other familiar words, but how much beyond that? Are you willing to move up a step higher in growth?

Let me challenge you to begin by selecting key verses or passages that you desire to remember. For example you may choose those Scriptures that explain the steps in becoming a Christian so you can share them with non-believers. Basic verses would include Romans 3:23, 6:23, 5:8-9, 10:9-10. This is sometimes called the Roman Road to Salvation. Selecting a biblical topic is another approach—such as verses related to some issue in your life where you need help. Write the verses on small cards so you can carry them with you. Then review them often during the day. Memorize the biblical references as well as the verses. Another helpful practice is that of meditating on these words and you memorize them—think about what they say and how they apply to your life. All this is part of the Spiritual Disciplines that contribute to your maturity.

Yahweh in Your Worship

I do praise and worship You, gracious Yahweh, for giving Your truth to me in a form I can understand. I ask You to help me hide Your words in my heart that I may live more like You. Lead me to those persons with whom You want me to share the good news of life in Christ.

January 18

Yahweh Wants Me to Be Disciplined to Meditate on His Word

Yahweh in the Word

> "This Book of the Law shall not depart from your mouth, but you shall meditate in it day and night, that you may observe to do according to all that is written in it. For then you will make your way prosperous, and then you will have good success" (Joshua 1:8 NKJV).

These words of wise counsel came directly from Yahweh to Joshua, just as he was taking over the leadership role Moses had filled. The Book of the Law would include the first five books of the Old Testament—the books written by Moses as he was inspired by Yahweh. Most reading in those days was done orally, thus the term "shall not depart from your mouth." Meditation was for the purpose of doing what Yahweh's law prescribed. The promise for doing these things was for true prosperity and success.

Yahweh in Your Walk

Today we come to another spiritual discipline—meditation on God's word. To meditate is to think carefully, slowly, and deliberately on some word, phrase, or sentence from the Bible. The word meditate is akin to ruminate which is what a cow does when she chews her cud. A cow takes a large bite of food, and then swallows it only to bring it back up later and chew on it before swallowing it again. In a similar manner we are to take a bite of Scripture and think carefully about it, turning it over and over in our minds, seeking to gain more insight and understanding.

The psalmist believed in the practice and value of meditation on Yahweh's word. He began the book of Psalms with these words: "How happy is the man who does not follow the advice of the wicked or take the path of sinners or join a group of mockers! Instead, his delight is in Yahweh's instruction and he meditates on it day and night. He is like a tree planted beside streams of water that bears its fruit in season and whose leaf does not wither. Whatever he does prospers" (Psalm 1:1-3). Notice the promise of prosperity in both these passages, not mere financial or worldly prosperity, but that which pleases Yahweh—true success in His sight.

Scripture memory and meditation go hand in hand. As you seek to memorize a verse, you will go over and over the words in your mind—as you do this, you must not just memorize the words but meditate on the meaning. Think deeply about each word as you ask the Holy Spirit to be your teacher and guide. Consider also how these truths apply directly to you and your life. Be ready to confess some sin revealed by your meditation; express yourself in worship as you understand Yahweh more completely. Always begin with a simple prayer like this: "May the words of my mouth and the meditation of my heart be acceptable to You, Yahweh, my rock and my Redeemer" (Psalm 19:14).

Yahweh in Your Worship

O Lord I long to think more deeply and accurately about You and Your ways. Teach me how.

January 19

Yahweh Wants Me to Be Disciplined to Pray

Yahweh in the Word

> *"Devote yourselves to prayer; stay alert in it with thanksgiving. At the same time, pray also for us that God may open a door to us for the message, to speak the mystery of the Messiah, for which I am in prison, so that I may reveal it as I am required to speak" (Colossians 4:2-5).*

The apostle Paul was in prison when he wrote these words to Christians in Colossae. His appeal in this text is for them to be devoted to prayer. The term "devoted" comes from two Greek words meaning to be strong toward, to endure in or persevere in. And "stay alert" means to be watchful. So, this command includes giving much attention and effort to being diligent regarding prayer, especially intercessory prayer for Paul to have opportunities to share the gospel message.

Yahweh in Your Walk

Have you ever thought of prayer as a ministry you could perform? Apparently the apostle Paul believed very strongly in the importance and effectiveness of intercessory prayer; he mentioned this often in his letters. From reading the Bible we must conclude that learning to pray and practicing praying is essential to a person's spiritual growth and maturity. Prayer is a God-given link that connects us and our needs to Yahweh's unlimited resources of grace and power. The writer of Hebrews encourages us to pray in these words: "Therefore let us approach the throne of grace with boldness, so that we may receive mercy and find grace to help us at the proper time" (Hebrews 4:16). The primary way we approach the throne of grace is through prayer. Think about the basic kinds of prayer for us to use. **Begin using these as you grow in Christ-likeness.**

First, worship utilizes prayer as our primary way of expressing our feelings toward Yahweh. Whether we are singing praise or offering thanksgiving or bringing our gifts and ourselves as offerings to Him, we do so by means of praying. All through every day, we should utter spontaneous prayers of worship to Yahweh, thanking and praising Him for His goodness and greatness. As you grow spiritually you will find yourself giving more time to personal worship.

Second, the ministry of interceding on behalf of others depends on prayer. In our text for this devotional, Paul requested that the Christians in Colossae pray for him and his fellow workers that Yahweh would open doors of opportunity for them. Let me suggest that you prepare a list of all the persons and needs you want to remember when you pray. Follow this list on a daily basis. Let intercessory prayer become an important ministry for you. You may be limited in where you can go and what you can do personally, but through prayer you can have a worldwide influence. I believe that one of the surprises for us in heaven will be to discover all who have prayed for us, and what a difference those prayers made.

Finally, give attention to your need for confessing your sin and claiming forgiveness.

Yahweh in Your Worship

Thank You, Father, for teaching me to pray and answering my prayers according to Your will.

January 20

Yahweh Wants Me to Be Disciplined to Worship

Yahweh in the Word

> *"Come, let us worship and bow down; let us kneel before Yahweh our Maker. For He is our God, and we are the people of His pasture, the sheep under His care" (Psalm 95:6-7).*

The book of Psalms is the worship book of the Bible. Many of its chapters are devoted to songs of praise, thanksgiving, and other expressions of both private and corporate worship. This text speaks of the reason for worshiping Yahweh—He is our Maker and the One who provides care for us, like a shepherd does for his sheep. We worship Him because of who He is and all He does for us. He is thus worthy of all praise and thanksgiving and the offering of ourselves to Him.

Yahweh in Your Walk

Today we continue our consideration of personal growth through practicing the various Spiritual Disciplines. **Our subject is worship.** How would you define worship? Some might say it is going to church, others would mention the reciting of certain forms of worship. Hopefully, your answer would be more accurate than these. Worship begins with an awareness of who Yahweh is, as our text declares—He is our Creator and Care-giver. The quality and meaningfulness of our worship is dependent on how well we know Yahweh. Worship includes the way we respond to our understanding of Yahweh—praise, thanksgiving, adoration, offering of oneself, and a devotion to being obedient to Him.

The extent of your spiritual growth is related directly to worship—as your worship of Yahweh becomes more frequent and meaningful, you experience greater spiritual maturity. Give attention to both private worship, when you are alone with Yahweh, and those occasions when you worship with others. Each of these has its advantages and must be included in this discipline. You will find an appeal in several of these devotionals to actively participate in times of worshiping with others—sing all the worship songs, orally or silently; pray along with others as they voice prayers; contribute generously and with intentionality to financial offerings; listen to sermons as an act of worship, claiming Yahweh's message for yourself. When an appeal is given for persons to openly declare their decision to be saved, pray earnestly for those needing help.

All this speaks of putting **actual** worship in your **acts** of worship. Whether alone or with others, be devoted to the worship experience—put yourself into your worship, never be a spectator or observer of others who worship. Corporate worship is not entertainment; it is involvement. Discipline yourself to being an active, eager, participant as you honor the One who is worthy.

Yahweh in Your Worship

Yahweh, Your Word calls me to present myself as a living sacrifice to You, declaring this to be my spiritual worship (Romans 12: 1). I long to worship in this authentic manner. Deliver me from being too casual and unengaged as I come before Your throne. Awaken me to Your greatness and goodness; call forth the appropriate praise, thanksgiving, and honor due to You.

January 21

Yeshua Wants Me to Be Disciplined as a Witness on Mission for Him

Yeshua in the Word

> "Then Jesus came near and said to them, 'All authority has been given to Me in heaven and on earth. Go, therefore and make disciples of all nations, baptizing them in the name of the Father and of the Son and of the Holy Spirit, teaching them to observe everything I have commanded you. And remember, I am with you always, to the end of the age'" (Matthew 28:19-20).

These final words of Jesus in the Gospel of Matthew are known as His Great Commission. His command is for all His followers to be devoted to the task of making disciples. His promise is to always be with his followers and to provide all the authority and power needed to accomplish this task. This commission is for everyone who claims Jesus as Savior and Lord.

Yeshua in Your Walk

Have you ever thought of Jesus' Great Commission to be His personal call to you? Or how about Paul's words: "We are ambassadors for Christ, certain that God is appealing through us. We plead on Christ's behalf, 'Be reconciled to God'" (2 Corinthians 5:20)? Do you think Yahweh is including you in these words of challenge? Let me assure you that every genuine follower of Jesus should consider himself or herself to be sent on mission by Him. We are all rescued from perishing not only that we be saved but that we, in turn, reach out to rescue others.

Your spiritual growth depends on your participation in the mission of Yeshua. His name means "I AM salvation," and we are to extend that offer of salvation to others. How can you do this? Does this mean you must be sent overseas as a career missionary? Yes, if that is Yahweh's plan for you. But there are many other ways of being on-mission for Him. For example, through your ministry of intercessory prayer, you can be a supporter of others in mission service, both near and far away. Pray for your church leaders and the mission efforts of your local church. Pray for various mission agencies and their workers.

Another direct opportunity is financial involvement through direct mission giving. Perhaps you can give to help send young people on short term mission trips. How about you going on a mission to another place or need? You might volunteer to serve in local outreach efforts to help others know the Lord. The point of all these suggestions is to see yourself as a person called to reach others however that works for you. My wife and I have occasional gatherings in our home for all our neighbors—at the Christmas season or other times. These are informal times of becoming better acquainted and giving some kind of Christian witness. **Perhaps you could seek to disciple some acquaintance, helping them grow in their faith. Ask Yahweh to use you, He will.**

Yeshua in Your Worship

Gracious Redeemer, help me see and seize opportunities to make You known to others, both near and far away. Deliver me from excuses for not being a bold, faithful witness.

January 22

Yahweh Wants Me to Be Disciplined as a Servant for Him

Yahweh in the Word

> *"Serve Yahweh with gladness; come before Him with joyful songs. Acknowledge that Yahweh is God. He made us and we are His—His people, the sheep of His pasture" (Psalm 100:2-3).*

This psalm of thanksgiving includes praise, celebration with joyful songs, and glad service to Yahweh as the means of worshiping Him. All this is appropriate because He is our Maker and our Owner—Yahweh deserves such recognition and honor.

Yahweh in Your Walk

We can easily see how Bible intake and meaningful prayer are essentials for spiritual growth, but may not think of serving Yahweh as something related to such a goal. And yet, **what could be more Christ-like than serving others.** You may recall the occasion when Jesus' disciples were having a dispute about who among them was considered to be the greatest. He reproved them for such concern and said, "I am among you as One who serves" (Luke 22:27). He demonstrated His servant role when He washed their feet, but even more so when He gave Himself to be the sacrifice for their sins.

By disciplining yourself to serve others, you will take a large step toward spiritual growth. However, you must do so with the proper motivation. Serving others must never be done as a means to gaining recognition from fellow believers or from Yeshua Himself. We serve out of a sense of gratitude to Him who gave Himself for us. Whenever I think of humble servants, I remember a widow in one of the churches we served. She did not have much to give materially but she made up for that by giving her time and words of encouragement and comfort. She had a true servant spirit about her—not wanting recognition—just the privilege of helping someone. And she did so with joy and enthusiasm.

You may already be serving Yahweh in meaningful ways, but if not, begin seeking opportunities to do so. Such service is never to be limited to church related actions, but seeks to help wherever there is a need. Let me suggest you begin at home with your family, if you have one. **Be an example to your loved ones of what it means to do helpful things in a spirit of love and kindness.** I think often of the apostle Paul's words at this point. He said, "Whatever you do, do it enthusiastically, as something done for the Lord and not for men, knowing that you will receive the reward of an inheritance from the Lord. You serve the Lord Christ" (Colossians 3:23-24). Apply this truth to your workplace or other avenues when serving is needed. The more you give of yourself, the more you will gain in terms of spiritual development and growth.

Yahweh in Your Worship

Thank You, Lord Jesus, for giving me the model of serving others out of love. Help me have a true servant spirit, and express it through meaningful ways of helping those who need my service. Today, I choose to seize opportunities to be a true servant of Yours.

January 23

Yahweh Wants Me to Be a Disciplined Steward of His

Yahweh in the Word

> *"Based on the gift each one has received, use it to serve others, as good managers (stewards) of the varied grace of God... so that God may be glorified through Jesus Christ in everything" (1 Peter 4:10-11).*

The apostle Peter appeals to his readers to recognize that whatever they have has come to them as gifts from Yahweh. They do not own these gifts but have temporary use of them; they are managers of what belongs to Yahweh, not owners. This concept is known as the biblical principle of stewardship. We are to use what Yahweh gives us in a manner that will glorify Him, and the only way we can do this faithfully is by the grace given us through Jesus Christ.

Yahweh in Your Walk

Another essential discipline to be practiced for spiritual growth is that of good and faithful stewardship. **A Christian must understand that whatever he or she possesses comes as a gift from Yahweh. He entrusts us with these gifts to be used, not primarily for our pleasure but for His glory.** This does not suggest that we cannot enjoy His blessings, but that we see them as temporary possessions for which we will someday give an account to Him for the way we used them. We are managers of what belongs to Him, not owners.

Consider two of your most important possessions—your time and your money. How well do you manage your time? Time is life; we live within the limits of time. Think of your time as Yahweh's gift to you, and seek to grow in managing your time in ways that honor Him. Wasting time is wasting life; therefore, seek to make better use of the hours of each day. Give priority to the time you need to spend in worshiping Him through the intake of His word and expressing praise and gratitude to Him. Be disciplined about this daily "quiet time," at the beginning of each day. Examine your daily schedule to discover ways of using time better—give attention to your family; be available to them, just to communicate better. Perhaps less television time or time spent just on yourself such as sports and hobbies. "People time" is usually a better use of time than project time. Your spiritual growth will reflect your management of time. Ask His help.

What about money and financial matters? How well is your management in these areas? The Scriptures teach us to bring a financial offering to Yahweh from the first-fruits of our income, not the left-overs. Have a plan of growing in the amount you give through your church for kingdom advance. Seek also to be a wise steward of the remainder of your money. Remember, it all belongs to Him; you are just His manager. Be preparing for that day of accountability.

Yahweh in Your Worship

Lord, You are so generous in giving me all the possessions I have. Surely, I do not deserve them. But I do want to grow as a manager of what belongs to You. Help me be a faithful steward of everything You entrust to my care. I claim Your wisdom and power to please You.

January 24

Yahweh Wants Me to Be a Disciplined Learner

Yahweh in the Word

> *"A wise man will listen and increase his learning...." (Proverbs 1:5).*

"Apply yourself to discipline and listen to words of knowledge" (Proverbs 23:12).

Many statements, such as these, point out the value of the discipline of being a learner. Of course a person can learn the ways of evil as well as good. But the Scriptures encourage Yahweh's people to be devoted to gaining knowledge of that which is good and pleasing to Him.

Yahweh in Your Walk

On January 13 we began this series of devotionals on Spiritual Disciplines. We pointed out that the term disciple means "one who is trained and taught." Most of the disciplines we have studied require reading and learning; anyone who is serious about becoming a disciple of Jesus must be committed to learning. Remember that He said, "Take My yoke upon you and learn of Me" (Matthew 11:29). Today's devotional will be the last in this series and will focus on the importance of an ongoing discipline of learning.

There are many ways to learn. Much of our learning comes from experiences in life. However, as one friend said, "Some people live and learn, while others just live." The point being—as we go through various life experiences we must also think about what occurs and consider the lessons we should gain from them. **Learning is an intentional discipline**.

Reading is one of the best learning opportunities. We have mentioned the importance of having a plan for Bible reading. But other fine resources also should be examined. Statistics show that 45 percent of Americans say they never read a book, and the average college graduate does not read one serious book in the course of a year. Hopefully these reports do not describe you. **Your spiritual growth will definitely be enhanced by having a plan for reading materials that increase your learning of that which makes a difference in life.**

As Christians we have a tremendous advantage over others when it comes to learning. Jesus promised the Holy Spirit to his followers. He is described as the One who would teach us all things and lead us into all truth. We have the best teacher—the One who knows all truth and is always with us. John Milton, the English writer of the famous poem "Paradise Lost," once said, "The end of learning is to know God, and out of that knowledge to love Him and to imitate Him." Consider the value of forming this habit: Begin each day with a simple prayer for the Holy Spirit to be your teacher that day. Each time you read a Scripture portion or a serious book, ask Him to teach you as you read. Seek His lessons in all of life. See yourself as His devoted student.

Yahweh in Your Worship

Holy Spirit, You are my special Teacher. Thank You for being patient with me as a learner. Guide me into all the truth I need to know. I long to know Yahweh better and be more like Him.

January 25

Yahweh Wants Me to Live in Fellowship with Other Believers

Yahweh in the Word

> *"They devoted themselves to the apostles' teaching, to fellowship, to the breaking of bread, and to the prayers" (Acts 3:42).*

This first description of the early church affords us good insight into what they felt was essential. First came instruction from the apostles, then fellowship with those of like faith, then having meals together which probably included the Lord's Supper, and finally, praying together. All this happened when they were all together. Thus fellowship with other believers was characteristic of the church from the beginning.

Yahweh in Your Walk

The term "**fellowship**" comes from a Greek word, ***koinonia***, which means "that which we have in common." This meaning is clear from the idea of fellows-on-the-same-ship—thus, fellowship. Christians all have much in common, but the most important commonality is the Spirit of Christ living in us. We literally share His life. For this reason we have much to gain from spending time with one another. (You will enjoy the devotionals in February on the biblical "one anothers.")

A local church is a fellowship of believers. The New Testament word church is ***ekklesia*** in the Greek language, meaning "a called out assembly." Yahweh has called out believers from the unbelieving world to join together in a fellowship of worshiping and fulfilling His purpose of sharing His love and truth with others. The so-called ordinances of the local church are baptism and the Lord's Supper. Together these are visual reminders of our spiritual experiences of death to sin, resurrection, and partakers of His life.

What about your involvement in a local church? Are you an active participant in a meaningful fellowship with other believers? If not, you are missing a vital aspect of Yahweh's plan for you. I urge you to become involved with other followers of Jesus, to carry out His Great Commission. As you do so, focus on what you can contribute to others, not what you can receive. Those who claim they do not "get anything" out of their church, have the wrong attitude. **You must see yourself as being a giver, not a getter**. Think of ways you can give more of yourself and your God-given abilities to enrich the lives of others—there is no limit to this opportunity. Here are some very practical suggestions: During worship sit close to the front of the room and always with someone else, never alone. **Participate** in all the songs, prayers, offerings, and listening, never be a spectator. **Reach out** to others in friendliness, greet others warmly, and get acquainted with those you do not know, especially newcomers. **Affirm those** who lead worship; let them know you appreciate their efforts. **Get involved** in a Bible study group; **open your home** to other believers and non-believers to share love and life together. Think of all this as your way of pleasing the Lord of His church—He deserves it!

Yahweh in Your Worship

Thank You, Lord Jesus, for including me in Your church. Help me to make a difference in fellowship with other believers. Make me a blessing to them.

January 26

Yahweh Plans for Me to Ultimately Be Gathered to My Family

Yahweh in the Word

> "This is the length of Abraham's life: 175 years. He took his last breath and died at a ripe old age, old and contented, and he was gathered to his people" (Genesis 25:7-8).

A clear theme running throughout the Bible is the fact of an afterlife—life beyond physical death. Several examples of this are found in references such as this and similar statements regarding other characters like Ishmael (Genesis 25:17), Isaac (Genesis 35:29), Jacob (Genesis 49:33), Moses and Aaron (Deuteronomy 32:50).

Yahweh in Your Walk

Yesterday's devotional spoke of the importance of our fellowship with other believers in a local church. There is where we find the best expression of our family of faith. Through the years, we experience the expansion of this family as we become acquainted with a larger community of believers. We are all brothers and sisters having been spiritually born of the same Heavenly Father. Ultimately, beyond the boundaries of this physical life, we will all be together in heaven.

Our text for today is one of the early indications of this destiny. The same words are given regarding the deaths of Abraham, Ishmael, Isaac, Jacob, Aaron and Moses—they died and were "gathered" to their people. This gathering speaks clearly of Yahweh's plan to have all His family together in eternity. The New Testament gives much more information about this final reunion. As Jesus said, "In My Father's house are many dwelling places; if not, I would have told you. I am going away to prepare a place for you. If I go away and prepare a place for you, I will come back and receive you to Myself, so that where I am you may be also" (John 14:2-3).

How does this truth affect your outlook on your life today? Most of us would have to admit that we seldom think of life beyond this present earthly existence. Perhaps occasionally we are reminded, by the passing of a friend or loved one, that there is more beyond the grave. But for the most part, we are creatures of the here and now. However, we would do ourselves a favor to give more thought to the realities of heaven and eternity. Such consideration can help us have a better perspective regarding this time in our existence. An old gospel song has these lines: "This world is not my home; I'm just passing through. My treasures are laid up somewhere beyond the blue. The angels beckon me from heaven's open door, and I can't feel at home in this world anymore." We all probably feel too much at home in this world. **Let's wake up to the fact that we are just pilgrims passing through on our way to our real and final home.** Such awareness can have a large effect on the way we value earthly possessions as well as our achievements. **This life is all temporary and preliminary to the ultimate gathering to our eternal family.**

Yahweh in Your Worship

Thank You, Yahweh, that You have a place prepared for me with all my Christian family. Help me look forward to this everlasting fellowship. Deliver me from valuing to this world too much.

January 27

Yahweh Wants Me to Know How Great Is His Love for Me

Yahweh in the Word

> *"I pray that you, being rooted and firmly established in love, may be able to comprehend with all the saints what is the length and width, height and depth of God's love, and to know the Messiah's love that surpasses knowledge, so you may be filled with all the fullness of God" (Ephesians 3:17-19).*

Here is one part of the apostle Paul's prayer for his readers in the church in Ephesus. Notice the emphasis is first of "being rooted and firmly established in love." Christians have this firm foundation upon which to build a life that is characterized by all the dimensions of love—"length and width, height and depth"—nothing is outside its reach. This love has its source in Yahweh (God) and Yeshua (Messiah). As we comprehend this amazing virtue, we become literally filled with the fullness of God—amazing!

Yahweh in Your Walk

As you progress through this day, you will have many opportunities to "seize the day with Yahweh" in the sense of expressing His love to others. If you feel overwhelmed by this responsibility, just remember—this is His love, not yours. He wants you to know how great is His love for you—a love of such great dimensions that you cannot contain it, and must let it spill over through you to others.

Years ago I was struggling with writing a definition of Yahweh's love for me—what does this actually mean? As I read descriptions of His love in the Bible, I noticed a small preposition that was often repeated—the word *for*. "Christ loved me and gave Himself *for* me." "Jesus laid down His life *for* us." "God sent His Son to be the atoning sacrifice *for* our sins." Many other examples could be given, but all of these declare the same amazing truth—to say that Yahweh and Yeshua love us means They are *for* us; They are on our side, reaching out to help us. This simple truth helps me comprehend the meaning of divine love.

Yahweh wants us to not only grasp the meaning of His love but also the vast dimensions of His love—"length and width, height and depth." In other words, nothing in all creation is outside His love; He is *for* this entire universe and all that is within it. How great is His love! Nothing we can ever think, say, or do is beyond the scope of His love. Here is why He can be so merciful and gracious towards us, and everyone else. Here is why He gave Himself *for* us upon the cross—He wants the best *for* us.

Now, our role in life is simply to pass this same love on to others—today! As you walk through this day, allow Him to extend His love through your words and actions. You will notice a difference—and so will others!

Yahweh in Your Worship

Make me an instrument of Your great love today. Deliver me from self-love to Your love.

January 28

Yahweh Wants Me to Share in His Delight

Yahweh in the Word

> "This is what Yahweh says: 'The wise man must not boast in his wisdom; the strong man must not boast in his strength; the wealthy man must not boast in his wealth. But the one who boasts should boast in this, that he understands and knows Me—that I am Yahweh, showing faithful love, justice, and righteousness on the earth, for I delight in these things.' This is Yahweh's declaration" (Jeremiah 9:23-24).

Notice the contrast between that which the world finds delightful: boasting in wisdom, strength, and wealth on the one hand, and what should be one's delight: boasting in knowing Yahweh who shows faithful love, justice, and righteousness.

Yahweh in Your Walk

We find greatest delight in that which is of most value to us. In this interesting text, Yahweh does not declare that being wise and strong and wealthy are wrong in and of themselves. However, if these become occasions for delight and boasting, then our values are misplaced. Think of these values like this: All human wisdom, strength, and wealth are temporary; they will not pass the test of time. Conversely, faithful love, justice, and righteousness are eternal, forever enduring. Which seems more important to you? Which brings greatest pleasure to you? Which do you prefer to reflect in all your relationships?

Yahweh reveals Himself in this text; here are those virtues that bring Him delight. Now that we understand this truth, we know Him better and can share in His joy. One of the few values worth boasting about is disclosed here—to be able to truthfully say that we understand and know Yahweh.

"Faithful love" translates the Hebrew word ***chesed***, which is used 248 times in the Old Testament, meaning "loyalty, steadfast love, grace." The term "justice" refers to Yahweh's provision for human needs according to His standards. And "righteousness" means that which is proper in His sight. All these are recurring themes throughout the Bible and speak clearly of Yahweh's character. His will is for all His people to reflect these same virtues and find delight in so doing. **As you walk through this day, and every day, seek to manifest these qualities in all your relationships.** Focus on treating everyone you meet, even the undeserving with these virtues—Yahweh will share your delight.

Yahweh in Your Worship

Thank You for revealing Yourself through words like these in our text today. Surely You are the only true and living God; the only One worthy of our worship and adoration. Today, I want to seize every opportunity to express Your faithful love, justice, and righteousness. Make me sensitive to those around me who need this kind of treatment. **Deliver me from boasting in vanity. Teach me those values that are worthy of my delight.**

January 29

Yahweh Wants Me to Sing to Him

Yahweh in the Word

> "And don't get drunk with wine, which leads to reckless actions, but be filled by the Spirit: speaking to one another in psalms, hymns, and spiritual songs, singing and making music from your heart to the Lord, giving thanks for everything to God the Father in the name of our Lord Jesus Christ, submitting to one another in the fear of Christ" (Ephesians 5:18-21).

In these words, the apostle Paul gives both a warning and positive instructions. He warns against drunkenness on the one hand and appeals to his readers to be filled with the Holy Spirit on the other. One evidence of the Spirit's control is that of singing to one another and to the Lord through various types of songs. Added to that is a spirit of gratitude to Yahweh along with mutual submission.

Yahweh in Your Walk

Not everyone has a good singing voice, but all can make a "joyful noise" to the Lord. Paul suggests here that we make "music from your heart to the Lord." Some worshipers have said to me, "Pastor, you don't want me to sing in church; it would drive people away!" My response to this excuse is to encourage non-singers to speak aloud from the heart the words of worship songs—the result is the same.

Christian Bateman was an English pastor who wrote many hymns. One had this challenge:

> Come, Christians, join to sing, Alleluia! Amen!
> Loud praise to Christ our King; Alleluia! Amen!
> Let all with heart and voice, before His throne rejoice;
> Praise is His glorious choice: Alleluia! Amen!

Notice the kinds of worship songs Paul mentions: "psalms, hymns, and spiritual songs." We can use a variety of music styles in worship. Every worshiper has preferences, growing out of traditions, but we can enjoy all kinds of worship music, as long as the songs are from a heart of worship and witness. Some of these songs should express gratitude "for everything to God the Father." And, most importantly, all come as the result of being filled with (controlled by) the Holy Spirit. **The songs on our lips are actually from the Holy Spirit who sings through us!**

Such personal worship is not limited to congregational experiences, but should occur as we walk through each day—singing our own, made-up expressions of praise and thanksgiving. Again, if you cannot "carry a tune," speak aloud the worship from your heart. Yahweh will be pleased.

Yahweh in Your Worship

You alone, O Yahweh, are worthy of my worship. Thank You for giving me the ability to sing unto You. Help me express the gratitude I feel for all Your wonderful, amazing gifts to me.

January 30

Yahweh Provides a Land of the Living for Me

Yahweh in the Word

> *"Then I heard a loud voice from the throne: 'Look! God's dwelling place is with humanity, and He will live with them. They will be His people, and God Himself will be with them and be their God. He will wipe away every tear from their eyes. Death will no longer exist; grief, crying, and pain will exist no longer, because the previous things have passed away.' Then the One seated on the throne said, 'Look! I am making everything new'"* (Revelation 21:3-5).

The apostle John recorded this vision as a message to be shared with all believers. Here is a revelation of how things will be in the future—a new intimacy with Yahweh, deliverance from all that brings grief, no more death or crying or pain—all these troublesome things will be over, everything will be new. This good news is the hope of all believers.

Yahweh in Your Walk

An elderly Christian gentleman was approached by a friend who greeted him this way, "Hey, it's good to see you in the land of the living." The older man replied, "Actually, I'm in the land of the dying. But I'm looking forward someday to being in the land of the living, where there is no more death!" How true! And how comforting to know Yahweh has made a place for us there.

Death is very much a part of our present experience—the death of loved ones and friends—death of so many others reported in the news media. We are literally surrounded by the reality of physical death. In fact, American society has been labeled as a "Death Culture," due to the large numbers of abortions, the growth of assisted suicides, and mass killings. All this is true because of sin; the wages of sin is death. But, as believers, we have the promise of life everlasting beyond this present age.

While none of us should look upon death as a friend, we have nothing to fear from it. For Christians death is actually a doorway to the land of the living where there is no more death. Our Lord said, "I am the resurrection and the life. The one who believes in Me, even if he dies, will live. Everyone who lives and believes in Me will never die—ever" (John 11:25-26). This wonderful promise gives hope to all who place their trust in Jesus.

We do well, in the light of these truths, not to place a major emphasis and undue value upon this present life. Our years here, however long, are just a time of warming up for the real deal—eternity with our Lord and all His redeemed children. The Bible describes our current life as a vapor that appears for a little while, and then it is gone.

Yahweh in Your Worship

Yeshua, You are not only my Lord but also my Life—eternal and abundant. I worship You.

January 31

Yahweh Wants Me to Stand Firm

Yahweh in the Word

> "But we must always thank God for you, brothers loved by the Lord, because from the beginning God has chosen you for salvation through sanctification by the Spirit and through belief in the truth. He called you to this through our gospel, so that you might obtain the glory of our Lord Jesus Christ. Therefore brothers, stand firm and hold to the traditions you were taught, either by our message or by our letter" (2 Thessalonians 2:13-15).

This brief personal letter from the apostle Paul to the church in Thessalonica is his second written message to them. In this text, he expresses his gratitude to them, reminding them of their indebtedness to the Lord for His salvation and call. His appeal is for them to stand firm.

Yahweh in Your Walk

You may have had experience in your workplace of seeking to build an effective team with employees who were not dependable. Hopefully, you also have learned the value of co-workers who were loyal and steadfast. What a difference! This same principle applies to the work of serving our Lord through His church. My wife and I have served as leaders in several churches through more than 50 years. Our most cherished memories are of fellow-laborers upon whom we could depend—in good times and in bad. They were as faithful as the sunrise, and right on time.

In all of his letters, Paul commended those who were steadfast, and warned those who weren't. His message on this subject is well stated in these words to the Corinthians: "Therefore, my dear brothers, be steadfast, immovable, always excelling in the Lord's work, knowing that your labor in the Lord is not in vain" (1 Corinthians 15:58). How do you measure up in this regard? **Are you a person who has learned the secret of standing firm, even when others fall away?** Do yourself and your Lord a big favor and engage in some self-evaluation at this point. Rate yourself from 1 to 10 (10 being the best) as you consider these statements:

> I am involved as a faithful worker in my church.
> My pastor and co-workers know they can depend on me to be available when needed.
> The Lord knows my commitment to be loyal to Him whatever the cost.
> I do not have to have my way in order to work closely with others.
> My example of steadfastness inspires others to do the same.

None of us will be a perfect 10 in all of these statements. However, we can learn the value of growing in these areas. **The secret of faithfulness is to rely on Him who is always faithful.**

Yahweh in Your Worship

Thank You, Yahweh, that You always stand firm in Your love for me. May Your faithfulness control me and be expressed through me in every aspect of life—for Your glory.

February 1

Yahweh Heals My Body

Yahweh in the Word

> "He said, 'If you will carefully obey Yahweh your God, do what is right in His eyes, pay attention to His commands, and keep all His statutes, I will not inflict any illnesses on you that I inflicted on the Egyptians. For I am Yahweh who heals you'" (Exodus 15:26).

As we noted on January 2, we will begin each month with a series of devotionals based on the 12 combination names of Yahweh. The first was Yahweh Yireh ("I AM the One who provides."). **Today we consider the second combination—Yahweh Rophe ("I AM the One who heals.").** The Hebrew term ***rophe*** (pronounced RO-fay) literally means "to restore," "to heal," or "make whole," and is found more than sixty times in the Old Testament. This work of restoration is applied to various areas of need, such as physical illnesses, broken relationships, spiritual maladies, and even the healing of nations. In other words, **Yahweh can restore wholeness wherever needed.**

Yahweh in Your Walk

Today we focus on our need for physical healing. Let's begin with this truth: **All physical healing is from Yahweh Rophe.** He created our bodies to heal themselves from most injuries and illnesses. But what about those times when we are unable to recover naturally—without outside assistance, such as surgery, medications, therapy, etc.? First, we can thank Him that He has led in all the medical research and development that assists this body to recover. Many physicians, surgeons, and those who develop various drugs and medications acknowledge their dependence upon God for their success. He is truly the Great Physician.

I know a Christian doctor who sees himself as God's hand reaching out to facilitate healing to each patient who comes to him. He admits that he cannot heal anyone—this is God's work. He also knows there will come a time when his patients will not recover from some ailment or accident or natural aging. Again, Yahweh Rophe will bring final, permanent healing in the sense of completely delivering us from this mortal "tent." Remember—all physical healing is temporary; this body must die. But then, we will receive a new, permanent "house in heaven."

Give thanks today to Yahweh Rophe for the physical body He has given you. Also, acknowledge your complete dependence upon Him for sustaining your health. However, give serious consideration to your own responsibility to maintaining a strong, healthy body as you follow good health practices, such as eating proper foods, exercising, getting adequate rest, and avoiding whatever is harmful to your body. Be a good steward of the health you have.

Yahweh in Your Worship

I offer praise and thanksgiving to You, Yahweh Rophe. You have faithfully healed me many times in the past, and will ultimately heal me completely and eternally. I rest in this blessed assurance. I seize this day knowing that You are with me as my strength and my health.

February 2

Yahweh Heals My Soul

Yahweh in the Word

> "I said, LORD (Yahweh) be gracious unto me; heal me, for I have sinned against You.... May Yahweh, the God of Israel be praised from everlasting to everlasting. Amen and amen" (Psalm 41:4, 13).

Our need for healing and restoration includes spiritual needs as well as physical. In fact, healing for our soul is far more important than healing from any illness or accident. We are not a body that has a soul, rather we are souls that live temporarily in a body. One day we will go on living without this body. The psalmist in this passage recognized his supreme need for healing from sin. Yahweh Rophe is the only One who can meet this most important need.

Yahweh in Your Walk

Spiritual healing begins with a new birth; a totally new creation is required since we were not just sick spiritually; we were dead. As the apostle Paul declared, "God, who is rich in mercy, because of His great love that He had for us, made us alive with the Messiah even though we were dead in trespasses" (Ephesians 2:4-5). The only cure for being spiritually dead is to be spiritually resurrected. Yahweh Rophe does not give us back our old nature made over, rather a new nature taking over! We must never assume that the old person we were before coming to Christ simply needs reformation—some improvements. Rather our need is for a totally new nature, the one given by a new birth. And this new nature is actually the life of Yeshua in us. As Paul declared, "Christ lives in me!" (Galatians 2:20). Can you recall a time when you, by faith, called upon Yahweh Rophe to make you alive spiritually? Pause now to thank Him for this miracle. Also, think seriously about sharing this good news with others. Your testimony can make an eternal difference for them. You can truthfully say, "I have found the Great Physician; let me introduce you to Him."

But our need for spiritual healing does not end with a new birth. Who of us has not experienced that spiritual malady called backsliding—times when we as a Christian walked contrary to Yahweh's will for us? Again, the Great Physician offers restoration to fellowship with Him. Note this promise: "Return you faithless children. I will heal your unfaithfulness" (Jeremiah 3:22). How can we return? By confessing our rebellion against Him, and claiming His promised forgiveness—such an action always brings needed restoration. We are healed by His gracious mercy and favor. Seize this day as one of spiritual health and wholeness.

Yahweh in Your Worship

My soul does magnify You, O Yahweh Rophe for You have raised me from spiritual death to spiritual life and health. I praise You as the One who has redeemed me and who brings spiritual renewal to me continually. Deliver me from Satan's attempts to lead me astray. I choose to present myself, body, mind, soul and spirit as a living sacrifice to You this day. Thank You O Yahweh for healing me—forever. Give me the courage and motivation to bear witness of Your healing to others. I long to see them made whole by Your mercy and grace.

February 3

Yahweh Heals My Emotions

Yahweh in the Word

> "The LORD (Yahweh) rebuilds Jerusalem; He gathers Israel's exiled people. He heals the brokenhearted and binds up their wounds" (Psalm 147:2-3).

The background for these comforting words finds God's people as captives in Babylon. They were hundreds of miles from their homes, and brokenhearted over their great loss. They may have been reasonably well physically, but they were heart-sick—emotionally depleted. But how encouraged they were to hear these words of promise. Their homeland was being rebuilt and Yahweh was gathering His exiled people for their return home—what healing this brought to them. Yahweh Yireh was restoring His people emotionally.

Yahweh in Your Walk

Isaiah the prophet was inspired by God to write words concerning the Messiah who came 700 years later: "The Spirit of the Lord God is on Me, because the LORD (Yahweh) has anointed Me to bring good news to the poor. He has sent Me to heal the brokenhearted...." (Isaiah 61:1). Jesus was just beginning His public ministry when he recited this same prophecy in His hometown synagogue (Luke 4:16-21). He concluded by saying, "Today, as you listen, this Scripture has been fulfilled." Jesus (Yeshua) came to restore all our brokenness. He followed this initial announcement with a ministry of bringing total healing to all who were in need.

We are emotional persons; we all experience joy and sorrow, love and hate, peace and distress, courage and fear, plus other feelings. Those emotions that cause distress can be extremely discouraging, even leading to illnesses. But **when we are troubled by our feelings, we can find relief by calling upon Yahweh Rophe.** The apostle Paul reminded the Corinthian believers that Yahweh was the God of all comfort, who comforts us in all our affliction (2 Corinthians 1:3-7). **Try calling upon Him for this comfort, using Yahweh Rophe, the special name we are studying in these devotionals.**

Has some situation left you feeling brokenhearted today? Yahweh welcomes your prayer for relief. Tell Him about your feelings; express your emotional pain. Then recall the promise of Jesus that He would send the Holy Spirit to be a personal "Comforter" (John 14:15-18)—a word meaning "one called alongside to help."

Yahweh in Your Worship

Thank You, Yahweh Rophe, that when I am feeling depressed, You lift me up by Your presence and promises of peace. I seize this day with confidence in Your Spirit of comfort within me. May I learn more of the emotional wholeness that only You can provide. Forgive me when I have tried to overcome my brokenness alone. Now I understand that You are present to bind up my wounds. Use me today to pass on this emotional healing to those around me who are brokenhearted.

February 4

Yahweh Heals Broken Relationships

Yahweh in the Word

> *"Be kind and compassionate to one another, forgiving one another, just as God (Yahweh) also forgave you in Christ" (Ephesians 4:32).*

Broken relationships between persons often occur because of some real or imagined offense. The apostle Paul recognized this possibility and urged the believers in Ephesus to seek reconciliation if this happened among them. Showing kindness, compassion, and forgiveness was essential to such healing. He appealed for this on the basis of the forgiveness received from Yahweh because of the sacrifice of Christ—"forgive because you have been forgiven."

Yahweh in Your Walk

Sin always results in brokenness—between us and Yahweh, and between us and others. Yahweh Rophe takes the initiative in bringing restoration—the healing of the relationship. When our Lord Jesus took our sin upon Himself at His cross, the way for restoration was made available to all who choose to believe.

Once we experience reconciliation with Yahweh, we are obligated to pass on to others that same forgiveness and healing. A well-known Christian leader was caught in an adulterous relationship. Later on a TV talk show, he and his wife were interviewed. Prior to the interview he had asked her forgiveness and she agreed. When the host of the show asked how she could be so forgiving, she replied, "I am simply passing on the forgiveness I have received from Jesus."

Jesus was very clear about this obligation when He said, "If you forgive people their wrongdoing, your Heavenly Father will forgive you as well. But if you don't forgive people, your Father will not forgive your wrongdoing" (Matthew 6:14-15).

Sometimes we are the offending one who needs forgiveness. Recently I found myself alienated from the college class I teach. My mistake was in scolding two students, in the presence of other class members, for their absence the precious class meeting. Later, the Holy Spirit made me aware of my mistake, so I offered an apology to the entire class. This was a very humiliating act for me but it was the only way to bring healing to a broken relationship. Class members were quick to forgive and the result was restoration.

We must not simply ignore our mistakes in situations like this. **Our place is to initiate confession of wrongs, make appropriate apologies, and bring forgiveness and reconciliation.** All this is the work of Yahweh Rophe.

Yahweh in Your Worship

Thank You, Yahweh Rophe, for assuring me of Your forgiveness for all my sins—past, present, and future. Now I claim Your grace to pass on to others that same kindness, compassion, and forgiveness. I seize this day with a forgiving spirit—Your Spirit in me.

February 5

Yahweh Heals All Things

Yahweh in the Word

> "Then he showed me the river of living water, sparkling like crystal, flowing from the throne of God and of the Lamb down the middle of the broad street of the city. The tree of life was on both sides of the river, bearing 12 kinds of fruit, producing its fruit every month. The leaves of the tree are for healing the nations, and there will no longer be any curse" (Revelation 22:1-2).

The apostle John recorded what he saw as an angel gave him a tour of the New Jerusalem. One important feature was the absence of any effect of sin—all evil and all results of evil were removed. The "healing of the nations" had occurred. Such healing restored a Garden of Eden reality. The "curse of sin" had been completely and finally removed.

Yahweh in Your Walk

We live in a sick world, surrounded by the consequences of sin. Yahweh Rophe has promised to bring total and final healing as He restores all creation to its original perfect condition. What a comforting truth! A recent Harris Poll revealed that only 67% of those surveyed were optimistic about the future. When we consider present trends of immorality and lawlessness, it is easy to see why many people are skeptical about the probability of things somehow getting better.

Statistics reveal a significant growth in various areas of our supposed advanced culture in America. We see an alarming rise in divorces, unmarried couples living together, homosexuality and other immoral practices. Along with this is the shocking number of political leaders who are caught in unlawful dealings. And, we note with shame how many religious figures fall from their places of respectability. All these facts reveal the activity of Satan, whose work is to steal, kill, and destroy. **Rather than panic in the light of such evil, we must maintain our trust in Yahweh's ultimate plan of bringing the restoration of righteousness and peace.**

The apostle Paul wrote these words to the Corinthian believers who were becoming discouraged regarding their depressing circumstances, "... do not focus on what is seen, but on what is unseen. For what is seen is temporary, but what is unseen is eternal" (2 Corinthians 4:18). The "unseen" includes all Yahweh is preparing for those who love Him. His ultimate plan is to bring complete healing in every dimension of life—physically (a new body), spiritually (an intimate fellowship with Him), socially (a peaceful relationship among all His children), emotionally (complete peace and wholeness), and a new heaven and earth where only righteousness is found.

Yahweh in Your Worship

I believe Your promises, Yahweh Rophe. Therefore I celebrate what I cannot see, but what, by faith, I know is coming. You are in ultimate control of all things and have promised the perfect health of everything, both physical and spiritual. **I reach forth and seize this day, believing that the best is always yet to be. And I praise You with all my being.**

February 6

Yahweh Is the Object of My Trust

Yahweh in the Word

>"It is better to take refuge in Yahweh than to trust in man" (Psalm 118:8).

Psalm 118 is the middle chapter of the Bible and verse 8 is the middle verse of the Bible. The words of this middle verse give the heart of the message of the entire Bible—"take refuge (trust) in Yahweh." Here is Yahweh's best counsel to us—trust Him.

Yahweh in Your Walk

The biblical word **trust** means to put confidence in someone or something. You know that American currency has the words "In God We Trust" prominently displayed. These words were also adopted as the national motto by an act of Congress on July 30, 1956. One source states that this affirmation was chosen as the result of a similar phrase found in the fourth stanza of "The Star Spangled Banner" which was written during the War of 1812. That statement is: "and this be our motto: In God Is Our Trust."

Having such a noble motto is certainly a good reminder of the importance of trusting God. However, having these words printed on U.S. currency and in our laws is one thing, actually trusting Yahweh is something far more. Trusting Him is the result of knowing that He is trustworthy. **We must become well acquainted with Yahweh before our trust in Him becomes a significant factor of our lives.**

We have one reliable source of knowledge about Yahweh—the Bible. He has chosen to reveal Himself to us through this sacred Book. There is no better way of growing in the knowledge of Yahweh than to become a serious student of God's Word. If you do not have a personal plan of daily Bible reading and study, begin developing one today. The psalmist said to Yahweh, "I have treasured Your word in my heart so that I may not sin against You" (Psalm 119:11).

Let the letters of the word HEART remind you of five ways to get His Word into your heart: **H-hear, E-examine, A-analyze, R-remember (memorize), T-think (meditate).** Include all of these as you seek to discover more about Yahweh, thus learning to trust Him more. Many serious students of the Bible keep a notebook to record discoveries they make in their study. Perhaps you will find help by such a personal discipline.

Yahweh in Your Worship

I do want to know You better and trust You more. Thank You for revealing Yourself in Your Word. Help me be more disciplined as a student of the Word. I seize the privilege of opening that Word today and learning of You, my Lord and my trust. Thank You for sending Your Holy Spirit as my personal teacher—One to guide me into all truth. And may Your truth come to me on its way to someone else. I long to become an effective witness of Your complete trustworthiness.

February 7

I Can Seek to Repay Yahweh for All His Goodness to Me

Yahweh in the Word

> "How can I repay Yahweh for all the good He has done for me? I will take the cup of salvation and call on the name of Yahweh. I will fulfill my vows to Yahweh in the presence of all His people" (Psalm 116:12).

The writer of this song of praise had a near-death experience (vv. 3, 8). But when he called on Yahweh, he was delivered from dying (vv.1, 5-8). As a result of Yahweh's goodness, the psalmist was determined to repay Him and mentions several ways he would attempt to do that.

Yahweh in Your Walk

Have you thought recently about how indebted you are for all Yahweh's expressions of goodness to you? Andrae Crouch voiced his sense of obligation in these plaintive words:

> How can I say thanks for the things You have done for me—things so undeserved, yet You give to prove Your love for me? The voices of a million angels could not express my gratitude—all that I am and ever hope to be, I owe it all to Thee. To God be the glory, to God be the glory, to God be the glory for the things He has done.

You probably feel yourself echoing these same sentiments. **The truth is, none of us can ever repay Yahweh for all He has done and continues doing for us.** However, like the psalmist, we can make a serious attempt. Notice how he decided to respond to Yahweh's favors: First, "I will take the cup of salvation and call on the name of Yahweh." **One basic way of showing gratitude for any gift is to receive it gladly while expressing gratitude to the giver.** Let Yahweh know how thankful you are for the "cup of salvation"—His grace that quenches your thirst for spiritual wellness.

Beyond this initial attempt at repayment is a more demanding one—"I will fulfill my vows to Yahweh in the presence of all His people." Each of us makes vows (promises) to serve Yahweh and to do whatever pleases Him. Making such commitments is a beginning, however, fulfilling those good intentions is far more demanding. **As you walk through this day, give serious thought to how you can live up to your promises to Yahweh**—this will be partial repayment. And this behavior is to be done openly, in the presence of His people. Participating actively in a local church fellowship is one very good way to do this. Start today working on repaying your debt. Make yourself available as a volunteer to help accomplish worthwhile ministries.

Yahweh in Your Worship

How truly grateful I am O Yahweh for all Your generous, undeserved gifts to me. Help me prove my sense of indebtedness by the sacrifices of praise, along with faithful service to You. Show me specific ways I can serve You by helping others. I want to be a doer of the word as well as a student of Your word. Set me free from any pretense of loving You that does not include self-sacrifice.

February 8

Yahweh Blesses Me as I Trust Him for Help

Yahweh in the Word

> "Hezekiah trusted in Yahweh God of Israel; not one of the kings of Judah was like him, either before him or after him. He remained faithful to Yahweh and did not turn from following Him but kept the commands Yahweh had commanded Moses. Yahweh was with him, and wherever he went he prospered" (2 Kings 18:5-7).

Hezekiah was a young 25 year-old when he became king of Judah. Many challenges came during his 29 year reign. He was, however, loyal to Yahweh, bringing many good reforms to his people, such as removing their idols and re-establishing the worship of Yahweh. At one time he became seriously ill, but Yahweh heard his prayer for healing and promised him 15 more years to live.

Yahweh in Your Walk

One of my favorite poems by Henry Wadsworth Longfellow is entitled "A Psalm of Life," and has these memorable lines:

> Lives of great men all remind us we can make our lives sublime,
> And, departing, leave behind us footprints on the sands of time.
> Footprints, that perhaps another, sailing o'er life's solemn main,
> A forlorn and shipwrecked brother, seeing, shall take heart again.
> Let us then be up and doing, with a heart for any fate;
> Still achieving, still pursuing, learn to labor and to wait.

Hezekiah has left good footprints for us on the sands of time. He was a man who, in spite of the influence of his wicked father, Ahaz, chose to follow Yahweh. Later, when threatened by Sennacherib, king of Assyria, and his huge army, Hezekiah turned to Yahweh for help. During the night, an angel of Yahweh destroyed all 185,000 Assyrian soldiers! (2 Kings 19:35)

We do well to follow this good man's example. **As we begin this new day, the wisest decision we can make is to commit ourselves and all we have to Yahweh, trusting Him to bring His will to pass in and through us.** Ask Him to help you be faithful to this commitment. If you stumble along the way, get back up and move forward, claiming His full restoration and strength.

Yahweh in Your Worship

Thank You, Yahweh, for the example of men like Hezekiah. You have proven Yourself to be faithful to all who place their trust in You. Help me this day to remember Your great promises and believe them. I choose to walk with You through all the challenges this day will bring. Keep me mindful of Your presence and guidance. I want to experience the true prosperity You provide, along with Hezekiah—the prosperity of honoring You in all I do.

February 9

Yahweh Welcomes My Worship of Him

Yahweh in the Word

> *"Come, let us shout joyfully to Yahweh, shout triumphantly to the rock of our salvation! Let us enter His presence with thanksgiving; let us shout triumphantly to Him in song... Come let us worship and bow down; let us kneel and bow down; let us kneel before Yahweh our Maker. For He is our God, and we are the people of His pasture, the sheep under His care" (Ps. 95:1-2, 6-7).*

Many of the psalms are worship songs. From them we learn truth about the meaning of authentic worship. In this text we find an invitation to worship Yahweh joyfully with loud songs of thanksgiving and praise. Notice the call to kneel before Him who is our Maker and Shepherd.

Yahweh in Your Walk

There are many opinions today regarding the nature of true worship. The same was true in Jesus' time. One day Jesus met a woman at a well in Samaria. She thought worship was primarily a matter of being in the right place—for her this meant on a certain nearby mountain where her ancestors worshiped. Jesus corrected her misunderstanding and declared, "An hour is coming and is now here, when the true worshipers will worship the Father in spirit and truth. Yes, the Father wants such people to worship Him. God is spirit and those who worship Him must worship in spirit and truth" (John 4:23-24).

Notice that Jesus affirmed that worship is not a matter of a physical location, like a mountain or even a temple, but worship is spiritual in nature—a person's spirit worshiping, and doing so according to truth. **We discover the truth about worship from Yahweh's Word—the Bible.** The better we know Him, the better our worship of Him will be. For example, our text today reminds us that He is our Maker and our Shepherd who cares for us. We are also admonished to express our worship of Him through loud, joyful songs of thanksgiving—along with bowing and kneeling before Him.

Today, we commonly speak of various types of worship services such as "traditional," "contemporary," and "blended." These terms refer primarily to the style of the music used in worship. Each of us has a preference for one of these—usually based on our traditions. However, **we must never assume that any one of these is "right" for everyone**. What matters most is not the style of worship but the heart of the worshiper. We can worship in spirit and in truth through many different expressions of music. Just remember that He is the object of our worship not us.

Yahweh in Your Worship

How about applying these truths as you worship today? First, kneel before Him, and then offer your own song of thanksgiving for Him as your Creator and Care-giver. Use your own words to express your spirit's praise and gratitude joyfully. This approach may seem a bit uncomfortable at first, but as you become more creative and expressive, you will find much pleasure as you worship in spirit and truth.

February 10

Yahweh Is Worthy of My Worship

Yahweh in the Word

> *"Ascribe to Yahweh, families of the people, ascribe to Yahweh glory and strength. Ascribe to Yahweh the glory of His name; bring an offering and come before Him. Worship Yahweh in the splendor of His holiness; tremble before Him, all the earth" (1 Chronicles 16:28-29).*

Here is a portion of the prayer King David offered when he brought the ark of Yahweh to Jerusalem and restored worship there. The term "ascribe" means to acknowledge that Yahweh is worthy of worship because of His glory and strength. Worshipers were to agree to this by bringing various kinds of offerings as they came before Him. All the earth should "tremble" before Him in the sense of recognizing Yahweh as Creator and thus worthy of worship.

Yahweh in Your Walk

We return to the subject of worship again today. The word ***worship*** comes from a root term meaning "worth-ship." That is, to worship someone or something is to attribute worth to them. And no one even begins to have the worth of Yahweh. Thus He alone is to receive our highest expressions of worship. Of all we are to do as believers and as a church, nothing is as vital and important as authentic worship. Think about these words of William Nicholls, "Worship is the supreme and only indispensable activity of the Christian Church. It alone will endure… into Heaven, when all other activities of the Church will have passed away."

Our text calls for us to "bring an offering and come before Him." **The primary and most important offering to express our belief in Yahweh's worth-ship is the gift of ourselves to Him.** As the prophet Isaiah declared in his most meaningful worship experience, "Here I am. Send me" (Isaiah 6:8). The offering of praise, thanksgiving, time, and money is likewise appropriate, but until we first offer ourselves, these are incomplete. During the time of the "offering" at your church always spend quiet time offering yourself and all you have to Yahweh—He alone is worthy of this kind of giving. I like to remember that when I place my financial offering in the plate, this money represents me in the sense of the time, effort, skill, etc. that I gave in earning it. I am giving a part of myself. And I do this with pleasure because Yahweh alone is worthy of such worship.

One caution is needed here: Remember that there is difference between entertainment and worship in our public services. There is nothing wrong with wholesome Christian entertainment, however, it must not be substituted for authentic worship. The question is: Who is the audience? God is the One to be honored in worship. Entertainment focuses on us and our pleasure.

Yahweh in Your Worship

Holy Yahweh, I seize this opportunity to begin this day worshiping You. I do so by offering not only praise and thanksgiving for all You are but also giving myself and all I have and can do to You. I ascribe glory and strength to You and You alone.

February 11

Yahweh Seeks for My Worship of Him

Yahweh in the Word

> *"But an hour is coming and is now here, when the true worshipers will worship the Father in spirit and truth. Yes, the Father wants such people to worship Him" (John 4:23).*

This text was part of our study two days ago, but needs further thought regarding worship. Our translation reads "the Father wants...." Earlier translations have, "the Father seeks...." The point being—Yahweh has a strong desire for us to worship Him in the proper fashion; He actively reaches out to us, appealing for our worship of Him.

Yahweh in Your Walk

What an interesting twist of reality—as we seek to reach out to Yahweh in worship; the truth is: He has first reached out to us! **Yahweh always takes the first step in all our relationships to Him, whether in worship or service.** He is the divine Initiator—first cause. What this means in practical terms is that our feeble efforts at worship are actually the result of His coming to us, awakening us to His worthiness, and assisting us as we seek to praise and honor Him. **When we see worship from this perspective, we are strongly motivated to participate more fully in all aspects of that worship.**

    Allow me to share how these truths have enriched my own experiences of corporate worship. When I meet with others to worship, I seek to actively participate in all that goes on. I sing all the hymns and choruses, I sing in my spirit with whoever is bringing some special message in song, I pray silently with whoever leads audible prayer, I focus on listening to the testimonies or preaching as Yahweh's word to me, I prayerfully place an offering in the plate as my gift of myself to Him. During the call for decisions, I respond in my heart to that invitation as well as pray for others to do so. In other words, **I am determined not to ever be a spectator or someone who is being entertained, rather, an active, fully involved worshiper.**

    All of this requires focus, concentration, and deliberate involvement. I want to be intentionally present for the purpose of what I can give toward true worship in spirit and in truth. Worship must never be about what we can receive, rather what we can give. Yahweh is the audience, we are the performers. Too often the reverse of this is what goes on—and some leave a worship service thinking, "I didn't get much out of that." What a false notion of what worship is all about! We worship to give, not to receive. If you have the opportunity to offer praise, thanksgiving, and honor to Yahweh, you have had an authentic, meaningful worship experience.

Yahweh in Your Worship

Gracious Yahweh, object of my worship, forgive me when I have failed to worship in a manner that pleases You. Help me seize every opportunity to please You with all my expressions of praise, adoration, and surrender. I do want to worship You in spirit and in truth. I claim the guidance of Your Spirit in making worship with others more conformable to Your will.

February 12

Yahweh Wants Me to Have Hope Beyond This Life

Yahweh in the Word

> *"Joseph said to his brothers, 'I am about to die, but God will certainly come to your aid and bring you up from this land to the land He promised Abraham, Isaac, and Jacob.' So Joseph made the sons of Israel take an oath: 'When God comes to your aid, you are to carry my bones up from here'" (Genesis 50:24-25).*

These are Joseph final words, and in this message is his firm belief that Yahweh would continue the work of ultimately restoring His chosen people to their original land of promise. His hope about this was based on Yahweh's promise to his forefathers, Abraham, Isaac, and Jacob. Joseph's final request was that the remains of his body be returned to the land of his birth for final burial.

Yahweh in Your Walk

One of the lesser known facts about the forty-year wandering of Yahweh's people in the wilderness is that they carried Joseph's bones with them. Our text reveals his instructions about taking his bones when they returned. He probably never imagined how long it would be before this vow would be fulfilled. There was a period of almost 300 years between the narrative that ends with Genesis and the events recorded in Exodus. As Moses led the people out of Egypt and on to the journey back to the promised land, we read this interesting account: "Moses took the bones of Joseph with him because Joseph had made the Israelites swear a solemn oath, saying, 'God will certainly come to your aid, then you must take my bones with you from this place'" (Exodus 13:19).

The next reference to this vow comes at the close of the book of Joshua. Joshua had died at the age of 110 years, and was buried. Then we read, "Joseph's bones, which the Israelites had brought up from Egypt, were buried at Shechem in the parcel of land Jacob had purchased...." (Joshua 24:32). Think about this rather bazaar and prolonged event. Joseph's body was embalmed and placed in a coffin when he died in Egypt. This coffin was preserved and cared for by the Israelites for the next 400 years, then buried as Joseph had requested.

Here we have an amazing expression of hope, based upon Yahweh's promise. Joseph believed that even though this promise had not been fulfilled in his lifetime, it would be someday—and it was! We have the same promise regarding our future. Jesus could return before our departure from this life. If so, we will be with Him. But if we pass before His return, the result is the same—we go to be with Him. Either way we win! **Having this assurance regarding the future enables us to face whatever comes with a solid hope based on His eternal promise.**

Yahweh in Your Worship

Thank You, Lord Yahweh, for the blessed hope I have in You and in Your promises. I rest in the peace of knowing that I will ultimately be with You in heaven forever.

February 13

Yahweh Wants Me to Pass on to Others What I Have Learned from Him

Yahweh in the Word

> "You, therefore, my son, be strong in the grace that is in Christ Jesus. And what you have heard from me in the presence of many witnesses, commit to faithful men who will be able to teach others also" (2 Timothy 2:1-2).

Timothy was the apostle Paul's son in the faith in the sense that Paul had nurtured him as a young disciple of Jesus. In this text Paul admonishes Timothy to be strong in the grace of Christ and also to pass on to others what he learned from Paul. These whom Timothy instructed would then be able to teach others what they had learned. Here then are potentially at least four generations of disciple-makers.

Yahweh in Your Walk

"Christianity is never more than one generation away from extinction." Years ago I heard this shocking statement of what could happen if one generation failed to teach the truths of the gospel to the next generation. Fortunately for us, all those generations of believers, beginning with the apostles, have been faithful to pass on to the next generation those truths they learned from Jesus.

Think about those persons who have shared the good news with you. These could include parents, friends, pastors, teachers, and many others. How thankful we must be for them and their willingness to teach us these life changing truths. But now it is time for us to take our place in becoming faithful witnesses to "teach others also." Let's think about some ways we can do this.

1. **Make an intentional decision to be a disciple-maker.** Jesus' final instruction to His disciples is called "The Great Commission." He said to them, "All authority has been given to Me in heaven and on earth. Go, therefore, and make disciples of all nations, baptizing them in the name of the Father and of the Son, and of the Holy Spirit. Teaching them to observe everything I have commanded you. And remember, I am with you always, to the end of the age" (Matthew 28:19-20). Basically, this is a command to disciples to be disciple-makers of disciple-makers.
2. **Ask Yahweh to show you that person or persons He wants you to teach.** You may not think of yourself as a gifted Bible teacher. However, you can teach what you know to one or more persons at a time. These whom you are to mentor may be from your family, friends, fellow-church members or other connections you have. Make this selection a matter of earnest prayer.
3. **Contact your chosen disciple or disciples.** Invite this person to have lunch with you, or whatever might be more appropriate, and share your interest in getting together for Bible study.
4. **Begin the process of learning together.** Meet on a regular basis, perhaps weekly, and begin working together through some simple Bible-based materials, plus sharing life together.

Yahweh in Your Worship Thank You, Yahweh, for sending those who have taught me; help me as I seek to pass on to others what I have learned—for Your glory and honor.

February 14

Yeshua Commands Me to Love Others as He Loves Me

Yeshua in the Word

> *"I give you a new command: Love one another. Just as I have loved you, you must also love one another. By this all people will know that you are My disciples, if you have love for one another" (John 13:34-35)*

These important words are part of Jesus' (Yeshua's) farewell discourse. He had just given an example of humble service by washing the feet of the disciples, including Judas. Then He told them of His being betrayed by one of them. This background makes the command to love as He loved much more significant.

Yeshua in Your Walk

Today is Valentine's Day—a celebration of love for one another. More than 2 million love notes and gifts will be shared today. How appropriate to have a special day to recognize the importance of letting others know of our love for them. **As followers of Jesus, we have been given a special love command—a new command—to love all others as He has loved us.** Why is this a "new command"? The previous command about loving others was "Love your neighbor as yourself" (Matthew 22:39)—an expression of human love. This new command features divine love—"as I have loved you." His love is far greater than ours—a self-sacrificing love (as shown on the cross), and a love for one's enemies (like Judas).

How can we as humans express divine love? The apostle John helps us with this answer: "No one has ever seen God. If we love one another, God remains in us and His love is perfected in us" (1 John 4:12). In other words, God provides the kind of self-sacrificing love He requires of us by literally living in us and loving through us. Amazing love! Our role is to welcome the Holy Spirit to live in us, control us, and express His fruit (love) in our words and actions.

As you walk through this day, claim Yeshua's love to be clearly revealed through you. Be willing to turn away from all selfishness (self-love) and reach out to all others, even enemies, with true compassion and kindness. Remember that Yeshua said, "By this all people will know you are My disciples, if you have love for one another." Tom M. Jones expressed his desire for this to happen with him as he wrote these challenging lines:

> Let the beauty of Jesus be seen in me, All His wonderful passion and purity. O Thou Savior divine, all my nature refine. Till the beauty of Jesus be seen in me.

Yahweh in Your Worship

Precious Lord, how great is Your love for me and for all others. As I bow in worship before You just now, I claim the promise of Your love filling me and overflowing to others. Use me as an example of what it means to love others as You have loved me. Lead me today to those who need an expression of Your love in some kind word or helpful deed; touch them through me.

February 15

Yahweh Wants Me to Guard My Heart Above All Else

Yahweh in the Word

> "My son, pay attention to my words; listen closely to my sayings. Don't lose sight of them; keep them within your heart. For they are life to those who find them, and health to one's whole body. Guard your heart above all else, for it is the source of life" (Proverbs 4:20-23).

Solomon wrote these words of wisdom to his son. He called on him to pay close attention to what was being said to him, and to keep these life-instructions in his heart. The result would be a meaningful life as well as good health. Both spiritual and physical benefits were promised if this father's wise counsel was heeded. What is most important, above everything else, is to carefully guard one's heart for it is the "source of life."

Yahweh in Your Walk

Your physical heart is the most essential organ of your body. And what an amazing creation it is. We are told that our heart pumps at a rate of 70-75 beats per minute. And although it weighs only about 11 ounces, it pumps around 2,000 gallons of blood through 60,000 miles of blood vessels every day. Your heart creates enough energy daily to drive a truck 20 miles, which in an average lifetime would equal going to the moon and back. But if your heart fails, all your body shuts down and you die. No wonder we give so much attention to having a healthy, functioning heart.

When Solomon spoke to his son about guarding his heart, he spoke of another very essential, life-giving part of you—your spiritual heart—that part of you that controls your thoughts, emotions, decisions, and actions. Your heart is the command center of your life. Another proverb affirms this truth in these words: "As a man thinks in his heart, so is he" (Proverbs 23:7 KJV).

So, how can you guard your heart today? Here are a few practical suggestions:

1. **Avoid anything that might cause "heart problems."** Your eyes and ears are the primary entry points to your heart. Be on guard against visual images that could corrupt your thoughts, such as pornography or reading material that provokes unwholesome thinking. Refuse to listen to false teachings, gossip, or stories that would corrupt your mind.
2. **Focus your attention on what is good,** as Paul told the Philippians: "Whatever is true, whatever is honorable, whatever is just, whatever is pure, whatever is lovely, whatever is commendable—if there is any moral excellence and if there is any praise—dwell on these things" (Phil. 4:8).
3. **Spend time each day in God's word—reading, meditating, and memorizing its truths.** The psalmist said, "I have treasured Your word in my heart so that I may not sin against You" (Psalm 119:11). The best defense against Satan's temptations is the sword of the Spirit.

Yahweh in Your Worship Today, I seize the opportunity to worship You, and claim Your protection of my heart. Create in me a clean, pure, and devoted heart—for Your sake.

February 16

Yahweh Has Inscribed Me on the Palms of His Hands

Yahweh in the Word

> "Zion says, 'Yahweh has abandoned me; Yahweh has forgotten me!' Can a woman forget her nursing child, or lack compassion for the child of her womb: Even if these forget, yet I will not forget you. Look, I have inscribed you on the palms of My hands; your walls are continually before Me" (Isaiah 49:14-16).

Isaiah imagines the city of Zion (Jerusalem) complaining that Yahweh had forgotten her, because He sent her children off into exile. However, Yahweh responds with strong assurance that just as a mother would not forsake her own child, He remembers His chosen people and even has them written on the palms of His hands. That same promise is made to you as His child today.

Yahweh in Your Walk

Have you ever written someone's name or phone number in the palm of your hand so you wouldn't forget it? I have done this many times. Such an action shows how important we consider that information to be. Recently I was in a restaurant and noticed a small tattoo on the inside of the food server's arm. When I inquired about it, she told me it was her boyfriend's name. Nowadays it's not uncommon to see special names, symbols, pictures, and even Scripture verses tattooed on various body parts. All this artwork is an attempt to make a statement about what that person considers important.

Notice in our text that Yahweh declares that He has His children inscribed on the palms of His hands—not their names, but them. How intensely personal is this image of His love and care for His people! **As you walk through this day, think about Yahweh's love for you.** He values you more than you realize because He created you for a special purpose. You exist because of His desire to have fellowship with you and to enjoy walking together through this day. Ask Him to make you sensitive to His divine appointments for you.

There may be times when you feel like Zion in our text—abandoned by Yahweh. But His comforting words assure you of His personal interest in you and His desire to remain in a close relationship with you. Jesus told His followers that they were secure in His hand and also in the Father's hand: "No one is able to snatch them out of the Father's hand. The Father and I are one" (John 10:29-30).

Joanie Yoder is one of my favorite devotional writers. Recently I read these words from her: "God bears the world's weight on His shoulder yet holds His children in the palm of His hand."

Yahweh in Your Worship

O Yahweh, how easy it is to worship One like You, who holds me in Your hand and promises to never forget nor forsake me. Thank You for reassuring me of Your strong and faithful love. Help me be a bold witness to others of Your goodness.

February 17

Yahweh Will Discipline Me as His Child

Yahweh in the Word

> "Consider Him who endured such hostility from sinners against Himself, so that you won't grow weary and lose heart. In struggling against sin, you have not yet resisted to the point of shedding your blood. And you have forgotten the exhortation that addresses you as sons: 'My son, do not take the Yahweh's discipline lightly or faint when you are reproved by Him, for Yahweh disciplines the one He loves and punishes every son He receives'" (Hebrews 12:3-6).

The first persons to read these words were experiencing hardships and various trials due to their Christian professions. The writer of Hebrews sought to encourage them by reminding them of two things: (1) the persecution Jesus received as a man, and (2) the fact that Yahweh is a good Father who disciplines His children for their benefit.

Yahweh in Your Walk

You probably know from experience that parents will discipline their children if they love them. We all have needed such correction as we grew to adulthood. If a child is left to follow his own inclinations, with no guidance, he will never develop properly. You may have children of your own and know how necessary firm discipline—tough love—can be.

As Yahweh's beloved children He will faithfully administer the correction we need as we walk with Him. Many biblical examples affirm this important truth. Job is known for all the hardships he endured—far beyond anything we have experienced. He suffered the loss of his possessions, his children, his health, his wife's support, and even the confidence of his friends. One of his friends sought to comfort Job with these words: "See how happy the man is God corrects; so do not reject the discipline of the Almighty. For He crushes but also binds up; He strikes, but His hands also heal" (Job 5:17-18). Although this friend did not fully understand Job's situation, he did give sound advice—our troubles may be Yahweh's way of helping us be better.

After Job endured much suffering and the misunderstanding of his wife and friends, he made this statement to Yahweh: "I had heard rumors about You, but now my eyes have seen You. Therefore I take back my words and repent in dust and ashes" (Job 43:5-6). The Father's discipline had its intended effect—Job became a better man through his trials. Yahweh worked through his troubles for Job's good and Yahweh's glory. What could have been a permanent loss became a lasting gain for Job.

How do you respond to trouble? Do you see the hand of Yahweh working to bring His loving discipline to you? **Rather than becoming discouraged and defeated by hardships, consider trials to be a means of learning, growing in character, and moving forward toward maturity.** Trust your loving Father who knows what's best—even His tough love.

Yahweh in Your Worship

Loving Father, I am your child. Give me the discipline I need. Thank You for helping me grow.

February 18

Yahweh Made His Beautiful World for Me

Yahweh in the Word

> "The heavens were made by the word of Yahweh, and all the stars by the breath of His mouth. He gathers the waters of the sea into a heap; He puts the depths into storehouses. Let the whole earth tremble before Yahweh; let all the inhabitants of the world stand in awe of Him. For He spoke, and it came into being; He commanded, and it came into existence" (Psalm 33:6-9).

Here is a clear call to worship Yahweh as the creator of the entire universe. His greatness is revealed by the fact that He brought all things into existence by simply commanding it to do so. No further theory or explanation of creation is offered; none other is needed. How awesome!

Yahweh in Your Walk

As you walk through this and every day seek to be mindful of all the wonders of creation—from the heavens above to the earth below; include the wonders of the creation of all humankind—each person completely unique and gifted by the Master craftsman. Take time to pause and observe these miracles; let each one provoke thoughts of praise and gratitude to such an amazing Creator/God. Seize these opportunities to worship.

The following hymn was composed by Maltbie Babcock (1858-1901) a gifted pastor who also loved running through the countryside near Lockport, NY. Before his morning run he would say to friends, "I am going out to see my Father's world."

> This is my Father's world, and to my listening ears
> All nature sings, and round me rings the music of the spheres.
> This is my Father's world; I rest me in the thought
> Of rocks and trees, of skies and seas—His hand the wonders wrought.
> This is my Father's world, the birds their carols raise,
> The morning light, the lily white, declare their Maker's praise.
> This is my Father's world; He shines in all that's fair;
> In the rustling grass I hear Him pass, He speaks to me everywhere.
> This is my Father's world, O let me ne'er forget
> That though the wrong seems oft so strong, God is the Ruler yet.
> This is my Father's world; the battle is not done;
> Jesus who died shall be satisfied, and earth and heav'n be one.

Yahweh in Your Worship

Today I choose to be a worshiper of You, gracious Yahweh, all day long. Assist me to see Your amazing hand in the wonders of nature—above and all around me. Open my eyes to see each person I meet as Your special masterpiece. Thank You for creating me in Your image and likeness. Use me this day as a witness of Your creative and re-creative power through Jesus. Thank You for all the amazing wonders of nature—both large and small.

February 19

Yeshua Invites Me to a Lifetime of Learning

Yeshua in the Word

> *"Come to Me, all of you who are weary and burdened, and I will give you rest. All of you, take up My yoke and learn from Me, because I am gentle and humble in heart, and you will find rest for yourselves. For My yoke is easy and My burden is light" (Matthew 11:28-30).*

These familiar words of Yeshua invite everyone to come to Him and find rest from the weariness and burdens of life. To "take up My yoke" means to become a disciple who learns from Him. His yoke is easy in the sense of being personally fitted to each individual's need. And His burden is light compared to the burden of seeking to bear life's trials alone.

Yeshua in Your Walk

John Stott departed this life in 2011. Before his passing he wrote many helpful books. In one of these I found this interesting statement: "Life is a pilgrimage of learning, a voyage of discovery, in which our mistaken views are corrected, our distorted notions adjusted, our shallow opinions deepened and some of our vast ignorances diminished." I like this description of life as a "pilgrimage of learning." No matter how old we become, we have the need and the possibility of continuing to learn. Jesus recognized this and invites us to keep on learning from Him every day.

None other has ever matched the skill of Yeshua as a teacher. His first disciples saw Him in that role as they followed Him about, listening to His teachings. Knowing that He would not always be around to teach His followers, He made this amazing promise: "I have spoken these things to you while I remain with you. But the Counselor, the Holy Spirit—the Father will send Him in My name—will teach you all things and remind you of everything I have told you" (John 14:25-26). And so now, our Teacher is the Holy Spirit. **Although He teaches us through many ways, such as the wonders of nature, life experiences, and the counsel of others, His primary textbook is the Bible.** As the apostle Paul declared, "For whatever was written in the past was written for our instruction, so that we may have hope through endurance and through the encouragement of the Scriptures" (Romans 15:4).

Every time you open the Bible, you give the Holy Spirit the opportunity to exercise His teaching ministry. Why not form the habit of opening your Bible along with a simple prayer like this: "Holy Spirit as I open this book in my hands, I ask You to open my heart to Your Word, and open Your Word to my heart." Be a life-long learner under the guidance of the life-way Teacher.

Yeshua and Your Worship

Lord Yeshua, thank You for sending the Holy Spirit to be my teacher. I claim His illumination as I seek to be learning from all of life's experiences. May I improve at being a doer of the Word and not a hearer only. And I want to be used by You to teach others what You teach me.

February 20

Yahweh Provides Guidelines for His People to Follow

Yahweh in the Word

> *"You shall have no other gods before me" (Ex. 20:3).*

The next ten devotionals will focus on the Ten Commandments. Consider how you can be obedient to these "God first" words.

Israel arrived at Mount Sinai three months after departing from Egypt. Immediately Moses went up the mountain to speak with the Lord, and there God offered to enter into the covenant with Israel.

He promised to make Israel His own special people, a kingdom of priests, and a holy nation. People who entered into the covenant with Yahweh would be God's treasured people immediately and forever. The Law was given only to Israel at that time to mark them as God's chosen people. The key to understanding the first commandment is the phrase "no other gods before me." These commands are not merely good advice or tips on etiquette, but what people must do for God. The Egyptians had numerous deities, but God claimed Israel for His own. The Hebrew people were to worship Him and Him alone with all their hearts. Since God was greater than all creation, idols carved from wood or stone were unacceptable. The Lord also forbade the Israelites to bow down before any image or to serve any god represented by an image.

Yahweh in Your Walk

One day in Hong Kong while visiting our missionary son, a special day was planned to include a visit to the Temple of a thousand Buddhas. Every wall inside the building was covered with theses gold idols, except for a huge 274,428 pound, manmade statue sitting in the middle of the room. I asked myself, "Why would anyone worship this ugly image?" Research about this man would be needed if I was to understand why people would bow down and worship him. So I decided to read some material about Buddha and found that he was born near Nepal on the Indian border. The historical details of the Buddha's life are hard to establish. According to tradition, the Buddha began his search for enlightenment at the age of 29. After a lifetime of missionary activity, the Buddha died in Kusinagare, Nepal, as a result of eating contaminated food. He was 80 years-old and his body was cremated. Today, Buddhism is a major world religion centered in India and based on the teaching of Siddhartha Gautama, who is known as the Buddha, or Enlightened One. As we left the temple, my heart grieved for these lost individuals who were so blinded by their false god. What needs to happen for these people to give up their lesser gods and know the real God?

Yahweh in Your Worship

Yahweh, I pray for wisdom to know the best ways to keep You first in my worship. Help me to stay focused on Your Word and Your guidance. Lead me to practice these Ten Commandments in my daily walk. Yes, Yahweh, I agree, we are to begin with You.

February 21

Yahweh Wants Me to Use His Name Only for Petitions and Praise

Yahweh in the Word

> "Do not make an idol for yourself, whether in the shape of anything in the heavens above or on the earth below or in the waters under the earth. You must not bow down to them or worship them; for I, the LORD your God, am a jealous God, punishing the children of the Father's sin, to the third and fourth generations; of those who hate Me, but showing faithful love to a thousand generations of those who love Me and keep My commands" (Exodus 20:4-6).

The Israelites had lived as captives in Egypt for over 400 years and had witnessed idols of gold made for worshiping flies. These idols had serious consequences. They distorted the fundamental reality of God as Creator. Idols make a god of something that is not God and gives allegiance to the father of lies, Satan. Now we understand why God gave **the second commandment.** The key to understanding this command is believing that God alone was to be worshiped. He would allow no other gods to stand or sit beside him on the throne of their hearts. The likeness of him would limit and dishonor Him. Moreover, human nature makes it inevitable that those who use such an image in worship sooner or later end up worshiping the image rather than God. **He will not tolerate divided loyalties.**

Yahweh in Your Walk

My husband and I have traveled to many countries around the world and I never cease to be shocked at some of the idols we encountered in homes and buildings. Idols come in all sizes; some so ugly they would scare a child away. Other idols are beautiful and have a special place in the room. The idol owners are sincere in their worship of some created god and will light candles and bring gifts to the image. Maria was a new Christian in the South American church. We were invited to her house for a meal during our visit to her village. Upon entering the dwelling, I noticed a wall dedicated to "gods." She immediately noticed my interest in this idol tribute. She said her father still believed in these false gods and would not allow her to remove the worship place.

Later, I asked Maria to explain what the wall had meant to her before she became a Christian. Her story was quite interesting and she carefully responded to my question. She knew that these images were harmless little statues. However, what if the idols were real? Until she met Jesus, she just chose to think the way of her ancestors. I asked for permission to take a picture of the worship wall, but she refused my request. Had she totally given up her faith in human ability to create gods for the truth that God is the holy and just God… no other thing will do?

Yahweh in Your Worship

Yahweh, lead me to be aware of the things of God and not human creations. Guide me to have a better understanding of people who worship false gods. Help me to really care what these people believe about their gods. Use me to be Your witness to them of the truth.

February 22

Yahweh Wants Us to Live and Speak the Truth

Yahweh in the Word

> *"Do not misuse the name of the Yahweh your God, because the Yahweh will punish anyone who misuses His name" (Exodus 20:7).*

This third commandment is probably the most misunderstood of all the commandments. The usual interpretation for this commandment is that it applies to cursing, to the use of some word for God in an expletive. This law clearly prohibits the use of the name of God in a crude way. People are to hallow Yahweh's name. However, **this command refers to far more than the careless use of His name in profane language.** Taking oaths in Yahweh's name is perhaps the primary prohibition here. You may have witnessed someone taking a political oath of office or making some other solemn vow and adding the words, "So help me God." To make such a promise in Yahweh's name and fail to live up to that vow is taking His name in vain. The same is true of marriage vows made "in the name of the Father and the Son and the Holy Spirit." If those sacred promises are not kept, God's name has been taken in vain.

Yahweh in Your Walk

Jesus warned His hearers against taking oaths and swearing by some sacred object, such as heaven or Jerusalem. His teaching was: "Let your word 'yes' be 'yes,' and your 'no,' be 'no.' Anything more than this from the evil one" (Matthew 5:37). In other words, He was saying we should be persons who speak truth without any need of adding some kind of oath. Just be sincere and truthful in all you say.

We Christians have taken the sacred name of Christ upon us; we are identified by His name. If we fail to allow Him to make a significant difference in our conduct and character, there is a real sense in which we have taken His name in vain; we have misused His name. We have claimed to belong to Him and said that we are His followers, and yet such boasting is meaningless if our behavior speaks otherwise. This hypocrisy is a violation of the Third Commandment.

Remember what we have shared earlier about Yahweh's name. This special word means, "I AM," and is the most frequently occurring noun in the entire Old Testament, some 6,828 times. No other word in any language is as significant as this one. The third of the Ten Commandments was given to safeguard the use of this sacred, holy name. The writer of the Psalms knew this. He declared: "Yahweh, our Lord, how magnificent is Your name throughout the earth" (Psalms 8:1); "Ascribe to Yahweh the glory due His name" (Psalm 29:2); "Proclaim Yahweh's greatness with me; let us exalt His name together" (Psalm 34:3). Indeed, as the songwriter said, "There is something about that name." Be diligent in showing the proper use of this name above all names.

Yahweh in Your Worship

Most Holy Yahweh, I speak Your name with utmost respect and reverence. Help me always remember who You are and thus guard against the improper use of Your name.

February 23

Yahweh Wants Us to Keep the Sabbath Day Holy

Yahweh in the Word

> "Remember to dedicate the Sabbath day; you are to labor six days and do all your work, but the seventh day is a Sabbath to Yahweh your God. You must not do any work—you, your son, or your daughter, your male or female slave, your livestock, or the foreigner who is within your gates. For Yahweh made the heaven and earth, the sea, and everything in them in six days; then he rested on the seventh day. Therefore Yahweh blessed the Sabbath day and declared it holy" (Exodus 20:8-11).

This fourth commandment is the longest, and is one of two such commandments that are stated positively. The term "Sabbath" means rest. Yahweh set an example of resting on the seventh day when He completed the work of creation: "By the seventh day God completed His work that He had done, and He rested on the seventh day from all His work that He had done. God blessed the seventh day and declared it holy, for on it He rested from His work of creation" (Genesis 2:2-3).

Yahweh in Your Walk

The seventh day of the week is our Saturday. The Christian Sabbath is on the first day of the week, Sunday. The major emphasis on this time is rest. Jesus had this in mind when he said, "The Sabbath was made for man and not man for the Sabbath" (Mark 2:27). **Yahweh intended for everyone to have respite from work and time for leisure.** "Holy" means that which has been set apart for God. A day that is holy is one which is devoted to God's special purposes, in this instance, a time of rest from common labor.

Our grandson and his wife are serious about setting aside one day each week for rest. Since they have a ministry of planting house churches among various ethnic groups, they find themselves very busy on Sundays. In fact, they have a small group meeting in their home each Sunday morning. In order to give themselves needed rest from normal ministry activities, they have chosen Mondays as their Sabbath day. They seek to avoid any meetings, performance of household tasks, and unnecessary contact with others on that day.

For some people such a practice would be impossible due to demands from their jobs. In that case, another period of time could be set aside for rest and focus on fellowship with Yahweh. **Whatever works for you is fine, just remember your need for planned times of rest and relaxation.** And such time should be devoted to Yahweh, in honor of His command. For example, most pastors will take a day off during the week since their Sundays are days filled with activities that can become very tiring.

Yahweh in Your Worship

Thank You, Holy Father, for Your example of resting from labors. Help me give respect to Your command for my rest. Teach me the value of setting aside a special time each week to cease from common employment and to focus more fully on Your purpose for me and my loved ones.

February 24

Yahweh Wants Me to Honor My Parents

"Honor your father and your mother so that you may have a long life in the land that Yahweh your God is giving you" (Exodus 20:12).

The Fifth Commandment to honor our parents forms a bridge between those Commandments relating to Yahweh and those relating to people. This Commandment is the last of our duties that focus on God and the first of our duties toward people.

Our parents are Yahweh's representative, for through them Yahweh has given us life and provides care for us. Moreover, through them He communicates His will to us and gives us guidance. Therefore, children need to develop an attitude of respect, reverence, and obedience on their part. Initially this duty must be instilled in children by their parents; children are not naturally obedient and respectful. The best way for this to occur is for parents to express honor for their parents. Such honor should be passed on from one generation to the next.

Yahweh in Your Walk

The erosion of moral values is shocking in American culture. Much of this can be traced back to a breakdown in family life. Yahweh's plan from the beginning has been for most men and women to marry and rear children. (Please note that we recognize this is not His plan for everyone. Some find fulfillment in serving Yahweh honorably as single persons.)

For example, our daughter, Martha, is a single mother—not by her choice—but due to an unfaithful husband. She is one of the best moms we know. And her daughter, Jordan, is developing into an outstanding leader in her school. But whether married or single, parents have the primary responsibility of teaching moral and spiritual values to their children. When we think of the good example Martha is to Jordan of how one should honor parents, we know this child will grow up to follow her mother's ways.

Think about your example at this point. Are you a person who gives proper respect and honor to your parents? Are they assured by you of your commitment to care for them when they no longer can care for themselves? Do you take time from your busy schedule to contact them frequently, just to let them know you love them and appreciate all they have sacrificed for you? One of the most common regrets people have is that of neglecting their aging parents when they should have reached out to them. So often, this concern comes after it is too late.

Another way of honoring "father and mother" is to adopt parents who have no children, or whose children neglect them. We have seen younger people do this and find great pleasure in such acts of compassion. You can bring tremendous joy to older adults who have no one to reach out in love to them. Perhaps Yahweh will lead you to meet someone like this, and become the child they never had. Just follow the Golden Rule and do to them as you would have them do to you!

Yahweh in Your Worship

Heavenly Father, You are so faithful to care for me; help me pass on that care to others.

February 25

Yahweh Wants Us to Reverence Human Life

Yahweh in the Word

"Do not murder" (Exodus 20:13).

Murder is the unlawful taking of a human life. **This Sixth Commandment** concerns the right to live and have human relationships. The primary reason Yahweh hates murder is that out of all creation only humans are made in His image. Jesus further clarified this command when He gave His Sermon on the Mount (Matthew 5:21-26). Hatred which is the same as murder is being vengeful, and hostile toward one's enemies. This commandment requires a spirit of kindness, patience, and forgiveness.

Some Bible students do not take these laws seriously. They consider them as merely general advice or tips of etiquette. The value of human life is not considered as important in their world. However, God demands respect for all people. An individual who has a violent temper should be considered dangerous. Someone who abuses another person is subject to fits of anger. No person has the right to take away the life of another person. **This Commandment forbids any unauthorized taking of human life.**

Yahweh in Your Walk

Life is God's gift; it is His first gift to us. How sad to see such disregard for the sacredness of human life. The media daily reminds us that people do not take this command seriously. Our state newspaper often has a horrible story involving murder featured on the front page of the paper. My personal experience with this commandment was serving on jury duty for my county. The foreman of the grand jury became ill and I was asked to serve for six weeks in his place. The only swearing-in I had ever witnessed was on the Perry Mason TV show. During those six weeks, I heard about terrible things that people did to others. Sleeping at night was difficult as I replayed the cases over in my mind.

One case that was so vicious was the abuse and murder of a little boy. How could this boyfriend of his mother be so insensitive to a small child? As the case unfolded in our grand jury, tears were shed by men and women because of the suffering of this small child. My emotions just ran wild because of the breaking of this Sixth Commandment. Fortunately, the murderer was sentenced to life in prison.

The most common form of murder today is abortion. Christians have different positions about this issue but the unfortunate victim, in most cases, is the unborn child. You may make a difference in this tragedy by helping in Right to Life causes and clinics.

Yahweh in Your Worship

Yahweh, help me to always consider that life is Your gift to humans and is sacred. Lead me to pray for people who are abused and who suffer any kind of brutality.

February 26

Yahweh Commands Faithfulness in Marriage

Yahweh in the Word

"Do not commit adultery" (Exodus 20:14).

This Seventh Commandment is a major step toward protecting the home. Adultery occurs when a married person is unfaithful to his or her companion sexually. A man was prohibited from taking another man's wife in a sexual relationship. God's plan for marriage is for one man to be joined together with one woman in a continual union. The sin of adultery breaks down the trust between a husband and his wife. A husband who is unfaithful violates his wife's confidence in him.

Jesus helped with the understanding of this problem in Matthew 5:21-26. He taught in the Sermon on the Mount that any sexual impurity between a man and a woman whether in thought, word, or deed, is wrong. The Hebrews viewed adultery as a sin both against an individual's body and against society. When marriage is not a secure relationship of trust and fidelity, all social relationships suffer. The choice to disobey this commandment leads a person down a path of destruction.

Yahweh in Your Walk

Perhaps the most well-known biblical account of an adulterous relationship is the one between King David and Bathsheba (2 Samuel 11:1-27). David lusted after this beautiful married woman when, from his rooftop, he saw her bathing. David forced her to have a sexual relationship with him, resulting in her pregnancy. In an attempt to cover his sin he tried to arrange for her to sleep with her husband, Uriah. When that failed he sent Uriah into battle so that he was killed. The Scriptures state: "The thing David had done displeased Yahweh" (v. 27). Later the child died and David's sin was exposed by Nathan, the prophet.

The reason for recounting this tragedy is to demonstrate the horrible consequences of adultery—how one brief sensual encounter often has such widespread and lasting effects on many innocent people. Because of David's sin, Uriah and other soldiers died, the baby died, Bathsheba suffered much grief, and David lost the respect of Nathan, God's prophet. Moreover David suffered greatly from his sense of remorse over his disobedience to Yahweh. Listen to these sad words from David regarding his sin: "Wash away my guilt and cleanse me from my sin... my sin is always before me. Against You—You alone—I have sinned and done this evil in Your sight" (Psalm 51:2-4). Fortunately, for David, Yahweh was merciful and forgave his sin. **We do well to be warned of the subtle power of our enemy, the devil, who deceived this very godly man.**

Yahweh in Your Worship

O Lord, thank You for creating marriage. Help me uphold the sacredness of this blessed relationship by adhering to Your command. Save me from speaking lightly of this tragic sin of adultery. I pray that our culture will repent of approving of this transgression.

February 27

Yahweh Wants to Maintain the Sacredness of Property

Yahweh in the Word

"Do not steal" (Exodus 20:15).

The Eighth Commandment forbids taking that which belongs to another person without their permission. Stealing another's possession is contrary to Yahweh's law. Why are people tempted to steal? It is one way of getting what a person is eager to possess without working to earn the money to purchase it. It's often getting something for nothing. Stealing also ministers to a person's conceit. The sense of being a bit smarter than others feeds the ego. Gangsters, embezzlers, and successful gamblers are fascinated by getting what they want without paying for it. These criminals will even steal the reputations of innocent people.

Yahweh in Your Walk

Jacob was an Old Testament person who was a thief. In fact his name means "supplanter" or "cheater." He prided himself on the fact that he could live by deceit. An example is the way he took advantage of his brother, Esau. Jacob offered to feed him in exchange for his birthright as the first born son. The famished brother sold Jacob his birthright for a bowl of stew! Later Jacob went on to deceive his father and stole the blessing that belonged to Esau. Subsequently, this deceiver was deceived by his father-in-law who tricked him into marriage with an unwanted daughter. Thus the principle of "what you sow, you will reap" was his experience. Fortunately, Yahweh was merciful in forgiving Jacob and ultimately changed his name to Israel, meaning "a prince with God." This thief became the Patriarch of the twelve tribes of Israel. What an example of how Yahweh can bring much good from what some would call a no-good person!

Stealing is a natural expression of our fallen human nature. Most of us, at some time, have taken something that was not ours to take—however small in value that item was. Or we may have taken credit for something we did not do—same principle. However, **our new nature in Christ is one that focuses on giving rather than getting.** Any form of stealing is completely contrary to this new quality of character. As Paul advised, "The thief must no longer steal. Instead, he must do honest work with his own hands, so that he has something to share with anyone in need" (Ephesians 4:28).

Again referring to Paul, who wrote this to his readers in Rome, "You then, who teach another, don't you teach yourself? You who preach, 'You must not steal?'—do you steal?" (Romans 2:21). We do well to examine ourselves carefully to be certain we are never guilty of stealing.

Yahweh in Your Worship

Yahweh, thank You for these special guidelines for living. Help me to resist every temptation to take anything that belongs to another. Teach me to be content with the abundance You have given me. I claim Your mercy and pardon for those times in the past when I have violated this commandment.

February 28

Yahweh Commands Me to Always Be Truthful

Yahweh in the Word

"Do not give false witness against your neighbor" (Exodus 20:16).

The Ninth Commandment seeks to maintain the truthfulness of a witness and thus to protect a person's right to a fair trial. The scene for this command is a court room drama. A person has knowingly made a false charge against his neighbor. A broader application of this law forbids telling any untruth.

Yahweh in Your Walk

We find many biblical examples of the grief caused by lying. Think about Simon Peter who was accused three times the same night of being a disciple of Jesus. He lied repeatedly by claiming to have nothing to do with Him (Matthew 26:69-75). Although Jesus knew in advance that this would happen, such a false witness from a trusted follower when He most needed support must have given Him much pain. In the book of Acts we read of many occasions when false witnesses were enlisted to speak untruths against Stephan (Acts 6:13) before he was stoned to death, and false charges were made against the apostle Paul in courts of law (Acts 25:7).

False statements made in public have continued through these centuries. Often in our own day the media has exposed such practices. You may remember the occasions when an outstanding American cyclist, who set numerous world records, was accused of using performance enhancing drugs. He repeatedly denied these incriminating charges until finally admitting his deceitful testimony. Countless other public examples of lying under oath have occurred in recent history.

As we said regarding stealing, the practice of lying is an expression of the old corrupt human nature common to every person. Satan works through this fallen nature to accomplish his evil purposes. As Jesus said of him, "He was a murderer from the beginning and has not stood in the truth, because there is no truth in him. When he tells a lie, he speaks from his own nature, because he is a liar and the father of liars" (John 8:44). **The only lasting remedy for this moral fault is a new birth which produces a new nature—one given to truth.**

The Holy Spirit is known as the Spirit of truth (John 16:13). We should begin every day by calling upon Him to control our thoughts and words so that when we speak, we speak truth. Our prayer should be that of the psalmist who said, "May the words of my mouth and the meditation of my heart be acceptable to You, Yahweh, my rock and my Redeemer" (Psalm 19:14). **Only He can overcome our natural tendency to be deceitful.**

Yahweh in Your Worship

Spirit of truth, thank You for revealing truth to me. I want to be a witness of Your truth in this world of false witnesses. Help me grow in the knowledge of who You are and all You want me to be. I claim Your merciful forgiveness of my dishonesty in the past. Fill me with Your power to resist the father of lies. Use me to declare Your gospel of truth to those in darkness.

February 29

Yahweh Wants Us to Deal with the Wicked Desires of our Hearts

Yahweh in the Word

> *"Do not covet your neighbor's house. Do not covet your neighbor's wife, his male or female slave, his ox or donkey, or anything that belongs to your neighbor" (Exodus 20:17).*

The tenth and last commandment focuses on what is known as "an ungoverned and selfish desire that threatens the basic rights of others." Covetousness grows out of a sense of greed wherein a person lusts after that which belongs to another. Various sins are an expression of covetousness, such as adultery and stealing. Yahweh demands that we respect the property rights of others. The covetous person is more concerned for personal material gain than human rights. Basically this sinful attitude reflects a discontent with that which Yahweh provides.

Yahweh in Your Walk

Once every four years we get an extra day, 366 rather than 365—called a Leap Year. This change occurs because the earth does not orbit the sun in exactly 365 days; that time is approximately six hours shorter than a solar year. Our calendar is called the Gregorian calendar and adding one day every four years compensates for the shortage. We have a friend whose birthday is February 29, so we tease him about celebrating his birth once every four years!

How interesting that our final devotional on the Ten Commandments occurs on this Leap Year day. This commandment is a prohibition against covetousness, or the improper desire for more. Leap Year occurs because of the desire for more! That is, our calendar wants another day in order to catch up to the solar calendar—we could say, it covets another day! Although this has absolutely nothing to do with the Tenth Commandment, it is an illustration of the meaning of covetousness—the desire for more.

Adam and Eve are notable biblical examples of violating this commandment. In the beginning God provided everything that this couple needed in their dwelling place called The Garden of Eden, and yet when the serpent showed Eve the fruit of the forbidden tree she realized that it was desirable as something she didn't have. So she ate, and sin and death entered the world.

The apostle Paul implored the Colossians to set their minds on the things that are above, not on the things that are on the earth. His list of undesirable practices to be cast off include: sexual immorality, impurity, evil desire, and greed (covetousness), which is idolatry (Colossians 3:5). Notice his designation of greed or covetousness as being idolatry; it is the worship of the material rather than the true spiritual worship of Yahweh. **Thus we learn that covetousness is a form of false worship.**

Yahweh in Your Worship

Yahweh, help me to recognize that coveting is a sin and to desire only what You have for me. Forgive me for wanting anything that displeases You. Teach me to be content with Your abundant provisions. Remind me that "Godliness with contentment is great gain" (1 Tim. 6:6).

March 1

Yahweh Nissi Gives Me Victory

Yahweh in the Word

> "Moses built an altar and named it 'The LORD is my banner (Yahweh Nissi)'" (Exodus 17:15).

Each month we will begin with a series of devotionals based on a different Yahweh combination. **This month the biblical term is Yahweh Nissi ("I AM the One who gives victory.").** The term *nissi* (pronounced NIS-see) is a Hebrew word meaning "ensign," "banner," or "standard." The usual reference is similar to our use of a flag, such as the American flag. Yahweh Himself is to be a believer's banner of victory.

The context for this biblical reference is the first warfare faced by God's people after they left Egypt on their way to the Promised Land. Moses stood on a hill top to watch the battle. As long as he held up his shepherd's rod, Israel prevailed. Aaron and Hur helped him hold up the rod till the battle was won. Then Yahweh told him to build an altar there which was named Yahweh Nissi (the LORD is my banner).

Yahweh in Your Walk

The authentic Christian life is one of continuous warfare—not a physical battle, but a spiritual conflict. As Paul reminded the Ephesians, "our battle is not against flesh and blood, but against the rulers, against the authorities, against the world powers of this darkness, against the spiritual forces of evil in the heavens" (Ephesians 6:12). In other words, Satan and all his demons are the enemies we must guard against.

As you walk through this day, be aware that your enemy will tempt you to disobey your Lord. Be alert to these subtle suggestions and respond, not trusting your own power and discernment, but by calling upon Yahweh Nissi for victory. James, Jesus' half-brother, was a leader in the church in Jerusalem. He wrote the very practical book of James in the Bible. Listen to his advice regarding our response to Satan, "Therefore, submit to God. But resist the devil, and he will flee from you" (James 4:7). Notice the order in which this command occurs—first, submit to Yahweh. That is, yield the control of yourself to Him, trusting Him for wisdom and strength for living a godly life. Second, "resist the devil." If we seek to resist the devil by our own ability, we will not succeed—he will not flee. However, **if we are fully yielded to Yahweh, we can be victorious over our enemy by Yahweh's power.**

William Cowper wrote a hymn with these words: "the devil trembles when he sees the weakest saint upon his knees." We find great comfort in knowing that Yahweh is sovereign over Satan, and will empower us to claim consistent victory over this subtle enemy.

Yahweh in Your Worship

O Yahweh Nissi, You alone are my hope of victory over the enemy today. My trust is in You. Thank You for Your promise to be with Me. I seize this day to be an experience of overcoming every attempt of Satan to distract me from following You.

March 2

Yahweh Nissi Provides All the Armor I Need

Yahweh in the Word

> *"Put on the full armor of God so that you can stand against the tactics of the Devil" (Ephesians 6:11).*

Yahweh Nissi does not fight our battles for us, but **He has provided all the armor and weapons we need to be victorious.** The apostle Paul describes this armament in detail, using the image of a Roman soldier like the ones who guarded him during the times of his imprisonments.

Yahweh in Your Walk

There are seven parts of this armor; **we will examine one for each of the next seven days**. First, "Stand, therefore with truth like a belt around your waist…." (Ephesians 6:14a). Jesus described Satan in this manner: "...there is no truth in him. When he tells a lie, he speaks from his own nature, because he is a liar and the father of liars" (John 8:44). The most effective defense against lying is truth, and the ultimate Source of all truth is the Spirit of truth—the Holy Spirit. As Jesus promised, "When the Spirit of truth comes, He will guide you into all the truth" (John 16:13).

The best way to know truth is by opening the Bible daily and claiming the teaching ministry of the Holy Spirit. Again, Jesus declared, "If you continue in My word, you… will know the truth, and the truth will set you free" (John 8:32). Reading these devotionals each day can be very helpful, but you need more exposure to God's Word than these brief writings. Discipline yourself to some plan of daily Bible study. Put on the belt of truth as you prepare to engage the enemy. As one friend says, "No Bible, no breakfast." He is committed to beginning every day by feeding on the truth of the Word.

I have found much help by memorizing biblical statements that apply to specific areas of life where I am weakest, then reminding Satan of these truths when tempted by him. For example, when Satan invites me to look at some image that could provoke lustful thoughts, I offer this prayer to Yahweh: "Turn away my eyes from looking at worthless things, and revive me in Your way" (Psalm 119:37). Or when tempted to worry, I declare, "My God will supply all your needs according to His riches in glory in Christ Jesus" (Philippians 4:19). These are practical expressions of using the sword of the Spirit to defeat the enemy.

Yahweh in Your Worship

Spirit of truth, today I worship You and thank You for opening my eyes to Your truth. I claim the protection Your Word gives to me in the warfare with Satan. Give me a greater hunger and thirst for the revelation You offer in the words of the Bible. Help me resist the devil and use the sword of Your Spirit effectively against him. I bless You for giving me authority over the devil by use of Your word of truth. I want to share this path of victory with others who are so often defeated by Satan. Remind me to reach out to these needy persons every day.

March 3

Yahweh Nissi Gives Me the Righteousness I Need

Yahweh in the Word

> *"Stand, therefore, with... righteousness like armor on your chest" (Ephesians 6:14b).*

Yahweh Nissi includes righteousness as another part of the spiritual protection we need for our battle against Satan. Paul compares this to the heavy armor worn over his chest by a Roman soldier to protect his vital organs. The term ***righteousness*** refers to two provisions made for us by Yahweh. One is known as **imputed righteousness**, referring to that right standing before God which believers receive as a gift by faith. The other is **imparted righteousness**, which means the work of the Holy Spirit to produce both thought and actions that please Yahweh—free from unrighteousness. Both of these are essential to protect us from Satan's attacks.

Yahweh in Your Walk

Satan is described as "the accuser" (Revelation 12:10). He often accuses us of being unrighteous in our relationship with God and with others. In other words, he reminds us of our sins. Our defense is to affirm that even though these accusations may be true, we have been forgiven and made righteous before God.

I recall times when Satan has reminded me of some transgression from my past. His purpose in doing this is to handicap me by causing feelings of guilt, shame, and remorse. But I have learned to overcome these charges by affirming the fact of Yahweh's forgiveness and restoration. He has declared me to be righteous in His sight, based on Jesus' payment for all my sin. Moreover, Yahweh goes on to produce righteous thoughts and actions toward others. **Thus the armor of righteousness protects and enables us to overcome the enemy and move forward in confident faith.**

Think about the author of our text for today—formerly known as Saul of Tarsus. He was a terrorist in the eyes of early believers in Christ. When we meet him for the first time, he is participating in the stoning of Stephen. Later, he is on a mission to locate, arrest, and imprison Christians in Damascus. But then came his dramatic roadside conversion. Subsequently, he became known as the apostle Paul, Yahweh's chosen missionary to the Gentiles. My point is: If Paul can be declared righteous before God, and experience His righteous kind of living, so can we. **We must never believe Satan's lying accusations that we are incapable of becoming persons who have the righteousness of God in Christ.** When we place our trust in Yeshua, He declares us to be righteous and begins His righteous transformation of us. (See June 1.)

Yahweh in Your Worship

"My hope is built on nothing less than Jesus' blood and righteousness; I dare not trust the sweetest frame, but wholly lean on Jesus' name. On Christ the solid Rock, I stand; all other ground is sinking sand." Thank You Yahweh Nissi for giving me the victory. I seize this day as an overcomer, by Your righteousness.

March 4

Yahweh Nissi Enables Me to Stand Firm Against the Enemy

Yahweh in the Word

"And your feet sandaled with readiness for the gospel of peace…" (Ephesians 6:15).

The image here is one of hand-to-hand combat, as was the common practice of Roman soldiers. Such warfare required sure footing; if a soldier slipped and fell, he was easy prey for the enemy. Thus, earlier in this passage Paul referred to the necessity of standing firm (vv. 11, 13-14). In order to stand securely, the soldier needed good sandals with tough tread. **In our spiritual warfare we find the solid stance we need in the gospel of peace.**

Yahweh in Your Walk

The biblical term ***gospel*** means "good news" or "glad tidings." This good news is the wonderful truth that we sinners can be completely forgiven and given a personal relationship with Yahweh, which means that we literally share His eternal, abundant life. Wow, this is the best good news we will ever hear! And all this is His gift to us because Jesus died to pay our sin debt, leaving us a right standing with Yahweh. As the apostle declared, "We have peace with God through our Lord Jesus Christ" (Romans 5:1).

Therefore, as we engage the enemy, we are able to stand sure-footedly against him because we are at peace with God, and have His power at our disposal. As the old gospel song declares,

> Standing on the promises of Christ the Lord, bound to Him eternally
> by love's strong cord,
> Overcoming daily with the Spirit's sword, standing on the promises
> of God.
> Standing on the promises, I now can see perfect present cleansing in
> the blood for me;
> Standing in the liberty where Christ makes free, standing on the
> promises of God.

One such promise on which we can stand is this one from Jesus, "Peace I leave with you. My peace I give to you. I do not give to you as the world gives. Your heart must not be troubled or fearful" (John 14:27). Another helpful promise is: "I am persuaded that not even death or life, angels or rulers, things present or tings to come, hostile powers, height or depth, or any other created thing will have the power to separate us from the love of God that is in Christ Jesus our Lord! (Romans 8:38-39). This kind of good news gives us sure footing as we stand against our enemy in spiritual warfare. **Now walk forward to seize this day, standing firm against the enemy with your feet planted on Yahweh's gift of peace.**

Yahweh in Your Worship

Today I choose to be in the spirit of worship continually. My heart overflows with gratitude and praise to Yahweh Nissi, who is my victory over every temptation from Satan. I desire to not only celebrate this peace but also communicate this good news to others. Oh Yahweh, make me aware of individuals around me whom You have prepared to receive this witness; speak Your truth through me.

March 5

Yahweh Nissi Provides a Shield to Protect Me from the Enemy

Yahweh in the Word

> *"In every situation take the shield of faith, and with it you will be able to extinguish all the flaming arrows of the evil one" (Ephesians 6:16).*

The Roman soldier carried a large wooden shield, usually about two feet wide and four feet long, covered with leather. When the enemy shot flaming arrows, the soldier would crouch down behind this shield for protection. Paul compares Satan's attacks to these flaming arrows; the temptations that come our way are like burning missiles from the enemy. **Faith is like a shield to protect us. The promise is that, using the shield of faith, we will be able to successfully extinguish every one of these temptations.**

Yahweh in Your Walk

Satan knows how to tempt us in ways that are especially appealing to us as individuals. For example, the temptation to drink alcoholic beverages has no appeal to me; I have never been attracted to this danger. However, some other believers are strongly tempted to imbibe. On the other hand, what tempts me may have no effect on others. Our enemy is skilled at knowing our areas of weakness and attacking us there. This fact means we must prepare for Satan's attempts to lead us astray by anticipating his particular "flaming arrows" and having our shield in place.

Regardless of what may attract us to evil, the effective response is the same—"the shield of faith." This kind of faith means choosing to believe what Yahweh promises in His Word. As we find in Romans 10:17, "So faith comes from what is heard, and what is heard comes through the message about Christ."

Here is an acronym for faith that helps me remember what this special term means for believers:

F-forsaking all. My hope is built on nothing other than Jesus blood and righteousness.

I-I make the choice to depend, not on myself, nor on others for deliverance, but solely on Him.

T-rust I take His word as being totally trustworthy and rely on His faithfulness.

H-Him Yahweh is the only true and living God; He provides all I need to be and do His will.

What works for me is to find some biblical promise regarding an area of my weakness, then memorizing this promise and raising it as a shield of faith each time the tempter comes. I urge you to try this strategy and experience the victory that comes with it.

Yahweh in Your Worship

Gracious Yahweh Nissi, You are so good to come to my aide as I struggle against the tempter. I praise You for always being with me and supplying all I need to overcome the enemy. Help me to be wise and skilled in choosing the most effective means of victory.

March 6

Yahweh Nissi Will Protect My Mind from Evil Thoughts

Yahweh in the Word

"Take the helmet of salvation…" (Ephesians 6:17).

The Roman soldier wore a helmet made of thick leather or some kind of metal. Protecting his head was essential to his survival. Paul may have mentioned this part of the armor to point out the importance of a believer's thought processes. He knew all about Satan's attempt to influence a person's thinking, thus actions as well. "Salvation" is used in the broad sense of Yahweh's deliverance from sin and every expression thereof. The experience of salvation begins with a new birth, but includes all of life. **We are to "take" this salvation in the sense of receiving the Savior by faith, and allowing Him to provide His deliverance from spiritual bondage.**

Yahweh in Your Walk

Hughie was a true oil field "roughneck." He looked the part and used typical roughneck language. After he became a follower of Jesus, he told me he had to relearn how to talk without a profane and vulgar vocabulary. But he knew his salvation experience was real; he definitely was a new creation in Christ.

For the remainder of his adult years, Satan was relentless in his attempts to cause Hughie to fall back to his old ways of thinking, speaking, and acting. Our church family reached out to this adult babe in Christ. Thereby he learned the meaning of salvation. He actually became a Sunday school teacher of young boys; they loved this burly, bald, tough-looking man.

What caused this dramatic miraculous change? Hughie's testimony reflected Yahweh's hand of grace reaching out to him and awakening him to his need of Jesus. When he came forward at our church, he cried out to me and said, "I need God!" The rest is history—the helmet of salvation became his deliverance.

As mentioned above, we need special protection for our mind. If Satan can deceive us into wrong thinking, he can affect all we are and do. Do you remember from the book of Acts about the first serious problem faced by the early church? A man named Ananias along with his wife Sapphira, noticed how others in the church were being recognized for selling their property and giving all the proceeds to help needy persons. So, they agreed to pretend to do the same thing, and brought a portion of their sale and gave it to the leaders. Peter discerned their hypocrisy and asked them, "Why has Satan filled your heart to lie to the Holy Spirit and keep back part of the proceeds from the field?" Upon being confronted with their sin, they both fell dead. (Acts 5:1-11). What a dramatic reminder of the important of integrity! We also must be on guard against Satan's lies.

Yahweh in Your Worship

Yes, Yahweh Nissi, I choose to seize this day by taking the helmet of salvation and living fully by Your protection of my mind and heart from the enemy's attacks. I bless You for so loving me.

March 7

Yahweh Nissi Will Provide the Weapons for My Warfare

Yahweh in the Word

> "Take... the sword of the Spirit, which is God's word" (Ephesians 6:17).

Notice the inclusion of an offensive weapon in this picture of the believer's armor. A short, sharp sword was used for hand-to-hand combat. The apostle compares this to the use of God's Word to defeat Satan and all his allies. The primary objective of our spiritual warfare is not simply defensive—resisting the enemy, but we are on the offensive—marching forward to win victories as we attack Satan's strongholds and set captives free.

Yahweh in Your Walk

Listen to this vivid description of Christians attacking enemy strongholds: "the weapons of our warfare are not worldly, but are powerful through God for the demolition of strongholds. We demolish arguments and every high-minded thing that is raised up against the knowledge of God, taking every thought captive to obey Christ" (2 Corinthians 10:3-6).

These weapons are the truths from the Bible—the sword of the Spirit. And they are effective. Do you remember Jesus' experience of being tempted in the wilderness by Satan? The Scripture tells us He was tempted for 40 days; three of these temptations are described for us in Luke 4:1-13. Each time Jesus responded to Satan's offers by quoting Scripture—the sword of the Spirit, and every use of this spiritual sword was successful.

This episode was recorded for our benefit—to show us how to respond to temptations. **Our own human efforts to repel the enemy will not be effective. We must depend upon the Word of God.** For example, there have been many times when Satan tempted me to be fearful and anxious about some situation. I have learned to respond by quoting some Scripture, such as, "Do not fear, for I am with you; do not be afraid for I am your God..." (Isaiah 41:10). **Try this strategy against the enemy as you seize this day for Yahweh.**

What I have just described is the recommended action of **taking** the sword of the Spirit. A physical sword, no matter how sharp and strong, is of no value unless a warrior actually grasps this weapon and uses it. So it is with God's Word as a weapon. You may own several Bibles and keep them displayed nicely; however, unless you **take this sword** and attack the enemy, you will never experience its power to overcome his strategies.

Yahweh in Your Worship

As you worship today, give thanks for each part of the armor Yahweh Nissi has given you. Claim His strength and wisdom in putting on the protection needed, and take His sword by faith. Commit yourself to being an effective warrior in the battle for righteousness and truth. Cease being passive about spiritual warfare, go on the offensive against the strongholds of evil. Become more serious about setting captives free through intercessory prayer, using the various part of the Christian's armor to fight the battles.

March 8

Yahweh Teaches Me How to Put On His Armor

Yahweh in the Word

> *"Pray at all times in the Spirit with every prayer and request, and stay alert in this with all perseverance and intercession for all the saints" (Ephesians 6:18).*

Yahweh Nissi provides all the right armor for our warfare against all the powers of darkness. However, we must be diligent to put on this armor daily. In this text, which follows a detailed description of the various parts of the armor, the apostle tells us how to be suited up for battle—"pray at all times in the Spirit."

Yahweh in Your Walk

> An old gospel song has these words in the third stanza:
> Stand up, stand up for Jesus, stand in His strength alone;
> The arm of flesh will fail you, ye dare not trust your own.
> Put on the gospel armor, **each piece put on with prayer;**
> Where duty calls or danger, be never wanting there.

Notice this sound advice, "Put on the gospel armor, each piece put on with prayer." Some mornings as I begin a quiet time of worship through prayer, I thank Yahweh Nissi for providing each piece of this armor, naming them one by one, and claiming their protection for that day. I encourage you to follow a similar procedure as you literally put on each piece of armor by prayer. Having done this you are fully armed and ready for the spiritual warfare of that day.

Notice how the apostle adds these words: "stay alert in this with all perseverance...." In other words, make a habit of doing this. Each day we face attacks from our enemy, therefore, each day we must put on the armor. Also, remember the words "intercession for all the saints." Paul would have us give prayerful concern not only for our welfare but also for others. As you think about others, such as missionaries, pastors, and Christians friends, include them in your prayers—asking that they also be fully armed against Satan's attacks.

We are not alone in this warfare, not just individual soldiers of the cross. We are part of a mighty army that circles the globe. Therefore intercessory praying is so important and necessary for the triumph of good over evil world-wide. **Keep a list of others to remember when you pray.**

Yahweh in Your Worship

Yahweh Nissi, thank You for providing all the armor I need in order to win the battle against Satan and his host of demons. I claim each piece as necessary for my protection as well as the mighty sword of the Spirit—Your Word. I praise You for winning the ultimate battle for me. Help me engage and defeat the enemy through intercession for other soldiers of the cross.

March 9

Yahweh Teaches Me to Pray

Yahweh in the Word

> "Stand up. Praise Yahweh your God from everlasting to everlasting. Praise Your glorious name, and may it be exalted above all blessing and praise. You alone are Yahweh. You created the heavens, the highest heavens with all their host, the earth and all that is on it, the seas and all that is in them. You give life to all of them and the heavenly host worship You" (Nehemiah 9:5-6).

Chapters 9 and 10 contain the longest recorded prayer in the Bible. Yahweh's people had returned from their captivity in Babylon and rebuilt the wall around Jerusalem. They also restored temple worship and this prayer is a part of their celebration. After this opening expression of praise it recounts the history of how Yahweh blessed His people. Then follows a rather lengthy confession of the sins of His people and a renewed commitment to serve Him.

Yahweh in Your Walk

One of the best ways to learn to pray in a way that pleases Yahweh is to study the various prayers of the Bible. Nehemiah 9-10 affords you a good opportunity to do just that. Notice the components of this cry from Yahweh's people and consider making them a part of your praying.

1. Learn to begin all praying with an appropriate introduction that includes a celebration of Yahweh's greatness and goodness. As you listen to others pray, notice how often this way of approaching Yahweh's throne of grace is omitted. So often prayers begin, not with worshipful praise, but with some kind of request. **Always take time to address Yahweh with respect and gratitude.** You will remember our Lord's Model Prayer—"Our Father which art in heaven, hallowed be Thy name...."
2. Give expression to remembering some of Yahweh's special favors. Thank Him for all He has already done in the past. If you read Nehemiah 9 you will see much of this kind of appreciation.
3. Always acknowledge your sin and unworthiness. **Make specific confession of wrongdoings, asking His forgiveness.** This biblical model reveals how detailed this should be.
4. **Commit yourself to renewed obedience and faithfulness**. You will see this vow in chapter 10. Notice those who offered this prayer made no requests for themselves. Their sole purpose was to exalt Yahweh and offer themselves as His servants to do His will.

Yahweh in Your Worship

Try following this biblical model as you worship Yahweh in your own words. Give thought and time to approaching His throne of grace with adequate praise for who He is and all He has done. Proceed to enumerate some of His blessings to you and others. Be especially grateful for His mercy and grace in the light of your sins and complete unworthiness. Include a renewed commitment of yourself to be all He would have you be. Affirm His presence with you always. Cease asking Him to be "with" you; rather thank Him for promising to never leave you.

March 10

Yeshua Teaches Me How to Pray

Yeshua in the Word

> "Therefore you should pray like this: 'Our Father in heaven, Your name be honored as holy'" (Matthew 6:9).

As part of His Sermon on the Mount (Matthew 5-7), Yeshua (Jesus) gave His disciples instructions on how they should pray. Notice in chapter 6, "Whenever you pray" is repeated in verses 5, 6, 7 followed by The Model Prayer (vv. 9-13).

Yeshua in Your Walk

For these next few days we will focus attention on Yeshua's words about how to pray. Let's begin by agreeing that Jesus is the world's foremost authority on the subject of prayer. Luke's Gospel relates an occasion when the disciples overheard Jesus praying and one of them said, "Lord, teach us to pray, just as John also taught his disciples" (Luke 11:1). When these men heard Jesus pray, they recognized that He was a true authority on this important subject. His praying must have been very impressive. This is the only time they asked Him to teach them something. He responded by giving them a model very similar to the one found in Matthew 6.

He began where all praying should begin—a proper way of addressing Yahweh. "Our Father" is a title that reminds us of our common family relationship. **He is our Father in the sense of being the One who brought us into His family—we are His by right of birth—the new birth.** This title also implies His fatherly care of us; He will provide everything we need at all times. We are secure because of who He is and what He does for all His family. Notice this model is inclusive of all His children—"our Father," not my Father. In fact, all the pronouns related to the person praying are plural—"our," and "us."

"In heaven" speaks of His dwelling place, as well as the location of our ultimate home. Our Lord once said He was going to prepare a place for us in His Father's house, and we would eventually be there with Him. The assurance of this wonderful heavenly home enables us to endure the trials of this life with a sense of future peace. Although Yahweh is "in heaven," He is also continually with us.

"Your name be honored as holy" focuses our attention on the privilege of honoring Yahweh as the Holy One—the One set apart from all that is unholy. Remember from our previous devotionals that the Father's name is Yahweh; "Father" is a title, not His name. We must always be careful of how we use this sacred name—never in profanity or in some form of slang or irreverence, but always with the utmost respect and honor.

Yeshua in Your Worship

Begin your prayer and worship by honoring the name of Yahweh. Take time to address Him properly. Avoid rushing into your prayer. Focus on His holy name. Using His appropriate titles such as God, Father, Lord, Savior, Master, and Almighty is a good way to call upon Him. But just quoting the Model Prayer is not adequate; let this be an example.

March 11

Yeshua Teaches Me How to Pray

Yeshua in the Word

> "Your kingdom come. Your will be done on earth as it is in heaven" (Matthew 6:10).

We continue our study of the Model Prayer. Those who know Yahweh as Father are presently citizens of His kingdom on earth. For His kingdom to come means that His will is being done. His will is always done in heaven; the prayer is that His will also be done on earth—now.

Yeshua in Your Walk

All Christians are citizens of two kingdoms—the kingdom of this world and the kingdom of Yahweh. The kingdom of Yahweh is one where His will is being done; where He rules as king. In order for Him to rule as king over us, we must first be born again. Jesus said to Nicodemus, "I assure you: Unless someone is born again, he cannot see the kingdom of God… Unless someone is born of water and the Spirit, he cannot enter the kingdom of God" (John 3:3, 5). At the moment of our spiritual birth, we become a part of the kingdom of God. In fact, the King Himself comes to dwell within us by His Holy Spirit.

When we become a part of Yahweh's kingdom, our primary concern should be to know and do His will. You may have asked the question: What is God's will in this situation? Only a kingdom-person is concerned about such a matter. But how do we know His will? Most of what we need to know about Yahweh's will is discovered by studying His Word. **His Holy Spirit has come to us as our Teacher so we can know His will.** Future devotionals will guide you in a study of many biblical passages on the subject of God's will.

However, there are times when our questions about His will in a given situation are not covered by His written Word. Here is where we must seek and find help from other sources, such as the wise counsel of godly persons. As we turn to such help, we must always ask the Holy Spirit to speak His guidance through these counselors. Let them know that you are trusting Yahweh to speak His wisdom to you through them.

Here is a statement that has always helped me: **"If we want to know and do God's will, we will find a way; if we don't want to know and do His will, we will find an excuse."** For His will to be done on earth, it must start with me—now. Make certain that as you offer this part of the Model Prayer, you are willing to actually do His will.

Yeshua in Your Worship

Precious Lord, I do worship You as my Savior and Lord. I desire to know and do Your will in every area of my life. Thank You for sending the Holy Spirit to guide me into all truth and to teach me all need to know. Holy Spirit, I depend on You to also motivate and empower me to do God's will on earth as it is done in heaven. Use me an as example to others of the joy that is found in knowing You and seeking to do Your will in every possible way.

March 12

Yeshua Teaches Me How to Pray

Yeshua in the Word

> *"Give us today our daily bread" (Matthew 6:11).*

These six simple words express the first personal request in this Model Prayer. The focus is on our physical needs—"daily bread." These two words cover all we need to live in this world—food, clothing, shelter—all the essentials.

Yeshua in Your Walk

The apostle Paul declared Yeshua's faithfulness to provide all we need in these strong words of promise: "My God will supply all your needs according to His riches in glory in Christ Jesus" (Philippians 4:19). In previous devotionals we have considered Yahweh Yireh, the One who provides whatever we need. **Remember, however, there is a vast difference between need and greed. Yahweh never promises to give us all we want (greed), but all we need.** And the request in this prayer for Him to provide all we need, is even further restricted to "our *daily* bread"—just enough for one day at a time. This request is a confession of our dependence upon Yahweh for everything we need, right down to food for today.

As mentioned earlier, notice that all the pronouns in this entire prayer are plural: "our," and "us." We are thus taught to include all of Yahweh's family in our requests. These truths are contrary to the false teachers who would have us believe that prayer is our way of getting whatever we want just for ourselves—the "name it and claim it" appeal. These hucksters promote a "health, wealth, prosperity gospel." They teach that Yahweh wants all His children to be healthy, wealthy, and prosperous; and if you have enough faith you can ask and will receive all these provisions.

Of course, every serious student of Scripture knows these teachings are not true according to the Bible. Some of Yahweh's best servants suffered in many ways. The history of the church is filled with accounts of how some of the finest Christians spent much of their lives in poverty, sickness, and persecution. The experience of the apostle Paul and his associates proves the fact that followers of Jesus should expect to be mistreated and suffer loss. However, the Father was with them, providing their basic needs, and ultimately welcoming them home to Heaven. We also can depend on our Father to care for us. **We should often express in our prayers our awareness that we must always look to Him for His gracious provision.**

Yeshua in Your Worship

Thank You, Holy Father, for always supplying every physical need of mine. I continue to look to Your open hand of provision every day. Forgive me when I worry about not having all I need. Help me claim the peace that comes from the assurance that You are faithful to supply, both materially and spiritually, all I actually require to be an effective servant of Yours. And I want to share what You give me with others who have far less. May You use me to be Your instrument in providing "daily bread" for others. **Forgive me when I complain about not having more.**

March 13

Yeshua Teaches Me How to Pray

Yeshua in the Word

> *"And forgive us our debts, as we also have forgiven our debtors"* (Matthew 6:12).

The subject of forgiveness was repeated several times in Jesus' teachings (see vv. 14-15). His hearers were subject to various kinds of mistreatment, sometimes from the Roman government and its representatives, sometimes from various religious leaders, and then also, from personal enemies. He wanted to make sure that His followers understood the importance of being forgiving because they had experienced the Father's forgiveness through Him.

Yeshua in Your Walk

Having all we need physically is vital; we cannot otherwise continue to live. But we also need the Father's help with spiritual and relational needs. That is, we must have His forgiveness as well as being forgiving of others. Notice here that forgiveness is related to "debts." We know that a debt is something we owe—a personal obligation. Because of our sins, we are indebted to Yahweh. The only adequate payment to Him for our sin is death. When we place our trust in the Lord Jesus and His death on the cross as the full payment for our sins, Yahweh forgives us completely, for Yeshua's sake. **The request for forgiveness in the Model Prayer is to acknowledge this gift as the reason for us being likewise forgiving of anyone who has wronged us in any way.**

Our forgiveness of others is not to gain Yahweh's forgiveness for us; rather, having experienced His forgiveness enables us and motivates us to forgive others. Recently, I read about a family whose son was killed in a car accident caused by a drunken driver. The young man's parents were in court when this driver was sentenced. To his total surprise, these Christian parents told them of their forgiveness for what he had done. They went on to share the fact that they wanted to forgive him because God had forgiven them many times. All this occurred without this driver offering any kind of apology and asking their forgiveness. What a powerful testimony!

Remember that our forgiveness of others must be available even if they never ask for it. I have a friend who was offended by another person. His word to me was, "I will forgive them if they will apologize and admit their wrong." Forgiveness should always come before any demand for appeasement. If we hold on to unforgiveness of others, we are only harming ourselves. No one should ever assume that they must in some way earn our forgiveness. **We forgive freely because we have been freely forgiven.**

Yeshua in Your Worship

I praise You, Yeshua, for making forgiveness available to me by taking my sin debt upon Yourself on the cross. How amazing that You loved me this much before I was even born. Thank You for teaching me the true meaning of forgiving others. Use me now to extend this good news to any who have wronged me.

March 14

Yeshua Teaches Me How to Pray

Yeshua in the Word

> *"And do not bring us into temptation, but deliver us from the evil one"* (Matthew 6:13).

Here is the final request in this Model Prayer. We recognize that we all have a very subtle and crafty enemy—Satan, the "evil one." His purpose is to tempt us to disobey Yahweh, even as he did Adam and Eve in the garden. This appeal for Yeshua's protection and deliverance admits our sense of needing help when facing temptation and dealing with all forms of evil.

Yeshua in Your Walk

Yeshua's disciples went with Him to the Garden of Gethsemane on the night before His crucifixion. While He was praying, they all went to sleep. Later He awakened them and said, "Stay awake and pray, so that you won't enter into temptation. The spirit is willing, but the flesh is weak" (Matthew 26:41). Unfortunately, the same thing occurred two more times. Such happenings are written as a clear warning to us. Our adversary is continuously seeking to lead us astray from loyalty to Yeshua. We must have His assistance as we deal with this enemy.

This request is for Yahweh's help as we face temptation, whether from Satan, the world, or our own fallen nature. An old gospel song, "Just a Closer Walk with Thee," expresses our need in these words:

> I am weak but Thou art strong. Jesus, keep me from all wrong. I'll be satisfied as long as I walk, let me walk close to Thee. Thro' this world of toil and snares, if I falter, Lord, who cares? Who with me my burden shares? None but Thee, dear Lord, none but Thee.

We all have a responsibility to do our part in avoiding and overcoming temptation; just voicing this request in prayer is not enough. **Yeshua expects us to do our part by staying clear of situations where we know we'll be tempted.** For example, we know of individuals who are likely to want us to join them in activities that are not pleasing to our Lord, such as the use of alcoholic beverages, recreational drugs, various kinds of immorality, and questionable behavior. We must consistently avoid these situations, not with a holier-than-thou attitude, but in the spirit of faithfulness to our Lord. Your testimony to friends requires that you steer clear of anything that could lead to you compromising Christian convictions.

Yeshua in Your Worship

Today I seize this opportunity to praise You for Your example of resisting temptation. Thank You also for always providing a way to escape the tempter through the use of Your Word. I claim Your help as I seek to resist every form and appearance of evil. Use me as a good example to others of someone who loves You more than the appeals of this world. And may I be more sensitive to those around me who struggle with temptation. I long to be of help to them.

March 15

Yeshua Teaches Me How to Pray

Yeshua in the Word

> "For Yours is the kingdom and the power and the glory forever. Amen" (Matthew 6:13b).

The model prayer ends as it begins, with praise to the Father who rules over His kingdom with sovereign power and deserves all glory forever.

Yeshua in Your Walk

One writer has stated that the true measure of a person's spirituality is the amount of praise and thanksgiving in his or her prayers. Notice that Yeshua calls for praise at the beginning and end of this Model Prayer. The closing sentence actually summaries and brings to a fitting conclusion all the words of this brief prayer.

The first request was: "Your kingdom come. Your will be done on earth as it is in heaven." Now the closing affirmation is: "Yours is the kingdom." The kingdom belongs to Yahweh because He created His kingdom by creating all humankind, then redeeming all believers as members of His kingdom. The kingdom is His because we are His—both the kingdom on earth and the kingdom of heaven. He rules over this kingdom by the sovereign control of Yeshua who is the King of all kings. There are many kingdoms in this world but all are temporary and in the process of fading away; only the Kingdom of God remains forever.

"Yours is… the power." The original word for "power" here is **dunamis** in Greek, a word indicating might and ability. He alone has the power to create all things, sustain all things, and cause His will to be done on earth as it is in heaven. Only He can provide for all our physical needs ("daily bread") as well as spiritual needs (such as forgiveness and deliverance from temptation and evil).

"Yours is… the glory forever." Glory refers to praise, honor, and the revelation of who Yahweh is—all of His greatness, majesty, and holiness are included. This world and all its kingdoms will fade and pass away, but He and His kingdom are forever.

The prayer ends, as do most prayers, with "Amen," which means "so be it." Here is final, concluding word—so, let all that is included come to pass just as it has been stated. What a masterpiece of brevity and beauty is this Model Prayer—or as some have described as the "Children's Prayer" because it begins with "Our Father." As His children, we come before Him with this kind of prayer and supplication. Notice **Yeshua did not say "pray this prayer," but "pray like this"—here is a worthy model to follow, not memorized words to quote.**

Yeshua in Your Worship

Thank You, Lord, for teaching me how to pray. Now help me to follow Your instructions.

March 16

Yahweh Wants Me to Help Reconcile Others

Yahweh and the Word

> *"So then, my brothers, you are dearly loved and longed for—my joy and crown. In this manner stand firm in the Lord, dear friends. I urge Euodia and I urge Syntyche to agree in the Lord. Yes, I also ask you, true partner, to help these women who have contended for the gospel at my side" (Philippians 4:1-3).*

The apostle Paul comes to the end of this very warm, personal letter with an appeal to help two women be reconciled—to "agree in the Lord." We do not know their problem, but the apostle desired a solution for their differences.

Yahweh in Your Walk

"As long as churches are made up of people, there will be problems." This wise counsel was given to me from an older, experienced pastor as I began my ministry. His words have proven to be very true. All the churches I have served as pastor or interim pastor have had situations where reconciliation among members was needed. **I have learned that there are no perfect churches because there are no perfect members.**

The text for this devotional reminds us of the importance of helping those who are not at peace with others in the church fellowship. These brothers and sisters need someone to assist them with their need of reconciliation. We must not simply stand by and expect them to resolve their problems on their own. But how can we best do this?

We begin our assistance by praying for them and with them. This kind of prayer is spiritual warfare because the real enemy is not the members who are alienated but the adversary, Satan, who is behind all conflict in the church. Until we recognize this, we will never be successful in resolving conflicts. Our prayers must first be against this subtle, crafty enemy. Then we attempt to meet privately with both parties of the conflict. Listen to each side carefully in an effort to understand the truth about what is going on—beware of forming opinions based on hearsay, get to the heart of the problem.

Finally, bring both sides together with an agreement to seek a peaceful resolution. Help them see the possible solutions and to be willing to arbitrate their separate positions. Most often, there needs to be some admission of wrong, followed by forgiveness. Seek to keep these discussions private, away from the congregation as a whole. And be trustworthy in not sharing confidential information. Always depend upon the Holy Spirit to do His work of healing broken relationships.

Yahweh in Your Worship

I worship You, Yahweh, as the supreme Reconciler of all. You have acted to bring reconciliation to Your entire creation. **I ask You to use me as a minister of reconciliation among my friends and fellow believers.** Help me always to be a peacemaker. I bless You for motivating our forgiveness of one another by Your pardon for all our transgressions.

March 17

Yeshua Assures Me of His Constant Presence

Yeshua in the Word

> "Be satisfied with what you have, for He Himself has said, 'I will never leave you or forsake you.' Therefore we may boldly say: 'The Lord is my helper; I will not be afraid. What can man do to me?'" (Hebrews 13:5-6).

The writer of Hebrews reminds his readers of Yeshua's promise to be with His followers always. Such assurance gives comfort and boldness to face all kinds of threats to safety.

Yeshua in Your Walk

March 17th is the traditional date for Saint Patrick's Day. Patrick was a 5th century Irish missionary who gave himself to the spread of Christianity throughout Ireland. He died on March 17th. He used a green shamrock leaf with its three leaves to illustrate the meaning of the doctrine of the Trinity—the Father, Son, and Holy Spirit. He reminded his hearers that although God reveals Himself as three persons, they are one in nature. **Here are words that come from what is known as "The Hymn of Saint Patrick":**

> Christ be with me, Christ within me,
> Christ behind me, Christ before me,
> Christ beside me, Christ to win me,
> Christ to comfort and restore me,
> Christ beneath me, Christ above me,
> Christ in quiet, Christ in danger,
> Christ in hearts of all who love me,
> Christ in mouth of friend and stranger.

Patrick was a believer who felt totally enclosed in space and experience by the presence of Yeshua. He found life's meaning in this intimate relationship. **The same peace and confidence can be yours as you simply acknowledge His promise to never leave nor forsake you.** As you walk through this day and face all its challenges, give thanks to Him for His inescapable presence.

How unfortunate that this day has become best known for beer-drinking parties, parades, and celebrations that have nothing to do with Patrick's devotion to Jesus (Yeshua) and his call to missionary service. **You can correct this for yourself by giving thanks for this soldier of the cross, and walking with confidence in the presence of Yeshua with you.**

Yeshua in Your Worship

Thank You, Yeshua, for Your presence within and without. I worship You as the Source of all I need in order to become all You want me to be and do—today. Use me as a witness to others of Your promise to be with us always. Help me live like a person who believes You are present.

March 18

Yahweh Wants Me to Keep in Touch with Friends

Yahweh in the Word

> *"Give my greetings to Prisca… Greet also the church that meets in their home… Greet Mary… Greet Urbanus… Greet Rufus… Philologus… Greet one another…" (Romans 16: 3-16).*

The apostle Paul probably wrote this letter to the church in Rome while he was in the city of Corinth, Greece. Although he had never been to this church, it is obvious that he had many friends there. In this final chapter of his letter he mentions 35 individuals to whom he sends his personal greeting. Paul often named persons in his correspondence showing that he valued their friendship and that he intended to keep in touch with them.

Yahweh in Your Walk

We have no way of knowing now many individuals have crossed our path during this earthly journey. But some of these have become friends who have influenced us in a positive manner. One indication of our maturity is the discipline of keeping in touch with many who have proven to be Yahweh's gifts to us. As I was writing this devotional a phone call came from a friend I first met several years ago. What a pleasant conversation we enjoyed as we exchanged information about ourselves and life experiences!

As you read these words perhaps Yahweh will bring to mind some person from your past who would be encouraged by a phone call, email, or personal note of appreciation from you—someone you have not reached out to for many years. I can tell you from personal experience that as we age our contacts with friends who are far away become less frequent. And when those friendships are brought up to date, we have a true sense of gratitude and appreciation.

Sometimes we wonder why friends do not call or send notes to us more often, but perhaps we are the ones who need to take the initiative and contact them. Several months ago I called an old friend that I had not heard from in a long time. He seemed so pleased to hear from me; he reminded me of some good times we had together—some very humorous! For years I have made a practice to keep a list of birthday dates and call family or friends on these special days. What a simple way to let a friend know they are loved and remembered. And occasionally I remove a name from my list when I hear they have passed on. One day in heaven I hope to see them again.

How about you making a list of persons you want to contact regularly—maybe even once a year on their birthday. I would especially encourage you to reach out to those older persons who were your teachers, pastors, or neighbors. Let them know you remember them with gratitude to God and want to thank them for their influence on your life. You would be surprised to know what a blessing this might be.

Yahweh in Your Worship

Thank You, Yahweh, for always staying in touch with me. I worship You for Your faithfulness as a Friend as well as my Savior and Lord. Help me pass on to others Your attentiveness.

March 19

Yahweh Wants Me to Be a Good Influence on Others

Yahweh in the Word

> "Hilkiah told Shaphan the court secretary, 'I have found the book of the law in Yahweh's temple,' and he gave the book to Shaphan. Shaphan took the book to the king… when the king heard the words of the law he tore his clothes" (2 Chronicles 34:15-19).

This incident of discovering the long-neglected book of Yahweh's law is part of the amazing story of Josiah who became king in Judah when he was only eight-years-old. Some years after he became king, this book of the law was found by Hilkiah, the high priest, who gave it to Shaphan, the court secretary, who passed it on to King Josiah. When this young king heard Yahweh's warnings against idolatry, he began reforms, including restoration of temple worship.

Yahweh in Your Walk

The words of today's Scripture text tell the story of how one person, Hilkiah, influenced another, Shaphan, who influenced another, Josiah, all for the good of Yahweh's people. You may have never heard of these individuals, but they are part of your spiritual heritage; they were used by Yahweh to make a difference in His people and their worship for many years to follow. We are indebted to all these, and so many, many others who have contributed to our knowledge of Yahweh today.

Recently, I read a book on leadership with this statement, "A leader is anyone who influences someone else." **This truth means that we are all leaders; we all have influence on others—either for good or bad.** Much of this influence is unintentional and unknown to us. When I was a young boy, I rode a bicycle to school each day. Since it had no chain-guard, I rolled up my right pant leg—and left it up during school. One of my young friends was Robert King who walked to school because he lived nearby. His mother told my mother this story: She noticed Robert came home with his right pant leg rolled up. When she asked why, and he said, "Jimmy Harvey wears his pants that way!" This simple story illustrates the fact that we all have influence on others.

Just as Yahweh has used many persons to influence you, He wants to use you to be a good influence on others. **As you walk through this day, be sensitive to the fact that others watch you, listen to you, and will be influenced by your words and behavior.** Consider this wise counsel given by the apostle Paul to young Timothy, "Let no one despise your youth; instead, you should be an example to the believers in speech, in conduct, in love, in faith, in purity" (1Timothy 4:12).

Yahweh in Your Worship

I worship You because of Your greatness, goodness, and grace toward me. Thank You for sending those whom You have used to influence me for good. Use me to do the same for others. May Your life be seen in all I say and do this day.

March 20

Yahweh Wants Me to Feed on His Word

Yahweh in the Word

> "Your words were found, and I ate them. Your words became a delight to me and the joy of my heart, for I am called by Your name, Yahweh God of Hosts" (Jeremiah 15:16).

The prophet Jeremiah speaks of the delight he found as he fed upon Yahweh's words; they became a source of pure delight and joy to him. He also celebrated the fact that as a prophet he was identified with Yahweh, the God of Hosts.

Yahweh in Your Walk

One of my favorite experiences is to see a person discover the sheer delight of digging into Yahweh's Word and finding the treasures of truth hidden there. I remember a young man who had recently trusted the Lord to be his Savior and Lord. Previously, Bible reading and study had been rather boring to him; he could not understand most of what he read, and was not impressed with it. But, after his heart was opened to the truth by the Holy Spirit, he had a new appetite for the Word that would not be satisfied. Like Jeremiah, when he fed upon the Word, he experienced the delight and joy he found there.

How do you perceive the value of Bible study? Is it a rather uninteresting duty that you feel you must fulfill, or can you identify with Jeremiah who found the Word a delight and joy? Job was another person who learned the pleasure of feasting on truth. He declared, "I have treasured the words of His mouth more than my daily food" (Job 24:3). Both of these students of Scripture compared the partaking of Yahweh's Word to the eating of food—one is for spiritual health, the other for physical nourishment; and both agreed—the Word is preferred!

Notice that Jeremiah spoke of **eating** Yahweh's words. He not only read the truth, but chewed on it and swallowed it! He learned the difference between a rather casual taste on the one hand and complete digestion on the other. Reading the Bible is just the beginning of receiving all the nourishment it provides. We must move on to in-depth study, meditation, memorization, and application to experience the intended complete benefit. **Allow us to encourage you to give more attention to your approach to your intake of Yahweh's Word.** Remember how your mother used to tell you to stop eating so fast—take smaller bites, slow down, chew your food well before swallowing it? Do the same with feeding on the nourishing, pleasure-giving Word of God—small bites, slowly considered, carefully thought-through, and absorbed completely.

Yahweh in Your Worship

Yahweh, You are the Word of life to me. I worship You as the giver of all the nourishment my spirit needs. Thank You for giving me Your Word in a language I understand. Forgive me for taking the Bible for granted. Help me learn to seize opportunities today to learn and grow through feasting on Your truth. Use me to encourage others to be consumers of Your truth. And thank You for calling me as one of Your own.

March 21

Yahweh Wants Me to Call on Him for Salvation

Yahweh in the Word

> *"Then the crowds who went ahead of Him and those who followed kept shouting: 'Hosanna to the Son of David! He who comes in the name of the Lord is the blessed One! Hosanna in the highest heaven!" (Matthew 21:9).*

This text comes from the Triumphal Entry of Jesus into Jerusalem a short time before His crucifixion. **Hosanna** is from the Hebrew word meaning "Please save!" It occurs 6 times in the New Testament and is based on this statement from Psalm 118:25 "Yahweh, save us! Yahweh, please grant us success! He who comes in the name of Yahweh is blessed."

Yahweh in Your Walk

Large crowds of people welcomed Jesus when He returned to Jerusalem for the last time. He knew that He was on His way to the cross. These excited adherents had all heard of Jesus, some personally heard Him teach in the temple area, others witnessed His miracles—He was the talk of the town. As he rode a donkey into Jerusalem, some cut palm branches (thus the term "Palm Sunday,") while others spread their robes on the ground to make a path for Him, all were crying out, "Hosanna!" ("Please save us.") Their plea was not so much for personal salvation but for deliverance from servitude to the Roman government. They believed His was the Messiah who would do this. Their concept of the promised Messiah was that He would be a political ruler.

During this Easter season, we remember events like this as part of the Holy Week celebration. How important for us to see the true meaning of what happened, beginning the Sunday of the Triumphal Entry, and climaxing with His resurrection from the dead one week later. All these familiar events were related to His coming to be our Yeshua ("I AM salvation"). Unlike this crowd at His entry event, we call out "Hosanna" to mean, "Please save us from our sins—from the power and consequence of such rebellion against You. Save us from our sinful nature; give us a new heart; put Your Spirit within us; deliver us from all that displeases You; take control of us and be Lord of all." **Our need is for a personal salvation more than a political one.**

Have you made a way for the Lord Jesus to come into your heart and life with His saving power? We must be sure that we do more than admire these biblical stories; we are to participate in what they mean for us personally. Not only do we need salvation from the consequences of our past sins but also deliverance each day from the practice of sin—a spirit of rebellion against Yahweh and His rule over us.

Yahweh in Your Worship

Today, I cry out **Hosanna** to the King of kings! You are the One who delivers me from my sin—continually. I praise You for coming as a lowly teacher, riding on a donkey, to become my Savior and Lord. I seize each opportunity to worship and serve You. You alone are worthy of honor and recognition as Yahweh Elohim Sabaoth (LORD God of Hosts).

March 22

Yeshua Wants Me to Kneel and Confess before Him

Yeshua in the Word

> "Make you own attitude that of Christ Jesus, who, existing in the form of God, did not consider equality with God as something to be used for His own advantage. Instead He emptied Himself… even to death on a cross. For this reason God highly exalted Him and gave Him the name that is above every name, so that at the name of Jesus every knee will bow—of those who are in heaven and on earth and under the earth—and every tongue should confess that Jesus Christ is Lord, to the glory of God the Father" (Philippians 2:5-11).

These words are some of the most sublime ever written; they describe the self-humiliation of Jesus for the sake of providing salvation for all who place their trust in Him. As a result of this sacrifice, Yahweh has exalted His Son to the highest position of honor in the universe—He is to be worshiped as Lord of all!

Yeshua in Your Walk

As we continue these pre-Easter meditations, this passage from Paul's letter to the Philippian believers serves as a powerful reminded of the kind of response we all should make to our Lord Jesus. Because of His willingness to empty Himself of all divine attributes and become a human sacrifice for the sins of all human-kind, He is worthy to receive our heartfelt worship and adoration—to the glory and praise of Yahweh.

Two expressions of this very appropriate honor are mentioned in this notable passage: "Every knee will bow, and every tongue should confess that Jesus Christ is Lord." Look more closely at these actions of worship. First, to bow one's knees means to kneel before Him as an expression of worship and submission. We find several occasions in Scripture of this posture of humility. The psalmist declared, "Come, let us worship and bow down; let us kneel before Yahweh our Maker" (Psalm 95:6). Several times in the Acts of the Apostles we read of believers kneeling to pray (Acts 9:40; 20:36; 21:5).

Then to confess with one's mouth that "Jesus Christ is Lord" was a common occurrence in the New Testament. Remember that "Jesus" is the English form of the Hebrew name "Yeshua," meaning **Yahweh is salvation**, and "Christ" is English for Messiah, the anointed One. Certainly these words should often be on our lips as we worship Him.

As you worship Yahweh this day, make certain you find some private place where you can kneel before Him and confess that He is Lord of you and of all creation.

Yeshua in Your Worship

O blessed Savior, I kneel down in my heart to acknowledge that You alone are worthy of all praise and worship. Thank You for emptying Yourself and sacrificing Yourself for my sake on the cross. I join all humankind in heaven above and in hell below to acknowledge that You are the Lord of lords and the King of kings. Get honor to Yourself through me this day.

March 23

Yeshua Wants Me to Remember Him

Yeshua in the Word

> "And He took bread, gave thanks, broke it, gave it to them, and said, 'This is My body which is given for you. Do this in remembrance of Me.' In the same way He also took the cup after supper and said, 'This cup is the new covenant established by My blood; it is shed for you'" (Luke 22:19-20).

Jesus (Yeshua) gave new meaning to a very familiar festive meal when He broke unleavened bread to symbolize His body being broken on the cross as a sacrifice for sins. He instructed His disciples to eat the bread in remembrance of Him and His death. The cup of juice was likewise given new significance by symbolizing the new covenant sealed by His blood.

Yeshua in Your Walk

The Festival of Unleavened Bread is called Passover because it commemorates Yahweh's deliverance of the children of Israel from their long bondage as slaves in Egypt. As part of this festival a lamb was slain and its blood smeared around the door of their houses, reminding them of the final miracle when all the firstborn males of the Egyptians died, but those of the Israelites lived due to the sacrificial lamb. Unleavened bread was also eaten for the next seven days to remind them that these ancestors left Egypt in haste with no time for their bread to rise. Jesus (Yeshua) used this occasion to establish what became known as the Lord's Supper to commemorate His death as the Lamb of God, sacrificed for our sins.

Today our churches observe this Communion or Lord's Supper, usually on varied time schedules—some every Sunday, others monthly, or once a quarter—whatever their custom may be. What is most important is not the frequency, but the meaning of this memorial event. **All believers should participate in the Lord's Supper regularly as an experience of worship and solemn celebration of His sacrifice for us.**

We are familiar with various kinds of monuments today, such as the Washington Monument, the Lincoln Memorial, and many others. We visit these sites and remember these heroes and their deeds on our behalf. The Lord's Supper is a similar monument with this important exception: here is the only memorial where we actually partake of its elements—we eat the bread and drink the juice. All this reminds us that what He did on the cross was for us—we are the benefactors of His sacrifice. **How very important it is to have a frequent reminder of this gift of life. Make certain that you participate regularly, with a spirit of worship and gratitude.**

Yeshua in Your Worship

Merciful Savior, I want to seize every opportunity to worship You by remembering Your sacrifice for me on the cross. How grateful I am that You laid down Your life that I might live. Help me to prove my gratitude by serving as Your witness this day. Guide me to participate more meaningfully in Your memorial feast.

March 24

Yeshua Completed His Redemption of Me on His Cross

Yeshua in the Word

> "When Jesus had received the sour wine, He said, 'It is finished!' Then bowing His head, He gave up His spirit" (John 19:30).

Only John's Gospel has this saying from the cross. And the prophet Isaiah records this prophecy which is fulfilled here: "Therefore I will give Him the many as a portion and He will receive the mighty as spoil, because He submitted Himself to death and was counted among the rebels; yet He bore the sin of many and interceded for the rebels" (Isaiah 53:12).

Yeshua in Your Walk

If you have placed your trust in Jesus as your Savior and Lord, you can walk through this and every day with the absolute assurance that His sacrifice provided full payment for your redemption—you are totally free from any penalty for sin. When Jesus gave Himself to die on the cross, His death for your sins was a complete payment to redeem you from the bondage of your sin debt.

The words "It is finished!" in this text are actually one word in the original Greek language—***tetelestai***, which means to bring to completion, to finish totally. My friend, Donnie Parker, decided to pursue a career as a barber, so he went to barber school, then completed his internship and opened his own business. Some of us went to his "grand opening" to celebrate with him. We took a wall plaque with the word "**tetelestai**" printed on it. We told him that when he completed a haircut he could repeat that word—finished! Since that time, many customers have noticed the wall plaque and asked about the meaning of the word. Their question has given him an opportunity to be a witness of what happened on the cross.

What good news for us sinners! What we could not achieve for ourselves, Yahweh has provided for us through the death of His Son. Our sin debt is fully paid and we are adopted into His forever family. Not only that but also the Spirit of Yahweh has now come to live in us and complete His plan for our final tetelestai! As the apostle Paul stated, "Don't you know that your body is a sanctuary of the Holy Spirit who is in you, whom you have from God? You are not your own, for you were bought at a price. Therefore glorify God in your body" (1 Cor. 6:19-20).

Perhaps as you proceed through this day, you will see a cross—on a church or worn as jewelry or some other display. If so, pause to give thanks for Yahweh's provision for your freedom.

Yeshua in Your Worship

I choose to seize this opportunity to worship You, Lord Jesus, and give You thanks for completing my salvation by Your sacrifice upon the cross. Use me as a witness of this event today. And every time I see a cross, help me remember what happened there for all humankind. And help me take up my own cross and follow You faithfully.

March 25

Yahweh Wants Me to Prepare the Way for Others to Believe

Yahweh in the Word

> *"A voice of one crying out: Prepare the way of Yahweh in the wilderness; make a straight highway for our God in the desert. Every valley will be lifted up, and every mountain and hill will be leveled; the uneven ground will become smooth and the rough places, a plain. And the glory of Yahweh will appear, and all humanity together will see it, for the mouth of Yahweh has spoken"* (Isaiah 40:3-5).

The prophet Isaiah was inspired to look forward to the day when Yahweh's people would return to their homeland from exile in Babylon. However, the ultimate fulfillment of these words occurred when John the Baptist came preaching to prepare the way for Jesus. (Mark 1:1-3)

Yahweh in Your Walk

Today is the birthday for my friend Kathryn who serves as a missionary with Wycliffe Bible Translators in West Africa. I like to pray for missionaries on their birthdays, but she and her family are special friends of ours so we support her with our prayers every day. When I contacted Kathryn for permission to mention her in this devotional, I asked about a favorite Scripture and she mentioned Isaiah 40. As I began reading this beautiful chapter, the words of our text for today seemed so descriptive of her work as a missionary.

Kathryn's ministry centers in languages. In college she studied Greek, the original language of the New Testament, and she spent years learning the French language, which is the primary language where she lives. Now she seeks to learn the language of a tribal group in order to work with educated speakers to translate Scripture into that language—sometimes teaching them to read their own language first. This work often requires that she and her coworkers spend time living among the people groups they serve to translate their spoken language into an alphabet, and then teach them to read while translating Scriptures into that language. All this work is done to fulfill Yahweh's call to prepare the way for Him "in the wilderness." **I have great admiration for those who do this tedious work.**

Have you ever thought of yourself as one whom Yahweh sends to prepare the way for Him? Each of is sent to be a missionary right where we live—our family, neighborhood, workplace, and wherever we go. **Your mission is to help smooth a path for the good news about Jesus.** As you reach out in friendship to those about you, you can help open the door for Him to enter.

Beyond this face-to-face ministry is the privilege of upholding servants like Kathryn when you pray. You become a co-laborer with those who serve far away as you intercede for them in prayer. All believers are involved in spiritual warfare against the powers of darkness; prayer makes a huge difference. Hopefully, you have a list of missionaries for whom you pray daily.

Yahweh in Your Worship

Thank You, Holy Father, for sending others to prepare the way for me to know You.

March 26

Yeshua Wants Me to Boast about His Cross

Yeshua in the Word

> "But as for me, I will never boast about anything except the cross of our Lord Jesus Christ. The world has been crucified to me through the cross and I to the world" (Galatians 6:14).

In this letter to the Galatians, Paul is careful to help them see the true meaning of the message of the gospel. This good news is for both Jew and Gentile, and both must come to Yahweh through faith in Jesus. In this text he is saying that although he is a Jew by birth his boast is not in keeping the Jewish law and ceremonies but he boasts in the fact that he has become right with Yahweh because Jesus died for him on the cross. The apostle goes on to declare that because of the cross, the world and all its allurement is dead to him and he is dead to the world.

Yeshua in Your Walk

Most of us are at least tempted to boast in some personal achievements. Perhaps you have excelled in some sport or accomplished status in the business or education world. Even religious leaders may take pride in their good works. The apostle Paul could have boasted about many things—such as his Hebrew heritage, the fact that he was a Roman citizen, his position as a Jewish rabbi, and more. However, when he came to understand what happened when Jesus died upon a cross, all his reasons for boasting changed; he took pride in, of all things, a cross. **What about you, do you find reasons to boast as you think about the cross? Here are some possibilities:**

1. I boast in the fact that Yeshua chose to reveal His great love for me by giving Himself as a sacrifice for my sins on the cross. "No one has greater love than this, that someone would lay down his life for his friends. You are My friends if you do what I command you" (John 15:13).
2. I boast in the cross because there He paid the full penalty for all my sins so that I might receive eternal life rather than eternal death. "For the wages of sin is death, but the gift of God is eternal life in Christ Jesus our Lord" (Romans 6:23).
3. I boast in the cross because there I died with Christ to an old life, to be raised to a new life in Him. "I have been crucified with Christ and I no longer live, but Christ lives in me. The life that I now live in the body, I live by faith in the Son of God, who loved me and gave Himself for me" (Galatians 2:20).
4. I boast in the cross because there the world has been crucified to me. "The world has been crucified to me through the cross and I to the world" (Galatians 6:14). Nothing else could have made such a lasting difference in my relationship to this world as His cross.

Yeshua in Your Worship

Gracious Savior, thank You for Your willingness to endure the cross for my sake. I worship You as my Redeemer, Lord, and Master. Use me as Your faithful witness this day.

March 27

Yeshua Wants Me to Celebrate His Resurrection

Yeshua in the Word

> *"Keep your attention on Jesus Christ as risen from the dead and descended from David. This is according to my gospel" (2 Timothy 2:8).*

The apostle Paul urged young Timothy to keep focused on Jesus Christ as the One who was raised from the dead—thus divine, but also a descendant from David—thus human. Only such a special Person could be the center of the gospel.

Yeshua in Your Walk

The true meaning of the Easter celebration can easily be lost due to all that accompanies this special Christian event—such as the Easter parades, Easter egg hunts, buying new clothes to wear Easter Sunday, and many other distractions. Paul advised his young friend to "keep your attention on Jesus Christ as risen from the dead." **Do yourself and others whom you may influence a huge favor this Easter by focusing on the central meaning of this special day.** As some have wisely said, "Keep the main thing, the main thing!"

A good example of this focus is found among the last words of a Chinese Christian leader named Watchman Nee (1903-1972). He was a missionary to his own Chinese people, starting many churches as well as writing excellent books. He died in prison where he was kept for the last 20 years of his life. After his passing his niece came to collect his few possessions and was handed a scrap of paper found by his bedside. On this paper Nee had written these final words: "Christ is the Son of God who died for the redemption of sinners and was resurrected after three days. This is the greatest truth in the universe. I die because of my belief in Christ."

Many outstanding persons have died throughout history; **what makes the death of Jesus so special?** The answer to this question is found in two facts found in Watchman Nee's brief note. **First,** unlike any other, the death of Jesus makes possible the "redemption of sinners. **Second,** only Jesus was "resurrected after three days," never to die again. This miracle sets Him apart from all others who have ever lived and died. How appropriate to "keep your attention" on this one-of-a-kind happening. Not because of its uniqueness but due to its significance for all persons. Join other believers as you sing this good news:

> Christ the Lord is risen today. Alleluia! Sons of men and angels say: Alleluia!
> Raise your joys and triumphs high. Alleluia! Sing, ye heav'ns, and earth reply: Alleluia!
> Lives again our glorious King. Alleluia! Where, O death, is now thy sting? Alleluia!
> Dying once, He all doth save. Alleluia! Where thy victory, O grave? Alleluia!

Yeshua in Your Worship

Yes, risen Lord, I join all creation in worshiping You this and every day. You alone are worthy of all our praise and celebration. Now live in me Your eternal life wherever I go.

March 28

Yeshua Wants Me to Participate in His Resurrection

Yeshua in the Word

> "Therefore we were buried with Him by baptism into death, in order that, just as Christ was raised from the dead by the glory of the Father, so we too may walk in a new way of life. For if we have been joined with Him in the likeness of His death, we will certainly also be in the likeness of His resurrection" (Romans 6:4-5).

Paul emphasizes the believer's identity with Christ in both His death and resurrection—we died with Christ to an old, sinful lifestyle, and likewise, we have been raised with Him to a new godly way of living.

Yeshua in Your Walk

The Easter season is a time for celebrating the miracle of the resurrection of Yeshua (Jesus) from the grave. **Here is the most amazing comeback story of all time.** Think of how totally defeated He appeared to be—His own disciples had abandoned Him; one had betrayed Him; another denied ever knowing Him; His claims to be sent from God seemed false; He who had saved many others could not save Himself—He looked to be a complete failure. It is no exaggeration to say that no one was ever so publicly humiliated as He.

But when He arose from the dead and came forth from the tomb, everything changed. His triumphant resurrection verified all He claimed for Himself. What an incredible victory over what seemed to be His final loss. **This good news gets even better for us when we are assured of our own participation in this wondrous event—all believers now share in the same resurrection, overcoming power!** Regardless of the overwhelming circumstances we may face, His victory is our victory—we live because He lives! Defeat and death hold no claim on us; we may sometimes be down, but never out.

As Paul declared, "If we have been joined with Him in the likeness of His death, we will certainly also be in the likeness of His resurrection." This glorious truth applies not only to life beyond the grave but also to this present life—"we may walk in a new way of life." Our new way of life is one in which various trials do not get us down because we share His resurrection—His overcoming—His comeback! **So as you walk through this and every day, be confident that absolutely nothing can ever get the best of you.** As the apostle went on to say, "I am persuaded that not even death or life, angels or rulers, things present or things to come, hostile powers, height or depth, or any other created thing will have the power to separate us from the love of God that is in Christ Jesus our Lord!" (Romans 8:38-39). Hallelujah!

Yeshua in Your Worship

I seize this opportunity to express heartfelt praise and adoration and thanksgiving to You, O Lord of life and death. Your death, burial, resurrection, ascension, and certain return—give me all the hope I need to face whatever challenges life may bring—even death itself. I praise You!

March 29

Yahweh Has Made Me to Be a Priest

Yahweh in the Word

> "You yourselves, as living stones, are being built into a spiritual house for a holy priesthood to offer spiritual sacrifices acceptable to God through Jesus Christ… you are a chosen race, a royal priesthood…" (1 Peter 2:5, 9).

The apostle Peter wrote to encourage his readers as they faced various kinds of persecution. He reminded them of their privileges as followers of Jesus, one of which was their role as priests. Just as the Levites in the Old Testament, believers in Christ become priests who offer the spiritual sacrifices of praise and thanksgiving to Yahweh.

Yahweh in Your Walk

What comes to your mind when you think of a priest? Probably some image of a Catholic priest who ministers to those of that church by hearing confession, offering the elements of the mass, and other services. Or you may remember the frequent Old Testament references to priests who served Yahweh's people when various sacrificial offerings were made. These men who were the direct descendants of Aaron were later known as Levites, one of the twelve tribes of Israel. We find an interesting reference to them when the land of promise was being settled. All the tribes were given a specific inheritance of land except for the Levites. "But Moses did not give a portion to the tribe of Levi. Yahweh, the God of Israel, was their inheritance, just as He has promised them" (Joshua 13:33). Although the Levites were given cities where they were to live, no land was theirs. Rather they were to be supported by the offerings of all the other tribes and Yahweh promised to provide for them—He was their inheritance. The same is true for us as His priests today—Yahweh is our inheritance!

Are you aware that according to the Bible all Christians are given the office of a priest? Our Scripture text for today is one of several references to this fact. Peter states that our priestly role is to offer spiritual sacrifices to Yahweh through Jesus Christ. Jesus is described as the "great high priest" due to His atoning sacrifice whereby He offered Himself as full and final payment for our sins. His death opened the way for us to have direct access to Yahweh through Him, no longer needing a human priest to intercede for us.

As you live this day, think about your service to Yahweh as His appointed priest. Give special time, as you do every day, to offering the sacrifices of praise and thanksgiving to Him. Also fulfill your priestly role as you intercede for others; bring them and their needs before Yahweh, asking His blessing and provisions for them, especially their need of forgiveness and restoration.

Yahweh in Your Worship

Holy Yahweh, I come before Your throne of grace as one of Your redeemed priests. I offer the spiritual sacrifices You so richly deserve—worship, adoration, praise, thanksgiving and love. Help me fulfill my role as an intercessor for others as I pray faithfully on their behalf.

March 30

Yahweh Always Offers Me Another Chance

Yahweh in the Word

"Bring Mark with you, for he is useful to me in the ministry" (2 Timothy 4:11).

These words from the apostle Paul reveal his forgiveness of young John Mark who had failed to stay with Paul and Barnabas on the first missionary journey. His restoration is an example of how those who experience personal failure in serving Yahweh, can be forgiven and become useful once more.

Yahweh in Your Walk

Have you ever felt like you messed up in some attempt to walk with the Lord, and then wondered if you could ever be forgiven and restored to usefulness? Most of us have been there. Our best encouragement and hope for another chance comes from many persons mentioned in the Bible who were pardoned, renewed, and made useful again. Mark is a good example for us. He started well, joining his cousin Barnabas and Paul on their initial missionary outreach. However, something happened to discourage young Mark and he left them. (Acts 13:13).

The next time Paul and Barnabas set forth on a mission trip, Barnabas wanted to take Mark along, but Paul was unforgiving. This disagreement led to a separation between Barnabas and Paul. Barnabas took Mark one direction while Paul chose Silas and went a different way. However, there are later references from Paul's letters showing his reconciliation with Mark (Philemon 24, Colossians 4:10, and our text 2 Timothy 4:11). In addition to these is the mention of Mark by the apostle Peter (1 Peter 5:13) where he calls Mark his son in the ministry. In fact Mark became a close associate of Peter and tradition says that Mark wrote his Gospel based on information he gained from Peter.

Peter is another example of someone who messed up and later was restored. Do you recall how Peter boasted of his loyalty to Jesus, and then later denied that he even knew Him? (See Matthew 26:35, 74). And yet, he was forgiven by Jesus and became a leader of the early church. His example, along with that of many others, gives us hope for a second chance (and even more chances than that!).

Do not listen to Satan when he tells you that you are finished because of your failures to be faithful. Rather, listen to the Word which promises: "If we confess our sins, He is faithful and righteous to forgive us our sins and to cleanse us from all unrighteousness" (1 John 1:9). **For the follower of Jesus, no failure ever needs to be final.** He forgives, restores, and teaches us from our mistakes. Let this truth be a personal encouragement—and pass this on to others.

Yahweh in Your Worship

Thank You most merciful Lord and Master. I claim today Your complete restoration. Use me to make a difference as Your faithful witness. May others see Your grace in my experiences. Help me to be the encourager that others need who have stumbled in their walk with You.

March 31

Yahweh Invites Me to Pray about Everything

Yahweh in the Word

> *"Don't worry about anything; but in everything, through prayer and petition with thanksgiving, let your requests be made known to God. And the peace of God which surpasses every thought, will guard your hearts and minds in Christ Jesus" (Philippians 4:6-7).*

Paul learned from his experiences that the cure for worry is prayer. He includes "everything" as being the proper scope of prayer. In other words, whatever causes us to worry is likewise a proper cause for prayer. Thanksgiving is to accompany our requests in the sense of thanking Yahweh in advance for hearing us and for answering according to His will and in His time. All this results in His peace (the opposite of worry) which goes beyond what we can even think. Such peace will stand like a guard over our hearts and minds.

Yahweh in Your Walk

Recently I misplaced my cell phone (again). I searched high and low; looking everywhere I might have left it. But it wasn't in all those places I had left it before. After two days of worrying about it, I decided to take Paul's advice and ask Yahweh for help. I said, "Lord, You know where this phone is; please help me find it." Then I sat down and began to mentally retrace my steps for those two days. As I recalled a time when I put on some old overalls for a special photo, I remembered making a call on my cell phone and putting the phone back in my pocket (very unusual for me). Later I folded these overalls, putting them away since I probably would not wear them again for a long time. Sure enough, when I unfolded them there was my phone—just waiting for me to use it again!! So, I paused to thank Yahweh for His help in a time of need.

Some might say we should not bother Yahweh with such minor requests, but I believe He wants to participate in every detail of our lives—even helping us find lost items. Here's the point: **Whatever becomes a worry for us is an appropriate subject for prayer**. Why worry when we can turn matters over to Yahweh in prayer with the thanksgiving that He hears and will take care of this concern in His way and in His time?

Let me suggest that you pause right now and think about something you are worried about—however small it may seem. Now, put that concern in the form of a request to Yahweh, thanking Him for hearing you and answering. Next, claim His peace about this matter since you have placed it in His hands. Satan will probably attempt to bring back the worry; simply resist him by quoting the words of our Scripture text for today. **Keep working at this cure for worry.**

Yahweh in Your Worship

Lord, I worship You with thanksgiving and praise because You care about every detail of my life. How blessed I am to know this truth; help me remember Your promise to hear and answer my every request. As I walk through this new day in fellowship with You, I want to share all my concerns with You. Thank You for Your amazing peace that passes all my understanding.

April 1

Yahweh M'Kaddesh Sets Me Apart for Himself

Yahweh in the Word

> "Consecrate yourselves and be holy, for I am Yahweh your God. Keep my statues and do them; I am Yahweh who sets you apart (Yahweh M'Kaddesh)" (Leviticus 20:7-8).

We come now to the fourth combination name—Yahweh M'Kaddesh (YAH-way ma-CAD-esh). The meaning of these words is "I AM the One who sanctifies you—Who makes you holy, sets you apart for Me." God was telling His people that because He was holy and had chosen them, they were a holy people—holy in the sense of being set apart from the rest of humanity for His special purpose.

Yahweh in Your Walk

Most churches have a place of worship called a sanctuary. This room is set apart from the rest of the building as a special location for focusing on Yahweh through various expressions of worship. I recall as a child being told that certain behavior was not appropriate in the church "sanctuary." I was not to run or talk loudly or laugh. There was something very special about that place. Now I understand that what makes any place "sacred" is Yahweh's presence, not the building. And since He is with us always, everywhere, we should show respect to Him wherever we happen to be. Running and talking and laughing can be pleasing to Him in any place where He is worshiped and honored.

The same root word in the Hebrew and Greek languages is translated as "holy," "saint," "sanctuary," and "sanctify." We use the word in a similar way to speak of an animal sanctuary—a place set aside for various animal species.

When the apostle Paul wrote to the "saints" in various churches, he was designating those believers who had been set apart and made holy by virtue of God's Holy Spirit living in them. **Yahweh is holy and all who trust Him for salvation likewise become holy because of His presence.**

As you walk through this day, pause at times to consider what Yahweh M'Kaddesh means to you in terms of setting you apart from this world. **You are a special sanctuary for Him.** What an amazing and wonderful truth!

Yahweh in Your Worship

Thank You, Yahweh M'Kaddesh that I do not have to be in a certain building in order to worship You. Because You reside in me, I engage You through praise and adoration whenever I so desire. Help me seize these glorious opportunities throughout this day. And use me as a witness to others of these amazing truths.

April 2

Yahweh Makes Me His Temple

Yahweh in the Word

> "Do you not know that your body is a sanctuary of the Holy Spirit who is in you, whom you have from God? You are not your own, for you were bought at a price. Therefore glorify God in your body" (1 Corinthians 6:19-20).

As noted in yesterday's devotional, Yahweh M'Kaddesh (I AM the One who sanctifies you) sets us apart for Himself, and He accomplishes this by literally coming to live within us. This amazing fact means that **our body becomes His temple—His dwelling place.** Therefore, we belong to Him—body, soul, and spirit—we are His, not our own because He purchased us with the price of the sacrifice of Jesus on the cross.

Yahweh in Your Walk

One very practical application of the truth of today's Word regards our physical body. You probably have concerns about maintaining good health—proper diet, exercise, rest, and regular check-ups from your physician. One motive for these disciplines is to feel better and live longer. However, in the light of Paul's words to the Corinthians, the primary reason for giving attention to this body is the fact that it is Yahweh's temple, and we are His temple-keepers! **The preferred motive for keeping fit physically is to provide the best dwelling place for Yahweh M'Kaddesh.**

Another application has to do with morality. Paul was cautioning the Corinthians to avoid sexual immorality (see vv. 12-20). **We must not allow Yahweh's temple—our body—to participate in sexual sins.** As he warned, "Don't you know that your bodies are a part of Christ's body? So should I take a part of Christ's body and make it part of a prostitute. Absolutely not!" (v. 15). Thus he declares, "Run from sexual immorality!" (v. 18). How unthinkable to deliberately cause Yahweh to participate in any form of sexual sin! Here again, is the ultimate motive for living a life that is wholly consecrated to the Holy One who lives in us and owns us.

Notice how Paul reminds his readers (and us) that "you are not your own, for you were bought at a price." **A major aspect of our stewardship responsibility is to give diligent care to that which Yahweh has entrusted to us.** In this instance that includes our physical bodies; we are literally caring for that which is not ours, but His—this human body. Even our appearance—the way we dress and groom this body—is included in this obligation. Let's be faithful stewards and responsible temple-keepers!

Yahweh in Your Worship

Today, O Yahweh M'Kaddesh, I bring myself—body, mind, and spirit, as a living sacrifice to You. I claim Your power to resist every temptation that would cause me to bring dishonor to Your temple. Deliver me from any human relationship that would displease You. Help me to seize this day for Your glory. Thank You for hearing and answering this prayer.

April 3

Yahweh M'Kaddesh Makes Me His Special Treasure

Yahweh in the Word

> *"Now if you will listen to Me and carefully keep My covenant, you will be My own possession out of all the peoples, although all the earth is Mine, and you will be My kingdom of priests and My holy nation" (Exodus 19:5-6).*

These words were spoken first by Yahweh to Moses regarding the Israelites, His chosen people. Many years later the apostle Peter applied these same expressions to describe Christians (see 1 Peter 2:9-10). The word "possession" in this passage translates the Hebrew term ***segullah*** (seg-ool-law) which means "a special treasure." Yahweh is telling Moses, and Peter is telling us that He owns all creation, yet He considers His people to be a special treasure to Himself.

Yahweh in Your Walk

My wife and I were college students living in an upstairs apartment owned by Mr. and Mrs. Yowell, who lived downstairs. One morning I passed Mrs. Yowell sitting in a rocking chair on her front porch as I left for my class. She greeted me and said, **"Now remember whose you are and whom you represent today."** I paused, asked her to repeat her words, and inquired about what she meant. She told me this was a saying she always gave her children when they left home—they were to remember that they belonged to the Lord and represented Him wherever they went. She wanted to help them be cautious about their behavior.

What wise and appropriate counsel! And I still remember these words some 60 years later. **All believers belong to Yahweh M'Kaddesh who has set us apart as His special treasures, and we represent our Owner at all times.** Could anything give us a greater sense of self-worth? Not **who** we are, but **whose** we are makes the most difference. We are all persons of infinite value and significance, because we are Yahweh's segullahs.

Think about how this should affect our lifestyle. Our values and actions, words and deeds, should reflect His life in every way. We are to be living examples of what it means to belong to Yahweh. Others should see His life in us. As Stuart Briscoe so aptly wrote, "Christianity is nothing less than all of Him in all of you." How about writing Mrs. Yowell's words on a card and taping it to your mirror where you will see them every day? Paul stated a similar truth when he declared, "We are ambassadors for Christ" (2 Corinthians 5:20). These reminders of our role as representatives of Yahweh can help us be more effective witnesses.

Yahweh in Your Worship

Thank You, Yahweh M'Kaddesh, for choosing me to be Your special treasure. May You use me to represent You accurately in all I say and do today. I am amazed over Your incredible love for me. What a privilege and pleasure to belong to You and be sent into this world as Your representative. Help me remember this solemn responsibility. Use me to encourage other fellow-ambassadors to be diligent and faithful to this noble calling.

April 4

Yahweh Is My Protector

Yahweh in the Word

> "Yahweh protects you; Yahweh is a shelter right by your side. The sun will not strike you by day or the moon by night. Yahweh will protect you from all harm; He will protect your life. Yahweh will protect your coming and going both now and forever" (Psalm 121:5-8).

If you read this entire chapter, you will find some form of the word "protect" five times. Notice the complete dimensions of this divine protection: protection from **all** harm, your coming and going—all **forever**! Earlier in the chapter we read, "the Protector of Israel does not slumber or sleep." Complete and continuous coverage!

Yahweh in Your Walk

You probably can tell stories of how Yahweh has protected you. Here is one of my favorite stories on this subject. Years ago I was teaching African pastors in a seminary in Jinja, Uganda. One of the missionaries offered to take me on a rafting trip down the Nile River. I was up for some excitement so we drove to the place where the river empties out of Lake Victoria. Eight of us put on life preservers and helmets as we boarded a rubber raft for the trip. The guide instructed us on what to do in the unlikely event of turning over in one of the rapids. He assured us that regardless of what happened, we would survive!

At first the river was smooth and slow as we floated downstream. I was enjoying the trip until I heard ahead of us the loud roar of the river flowing between huge boulders. We made it safely through the first series of rapids. Then the guide said, "Hold on, here come the big ones!" We paddled as hard as we could but just before passing through the last rapid, the raft hit a large rock and turned over, spilling all of us into the swift water. My seat was on the lower side of the raft as it turned over, so everyone came down on top of me, forcing me down to the bottom of the river. I still have a scar on my shin from hitting a sharp rock, but fortunately my life vest forced me up and back on the surface of the river. We all floated downstream and recovered the raft for a peaceful completion of our journey. Needless to say, I was quite shaken by this venture that appeared at first to be a pleasant and calm float trip.

This could well have been my final venture, however, Yahweh was with all of us and we survived. He protected us from all harm. As you walk through today, there will be dangers of all kinds. But rest assured that **Yahweh is with you as your personal Protector**. He knows the dangers long before we do; He provides for our survival. And even if we are overcome by some unforeseen threat, we are assured of being at home in heaven with Him forever; we cannot lose!

Yahweh in Your Worship

Today I make the choice not to fear the unknown but to rest in the security of Your protection and everlasting care. Thank You for being faithful in Your kind deliverance. I worship You with praise and adoration.

April 5

Yahweh Is Worthy of All I Give Him

Yahweh in the Word

> *"Ascribe to Yahweh the glory of His Name; bring an offering and come before Him. Worship Yahweh in the splendor of His holiness" (1 Chronicles 16:27).*

This verse comes from a longer song of thanksgiving composed and sung by King David on the occasion of the return of the Ark of the Covenant to Jerusalem. To "ascribe to Yahweh" means to acknowledge that Yahweh's name is glorious; that is, He is to be worshiped and praised for being so great and holy. Furthermore, David exhorted the people to "bring an offering and come before Him." This offering included various animals to be offered as sacrifices, as well as the offering of themselves to sing praises to Yahweh as they worshiped Him.

Yahweh in Your Walk

What will you give Yahweh as an expression of worship today? Why not begin each day by offering yourself to Him. My habit is to think of my bed as an altar. Before I get out of bed, I lie on my back and pray something like this: "Yahweh, this is the day You have made. I offer myself as a living sacrifice to You. I ask You to use me and all I have for Your glory today. Amen."

Although this is a very brief prayer, it starts the day right. One thing this means is that I am never more than 24 hours away from a full surrender of myself to Yahweh. I believe He takes this offering of myself seriously and answers this simple prayer in ways beyond my imagination. During each day I become aware of His control in small and sometimes larger ways.

One further suggestion at this point is that we must seek to grow in our understanding of such a full surrender. **To give oneself includes every thought, word, and action, as well as all possessions.** I often quote these words from an old hymn by Kate Wilkinson:

Yahweh in Your Worship

> May the mind of Christ my Savior live in me throughout this day,
> By His love and power controlling all I think and do and say.
> May the Word of God dwell richly in my heart from hour to hour,
> So that all may see I triumph only through His power.
> May the peace of God my Father rule my life in everything,
> That I may be calm to comfort sick and sorrowing.
> May the love of Jesus fill me as the waters fill the sea;
> Him exalting, self-abasing—this is victory.
> May I run the race before me, strong and brave to face the foe,
> Looking only unto Jesus as I onward go.
> May His beauty rest upon me as I seek the lost to win;
> And may they forget the channel, seeing only Him.

April 6
Yahweh Deserves My Complete Loyalty

Yahweh in the Word

> "Do not persuade me to leave you or go back and not follow you. For wherever you go, I will go, and wherever you live, I will live; your people will be my people, and your God will be my God. Where you die, I will die, and there I will be buried. May Yahweh punish me, and do so severely, if anything but death separates you and me" (Ruth 1:16-17).

The story of Naomi and her daughter-in-law Ruth is one of the most beautiful in the entire Bible. Naomi and her husband took their two sons and moved to the land of Moab due to a famine in Judah where they lived. Both sons married Moabite women. One son married a Moabite named Ruth. Later when Naomi's husband and both sons died, she decided to move back to Judah where conditions had improved. One daughter-in-law agreed that she should remain in Moab with her own people. However, Ruth had such love for Naomi that she was determined to return with her. In spite of Naomi's advice, Ruth expressed her loyalty in the verses above. Apparently she had observed the devotion of Ruth and her family to Yahweh and wanted to become a worshiper of Him, rather than her pagan gods. Yahweh rewarded her decision and later gave her a godly man named Boaz to be her new husband. We are told in Matthew's genealogy of Jesus (Matthew 1:1-16) that Boaz and Ruth were part of Jesus' family tree.

Yahweh in Your Walk

Today will be a new adventure for you; you have never been on this portion of your life journey before. What makes this walk into the unknown exciting is the possibility of helping another person know more about your God—Yahweh. Apparently Naomi was careful to show her daughter-in-law that worshiping Yahweh made a significant difference in her life experiences. Perhaps through the loss of her husband and both sons, Ruth saw how Naomi handled these times of grief with unusual strength and peace. Although we are not told the exact cause of Ruth's desire to become a worshiper of Yahweh, we know she made the decision to leave both her homeland and her gods to cling to Naomi.

Will you commit yourself this day to giving evidence that your loyalty to Yahweh is complete and unshakeable? Ask Yahweh to open a door of opportunity for you to be a witness of how worthy He is of your allegiance. Then be alert for those occasions that only He can create. **Only Yahweh knows how some small act of kindness on your part can have far reaching consequences.** Trust Him to use you for His purposes as you walk confidently through this new adventure of service to Him.

Yahweh in Your Worship

Yahweh, You are my God, the One I worship and live for. You alone are worthy of my heartfelt devotion and loyalty. I praise You for proving Yourself to be merciful and gracious to me.

April 7

Yahweh Will Never Give Up on Me

Yahweh in the Word

> *"Jonah prayed to Yahweh his God from inside the fish" (Jonah 2:1).*

No one else in the Bible ever prayed from such an unlikely place! And yet, Yahweh heard and answered him. The story of this prophet is a clear and powerful account of Yahweh's persistent pursuit of one of His chosen servants. We first meet Jonah as he decides to refuse Yahweh's call to warn the people of Nineveh that judgment is coming upon them. Jonah boards a ship headed as far from Nineveh as he can go. But Yahweh goes with him and through a series of miracles leads him to return and fulfill his mission to the Ninevites.

Yahweh in Your Walk

Jonah was determined to flee from Yahweh's presence. As the Scripture says, "Jonah got up to flee to Tarshish from Yahweh's presence" (Jonah 1:3). However, Yahweh went with him! Even when the sailors finally decided to throw Jonah overboard into the stormy sea where he was swallowed by a huge fish—Yahweh was right there beside His servant. In spite of Jonah's rebellion, Yahweh never gave up on this most reluctant prophet.

Most of us have our ups and downs in life. An old gospel song entitled "Nobody Knows the Trouble I've Seen" has these sad lines: "Sometimes I'm up; sometimes I'm down; sometimes I'm almost to the ground." Jonah was lower than the ground—deep in the sea and deep inside a fish where he remained for three days and nights. But even there Yahweh came to him and gave him a second chance.

Jonah illustrates an important truth for us to always remember: Yahweh will never give up on us. He loves us too much to let us go our own way without reaching out to rescue us from our sins. The psalmist asked Yahweh, "Where can I go to escape Your Spirit? Where can I flee from Your presence? If I go up to heaven, You are there; if I make my bed in Sheol, You are there. If I live at the eastern horizon or settle at the western limits, even there Your hand will lead me; Your right hand will hold on to me" (Psalm 139:7-10).

Sometimes you may be tempted to give up on yourself as Satan tells you that you are of no value to Yahweh or anyone else. Don't you believe it! Your faith in Yahweh may falter, but He never quits believing in you. He is always ready to forgive you and restore you to His fellowship and service—just as He did Jonah. If you feel like you're in the belly of a fish, just know you aren't there alone. Yahweh is in the restoration business and He is ready to restore you.

Yahweh in Your Worship

Thank You Yahweh for Your patience and persistence toward me. Forgive my waywardness and turn me back to Your good ways. I worship You for being so merciful and gracious in all Your dealings with me. Help me pass this on to others.

April 8

Yahweh Wants Me to See Him in All of Life

Yahweh in the Word

> "He (Moses) said about Joseph: 'May his land be blessed by Yahweh with the dew of heaven's bounty and the watery depths that lie beneath; with the bountiful harvest from the sun and the abundant yield of the seasons; with the best products of the ancient mountains and the bounty of the eternal hills; with the choice gifts of the land and everything in it; and with the favor of Him who appeared in the burning bush. May these rest on the head of Joseph, on the crown of the prince of his brothers'" (Deuteronomy 33:13-16).

Shortly before he died, Moses pronounced a blessing upon the individual tribes of Israel including the one for Joseph in our text for today. You will notice the numerous references to the best gifts that nature can supply. He concluded with a request that Yahweh bless the land of Joseph's descendants "with the favor of Him who appeared in the burning bush." Moses was present at that burning bush encounter with Yahweh and knew what that meant to him.

Yahweh in Your Walk

Elizabeth Barrett Browning wrote a very lengthy literary piece entitled "Aurora Leigh" in which she included these lines:

> Earth's crammed with heaven, and every common bush afire with God,
> But only he who sees takes off his shoes; the rest sit round it and pluck blackberries.

The point she made is very true—evidences of Yahweh and His wondrous works literally fill the earth, even in common bushes. But the only ones who become aware of these evidences of His work and "take off their shoes" (as Moses did) in a spirit of worship are those who are looking for them. Most people miss these revelations of the hand of Yahweh and simply pluck the blackberries without ever pausing to see the wonder of God in that very bush.

Here is a worthy challenge for you as you walk through this day: **Look for the evidences of Yahweh's presence and power in the common things around you.** For example, see Him in trees, as Joyce Kilmer reports in these beautiful words:

> I think that I shall never see a poem lovely as a tree.
> A tree whose hungry mouth is pressed against the earth's sweet flowing breast;
> A tree that looks at God all day and lifts her leafy arms to pray;
> A tree that may in Summer wear a nest of robins in her hair;
> Upon whose bosom snow has lain; who intimately lives with rain.
> Poems are made by fools like me, but only God can make a tree.

Yahweh in Your Worship

Creator of all things, open my eyes to see You and Your works all about me today.

April 9

Yahweh Invites Me to Call on His Name

Yahweh in the Word

> "Then everyone who calls on the name of Yahweh will be saved" (Joel 2:32).

The prophet Joel's name means "Yahweh is God." He was sent by Yahweh to call His people to repent and prepare for a coming day of judgment. Our text gives this promise to all who acknowledge their need for Yahweh to deliver them from their sins, as well as from their enemies.

Yahweh in Your Walk

Has there been a time in your life when you realized you needed to be saved from the consequence of rebelling against Yahweh and you cried out to Him to save you? Can you give a testimony of this experience, explaining how this happened? If so, then you know the truth of the text we consider today. You have been saved from spiritual death forever. And you are secure in this salvation because of Him who is your Savior—the Lord Jesus. As mentioned in the Introduction to this book, the name Jesus in Hebrew is **Yeshua**, meaning "Yahweh is salvation." You know His name is appropriate because you have experienced His saving power.

These words of our text were quoted by the apostle Peter when he preached to those assembled on the Day of Pentecost, described in Acts 1-2. He said, "Everyone who calls on the name of the Lord will be saved" (Acts 2:21). We are told that of those who heard this message about 3,000 responded in faith and became the first church in Jerusalem. Since that memorable day, every person who has believed on and received Yeshua has been permanently delivered from the final consequence of sin—eternal separation from Yahweh.

However, being "saved" includes more than being rescued from going to hell. Salvation is a much broader experience than that. **Every day we need to be saved, not only from the penalty for sin, but from the practice of sin.** Our new birth must be followed by a new life—one that is no longer characterized by disobedience to Yahweh. The only way this can happen is by learning to call on Yeshua each time we are tempted to sin or yield to sin. He wants to save us moment by moment because we cannot save ourselves. The chorus to an old hymn puts the truth in these words:

> Moment by moment I'm kept in His love; moment by moment I've life from above.
> Looking to Jesus till glory doth shine; moment by moment, O Lord, I am Thine.

Yahweh in Your Worship

Blessed Yeshua, I seize this opportunity to call on You for deliverance from all my sin. I have learned by experience that I can never save myself. Thank You for inviting me to call on You throughout each day. Remind me of this important action. May I be a faithful witness to others of Your saving power.

April 10

Yahweh Should Have Praise from Me as Long as I Live

Yahweh in the Word

> *"Hallelujah! My soul, praise Yahweh! I will praise Yahweh all my life; I will sing to my God as long as I live" (Psalm 146:1-2).*

The psalmist began this song with the biblical word "Hallelujah" which means "praise Yahweh." He cried out this praise from his soul—his innermost being, and declared that his praise would continue throughout his entire life, singing to his God as long as he lived.

Yahweh in Your Walk

John Wesley (1703-1791) is known as one of the founders of the Methodist movement which later became the Methodist Church. One of his contemporaries was Isaac Watts (1674-1748) the writer of many well-known hymns. When John was nearing death, his family and friends gathered around his bed and heard him singing these words from a hymn by Isaac Watts:

> "I'll praise my Maker while I've breath; and when my voice is lost in death,
> Praise shall employ my nobler powers; my days of praise shall ne'er be past,
> While life, and thought, and being last, or immortality endures."

This beautiful hymn is a paraphrase of our text, Psalm 146:1-2. Although John Wesley died, according to his own testimony, his praise of Yahweh continued on—in heaven. **We do well to form the habit now of giving much time to praising Yahweh, in preparation for our more informed praise in heaven.** We know this will be true because of the vision of heaven given to the apostle John, who wrote: "Then I heard something like the voice of a vast multitude, like the sound of cascading waters, and like the rumbling of loud thunder, saying:

> Hallelujah, because our Lord God, the Almighty, has begun to reign!
> Let us be glad, rejoice, and give Him glory, because the marriage of the Lamb has come,
> And His wife has prepared herself. She was given fine linen to wear, bright and pure."
> Revelation 19:6-7

Yahweh in Your Worship

Take some time to simply think on Yahweh's greatness and express praise to Him. You may want to use the words of this quote from Revelation 19 or other biblical expressions of praise. Make a covenant with Yahweh that you will continue to praise Him as long as you live. Use the time when you are alone driving your car, to turn off the radio and simply give expression to praise and adoration. Ask Him to remind You of various reasons to praise Him.

April 11

Yahweh Is Worthy of My Heartfelt Worship

Yahweh in the Word

> "Shout triumphantly to Yahweh, all the earth. Serve Yahweh with gladness; come before Him with joyful songs... Enter His gates with thanksgiving and His courts with praise. Give thanks to Him and praise His name" (Psalm 100:1-2, 7).

These words reflect the message of many of the psalms. Worship must become a priority for all Yahweh's people, for nothing affects our relationship with Him as much as heartfelt worship. Notice what worshipers are commanded to do by this text: shout, serve, sing songs, give thanks, and praise His name. All of these are appropriate aspects of authentic worship.

Yahweh in Your Walk

Could it be said truthfully of you that you are a genuine, enthusiastic worshiper of Yahweh? Are you aware that you can attend worship services and never actually worship? We have become a generation of persons who are so programmed by watching television, movies, and other venues that we go to a church service expecting to be entertained by the music and comforted by the sermon. And if we don't get what we expect, we leave disappointed and critical. But these are not components of authentic worship—the worship we find in the Bible. We must never become consumers regarding worship—looking for the best deal, that which is best suited to our taste.

Biblical worshipers assembled to participate in a celebration of Yahweh's greatness and goodness. They often confessed their sins to Him and sought His mercy. There was no entertainment, no promises of health, wealth, and prosperity. Everything focused on Yahweh, not the worshipers. In these daily devotionals you will find repeated appeals to learn how to worship in a manner that is true to what is found throughout the Bible. Above all, worship is participation in heartfelt praise, thanksgiving, and the offering of oneself to serve Yahweh.

Let me challenge you to begin actively participating in every aspect of a worship service. Give your voice in every song or hymn, either singing or saying aloud the words. If person or group sings, join them by repeating their words in your spirit. When someone leads a prayer, pray silently with them. As the minister is preaching receive what is said as Yahweh's message to you. And as you place your money in the offering plate, offer yourself to Yahweh in a silent prayer. If there is a closing invitation, respond in your heart with a new surrender of yourself to Him.

Yahweh in Your Worship

Gracious Yahweh, I do worship You in my spirit and in truth. Deliver me from being an observer in congregational worship. I want to seize every opportunity to participate in worshiping You.

April 12

Yahweh Wants Me to Be Strong

Yahweh in the Word

> "Even so, 'Be strong, Zerubbabel'—this is Yahweh's declaration. 'Be strong, Joshua son of Jehozadak, high priest. Be strong all you people of the land'— this is Yahweh's declaration. 'Work! For I am with you'—the declaration of Yahweh Sabaoth. 'This is the promise I made to you when you came out of Egypt, and My Spirit is present among you; don't be afraid'" (Haggai 2:4-5).

Haggai was Yahweh's prophet to His people after they returned from many years in Babylonian exile. When they first returned, they began rebuilding the temple in Jerusalem. Due to opposition they left that project before it was finished. Haggai was sent to encourage them to be strong and get back to their task. Zerubbabel was their governor and Joshua was the high priest.

Yahweh in Your Walk

You may have experienced the fact that beginning a project often is easier than completing it. Most of us are better starters than finishers. Sometimes, after the "new" wears off, we tend to lose our initial enthusiasm. Yahweh's people were like this when they returned from exile and began reconstructing their temple. Although they laid the foundation and began building, they lost the needed perseverance when opposition arose from their enemies. Yahweh sent Haggai to call His people to be strong and complete the task.

Consider Yahweh's message: "Be strong" (three times), "Work! For I am with you," "My Spirit is present among you; don't be afraid." **All these words can be applied to us whenever we become discouraged.** Let's examine each of these more closely. First, "Be strong," addresses the need for the strength to keep on keeping on. Where do we obtain this kind of endurance? The psalmist declared, "Yahweh is my strength." **As we call upon Him, He provides both the motivation and the power we need to stay with the task, whatever that may be.** As the song says, "I am weak but Thou art strong."

Then He said, "Work! For I am with you." Yahweh does not build temples; people must do that kind of work. So it is with the tasks we face—He is with us, supplying the needed strength, but we must do the actual construction. I like the way the apostle Paul expressed this joint working relationship with Christ when he wrote: "I labor for this, striving with His strength that works powerfully in me" (Colossians 1:29). When we see ourselves as co-laborers with Him, the task is not only do-able but pleasurable. Having His Spirit present also gives us the needed courage.

Yahweh in Your Worship

O God of my strength, I give praise and thanksgiving to You. Apart from You, I can do nothing. But when We work together, all things are possible. Teach me to be a strong worker with You.

April 13

Yahweh Will Complete the Work He Began in Me

Yahweh in the Word

> "I am sure of this, that He who started a good work in you will carry it on to completion until the day of Christ Jesus" (Philippians 1:6).

These reassuring words of the apostle Paul were written to all the believers in the church at Philippi. He knew that the "good work" of saving them and calling them out to be His church was the work of the Lord Yeshua, and that He would continue doing that work until His return.

Yahweh in Your Walk

Some of my favorite Scripture verses are those that speak of Yeshua's work in us—the work of saving us from our sins and forming us into His likeness. For example, later in this letter, Paul says, "For it is God who is working in you, enabling you both to desire and to work out His good purpose" (2:13). Again in Colossians 1:29 we read, "I labor for this, striving with His strength that works powerfully in me." Notice that in our text and in the second reference (2:13), the apostle refers to Christ working in His church as a whole; this last statement speaks of Him working powerfully "in me" as an individual. **The message for us is that Yahweh is working powerfully in both individual believers and in their fellowship together.**

Sometimes we may think we have accomplished something rather significant in terms of our service for Christ or in our personal development in the faith. The truth is—He is the One who does all this good work; **we are simply His tools and His workshop!** And the good work He began in us and keeps doing in us will finally be carried to "completion." The word Paul used here has the same root as Jesus' word from the cross when He said, "It is finished!" (John 19:30). The idea conveyed is that Jesus' death fully completed all that was essential for our salvation. Now He is working to complete the ultimate result of that salvation—our becoming like Him.

Joel Hemphill wrote these words for a children's song, but it applies equally to adults:

> He's still working on me—to make me what I ought to be.
> It took Him just a week to make the moon and the stars,
> The sun and the moon and Jupiter and Mars.
> How loving and patient He must be 'cause He's still working on me.

How important for us to be working with Him and being fully yielded to His work in and through us. Begin your walk with Him today by surrendering control of your life to Him.

Yahweh in Your Worship

Thank You, Lord, that You will finish what You began in me. I offer myself to be Yours today.

April 14

Yahweh Deserves to Receive Glory from Me

Yahweh in the Word

> *"Ascribe to Yahweh, you heavenly beings, ascribe to Yahweh glory and strength. Ascribe to Yahweh the glory due His name; worship Yahweh in the splendor of His holiness" (Ps. 29:1-2).*

To ascribe glory to Yahweh means to acknowledge that He is worthy of all praise and honor; He is the sovereign Lord of this entire universe. All "heavenly beings" refers to the total host of angels in heaven; they know Yahweh intimately and join all redeemed humankind in exalting Him through worship.

Yahweh in Your Walk

You will notice the term "worship" in the midst of this text. The psalmist is calling for all created beings, in heaven and on earth, to join together in worshiping Yahweh. A noted theologian once declared, "Christian worship is the most momentous, the most urgent, and the most glorious action that can take place in human life." **Of all the varied aspects of the Christian life, none is as influential upon us as our understanding and practice of worshiping Yahweh.**

How can we improve the quality of our worship? Consider this statement made by A.W.Tozer (1897-1963) a highly respected biblical scholar: "The quality of our worship is enhanced as we move away from the thought of what God has done for us, and move nearer the thought of the excellence of His holy nature... We begin to grow up when our worship passes from thanksgiving to admiration." Another leader expressed the same truth in these words: "We should seek God's face and not His hand. When you seek God's face, you seek Him for Himself. You seek to know Him and to please Him. When you seek God's hand, you seek just His blessings, His gifts."

Too often our worship with other believers becomes more concerned with **how** we worship—the various worship styles—than with **who** we worship. **Authentic worship is not about us—our taste for music or our preference for an atmosphere conducive to our kind of worship—it is about Him, pleasing Him, honoring Him, offering ourselves to Him**. William Temple (1881-1944) described worship like this: "To worship is to quicken the conscience by the holiness of God, to feed the mind with the truth of God, to purge the imagination by the beauty of God, to open the heart to the love of God and to devote the will to the purposes of God."

Most of our worship experiences should occur when we are alone with Yahweh; all through the day we lift our hearts in adoration and praise, ascribing glory to Him. But remember, worship that is genuine makes a difference in our walk; words of praise must become works of service.

Yahweh in Your Worship

Holy Yahweh, creator and sustainer of all things, I join all creatures in offering praise to You. You alone are worthy of my worship because of who You are.

April 15

Yahweh Wants Me to Pay What I Owe

Yahweh in the Word

> "Then they sent some of the Pharisees and the Herodians to Him to trap Him by what He said. When they came, they said to Him, 'Teacher, we know You are truthful and defer to no one, for You don't show partiality but teach truthfully the way of God. Is it lawful to pay taxes to Caesar of not? Should we pay, or should we not pay?' But knowing their hypocrisy, He said to them, 'Why are you testing Me? Bring Me a denarius to look at.' So they brought one. 'Whose image and inscription is this?' He asked them. 'Caesar's,' they said. Jesus told them, 'Give back to Caesar the things that are Caesar's, and to God the things that are God's.' And they were amazed at Him" (Mark 12:13-17).

The Pharisees and the Herodians were Jews who had strong disagreements regarding the relationship of Jews to the Roman government. The Pharisees resented Roman rule over them while the Herodians favored Herod Antipas, the Roman governor of Galilee. These two enemies got together and came up with a trick question for Jesus. They knew that whichever way He answered would cause Him trouble. But, with great wisdom, Jesus gave an answer that satisfied both sides. They were amazed at the unexpected way Jesus answered them.

Yahweh in Your Walk

Today is known as "Tax Day." Since 1955 Federal Income Taxes are due to the US government on this date. On this day most US citizens are required to file a tax return reporting what has been paid and what may be owed for the previous year. As Christians we should participate gladly as an expression of gratitude for all we receive from our government as US citizens. This is our way to obey Jesus' command to "Give back to Caesar the things that are Caesar's."

The apostle Paul wrote about the civil responsibility of believers when he said, "Everyone must submit to the governing authorities, for there is no authority except from God, and those that exist are instituted by God… For government is God's servant for our good… and for this reason you pay taxes, since the authorities are God's public servants" (Romans 13:1, 4, 6). **We owe taxes to support the government that, in turn, supports us in many practical ways.**

But we also have an obligation to "give back to God the things that are God's" which includes far more than money. We are indebted to Him for everything we have—even the air we breathe. How then can we possibly repay Him? By being good stewards of all He entrusts to our care. **We are not owners, but possessors and a manager of all Yahweh gives us.** Our responsibility is to use what we have in a manner that pleases Him and honors Him. What a privilege!

Yahweh in Your Worship

Today, I choose to seize every opportunity to worship You by being a good steward of all You give to my care. Thank You for giving me such a great country where I am free to worship.

April 16
Yahweh Asks Me to Give Myself to Him

Yahweh in the Word

> "I testify that, on their own, according to their ability and beyond their ability, they begged us insistently for the privilege of sharing in the ministry to the saints, and not just as we had hoped. Instead, they gave themselves especially to the Lord, then to us by God's will" (2 Corinthians 8:3-5).

The apostle Paul wrote these words to Christians in Corinth. He told about Christians in Macedonia who, in spite of severe afflictions, had begged him to accept their offerings to help others. Paul notes that such generosity was the direct result of first giving themselves to the Lord.

Yahweh in Your Walk

One of the freedoms we have is that of self-determination, that is, deciding what to do with our lives. We can choose to live primarily for ourselves, doing what we do for self-gratification, or we can select someone else or some other cause as our reason for what we do. When Jesus called others to follow Him, He was clear about the cost of such a decision. He said, "Deny yourselves, take up your cross and follow me." To deny oneself means to say no to self-centeredness and taking our cross means we choose to die to self. And following Him means we give ourselves to Him as the Lord and Master of all we are and have and do. This commitment involves a major change in one's lifestyle and values and purpose for living—not an easy nor simple decision.

What can motivate a person to make such a life-altering choice? Part of the answer is found in this interesting story: Fannie Crosby became blind due to a physician's error shortly after her birth in 1820. When she was 31 years old, she attended a revival service at John Street Methodist Church in New York, City. As the hymn: "Alas! And Did My Savior Bleed" was being sung, she listened to these words from the fifth stanza: "But drops of grief can ne'er repay the debt of love I owe. Here, Lord, I give myself to away, 'tis all that I can do." Her testimony is that as these words were being sung, "my very soul was flooded with celestial light" as she gave herself to serve Jesus. As a result of this commitment, she went on to become "The Queen of Gospel Music," composing over 8,000 hymns and gospel songs.

Just like Fannie Crosby, when we become aware of the tremendous sacrifice Jesus made for us upon His cross, we will also want to offer ourselves to worship and serve Him. And this gift will increase the better we come to know Yeshua and His love for us.

Yahweh in Your Worship

All praise and honor belong to You, Holy Master. Your gift of life to me motivates me to return this gift to You; take me and make me all You want me to be. I love You and worship You as my eternal King.

April 17

Yahweh Wants Me to Treat Others with Kindness

Yahweh in the Word

> "Be kind and compassionate to one another, forgiving one another, just as God also forgave you in Christ" (Ephesians 4:32).

Earlier in this passage the apostle Paul speaks of putting off the old self and putting on the new self which is created according to God's likeness. He then describes how these new Christ-like attributes replace the old sinful ones. The text here points to kindness, compassion and forgiveness as examples of this change.

Yahweh in Your Walk

When I ask my wife what kind of gift she would like from me for Easter, I know beforehand what her answer will be—a Cadbury chocolate egg! What neither of us knew before doing some recent research is the interesting story behind this tasty product. Here are some noteworthy facts: John Cadbury began this company in his native England in 1824. He and his family were Quakers and were concerned about the deplorable working conditions for laborers at that time. His son, George, developed the Bournville estate, a model village that was designed to give their employees improved living conditions. In addition they built a state-of-the-art factory with heated dressing rooms, a kitchen, and recreational areas. In order to meet the spiritual needs of their employees, each workday began with a brief time for Bible study and prayer. Yahweh blessed the kindness of this family business, and it has grown to a very large company.

There is an important lesson here for all of us. **Yahweh loves everyone equally. And His will is that all of His children treat one another with kindness and compassion.** Let's consider some practical ways this can be lived out.

We must always begin expressing His kindness at home, with our family members. Examine the way you relate to your immediate family—are you known and appreciated as being kind and compassionate by those with whom you live? Are your words and actions expressions of love?

> Next, think about your workplace or school or wherever you go as you leave home. If you have employees, are you treating them as you would like to be treated if you were in their place?
> How about your reputation at your church, would fellow believers describe you as being kind and caring? Do you take the initiative in reaching out to help others?

If you are not expressing the kindness of Jesus in all these areas, begin now to make changes!

Yahweh in Your Worship

Gracious and kind Yahweh, I worship You for being so merciful and forgiving of me and all others. You are to be continually praised for Your goodness. Help me be more like You.

April 18

Yahweh Wants Me to Know that I Have Died with Christ and Been Raised Up with Him

Yahweh in the Word

> "If you died with the Messiah.... you have been raised with the Messiah, seek what is above, where the Messiah is, seated at the right hand of God" (Colossians 2:20; 3:1).

The apostle Paul sent this message to readers in Colossae to remind them of their identity with Christ in both His death and His resurrection.

Yahweh in Your Walk

Easter is a season of the year with very a significant meaning for Christians. We remember how our Lord was first betrayed by Judas, humiliated through the various legal trials before both civil and religious leaders, forsaken by his own disciples, then horribly mistreated by merciless beatings, shamefully striped of His garment and nailed to a cross. His agony was more than we can ever imagine as He endured such physical pain. And yet, none of that compares to His spiritual suffering as He carried in Himself the total sin debt of all humankind, both past, present, and future. Surely this was the worst expression of the wages of sin in all the history of the ages.

But we also remember the incredibly good news of His victory over all this evil as He arose from the grave on the third day. What an amazing reversal—first, He went **down** under the power of sin and guilt, then—He came **up** from the grave as the ultimate victor over all that evil powers could combine to do. This glorious victory proves beyond all doubt that He is the Son of God!

However, there is another aspect of this Easter story that provides tremendous benefits for us as we walk through this world where we are faced with our own trials and temptations. **Paul reminded all believers who would read his letter that there is a sense in which we all actually died with Christ and also joined Him in His triumphant resurrection.** How can this be? Think about this wonderful truth: We died with Christ because He died to pay our sin debt. This means we are dead to any future penalty for our sins—our debt is paid in full by His death. Also, we are united with Him in His resurrection because we have been spiritually raised from our old dead nature to a new life—His resurrected life in us.

On Easter Sunday in 1993, a man named Bernhard Langer won the Masters golf tournament. As he received his coveted green jacket, a reporter said to him, "This must be the greatest day of your life." Langer replied, "It's wonderful to win the greatest tournament in the world, but it means more to win on Easter Sunday—to celebrate the resurrection of my Lord and Savior."

Yahweh in Your Worship

I worship You, O Resurrected Lord, because of Your great sacrifice for me. I join all believers in celebrating Your risen life. Thank You for making all this new life possible.

April 19

Yahweh Always Treats Me Better Than I Deserve

Yahweh in the Word

> "He (Yahweh) has not dealt with us as our sins deserve or repaid us according to our offenses" (Psalm 103:10).

In this memorable psalm, David celebrates Yahweh's goodness to him. He calls upon his readers to remember how merciful and gracious Yahweh has been and always will be.

Yahweh in Your Walk

Recently I asked a friend, "How are you doing?" His reply was interesting, "Much better than I deserve!" As I have thought about this, I realize how true this is. If Yahweh were to give us what we deserve, it would be hell. Our sins have earned for us this return.

Satan would like for us to think we are a good person simply because we aren't criminals who have to be locked up in prison. However, the truth is—we are all sinners; we have chosen our ways over Yahweh's ways. And because He is just, we deserve to be punished by being separated from Him forever in a place of endless torment; that's what every one of us deserves.

Were it not for Yahweh's mercy and grace, we would all perish. David was keenly aware of this fact so he began this beautiful psalm by saying, "My soul, praise Yahweh, and all that is within me, praise His holy name. My soul, praise Yahweh, and do not forget all His benefits" (vv. 1-2).

As you walk through this day, a day you have never lived before, a day which is Yahweh's undeserved gift to you, think about His favors to you. **Remember that He is far better to you than you could ever deserve.** Begin making a list of some of His grace-gifts to you. Pause to thank Him for each one. Ask Him to open your eyes to evidences of His mercy; worship Him in the light of these expressions of love.

The next time someone asks you, "How are you doing?" Respond like my friend, and then explain more fully why you gave that answer. **Be a bold witness of His goodness to you.** Your testimony could make a difference in the attitude toward life of your friend. Some of those you will meet today struggle with feeling that they aren't receiving from God what they really deserve. Your words can help them see the truth about sin, compared to Yahweh's mercy and grace.

Yahweh in Your Worship

Gracious Yahweh, I worship You because You are so great, so good, so merciful, and so kind to me. Forgive me when I have forgotten how Your love is far greater than my sin. Use me today to share with others Your blessings upon me. Help me pass on what You have bestowed upon me.

April 20

Yahweh Is Always on My Side

Yahweh in the Word

> "If Yahweh had not been on or side… If Yahweh had not been on our side… Our help is in the name of Yahweh, the Maker of heaven and earth" (Psalm 124:1-2, 8).

In this song of deliverance, David celebrates Yahweh's protection and provision for His chosen people. He observes that if Yahweh had not been on Israel's side, their enemies would have overcome them. This same truth applies to us today.

Yahweh in Your Walk

Do you recall times in your childhood when you played games where you had to choose sides for some kind of contest? I always hoped to be chosen for the best side—the one with the best team members. The point of this devotional is that **we who are Yahweh's children can be sure that He has chosen to always be on our side in this contest called life.** No matter how bleak our circumstances may appear, Yahweh is for us; He is on our side—you can bet your bottom dollar on this fact!

The apostle Paul affirmed this same truth when he wrote to believers in Rome about all the great blessings Yahweh had bestowed on them. He concluded his remarks in these memorable words: "What then are we to say about these things? If God is **for us**, who is against us? He did not even spare His own Son but offered Him up **for us** all, how will He not also with Him grant us everything?" (Romans 8:31-32). His reasoning is that since Yahweh has proven that He is **for us** by giving us His best, surely we can expect Him to give us whatever else we need.

Let this wonderful truth accompany you as you walk through this and every day of your life—**Yahweh, the sovereign God of this universe is on your side—that is, He is providing everything you need to become all He wants you to be.** Your part is to simply be available to Him, to place yourself and all you have in His hands.

Remember, because He is on your side, you are on the winning team. As Paul stated when he concluded his message, "In all these things [various severe trials] we are more than victorious through Him who loved us. For I am persuaded that not even death or life, angels or rulers, things present or things to come, hostile powers, height or depth, or any other created thing will have the power to separate us from the love of God that is in Christ Jesus our Lord" (8:37-39).

Wow! Life just doesn't get any better than this. Do you really believe He is on your side—today?

Yahweh in Your Worship

Gracious Lord, You are so good to me. I worship You with gratitude and praise in my heart. May Your purpose for me be fulfilled this day; make me aware of Your presence and help at all times.

April 21

Yahweh Is Able to Do Far More than I Can Imagine

Yahweh in the Word

> *"Now to Him who is able to do exceedingly abundantly above all that we ask or think, according to the power that works in us, to Him be glory in the church by Christ Jesus to all generations, forever and ever. Amen" (Ephesians 3:20-21 NKJV).*

The apostle Paul often spoke benedictions in his letters to the churches. Here is one of the most inspiring. All glory belongs to Yahweh because of all He is capable of doing in and through His people.

Yahweh in Your Walk

There have been times when all of us have felt that we were unable to do what we wanted to do and knew we should do; we were keenly aware of our weaknesses. How comforting and reassuring to know that Yahweh is never like that; He is always fully able to do what needs doing. As our Scripture text for today declares, He is able to do, not just enough to get by, but "exceeding abundantly above all that we ask or think." **Take a moment to meditate on these amazing words: exceeding—abundantly—above—all that we ask—or even think.** Wow! Talk about superlatives—here is a string of words that is totally overwhelming! **How can we ever again feel inadequate to any task?**

Notice how this amazing ability is expressed: "according to the power that works in us." The original word here for "power" is the same root as our English word ***dynamo*** or ***dynamite***. As believers we literally have the power (dynamo) of the Holy Spirit living in us and working in us to accomplish God's will—all the time. This truth is the reason Paul said, "I can do all things through Christ who strengthens me" (Philippians 4:13). **You can say the same thing because you have the same resource of power living in you!**

As you walk through this day, use the faith Yahweh has given you to claim this ability to handle whatever challenges come your way. Rather than focusing on your inability, claim His ability and prove His word to be more than adequate for your need. Again, notice in the text the fact of doing **much more** than what is needed—**exceeding, abundantly, above, all we ask or think.** Remember, this is not dependent on what you can do, rather what Yahweh can do in and through you—what a tremendous difference!

Yahweh in Your Worship

How wonderfully blessed am I to know You, O Yahweh! You supply more power than I could ever need to do Your will and be Your person. I praise You for being so gracious toward me and to all others. Thank You that I truly can do all things through the One who strengthens me today. Help me share this good news with others who struggle because of dependence upon themselves.

April 22

Yahweh Helps Me When I Pray

Yahweh in the Word

> "In the same way the Spirit also joins to help in our weakness, because we do not know what to pray for as we should, but the Spirit Himself intercedes for us with unspoken groanings. And He who searches the hearts knows the Spirit's mind-set, because He intercedes for the saints according to the will of God" (Romans 8:26-27).

Paul wanted his readers to be confident of Yahweh's effective help when they prayed. Although we are weak when it comes to knowing exactly how to pray, the Holy Spirit, who lives within us prays for us (intercedes) according to God's perfect will.

Yahweh in Your Walk

Hopefully, you will offer many prayers during this day—some very brief as you face various people and needs, other times, longer periods of fellowship with Yahweh in prayer. Some of your prayers will be expressions of praise and thanksgiving—always appropriate. However, there may be those situations where you aren't sure just how to pray—what to ask. Today's Scripture text gives you assurance that Yahweh has provided an effective Helper—the Holy Spirit to make your requests conform to God's will.

The term "groaning" occurs several times in this chapter (vv. 22, 23, 26). The idea found in this word is that of inward feelings of concern, too profound to be expressed in words. You may recall times when something affected you so deeply that you had no words to express your feelings; you simply groaned within. In a similar way the Holy Spirit "intercedes for us with unspoken groanings." How encouraging to remember this profound truth when you pray. He understands your heart—your deepest concerns—and expresses those requests before Yahweh in a manner that conforms to His will. **You never need to worry about whether you are offering your prayers in just the right words; He helps your prayer be pleasing to Yahweh.**

Consider an application of this truth. You have often prayed for someone with an illness or injury to be healed because you believe that Jesus is the Great Physician who can restore good health. Sometimes your prayer has been answered, just as you asked. Other times, nothing seemed to change. Why? There are times when Yahweh's will for an individual is best accomplished through suffering, so His answer to your request is no, or later, but not now. The Holy Spirit will intercede and will conform your request to Yahweh's will. Thus, all our requests should agree with Jesus as He faced the cross, "Nevertheless, not My will but Yours be done."

Yahweh in Your Worship

Yahweh, I bow before You with praise and thanksgiving. You are the One who hears and answers my prayers, according to Your will. Thank You for Your supreme wisdom in all things.

April 23

Yahweh Gives Me Reasons for Smiling

Yahweh in the Word

> "Yahweh spoke to Moses: 'Tell Aaron and his sons how you are to bless the Israelites. Say to them: "May Yahweh bless you and protect you; may Yahweh make His face to shine on you and be gracious to you; may Yahweh look with favor on you and give you peace"' (Num. 6:24-26).

Yahweh gave clear instructions about the way Aaron and his sons, the priests, were to speak words of blessing to His people. Yahweh's desire was to favor them with His continuous protection, grace, and peace.

Yahweh in Your Walk

Have you ever noticed how a newborn infant often responds to attention with a smile? Smiling seems to be a natural instinct with babies. At the other extreme, how sad to see a frown on the face of someone who is advanced in age; it seems that their natural countenance often is a wrinkled scowl. Researchers have discovered that smiling is good for a person's health—it slows down one's heart and reduces stress. But smiling is of value for other reasons than improved health. **How important it is that we make a habit of smiling when we meet a person, whether a stranger or friend.** Our smile can open a door for further communication. A friendly smile lets a person know we are focused on them and ready to reach out to them in other ways. As one writer said, "A smile can hug someone with love without giving them even the slightest touch." **Consider several reasons for why we should be characterized as "smilers."**

Although the word *smile* does not appear in most translations of the Bible, there are many references to the importance of our countenance (face), such as "A joyful heart makes a face cheerful but a sad heart produces a broken spirit" (Proverbs 15:13). In other words, your face reveals the condition of your heart—cheerful face, joyful heart—troubled face, sad heart. We believers have multiple reasons for a joy-filled heart. One of which is the fact that **Yahweh smiles on us** with innumerable blessings. Where our text reads "may Yahweh make His face to shine on you," the New Living Translation is, "may the LORD smile on you." **When our ways are pleasing to Yahweh, He responds with a smile!**

Moreover, we can have a joyful heart when we pause to remember specific ways Yahweh shows His favor to us. An old gospel song gives this good advice: "Count your many blessings, name them one by one; count your blessings, see what God hath done. Count your blessings, name them one by one; count your many blessings; see what God has done." That will make you smile.

Yahweh in Your Worship

How grateful I am for Your smiling countenance toward me, Lord. Help me pass that look of favor on to others today. May You bless others with Your smiling face through me.

April 24

Yeshua Wants Me To Avoid Mistakes In Life

Yeshua in the Word

> "Paul and his companions set sail… Mark however left them and went back to Jerusalem" (Acts 13:13).

The next seven devotionals are a study of biblical people who faced restarts, endings, beginnings, and change. John Mark was the nephew of Barnabas and joined Paul and his associates on some of the early missionary journeys. Once the Sprit had spoken and the missionaries were prepared to leave, the believers fasted, prayed, and laid their hand on the missionaries. The church at Antioch launched a movement to evangelize the world. Mark was apparently a young man and could not handle the many crises on this trip. These dramatic episodes of travel, confrontation, desertion, opportunity, success, jealousy, hostility, courage, and threat of death were too much. So in Perga, of Pamphylia, he decided to leave the group and return to Jerusalem. The apostle Paul did not like this young man's decision and refused to allow him to be a part of this opportunity to share the gospel with the Gentiles. However, amid many trying circumstances, churches were planted and strengthened there.

Much later in the letter of 2 Timothy, Paul longed to see Mark again. Even though Mark had failed to be what others expected him to be, he made an effort to restart his life and worked with Barnabas in Cyprus. **Mistakes do not need to be final.** Apparently Mark grew in his ability to work on the road ministry and be away from home. He did restart his life. Lesson learned.

Yeshua in Your Walk

Mildred has a reputation for being a starter and a quitter! She is the first to volunteer when any need surfaces in our church. Aggressive is a good word to describe her… for a while. However, after the initial excitement of a project ends, she quits. Someone else has to assume the responsibility for her lack of commitment.

One day, a plea was issued for someone to begin the Women's Ministry of our church. I knew she would eagerly take the position. Her organizational skills were good; many women became involved in this needed work. About six months later, she would not come to the planning meetings and allowed a banquet to be a complete failure. She left our church after that problem.

Good news came to me several years later from a former friend who now knew Mildred. She was pleased that my friend had restarted her service in the new church and was staying with the ministry. I rejoiced that her mistakes from the past were not hindering her work in the present. However, many people had difficulty believing Mildred was being successful in her new location.

Yeshua in Your Worship

Yeshua, forgive my mistakes from the past and help me learn to start over, depending on You.

April 25

Yeshua Wants Me to Be Available for His Work

Yeshua in the Word

> *"To Timothy, my true son in the faith..." (1 Timothy 1:2).*

Timothy was one of Paul's special associates. His name means "one who honors God." This young man, born of mixed parentage, along with Titus, dealt with some of the rough assignments in the churches Paul had established. As an eager young man, he was recruited to work among the churches. **He is an example of someone who begins his work for the Lord and stays faithful until the end.** He was Paul's protégé, his spiritual son, the most genuine reflection of the apostle. Timothy probably knew the apostle Paul better than any other person. He joined the missionary on Paul's first journey.

His mother and grandmother had taught him the Scriptures. The supreme joy for any parent is to see their child grow into a mature, well-developed adult. However, **he struggled with his youthfulness and shyness, especially involving the church at Ephesus.** The city was devoted to worship of Diana, who promoted sexual immorality of all kinds. Timothy was a beginner in the church work. Paul was a Roman prisoner when he wrote his second letter to his young friend. Sound words of advice came from the aging missionary. He wanted Timothy to rightly handle the Word of God. Apparently he pursued this task and remained faithful in his ministry. The pattern of his life was obedience.

Yeshua in Your Walk

This advertisement appeared in a city newspaper:

> Men wanted for hazardous journey, small wages, bitter cold, long months of complete darkness, constant danger, safe return doubtful. Honor and recognition in case of success.

Thousands of men responded to Sir Ernest Shackleton's search for his Artic expedition. If Jesus had advertised for workers in the Ephesus church with the priority assignment of teaching sound doctrine, how many individuals would respond? **Even today the call to missions involves many dangers.** Many young married couples and singles are willing to begin serving wherever Yahweh leads them. Our son, Mark, and his wife, Judy, received a clear call to serve God in Asia. No doubt existed about their calling. So, they left our home and spent the next 35 years proclaiming the good news to people on the Pacific Rim. As retirement nears, Yahweh will surely say of them, "Well done, good and faithful servants."

Yeshua in Your Worship

Lord, help me to rely on the spiritual insight You provide in Your Word. I want to be available to whatever You call me to do. Thank You that Your call to service always includes all I need to perform whatever You ask me of me.

April 26

Yahweh Wants Me to Be a Godly Example During Difficult Times

Yahweh in the Word

> "Do not persuade me to leave you or go back and not follow you. For wherever you go, I will go, and wherever you live, I will live; your people will be my people, and your God will be my God" (Ruth 1:16).

Ruth was from Moab and met her husband, Mahlon, when his family migrated to her country because of a severe famine in Bethlehem. Naomi was her mother-in-law. Their cultures and ages were very different. During the stay of Naomi's family, her husband and two sons died. Only three widows and no children were left in Elimelech's family. This grieving widow decided to return to her homeland and Ruth accompanied her.

The return of these two widows to Canaan caused quite a stir. However, Ruth, the Gentile Moabitess, was accepted and blessed of the Lord. Harvest season was in progress and Ruth found a job gleaning in the field of Boaz, a relative of her husband. This was good news for Naomi and she quickly arranged a marriage following the levirate law.

The story of Ruth teaches that Yahweh's people today should be more considerate of the stranger and sojourner among us. This consideration includes sharing the gospel—the good news of Jesus who became Ruth's greatest descendant.

Yahweh in Your Walk

The story of Ruth is about change. A young heathen became a member of a family of Yahweh-worshipers. Her experience reminds me of a young woman who came into my life many years ago. First, she was different, a Japanese by birth, and worshiped a different god than mine. She met her American military husband after World War II. Their love grew and the day came when he was to be shipped home after two years in Japan. Loi Kei desired to return home with her new husband, Ben.

The family was shocked that their son would marry "the enemy." Japan was responsible for the terrible war our country had just experienced. However, this loving, Christian family did their best to accept this foreign woman. They prayed and read their Bible and sought counsel from other believers. I participated in the major change in her life and became her friend. My feelings about her were difficult at first and I spent much time in prayer about my attitude. "Why me?" was my response when Ben asked me to teach her our American ways and I did!

Yahweh in Your Worship

Thank You for teaching me to accept change in my life. LORD, help me to realize that ALL people need You, no matter the race, color, or language barriers. Let me be Your witness to the world around me. You can cause me to love all people and Your Word will be my guide in the remaining days of my life.

April 27

Yahweh Wants Me to Be a Barefoot Saint

Yahweh in the Word

> *"Moses was shepherding the flock of his father-in-law Jethro... Then the Angel of Yahweh appeared to him in a flame of fire within a bush. As Moses looked, he saw that the bush was on fire but was not consumed... God called out to him from the bush, 'Moses, Moses!' 'Here I am,' he answered. 'Do not come closer,' He said, 'Remove the sandals from your feet, for the place where you are standing is holy ground'" (Exodus 3: 1-5).*

This dramatic encounter with Yahweh was a turning point in Moses' life. For the past forty years he had been living in the Sinai Desert as a shepherd, having run away from his home in Egypt where he was wanted for killing an Egyptian. Yahweh had other plans for this chosen servant. Following this burning bush episode, He sent Moses back to Egypt to lead His people out of their bondage there, and onto a forty-year-journey to their future home.

Yahweh in Your Walk

Moses is another biblical figure who recovered from a bad start to become one of Yahweh's greatest leaders. His personal history included beginning as an adopted and favored member of Pharaoh's family, to being a fugitive/shepherd, to serving as Yahweh's chosen representative to His special people. These were three forty-year segments of Moses' life. The final forty were the most significant.

At the burning bush, Yahweh revealed Himself and His special name to Moses for the first time. To add gravity to this encounter, Yahweh told Moses to remove His sandals because he was standing on "holy ground." That place was holy because Yahweh, the holy God of the universe, was present. Years later, Moses' assistant, Joshua, had a similar experience when Yahweh gave him the same instructions, "Remove the sandals from your feet, for the place where you are standing is holy" (Joshua 5:15). **Wherever Yahweh is, is a holy place—because He alone is completely and eternally holy.**

Think of the implications of this truth today. Since the Day of Pentecost, when the Holy Spirit was given as a permanent resident to every believer, all Christians have been saints—holy ones; not because we are holy in and of ourselves, but because the One who now lives in us is holy. Therefore, **we are to be "barefoot saints" in the sense of living continually in the presence of holiness—the Holy Spirit.** When my bare feet touch the floor each morning, I pause to acknowledge His presence and commit myself to His control for that day. **Just as Yahweh's presence was a turning point for Moses and Joshua, so He wants to be that for you.**

Yahweh in Your Worship

I praise You, holy LORD, for Your continuous presence with me. Help me be aware of You.

April 28

Yeshua Offers Restoration to All Who Come to Him

Yeshua in the Word

> "They seized Him (Jesus), led Him away, and brought Him into the high priest's house. Meanwhile Peter was following at a distance... When a servant saw him sitting in the firelight, and looked closely at him, she said, 'This man was with Him too.' But he denied it: 'Woman, I don't know Him!'" (Luke 42: 54-57).

This sad event regarding Peter's denial of Jesus is recorded in all four Gospels. Jesus had warned Peter that this would happen, but Peter boldly maintained that he would die with Jesus rather than deny Him. But when accused three times of being one of Jesus' disciples, he shamefully denied even knowing Him.

Yeshua in Your Walk

Here is another example of how Yeshua forgives and restores those who stumble in their walk as a believer. You will recall that Peter was the first of the disciples to make the bold statement, "You are the Messiah, the Son of the living God" (Matthew 16:16). Our text for today records a later occasion when three times he repeated his cowardly plea that he did not even know Jesus. However, he was obviously restored to the point of being the bold preacher on the Day of Pentecost when several thousand were saved (Acts 2:14-41).

Subsequently, he was the first disciple to be sent to evangelize a Gentile and his entire household—Cornelius (Acts 10). But another defect occurred when Peter went to Antioch, eating with Gentile believers until he feared that Christian Jews who came from Jerusalem would be displeased with his compromising behavior. Paul recorded a stern rebuke of Peter for this hypocrisy (Galatians 2:11-14). So, Peter was a vacillating disciple, sometimes bold, and other times cowardly. And yet, he remains one of the most influential of Yeshua's followers, all because of His mercy and grace.

Here is the message for us from this well-known Christian leader: **Even those who profess most strongly to be trustworthy and faithful, may falter and fail.** However, like Peter, if we genuinely repent and seek His pardon, we will be fully restored and used in a powerful manner to extend His kingdom in this world. A clear word of hope is found in these solemn words: **"For a believer in Jesus, no failure ever needs to be final."**

Yeshua in Your Worship

I worship You, Holy Savior, for You are a God of mercy, patience, and grace. Thank You for restoring me when I have failed to be faithful to You. Use me to share this good news of restoration to others.

April 29

Yahweh Wants Me to Be Loyal to Him

Yahweh in the Word

> "He raised up David as their king and testified about him: 'I have found David the son of Jesse, a man loyal to Me, who will carry out all My will'" (Acts 13:22).

These words are from a message Paul delivered in a synagogue in Antioch of Pisidia on his first missionary journey. He recounted Israel's history from their bondage in Egypt up to the resurrection of Jesus.

Yahweh in Your Walk

Most of us can remember times when we have been loyal to Yahweh, and other times when we have been disloyal. None of us has been as faithful as we could and should have been. **We can take heart and be encouraged by the biblical example of David.** You may recall his beginning as a shepherd boy who was called out of his large family and anointed as the future king by the prophet Samuel (1 Samuel 16:1-13).

First, he became Saul's armor bearer who would at times sing songs to comfort the king. Later David rose to prominence by slaying Goliath, the giant, and showing loyalty to King Saul. After the death of Saul, David became king of Judah and later united Judah and Israel as one nation. But his service to Yahweh was marred when he engaged Bathsheba, Uriah's wife, in an illicit sexual relationship. This act of lust grew to become murder as he had Uriah killed in battle. Later the prophet Nathan was sent by Yahweh to confront David with his sins. David confessed and found Yahweh's forgiveness, however, the consequences of his foolish acts remained for the rest of his life.

Here is another example of a person whom Yahweh used in a very significant manner in spite of his shortcomings and failure to always be loyal to his calling. Many of the psalms were written by David, and in several of these he acknowledges his sins against God: "Be gracious to me, God, according to Your faithful love; according to Your abundant compassion, blot out my rebellion. Wash away my guilt and cleanse me from my sin" (Psalm 51:1-2). His example of a repentant heart, followed by confession of sin shows us how any person can be restored through calling upon Yahweh for mercy and pardon. Yahweh's purpose for David was hindered by the sin of this chosen servant, and yet, he was fully reconciled and used mightily once more.

Yahweh in Your Worship

Thank You, Holy Yahweh, for Your mercy and compassion toward me and all sinners. I claim Your forgiveness for all my expressions of rebellion against You. I appreciate Your patience in dealing with me. Help me become more loyal to You and more consistent in that loyalty.

April 30

Yahweh Gives Me Victory Over Past Mistakes

Yahweh in the Word

> "I myself supposed it was necessary to do many things in opposition to the name of Jesus the Nazarene. I actually did this in Jerusalem, and I locked up many of the saints in prison… When they were put to death, I cast my vote against them. In all the synagogues I often tried to make them blaspheme by punishing them. I even pursued them to foreign cities since I was greatly enraged at them" (Acts 26:9-11).

These words are a portion of the apostle Paul's testimony before King Agrippa when he was on trial in Caesarea. At this time Paul was under arrest and on his way to Rome where he would be tried before Caesar. He spoke here of the transforming power of the resurrected Christ.

Yahweh in Your Walk

This is the last in a series of seven devotionals on the subject of biblical characters who, by Yahweh's grace, overcame significant obstacles to become useful to Him. **How interesting and helpful for us to remember that many of the outstanding persons found in the Bible faced major problems during their formative years**. We have considered John Mark, Timothy, Ruth, Moses, Peter, David, and now Paul. Each of these is an example for us of Yahweh's power to redeem and restore His chosen servants. **He can do the same for us if we are willing.**

Apart from Jesus, Paul is the leading figure of the New Testament. He is the author of 13 of the letters and his story occupies a large amount of the book of Acts. This means he is the author or subject of nearly one-third of the New Testament as well as the major interpreter of Jesus' life and teachings. His book of Romans is the most complete expression of Christian doctrine.

However, all this stands in stark contrast to his early years when he was literally a terrorist against Christians, as our Scripture text for today shows. Because of his religious beliefs, he vigorously sought to stamp out Christianity by having believers arrested, beaten, and even put to death. His dramatic conversion, followed by years of missionary service is a clear expression of the miraculous transforming power of the gospel.

In addition to assuring us of Yahweh's power to bring good from our lives, however scarred by sin, **this redemptive truth encourages us to pray for those who are the enemies of the cross today.** Do you suppose any in Paul's day were praying for his conversion? Let's believe that Yahweh can change anyone and pray for today's terrorists to become missionaries like Paul.

Yahweh in Your Worship

Help me, Holy Father, to believe that You can and will change Your enemies into servants.

May 1

Yahweh Shalom Provides All the Peace I Need

Yahweh in the Word

> *"When Gideon realized that He was the Angel of Yahweh, he said, 'Oh no, Lord God! I have seen the Angel of Yahweh face to face!' But Yahweh said to him, 'Peace to you. Don't be afraid, for you will not die.' So Gideon built an altar to Yahweh there and called it Yahweh Shalom" (Judges 6:22-24).*

Gideon was chosen by Yahweh to bring peace to His people by delivering them from their enemies. Notice His first words in this conversation, "Peace to you." Shalom (pronounced sha-LOME) is the Hebrew word for peace, a word with a rich meaning, including health, prosperity, wholeness, fulfillment, and completeness. One definition is: "Shalom means that kind of peace that results from being a whole person in right relationship to God and to one's fellow man."

Gideon built an altar and properly named it "Yahweh Shalom (I AM peace)." An altar is a place of worship. Gideon chose to worship the One who promised him life and prosperity in all his endeavors.

Yahweh in Your Walk

The term **shalom** occurs more than 170 times in the Old Testament. Yahweh wants us to know that He is the source of true and lasting peace—in the fullest sense of that word. An older classic writing is Billy Graham's popular book *Peace With God* (1953). In this book he declares, "All mankind is searching for happiness and peace with God." He goes on to point to Jesus' death on the cross as Yahweh's provision for this peace. **Every person, regardless of their past, can know this eternal wholeness by turning from sin and receiving Yeshua by faith.**

The apostle Paul wrote, "Therefore, since we have been declared righteous by faith, we have peace with God through our Lord Jesus Christ" (Romans 5:1). Over 2700 years ago another servant of Yahweh made a similar statement "The result of righteousness will be peace (shalom); the effect of righteousness will be quiet confidence forever" (Isaiah 32:17). The central message of the entire Bible is the truth that Yahweh loves every person and has made provision through His Son for all to be fully reconciled to Him—experiencing a peaceful relationship.

You can experience this promised peace by turning from the sin of unbelief and receiving the Lord Jesus by faith. He promises to forgive you and welcome you into a right relationship with Him. Then you will become His witness to others—your peace can become theirs.

Yahweh in Your Worship

Yahweh Shalom, thank You for being my peace. I seize this day believing Your promise of complete forgiveness. Use me to bring others to know Your peace and quiet confidence. I want to be Your peacemaker, Your ambassador of peace to this troubled world.

May 2

Yahweh Shalom Helps Me Maintain His Peace

Yahweh in the Word

> "You will keep in perfect peace the mind that is dependent on You, for it is trusting in You. Trust in Yahweh forever, because in Yahweh, Yahweh is an everlasting rock" (Isaiah 26:3-4).

These words, beginning in verse 1, are part of a song. The term "perfect peace" translates the Hebrew words ***shalom, shalom***. By repeating a word like this, the singer gives added emphasis to it. This song celebrates what Yahweh will do for His people, such as keeping them in a state of "perfect peace."

Yahweh in Your Walk

We receive the peace of Yahweh Shalom by calling upon Him for salvation. However, maintaining that sense of peace requires a focused discipline. Note in the verse for today, "the mind that is dependent on You, for it is trusting in You" is necessary for keeping Yahweh's peace. You may well ask, how do we achieve this?

Trust in a person comes as a direct result of knowing that this individual is trustworthy. Thus our trust in Yahweh grows stronger the better we know Him. And we know Him by examining what He reveals to us about Himself in the Bible. **Here is why a consistent study of the Bible is essential to developing a strong trust in Yahweh.** What is your personal plan for reading and studying Yahweh's Word? This daily devotional is a good beginning, but a more extensive search of the Scriptures is needed. Listen to these words of Paul regarding the believers in Berea, "...they welcomed the message with eagerness and examined the Scriptures daily to see if these things were so" (Acts 17:11). Could these words also describe you? Are you a serious student of biblical truth?

Let me encourage you to develop your own procedure for personal Bible study. Include both reading Scripture passages, analyzing them by using study helps like a Bible dictionary and concordance, and keeping notes on what your discover. An additional helpful discipline is Scripture memory. As the psalmist said, "I have treasured Your word in my heart so that I may not sin against You" (Psalm 119:11). Select special verses and entire passages for memorizing. I write these on small cards and carry them with me so I can review them through the day. As you memorize you can also meditate on each phrase to obtain greater spiritual nourishment. The practice of meditation on Scripture words, verses, and entire chapters can build your faith as you become increasingly immersed in the truth of who Yahweh is and all He has promised you.

Yahweh in Your Worship

Yahweh Shalom, I choose to be like Gideon as I erect in my heart an altar to honor You as my peace-giver. Here I worship You and claim all the peace I need. Use me as Your peacemaker in my world today. Help me become more aware of persons around me who need to discover the way to peace with You and others.

May 3

Yahweh Shalom Enables Me to Be a Peacemaker

Yahweh in the Word

> *"The peacemakers are blessed, for they will be called sons of God" (Matthew 5:9).*

Here is one of Jesus' Beatitudes. He declares that those who seek to help others discover peace with Yahweh and with others will themselves be blessed. The term "peacemakers" occurs just this one place in the Bible. We know that Jesus (Yeshua) came into this world to be the Prince of Peace. As we follow Him we also will be His ambassadors for peace wherever we are.

Yahweh in Your Walk

The Bible contains many examples of how Yahweh's people experienced times of reconciliation following some disagreement or mistreatment of one another. One of my favorite peacemakers is Joseph as described in Genesis 37-50, the longest account of one person in the Old Testament. You may recall how his older brothers, due to their jealousy of him, sold him into slavery. Many years later they found themselves down in Egypt where Joseph had become the trusted servant of Pharaoh, the ruler. Although his brothers did not recognize Joseph after so many years, he knew them and decided to be merciful and forgiving of their wrong. Here is one of the best examples of how a spirit of forgiveness brings healing to broken relationships.

Can you think of anyone against whom you bear a grudge, or perhaps they have ill will toward you? Why not take the initiative to be a peacemaker toward them? Let them know you are ready and willing to let go of the past and forgive whatever happened. Yahweh promises to bless you as you do this. Or how about those persons you may know who have had a falling out with one another over some issue? Are you willing to be Yahweh Shalom's ambassador of peace for them? Perhaps you can help them be reconciled. Think of what a blessing that would be for them.

Most importantly is one's need of being at peace with God. Here is where every Christian finds a calling from Yahweh to be His witness. **We are actually sent by Yeshua to be "ministers of reconciliation."** We have the good news that every repentant person can experience forgiveness and peace with Yahweh. This gift is the ultimate offer of shalom.

My friend Dan Marshall and his wife Diana are serious about this ministry of reconciliation. In addition to being a professional counselor where he helps clients learn to live in peace, he and Diana lead the outreach evangelism ministry of our church. They have a burden to train others to share their testimony about Jesus, and have seen many lost persons find peace with Yahweh.

Yahweh in Your Worship

How grateful I am for Your gift of peace to me. Thank You for paying the price for this wonderful gift. Today I want to seize every opportunity to celebrate this peace and pass it on to others.

May 4

Yahweh Shalom Gives Me Peace in Times of Trouble

Yahweh in the Word

> "The LORD (Yahweh) gives His people strength; the LORD (Yahweh) blesses His people with peace (shalom)" (Psalm 29:11).

The psalmist (probably David) uses images from a thunderstorm and flood in this song. He points to Yahweh as being sovereign over all this turmoil. Yahweh provides the strength and peace His people need in the midst of frightening storms. This same truth applies to those storms of trouble that come to everyone. "God is our refuge and strength, a helper who is always found in times of trouble" (Psalm 46:1). How comforting to know we always have this faithful provision whatever our need.

Yahweh in Your Walk

My neighbor, Frank, is a farmer as well as a fine Christian man. Recently he was driving his small ATV as he sought to herd some cows out of one pasture to another. Unfortunately, as he looked back at the cattle, he ran into a rather large tree. The result was a serious injury to his leg, requiring numerous stitches. After I heard about this misfortune, I went to his house to visit him. He greeted me from his recliner, "Hello, good neighbor. Thanks for coming by; I look forward to what the Lord will teach me through this accident!" (I started to say, "The Lord will teach you to watch where you are going!" But I knew he was serious about learning spiritual lessons.)

Frank's attitude is a fine example of how we should always be alert to those life-lessons Yahweh will teach us through various life-experiences. One such lesson has to do with Him always being with us to bring peace in the midst of trouble. Jesus was very near to His time for enduring the cross and all its suffering when He said to His disciples, "Peace I leave with you. My peace I give to you. I do not give to you as the world gives. Your heart must not be troubled or fearful" (John 14:27). A short time later Jesus told them how they would all leave Him alone, but He said "I have told you these things so that in Me you may have peace. You will have suffering in the world. Be courageous! I have conquered the world" (John 16:33).

Yes, trouble will come to all of us; but we can cope with it and even learn from it because of Yahweh Shalom. Recently I read this thought-provoking truth: "God often allows us to learn in the sunshine what we will need to lean on in the darkness."

Yahweh in Your Worship

I seize this day knowing that because You are always with me, I can do whatever is necessary. I worship You as the One who gives me the strength I need, as I need it. My trust is in You alone as the ultimate Resource of spiritual power; apart from You, I can do nothing that is of eternal significance. Help me this day to show others the way to discover peace with You and the difference that can make for them. I enter this part of my life-journey knowing that whatever happens to me and my loved ones is in Your plan for our good.

May 5

Yahweh's Peace Is to Be Extended to Others

Yahweh in the Word

> "Yahweh spoke to Moses, 'Tell Aaron and his sons how you are to bless the Israelites. Say to them: May Yahweh bless you and protect you; may Yahweh make His face shine on you and be gracious to you; may Yahweh look with favor on you and give you peace.' In this way they will pronounce My name over the Israelites, and I will bless them" (Numbers 6:22-27).

This familiar passage is often called the "Aaronic Benediction." A benediction is a spoken blessing. Yahweh told Moses to instruct Aaron, the priest, and his sons to speak the words of this blessing to the people. Included in this gift from Yahweh are the promises of His protection, grace, favor, and peace. What a beautiful expression of Yahweh's love for His people! Notice that at the heart of this blessing is the fact of pronouncing Yahweh's name over the Israelites. There is great favor in His name—Yahweh.

Yahweh in Your Walk

Recently I called an auto insurance company to ask a question about my policy. A woman answered and gave me the information I needed. When the conversation ended she asked, "May I help you with anything else?" To her surprise, I said, "No further questions, but may I offer something to you?" She was quiet for a moment then said, "Yes, of course." I told her how I appreciated her helpfulness, then said, "I want to give you a blessing from the Lord." I proceeded to quote most of the scripture printed above—Numbers 6:22-26.

When I finished she said nothing for a while, but then said, "Thank you, I really needed to hear that and I appreciate you sharing these beautiful words. Where is this found in the Bible?" I gave her the reference before putting down the phone. Afterwards, I sensed in my spirit that Yahweh had led me to extend this message of peace to this unknown listener. And I wondered if she found this Scripture and was blessed by reading these words again. Moreover, who knows how she may have passed them on to others?

As you walk through this day, you may have a similar opportunity to share Aaron's benediction with others. Why not make a copy of these words and keep them handy for just such a love gift. I have shared this blessing many times to unknown callers; sometimes it was an unwelcomed solicitation call. Rather than hang up abruptly or give a rude response, I gave the caller this blessing. I'm sure it came as a real surprise! I certainly felt better than if I had been unkind. I suggest you try this and see how you are blessed when you seek to bless others!

Yahweh in Your Worship

Yahweh Shalom, You are the Source of all peace and of all blessings. I worship You as the Fountain of all that is good. May the healing waters of Your peace flow through me today. Make me aware of those I meet who may need a refreshing drink from Your streams of love and grace. Give me boldness to offer Your words of blessing to others.

May 6

Yahweh Enables Me to Make the Choice to Rejoice

Yahweh in the Word

> "Though the fig tree does not bud and there is no fruit on the vines, though the olive crop fails and the fields produce no food, though there are no sheep in the pen and no cattle in the stalls, yet I will triumph in Yahweh; I will rejoice in the God of my salvation!" (Habakkuk 3:17-18).

This prophet describes the worst kind of situation economically—no figs, no fruit, no olives, no food, no sheep, and no cattle—absolute disaster in an agricultural setting! In spite of this total loss, however, Habakkuk makes a determined choice to triumph over his bleak circumstances by focusing on the salvation provided by Yahweh. What an amazing expression of trust!

Yahweh in Your Walk

My wife and I grew up in a small farming community in southwest Oklahoma. The economy depended entirely on the crops and the cattle. If the rains came at the right time and the right amount, the results were good. But there were times of drought or flooding when the wheat and cotton crops failed to produce. As old timers said, "We either have a feast or a famine!"

After finishing our seminary training, we returned to this area for our first pastorate. One of the men in that church taught us a valuable lesson. Following the harvest each season, he would say, "Preacher, the good Lord knows our needs and always comes through—sooner or later." This deacon was a faithful worker in that church regardless of the crop successes or failures. He always had a smile on his face and a song in his heart. He had learned to trust in Yahweh who never changes rather than trust in the uncertain harvests. He believed that the One in control of all circumstances, whether they seemed good or bad, would bring His good purpose to pass in His chosen time.

How about you? Are you sometimes up and sometimes down—depending on circumstances, or **have you learned that because of Yahweh's faithfulness, you can always make the choice to rejoice?** The apostle Paul is a fine example of this power to choose. He was a prisoner, facing possible execution when he wrote these words to encourage his readers: "Rejoice in the Lord always. I will say it again: Rejoice!" (Philippians 4:4). **In spite of his miserable circumstances, he made the choice to rejoice and to call on others to do the same. He was able to do this by looking beyond his situation to his Savior and Lord. We can make the same choice—every day!**

Yahweh in Your Worship

O Lord Yahweh, You are so good to me. No matter what my circumstances may be, You are the same loving Father. I choose to seize every opportunity today to give honor and praise to You. Help me to always focus on Your presence and provisions for all my needs. Forgive me when I complain and give way to discouraging thoughts. Use me to encourage others who may feel defeated. May I be a witness to Your faithfulness today.

May 7

Yahweh Demands and Deserves My Love for Him

Yahweh in the Word

> *"Love Yahweh your God with all your heart, with all your soul, and with all your strength" (Deuteronomy 6:5).*

Moses gave these solemn words to Yahweh's people to make them aware of what Yahweh expected of them. Their entire being—heart, soul, and strength—was to be included in their expression of love for Yahweh. Later when Yeshua (Jesus) was asked to give the greatest commandment from Yahweh, He responded with these same words. We cannot over-emphasize the importance of this simple command.

Yahweh in Your Walk

When my wife and I visited the Holy Land several years ago, our guide took us to a portion of an old wall called the "wailing wall" near the temple in Jerusalem. Here we saw Jewish men standing near the wall, swaying back and forth as they read various portions of their Hebrew Scriptures and prayed. Each man had a small leather box tied to his forehead. Our guide told us these boxes were known as "phylacteries" and contained words from Moses printed on slips of paper. Included would be our text for today. If you read Deuteronomy 11:18, you will see where this custom of phylacteries originated. Moses offered this means of reminding worshipers of their first and foremost obligation to Yahweh.

We all need reminders of this great commandment and of its importance. But as you well know, it is one thing to say we love Yahweh and sing about our love for Him, but something far more demanding to actually practice loving Him. What is the best evidence to prove we actually love Yahweh as we should? Yeshua gave a clear answer when He said on numerous occasions, "If you love Me keep My commandments." **The ultimate test of love is obedience.** This truth means we should respond to the great commandment with a great obedience—of heart, soul, and strength.

Such obedience requires more than human determination. None of us can keep Yahweh's command in our own strength. Yeshua said, "Without Me you can do nothing" (John 15:5). We need more than a black box to remind us of His will; we must rely on Him for both the motivation and power to obey. **As you walk through this day, lean on His indwelling Spirit to produce the love that seeks to conform to His commands.**

Yahweh in Your Worship

Yahweh, You are so worthy of all my love; You deserve my total obedience to all Your will for me today. Help me seize every opportunity to prove my love for You. I depend on You, Lord Yeshua, for the power to conform to all You would have me be and do. Use me to help others know of Your love, Your commandments, and the joy of obeying You. I do rejoice in knowing that You are pleased with my desire to honor You in all things.

May 8

Yahweh Wants Me to Lean on Him

Yahweh in the Word

> "For they are named after the Holy City, and lean on the God of Israel; His name is Yahweh of Hosts" (Isaiah 48:2).

Yahweh sent Isaiah to bring His messages to His people. Some were messages warning of coming judgment, while others offered hope if the people turned back to Him. In this text Yahweh calls for His people to remember whose they are and to put their trust in Him as they lean on Him.

Yahweh in Your Walk

A friend of ours recently suffered a broken hip. After several weeks of therapy, he was shown how to use a walker so he could begin resuming normal activities. He told me this whole experience taught him to be less independent and allow others to help him. The hardest part was learning to lean on the walker as he moved about.

Here is an illustration of how Yahweh wants us to become aware of our constant need of Him as we go through each day. We must learn, sometimes through painful "falls," the importance of leaning on Him. The words of this chorus from a song by John Stallings says it best:

> I'm learning to lean, learning to lean, learning to lean on Jesus.
> Finding more power than I'd ever dreamed, I'm learning to lean on Jesus.

The alternative to leaning on Yeshua is to lean on ourselves and follow what we think is best and what we think we can do without Him. Solomon gave wise counsel when he wrote: "Trust in Yahweh with all your heart, and *lean not on your own understanding*; in all your ways acknowledge Him and He will direct your paths" (Proverbs 3:5-6).

As you think about your walk through this day, can you say you are learning to lean on Yahweh more than being independent of Him? **He invites you to put your trust in Him as you seek to make wise decisions—about everything.** Make a habit of pausing before each choice you make and offer a brief prayer asking Yahweh to guide you. He will hear and answer your request.

At the end of each day, take time to reflect on your experiences. Thank Him for those times you can perceive His guidance and care. Also, claim His forgiveness for the times you acted independently of Him, going your own way. Ask Yahweh to help you learn to lean more on Him.

Yahweh in Your Worship

I praise You, Yahweh, for Your willingness to allow me to lean on You for wisdom and strength. Today I choose to seize every opportunity to seek Your help with all my needs. Thank You for being faithful as my Teacher in all of life.

May 9

Yahweh Wants Me to Know His Name

Yahweh in the Word

> "Then God spoke to Moses, telling him, 'I am Yahweh I appeared to Abraham, Isaac, and Jacob as God Almighty but I did not reveal My name Yahweh to them.... Therefore tell the Israelites: I am Yahweh and I will deliver...'" (Exodus 6: 2-3, 6).

Moses was the first to know God's name. At the burning bush this special revelation was made for the first time. Thereafter, Yahweh wanted all people to know His special name, a name that means "I AM." This word is the most frequently occurring noun in the Old Testament, found more than 6,800 times. Now we who know this name are to use it as we speak to Yahweh and as we make this sacred name and its meaning known to others.

Yahweh in Your Walk

Early in their history the Hebrew people came to have a very strong respect for God's name. The third of the Ten Commandments states: "Do not misuse the name of Yahweh your God, because Yahweh will not leave anyone unpunished who misuses His name" (Deuteronomy 5:11). Rather than risk misusing His sacred name and thus violating this command, the Hebrews refrained from using it altogether. They formed a new word to represent God's name, a word translated in English as LORD (all capital letters). The translators of the King James Version used the term *Jehovah* several times for God's name, but this also is a substitute word. **His name, as revealed to Moses is Yahweh and He wants us to know and use this special name.**

Many years ago I came across this anonymous poem that reminds me of the wonder of this name:

> I know a soul that is steeped in sin, that no man's art can cure;
> But I know a Name, a precious Name, that can make that soul all pure.
> I know a life that is lost to God, bound down by things of earth;
> But I know a Name, a precious Name, that can bring that soul new birth.
> I know of lands that are sunk in shame, of hearts that faint and tire;
> But I know a Name, a precious Name, that can set those lands on fire.
> Its sound is a brand, its letters flame like glowing tongues of fire
> I know a Name, a precious Name, that will set those lands on fire.

The power of this name is not in the letters that compose it, rather in the Person it represents—the only true and living God. We must revere this Name above all names and use it with respect.

Yahweh in Your Worship

Holy, holy, holy is Yahweh, the only true and living God. I hallow Your name and worship You and thank You for revealing Your name to me. May I so live that Your name will be honored.

May 10

Yahweh Wants Me to Have Fullness of Joy

Yeshua in the Word

> *"We are writing these things so that our joy may be complete" (1John 1:4). "I hope to be with you and talk face to face so that our joy may be complete" (2 John 12). "I have no greater joy than this: to hear that my children are walking in the truth" (3 John 4).*

The apostle John probably wrote these three letters from Ephesus where he was a leader in the church. All three are addressed to different readers; all three mention the joy this servant of Yahweh experienced in spite of being persecuted and placed in exile on the island of Patmos.

Yeshua in Your Walk

There are numerous examples in the Bible of godly persons who found themselves in very miserable circumstances and yet, testified about their joy. How can this be? Take for example Paul and Silas who were preaching in the city of Philippi when they were arrested, beaten, and cast into prison. The account of this, found in the book of Acts reports: "About midnight Paul and Silas were praying and singing hymns to God" (Acts 16:25). Can you imagine how amazed the other prisoners were, as well as the guards? They must have thought these men were either drunk or insane. Truth is, these servants of Yahweh had found a source of joy far greater than their harsh circumstances. Years later, Paul wrote back to the believers in Philippi, "Rejoice in the Lord always. I will say it again: Rejoice! (Philippians 4:4).

You and I have the same resource—the unchanging joy in knowing and fellowshipping with our Lord Jesus Christ. There are times when all of us feel unhappy. But remember, there is a vast difference between happiness and joy. Happiness is usually the result of what happens-to-us; it is circumstantial. As one observer has said, "If happenings happen to happen happily, we are happy. But if happenings happen to happen unhappily, we are unhappy!" In other words, happiness is a feeling of well-being, often the result of some pleasant event or situation. But joy is not basically an emotion. **Joy is the inner pleasure that comes from being in a right relationship with the Lord. Thus joy is independent of circumstances**. Paul and Silas could rejoice in spite of their suffering because they knew God was with them in their pain and misery.

Jesus said to all who follow Him, "These things I have spoken to you, that My joy may remain in you, and that your joy may be full" (John 15:11). Fullness of joy is His gift to you—claim it!

Yeshua in Your Worship

Thank You, Lord Jesus, for the gift of joy that is full and unchanging. I choose to seize this new day as an opportunity to experience fullness of joy in spite of whatever circumstances may come. Now use me to share the good news of this kind of joy with others today.

May 11

Yahweh Needs My Help in Doing His Work Today

Yahweh in the Word

> "Yahweh took the man and placed him in the garden of Eden to work it and watch over it... the man gave names to all the livestock, to the birds of the sky, and to every wild animal" (Genesis 2: 15,20).

One part of Yahweh's amazing creation was to make a man in His own image. He also gave this man work to do; he was to be Yahweh's gardener. In addition, this man was to give names to all other creatures.

Yahweh in Your Walk

The story of creation is filled with interesting revelations about Yahweh as well as His plan for humankind. **One important truth we find is that He intended, from the beginning, to have a partnership with all those created in His image**. Yahweh is a worker and those created in His image are to work in cooperation with Him. For example, we are told that Yahweh planted the first garden and caused all plants to grow there (Genesis 2:8-9). But Yahweh's plan was for Adam to "work it and watch over it," as well as give names to all animal life; Yahweh and Adam were to be co-laborers, each doing his part.

Throughout the Bible we see this partnership continued. Yahweh planned the ark and gave Noah all the specifications, but Noah did the building. Yahweh planned the tabernacle, with all the dimensions and items to go in it, but Moses and his people built it. Many such examples are found throughout the Scripture.

What can we learn from these truths? Could it be that Yahweh desires to work together with us in accomplishing His will? Is it possible for us to have a personal partnership with Him? Consider these words from the apostle Paul as the biblical answer to our question: "We are God's coworkers" (1 Corinthians 3:9) and "Working together with Him" (2 Corinthians 6:1). He was referring to the building of the members of a local church there in Corinth. **Likewise, we should see ourselves as coworkers with Yahweh to build His church in this world.**

The same principle of partnering with Yahweh applies to each of us in whatever we seek to do in serving Him. Another vital area of co-laboring is that of building a marriage and home. Yahweh wants to be our partner in this important ministry for Him. Add to this your vocation and, in fact, whatever you do that is honorable in His sight—let Him do His part as you labor in doing yours.

Yahweh in Your Worship

Give some time to thanking Yahweh for His partnership in all areas of your life. Acknowledge your total dependence upon Him in order to do your part well.

May 12

Yahweh Wants Me to Know His Will and Do His Will

Yahweh in the Word

"Your kingdom come, Your will be done on earth as it is in heaven" (Matthew 5:10).

This portion of the Model Prayer clearly reveals that Yahweh wants us to know and do His will. The term "Your will" refers to that which Yahweh wants to happen—that which pleases Him the most. He has chosen to make His will known to us primarily through the Bible.

Yahweh in Your Walk

Every Christian should desire to know God's will and do it. We agree with the psalmist who said, "I delight to do Your will, my God; Your instruction lives within me" (Psalm 40:8). But we cannot do His will until we know what His will is. During these next six days we will examine those statements in God's Word that relate clearly to His will. As we look at these passages, we do so with this simple prayer: "Teach me to do Your will, for You are my God" (Psalm 143:10).

Let's begin with these words of Jesus: "This is the will of Him who sent Me: that I should lose none of those He has given Me but should raise them up on the last day. For this is the will of My Father: that everyone who sees the Son and believes in Him may have eternal life, and I will raise him up on the last day" (John 6:39-40). Bible students refer to the doctrine of eternal security which means that Jesus will eternally keep all who come to Him, trusting Him as their Savior and Lord. Listen to these words from Jesus on that subject: "My sheep hear My voice, I know them, and they follow Me. I give them eternal life, and they will never perish—ever! No one will snatch them out of My hand. My Father, who has given them to Me, is greater than all. No one is able to snatch them out of the Father's hand. The Father and I are one" (John 10:27-30). **Our security is in the faithful preservation of Yahweh, not in our faithful perseverance.**

When we understand and believe that Yahweh's will is for us to be eternally secure in His hands, we can cease having any anxiety about someday being lost from Him. As we rest in His promise to keep us from falling away spiritually, we have peace and a strong sense of security in Him. Satan is the one who tries to deceive us at this point. He is known as "the accuser," and will seek to cause us to doubt our security by accusing us of sins—both in the past and present. We must resist him by reminding him of Yahweh's promise to keep us safe, eternally. Use this "sword of the Spirit"—the Word of God to defeat every attack of the enemy. Security is God's will for you.

Yahweh in Your Worship

Thank You, Yahweh, that You reveal Your will for me to be eternally saved and secure in Your hands. I do trust You to keep me from yielding to Satan's attacks. You are my Lord and my Life. I choose to seize every opportunity this day to celebrate Your eternal salvation, and tell others about this comforting truth.

May 13

Yahweh Wants Me to Give Thanks in Everything

Yahweh in the Word

> *"Give thanks in everything, for this is God's will for you in Christ Jesus" (1 Thessalonians 5:18).*

These words are found in a long list of commands given by the apostle Paul near the conclusion of his first letter to the believers in Thessalonica. He appeals for them to exhibit those virtues that are consistent with their professed new life in Christ.

Yahweh in Your Walk

Today we continue our consideration of the will of God. Numerous references are made on this subject throughout the Bible. Our text gives one of those clear statements regarding this vital matter. If you are serious about knowing and doing Yahweh's will, you will take these words to heart and seek to obey this simple command.

As Yahweh's children we have so much for which to give thanks. Notice that these words from Paul go beyond **being** thankful. We are not only to be thankful but also **give** thanks, that is, give verbal expression to our felt gratitude. I read a recent comment made by an older Christian writer. He said, **"One good measure of a Christian's maturity is the amount of praise and thanksgiving in their prayers."** Are you being careful to speak your gratitude to Yahweh when you pray? I practice doing this often during the day as the Holy Spirit prompts me to think of the many reasons for giving thanks.

Notice also the little word "in" found in this text. The apostle did not tell his readers to give thanks **for** everything, rather **"in"** everything. There is a big difference here. We cannot be thankful for everything—not for all the evil and injustice in the world, not for all the suffering and hardship, not that many are starving to death, and on and on. However, we can give thanks in the midst of whatever is happening to us, because we know Yahweh can work through all our experiences for our ultimate good. Just today I had lunch with a friend, Don Gower, whose wife died several years ago. He told me how thankful he was for Yahweh's comfort and strength during the days of her passing, and what he had learned from that painful experience.

How about giving more attention today to expressing thanks for all the rather small blessings that you often take for granted? Or perhaps to sit quietly for a few minutes before going to bed, just to recall Yahweh's favor in so many ways during the past twenty-four hours, and give thanks for everything you can remember. This is God's will for you.

Yahweh in Your Worship

O Yahweh, how blessed I am to know You and to understand how much You love me and how You prove that love through countless blessings every day. Help me be more prompt to give You thanks. Open my eyes to see Your hand at work on my behalf through all my life experiences.

May 14

Yahweh Wants Me to Avoid Every Kind of Sexual Sin

Yahweh in the Word

> "This is God's will, your sanctification: that you abstain from sexual immorality, so that each of you knows how to control his own body in sanctification and honor, not with lustful desire, like the Gentiles who don't know God. This means one must not transgress against and defraud his brother in this matter, because the Lord is an avenger of all these offenses" (1 Thess. 4: 3-6).

Paul appealed to his readers to guard against all expressions of sexual gratification outside of marriage. The term "sanctification" could be translated ***holiness***, meaning "set apart for God." To "defraud your brother" assumes one's sexual partner is married to another Christian person; to engage this person in a sexual relationship is to "defraud"—steal from their husband or wife. The serious warning here is that Yahweh will punish the offender in such matters.

Yahweh in Your Walk

We live in a culture of sexual permissiveness. **One distinctive of Christian living is the absence of immoral behavior.** The apostle Paul gave this clear warning to his readers because he was aware of how believers were immersed in an ungodly society. Our text begins with the subject on which we are focusing—the will of God. His will is that His children not be controlled by "lustful desire." Rather, we are to be sanctified, that is, set apart from those who follow after their old carnal nature.

We are created with sexual desires and the capacity to fulfill those desires as long as they are limited to the marriage relationship. The forbidden sexual practices include: premarital sex, incest, homosexuality, polygamy, bestiality, and adultery. Unfortunately, many in our society not only practice these perversions they also want them to be made legal and recognized as normal behavior. **As Christians we must love all persons, but we must not approve of lifestyles that are practiced contrary to biblical standards**. This means, we love sinners, but not their sin. Our mission is not only to avoid immoral practices but to help rescue others who live in a manner contrary to God's will.

Sexual purity is very difficult for most Christians to maintain. Yahweh gives us His Holy Spirit (see verse 8) to enable us to resist temptation in this area. He alone can deliver us from our old nature. Our part is to avoid those situations where appeals to the lust of the flesh are found. We must put on the whole armor of Yahweh and pray for deliverance by the Holy Spirit.

Yahweh in Your Worship

Yahweh, I claim by faith Your strength to resist the temptations to satisfy fleshly lusts. Your will is for me to maintain purity, for Your sake. Thank You for helping me think pure thoughts.

May 15

Yahweh's Will for Me May Include Suffering

Yahweh in the Word

> "But even if you should suffer for righteousness sake, you are blessed.... For it is better to suffer for doing good, if that should be God's will, than for doing evil. For Christ also suffered for sins once for all, the righteous for the unrighteous, that He might bring you to God...." (1 Peter 3:14, 17-18).

The apostle Peter wrote this letter to Christians who were suffering due to persecution. He reminded them that Jesus also had to suffer in order to fulfill Yahweh's purpose for Him. As long as believers were mistreated for doing what was right, they could expect Yahweh to bless them. Their example of accepting persecution in a spirit of submission would be a clear witness.

Yahweh in Your Walk

Here are words to an old song by Annie Johnson Flint that communicate biblical truth:

> God hath not promised skies always blue, flower-strewn pathways all our lives through;
> God hath not promised sun without rain, joy without sorrow, peace without pain.
> But God hath promised strength for the day, rest for the labor, light for the way.
> Grace for the trials, help from above, unfailing sympathy, undying love.

Being in God's will does not make us immune to suffering. Sometimes that suffering is in the form of persecution, as it was in our text for today. These followers of Jesus were hated by non-Christians and mistreated for their loyalty to Him. We are told that there is more persecution against Christians in our world today than ever before. Some are beaten, imprisoned, and put to death because of their faith in Him. Peter wrote to encourage such believers, assuring them of Yahweh's blessing and of His use of their example as a powerful witness of Him.

Peter mentions another outcome of suffering according to God's will in these words: "You rejoice in this, though now for a short time you have had to struggle in various trials so that the genuineness of your faith—more valuable than gold, which perishes though refined by fire—may result in praise, glory, and honor at the revelation of Jesus Christ" (1 Peter 1:6-7). **Undeserved suffering may also be Yahweh's way of refining and testing one's faith—resulting in a much stronger trust in Him.**

Another type of suffering within Yahweh's will may take the form of physical illness. The apostle Paul speaks of some malady he experienced, calling it a "thorn in the flesh," for which he prayed to be delivered. Yahweh's answer was no, with this addition: "My grace is sufficient for you, for power is perfected in weakness" (2 Corinthians 12:9). Illness can be a blessing.

Yahweh in Your Worship

You know what is best for me; I gratefully accept what You give

May 16

Yahweh's Will Is for Me and Everyone to Be Saved

Yahweh in the Word

> "...It is not the will of your Father in heaven that one of these little ones perish" (Matthew 18:12). "This is good, and it pleases God our Savior, who wants everyone to be saved and to come to the knowledge of the truth" (1 Timothy 2:2). "The Lord does not delay His promise, as some understand delay, but is patient with you, not wanting any to perish but all to come to repentance" (2 Peter 3:9).

These three statements made by three different persons (Jesus, Paul, Peter) make a strong affirmation that the will of Yahweh is for everyone to experience salvation from sin. He has made this deliverance possible and available, but not everyone has heard this good news and therefore cannot respond with repentance and faith.

Yahweh in Your Walk

What an amazing truth—Yahweh loves all persons, regardless of how sinful and rebellious against Him they have been. And, because of this great love, He has gone to the extreme of giving His Son, the Lord Jesus, to take upon Himself the sin debt of every person and die in their place. Now, all who believe this good news and receive Jesus by faith, are forgiven their sin debt, given a new nature, and welcomed into Yahweh's everlasting family. This is Yahweh's will for everyone.

Yes, there is a way for everyone to be saved—but only one way, the way of believing on Jesus. Humankind desperately needs to hear this message and choose the way to life everlasting. Unfortunately, most people believe there are many ways that lead to heaven—that all religions help people be saved. Is this true? Not if we take Jesus at His word. He said, "I am the way, the truth, and the life. No one comes to the Father except through Me" (John 14:6). The apostle Peter agreed with Jesus and said, "There is salvation in no one else, for there is no other name under heaven given to people, and we must be saved by it" (Acts 4:12).

Herein lays the motivation for all missionary outreach. Every person who has not heard this message has no hope of eternal life. Every person who has heard this message and has chosen not to believe it has no hope of eternal life. Paul expressed his motive for traveling and preaching in these solemn words: "Everyone who calls on the name of the Lord will be saved. But how can they call on Him they have not believed in? And how can they believe without hearing about Him? And how can they hear without a preacher? And how can they preach unless they are sent?" (Romans 10:13-15). Whether you preach or send or pray, you are part of this mission.

Yahweh in Your Worship

Thank You for loving me and sending this message to me. Now, use me to pass it on to others.

May 17

Yahweh Wants His Will to Have Priority in My Life

Yahweh in the Word

> *"'My food is to do the will of Him who sent Me and to finish His work,' Jesus told them" (John 4:34).*

Jesus gave a clear statement of His life purpose in these brief words—to do Yahweh's will.

Yahweh in Your Walk

Suppose someone asked you, "What is your purpose for living?" What would you say? Surely this is a matter worth considering. We all should think seriously about such an important subject. What is our life goal; why do we do what we do? Our text reveals Jesus' answer to the question of His life purpose—to do His Father's will, that's it—pure and simple. You may respond to this question by saying, "That's great for Jesus, and I admire Him, but I'm not Jesus—therefore I could never live up to such a high standard."

Let's consider an ordinary person, one like you and me—the apostle Paul. He began five of his New Testament letters with this same phrase, "Paul, called as an apostle of Christ Jesus by God's will" (1 and 2 Corinthians, Ephesians, Colossians, and 2 Timothy). Moreover, he often referred to his plans as being "according to God's will" (see Romans 1:10; 15:32; Ephesians 6:6). He told the Colossians that in his prayers for them he was "asking that you may be filled with the knowledge of His will in all wisdom and spiritual understanding" (Colossians 1:9). All these and more references are found in his writings to validate the claim that this man lived for one purpose—to know and to do Yahweh's will.

He also recommended this same worthy purpose for his readers. For example, in his letter to the Christians in Rome he made this appeal: "Therefore, brothers, by the mercies of God, I urge you to present your bodies as a living sacrifice, holy and pleasing to God; this is your spiritual worship. Do not be conformed to this age, but be transformed by the renewing of your mind, so that you may discern what is the good, pleasing, and perfect will of God" (Romans 12:1-2). Think about these last words where he declared that the will of God is "good, pleasing, and perfect." **This truth is the reason we should have as our life purpose to know and do His will.**

Yahweh in Your Worship

O Yahweh, how amazing that You love me so much that You have a definite plan for my life. Therefore, I choose to seize every opportunity to understand and do Your will. I humbly ask that You make me aware of Your will in every decision I make today. Thank You for hearing and answering me. Help me share this good news with others as You lead me.

May 18

Yeshua Calls Me to Serve Others

Yeshua in the Word

> "When Jesus had washed their feet and put on His robe, He reclined again and said to them, 'Do you know what I have done for you? You call me Teacher and Lord. This is well said, for I am. So if I, your Lord and Teacher, have washed your feet, you also ought to wash one another's feet. For I have given you an example that you also should do just as I have done for you... If you know these things, you are blessed if you do them'" (John 13:12-15, 17).

The custom in Jesus' day was for the host at a meal to have a large basin of water ready to wash the grimy feet of guests when they arrived. This washing was usually done by a non-Jewish slave. On this occasion, no slave was present so Jesus and his disciples proceeded to eat their meal. Jesus "got up from supper" and to the utter surprise of everyone, washed their feet, including those of Judas. He then called their attention to His example of humble service, which He commended to them.

Yeshua in Your Walk

Today, as in most days, you will have an opportunity to "wash feet." That is, to perform some service for another person, even a stranger. **How about examining yourself now to see if you have a true servant spirit when it comes to helping others?** One truth that has helped me at this point is what Yeshua said on another occasion as He told the story of how someday all nations would come before Him to be judged and rewarded for their deeds. He said the righteous would be reminded of how they had performed various charitable deeds for Him, but would ask, "When did we do these things for You?" His answer was interesting, "I assure you: Whatever you did for one of the least of these brothers of mine, you did for Me" (Matthew 25:40). **How helpful to remember that any act of kindness done to others, regardless of how unworthy they may seem, is actually being done for Yeshua, who identifies with the needy.**

General William Booth (1829-1912) was the founder of the Salvation Army, a Christian organization that has ministered to human need for more than 100 years. His "soldiers" had gathered for their international convention, but Booth was gravely ill and unable to attend. Those gathered had hoped to hear him give the main address, so they asked for some word from him. He sent a telegram from his sickbed with this final message to them: **"Others!"** How appropriate for the servant whose life had been dedicated to serving his Lord by helping others.

I read these challenging words from the pen of Jodie Yoder, "The opposite of love is not hate—it's self!" If we live a self-centered life, we cannot honor the life of Yeshua; we must be servants.

Yeshua in Your Worship

O Master, may Your servant spirit be seen in all I do. I worship You because of Your service.

May 19

Yahweh Keeps Me as the Apple of His Eye

Yahweh in the Word

> *"He found him in a desert land and in the wasteland, a howling wilderness; He encircled him, He instructed him, He kept him as the apple of His eye" (Deuteronomy 32:10 NKJV).*

These interesting words are a part of Moses' farewell song to his people. In this verse he reminds them of how Yahweh chose them and provided for them—giving them His protection because they were special to Him.

Yahweh in Your Walk

You may have heard an expression of affection somewhat like this, "His granddaughter is the apple of his eye." Have you ever wondered what that means, and where that expression comes from? These words occur several times in the Bible and refer to the fact that when you look at someone, their image is reflected in the pupil of your eye which is at the very center of your eye—sometimes called the "apple" of your eye because it is round like an apple. From that comes the idea that the apple of your eye is someone who is especially cherished by you.

Moses sang about Yahweh finding His chosen people, surrounding them with His care, instructing them in His ways, and preserving them as "the apple of His eye." The same wonderful, comforting truths may well be said of all His people, including you, today. **You are very precious in His sight.** In fact, Yahweh values you so highly that He went to the ultimate extreme of sending His Son to become your Savior, Lord, and Life!

Today we hear from counselors about the importance of an individual having a healthy self-image—a sense of personal value. Where does this self-esteem come from? Some seek to find it in their personal achievements or the contributions they make. However, true self-worth is not dependent upon what we do, rather by who we are—persons created by Yahweh and for Him. He determines our worth by His own standards, not ours. **The truth is that we are of infinite worth simply because we are made in the image and likeness of God.**

A comic once said, "I know I'm important because God made me and God don't make no junk!" Very true! Therefore, walk through this day with your head up, your shoulders back, and a smile on your face because you know that you are the apple of Yahweh's eye; regardless of anything in your past, you are cherished by Him, protected by Him, and encircled by His love and care. Believe it; behave like it; and celebrate it! And—pass this truth on to others; they need to hear it.

Yahweh in Your Worship

I come before You as a worshiper today, Precious Yahweh. You are so good to me; I can never praise You enough. You are the apple of my eye, the One I adore more than any other.

May 20

Yahweh Teaches Me Valuable Lessons Through Trials

Yahweh in the Word

> "Therefore, so that I would not exalt myself, a thorn in the flesh was given to me, a messenger of Satan to torment me so I would not exalt myself. Concerning this, I pleaded with the Lord three times to take it away from me. But He said to me, 'My grace is sufficient for you, for power is perfected in weakness.' Therefore I will most gladly boast all the more about my weaknesses, so that Christ's power may reside in me. So I take pleasure in weaknesses, insults, catastrophes, persecutions, and in pressures, because of Christ. For when I am weak, then I am strong" (2 Corinthians 12:7-10).

These remarks from the apostle Paul are his personal testimony regarding his experience of being caught up into heaven where he heard "inexpressible words" (v. 4). The Lord gave him a "thorn in the flesh" in order to prevent him from becoming overly proud about this revelation. As a result of not receiving the answer he wanted from his prayer, he learned a valuable lesson regarding Yahweh's grace being sufficient in all situations of life.

Yahweh in Your Walk

How do you usually respond to unpleasant and even painful situations that come to you? You have a choice—you can either resent the trial or you can ask Yahweh to help you learn from it. Paul is an excellent example of how believers should deal with personal troubles. First, he asked Yahweh to remove the pain from him—"take it away from me." Next, after three unsuccessful attempts to get the answer he wanted, he chose to stop talking and start listening to Yahweh—whose answer was, "My grace is sufficient for you." The master Teacher was instructing him.

You can probably identify with Paul at this point. **Sometimes Yahweh's answer to our earnest, repeated requests is "No, I have something better for you."** Our personal prayer requests should always include, "Not my will but Yours be done." Yahweh may have some important lesson for us to learn through trials. His will for allowing our suffering is always for our benefit.

Notice the bottom line in Paul's testimony—he learned this paradox: "When I am weak, then I am strong." How can this be true? When we are mindful of our weakness, we are forced to depend on Him for needed strength in order to cope with life's challenges. And His strength and grace is always sufficient for all our needs. So, join Paul in celebrating the fact that you are too weak to make it on your own—you need Yahweh's grace and strength—today and every day!

Yahweh in Your Worship

Holy Teacher, thank You for using my life experiences—both good and painful—to instruct me in ways I could never learn otherwise. Help me be a good learner; teach me to be patient. And use me to help others as they learn more of Your matchless ways.

May 21

Yahweh Wants to Help Me Have a Good Attitude

Yahweh in the Word

> "Make your own attitude that of Christ Jesus: Who existing in the form of God, did not consider equality with God as something to be used for His own advantage. Instead He emptied himself by assuming the form of a slave, taking on the likeness of men. And when He had come as a man in His external form, He humbled himself to become obedient to the point of death—even to death on a cross!" (Philippians 2:5-8).

The apostle Paul wrote these words when he was in prison, facing the real possibility of being executed for his work as a missionary. He commends to his readers the servant attitude of Jesus.

Yahweh in Your Walk

Today you will make many choices, some are of small significance, and others have major consequences. One of these choices has to do with your attitude. Charles R. Swindoll wrote an excellent article on attitude in which he says, "The remarkable thing is we have a choice every day regarding the attitude we will embrace for that day.... I am convinced that life is ten percent what happens to us and ninety percent how we react to it. And so it is that we are in charge of our attitudes."

The fact that you claim to be a follower of Jesus should have a strong influence upon the attitude you choose for today. As Paul wrote, "Your attitude should be the same as that of Christ Jesus." How is this possible? The apostle also said, "Christ lives in me" (Galatians 2:20). If you begin this day by submitting yourself to the control of Jesus, He will manifest His attitude in and through you. Among other things, this means your attitude will reflect His love, kindness, patience, and a positive outlook on life.

You have heard of Fannie Crosby, the well-known writer of gospel songs. Her life was spent in physical darkness due to blindness. On one occasion she wrote: "Oh, what a happy soul am I! Although I cannot see, I am resolved that in this world, contented I shall be. How many blessings I enjoy, that other people don't. To weep and sigh because I'm blind, I cannot—and I won't." Here is a good example of a person who made the choice to have an attitude toward life that expresses the Spirit of Jesus. Even when facing death on a cross, He said to His disciples, "I have spoken these things to you so that My joy may be in you and your joy may be complete" (John 15:11). **Today you can choose to have an attitude of joyful gratitude, not because of pleasant circumstances but due to the One who lives in You and controls your thoughts.**

Yahweh in Your Worship

Today, I choose to seize this opportunity to worship You, O Lord of life. How thankful I am to know that You live in me by Your Holy Spirit. May Your control be seen in my attitude today.

May 22

Yahweh Wants Me to Be a Confident Leader

Yahweh in the Word

> "Then Caleb quieted the people in the presence of Moses and said, 'We must go up and take possession of the land because we can certainly conquer it!'" (Numbers 13:30).

Moses sent 12 spies to search out the land Yahweh promised to give His people. They returned after 40 days, showing some of the luscious fruit they found. However only Caleb and Joshua gave a favorable report. All the others were fearful of the strong inhabitants of the land.

Yahweh in Your Walk

Do you see yourself as being a leader of others? One writer states, "Leadership means influence. If you influence others, you are a leader." In light of this definition of leadership, let's restate the original question: Who do you influence? You can begin with those nearest to you—your family members; then consider your friends, co-workers, fellow Christians, etc. You may not see yourself as a leader, but you are because you have influence on others, more than you realize. So the question goes on to become: Are you a good influence? **Does your influence make a positive difference in those who know you?**

The challenge of this devotional is to help you become more like Caleb—a man who provides a strong example of a leader who was confident because of his trust in Yahweh. The secret of Caleb's effective leadership is found in these words: "If Yahweh is pleased with us, He will bring us into this land, a land flowing with milk and honey, and give it to us. Only don't rebel against Yahweh, and don't be afraid of the people of the land, for we will devour them. Their protection has been removed from them, and Yahweh is with us. Don't be afraid of them" (Numbers 14: 8-9).

His attitude reminds us of another biblical leader who boldly stated: "I am able to do all things through Him who strengthens me" (Philippians 4:13). Effective Christian leaders exhibit confidence—not confidence in themselves but in the One who gives them strength and clear guidance. **Your life will touch others today; make certain your touch will be positive and show confidence in Yahweh's faithfulness to lead in His ways.** When it comes to opportunities for serving Yahweh, remove the words "I can't" from your vocabulary; always be an "I can" person, not because you are wise and strong, but because He is. Remember "Yahweh will be your confidence and will keep your foot from a snare" (Proverbs 3:26).

Yahweh in Your Worship

Yahweh, You are my leader, the One who influences me in all the right ways. My confidence is totally in You. I worship You for being so gracious and kind and faithful to me. May I be the influence You would have me to be. Manifest Your wisdom and power through me today.

May 23

Yeshua Intends for Me to Be a Generous Giver

Yeshua in the Word

> *"You yourselves know that these hands have provided for my needs and for those who were with me. In every way I've shown you that by laboring like this, it is necessary to help the weak and to keep in mind the words of the Lord Jesus, for He said, 'It is more blessed to give than to receive'" (Acts 20:34-35).*

Paul gave this message to leaders from the church in Ephesus as he left them on his journey to Jerusalem. He reminded them of how he provided financial support for himself and his helpers during the years he spent with them. He probably did this through his trade as a tentmaker.

Yeshua in Your Walk

Are you generous in giving to help others—through your church and your own personal gifts? **Yeshua (Jesus) will lead you to grow in giving as you follow Him**. Paul's quote of Jesus' words from our text about giving are found only here. However, His teachings about giving are found often in the Gospels. For example He said, "Give, and it will be given to you; a good measure—pressed down, shaken together, and running over—will be poured into your lap. For with the measure you use, it will be measured back to you" (Luke 6:38).

I share this personal testimony: When my wife and I first married we agreed to give 10% of all our income through our local church. That seemed like a large gift compared to our limited income. However, after one year of doing this we decided to increase the amount by 1% each year. During the years that followed, all our financial needs were met, plus much more. And that percentage continued to grow for many years (not for our full 61 years together, but beyond 40 %). We have chosen to accept the challenge Yahweh gave His people in these words, "Bring the full tenth into the storehouse so that there may be food in My house. Test Me in this way, says Yahweh of Hosts. See if I will not open the floodgates of heaven and pour out a blessing for you without measure" (Malachi 3:10). Here is the one place in the Word where **Yahweh invites us to put Him to a test—to prove Him.** We have found Him faithful to His promise.

Tithing (bringing the first tenth of our income to Yahweh) is not a legal requirement for believers, rather a principle for honoring Yahweh with our financial gains—a way to acknowledge Him as the ultimate Source of all we receive. But moving beyond that basic tenth allows us to grow in giving and discover the truth that "it is more blessed to give than to receive." Remember: you make a living by what you receive; you make a life by what you give.

Yeshua in Your Worship

> Lord Jesus, You set the example for me by giving Yourself for me and to me. Teach me to be a generous giver—of myself and all I possess. Help me grow is this area of being a liberal servant.

May 24

Yahweh Has My Name Written in His Special Book

Yahweh in the Word

> "So a book of remembrance was written before Him for those who feared Yahweh and had high regard for His name. 'They will be Mine,' says Yahweh of hosts, 'a special possession on the day I am preparing.'" (Malachi 3:16-17).

Yahweh spoke through His prophet Malachi to encourage all those who reverenced Him and had great respect for His name. He assured them of being remembered by Him as a special treasure being prepared for a future day.

Yahweh in Your Walk

The Bible has several references to Yahweh's written records. One is in our text for today—"a book of remembrance." Another volume is known as "the book of life" (Philippians 4:3) or "the Lamb's book of life," mentioned six times in the Revelation (3:5; 13:8; 17:8; 20:12, 15; 21:27). Both of these books contain all the names of Yahweh's people. **If you have believed in Jesus as your Savior, your name is written there and will never be removed.** Do not ever allow Satan to deceive you with his lies about someday losing the salvation purchased for you by the Lord Jesus—you are eternally secure, not because you are strong and faithful, but because He is. He said of His chosen ones, "I give them eternal life, and they will never perish—ever! My Father, who has given them to Me, is greater than all. No one is able to snatch them out of the Father's hand. The Father and I are one" (John 10:28-30). Here is your eternal security!

If you could earn salvation by doing works of righteousness, then you could lose that salvation if your good works did not measure up to God's standard. Fortunately, eternal life is the gift of God, not of works lest anyone should boast. You can walk through life with the peace of knowing you are in your Savior's hand; His Spirit lives within you and will keep you securely through this life and for all eternity. The apostle Paul wrote these comforting words to young Titus, a pastor in Crete:

> But when the goodness of God and His love for mankind appeared,
> He saved us—not by works of righteousness that we had done,
> But according to His mercy, through the washing of regeneration and
> Renewal by the Holy Spirit. He poured out the Spirit on us abundantly
> Through Jesus Christ our Savior, so that having been justified by His grace,

We may become heirs with the hope of eternal life (Titus 3:4-7).

Yahweh in Your Worship

Holy Father, I come before Your throne of grace to worship You and to express my deepest gratitude to You for including me in Your Book of Life. I confess that I am not worthy of such favor, but I know You are gracious and forgiving. Help me pass on to others this good news.

May 25

Yahweh Wants Me to Seize Opportunities

Yahweh in the Word

> "While they were traveling, He entered a village, and a woman named Martha welcomed Him into her home. She had a sister named Mary, who also sat at the Lord's feet and was listening to what He said. But Martha was distracted by her many tasks, and she came up and asked, 'Lord, don't You care that my sister has left me to serve alone? So tell her to give me a hand.' The Lord answered her, 'Martha, Martha, you are worried and upset about many things, but one thing is necessary. Mary has made the right choice, and it will not be taken away from her'" (Luke 10:38-42).

Martha, Mary, and their brother Lazarus became special friends of Jesus. Their home in Bethany was only a short distance east of Jerusalem and Jesus apparently visited them often. Lazarus is the one Jesus raised from the dead at a later time (John 11:1-44). In this episode Martha complains to Jesus that her sister has neglected her hospitality duties; Jesus replies by commending Mary's choice to listen to His teachings.

Yahweh in Your Walk

Every day you make decisions based on various opportunities. For example, most days you choose to either get up just in time to get dressed, have breakfast, and begin the tasks of that day, or to get up early enough to spend some quiet time with Jesus in His Word and conversing with Him in prayer. Which would you say is the best use of an opportunity? Hopefully, you would follow the example of Mary and give your attention to your Savior and Lord. Other duties, however important, do not compare to this privilege. **If you put Him first, Jesus will say to you as He said of Mary, "You have made the right choice."**

Why is this simple discipline so essential? Notice what Jesus said to Martha about her sister's decision to sit at His feet and learn from Him, "One thing is necessary." He was saying, "Many things need to be done, but one thing is necessary if we are to become all God wants us to be." And **that one necessary choice is to give priority to fellowship with Jesus**. Nothing else is as important as this. Here is the reason for beginning the day with a quiet time of meditation and prayer—searching the Scripture to learn more of Yahweh's truth, and offering oneself to Him as a living sacrifice for that day.

Seize the Day with Yahweh is the title we have chosen for this book of daily devotionals. We have found that taking advantage of this opportunity makes a real difference in us each day. We hope you will discover how helpful these few minutes of meditation and prayer can be.

Yahweh in Your Worship

Lord, I choose to sit at Your feet and learn of You. Help me become all You want me to be.

May 26

Yeshua Will Determine My Rewards on His Day of Judgment

Yeshua in the Word

> "We make it our aim to be pleasing to Him. For we must all appear before the tribunal of Christ, so that each may be repaid for what he has done in the body, whether good or worthless" (2 Corinthians 5:10).

We are reminded here of our individual accountability to the Lord. The day of judgment is certain to come and Christians will gain or lose rewards according to our works.

Yeshua in Your Walk

A very sobering thought is that of your personal accountability to Yeshua. **What you say or do today will make a difference for you on the day of judgment.** As a believer this event will not be to determine whether you make it to heaven; that decision was settled once for all when you placed your trust in Jesus as your Savior. He has suffered the penalty for all your sins, however, you are responsible and accountable for the way you serve Him each day.

Yeshua spoke of this event on several occasions: "I tell you that on the day of judgment people will have to account for every careless word they speak. For by your words you will be acquitted, and by your words you will be condemned" (Matthew 12:36). "For the Son of Man is going to come with His angels in the glory of His Father, and then He will reward each according to what he has done" (Matthew 16:26). And among the last words of the Bible are these words of Jesus: "Look! I am coming quickly, and My reward is with Me to repay each person according to what he has done" (Revelation 22:12).

These truths should cause you to think carefully before you act or speak—**Someone is hearing what you say and observing all you do.** And He is keeping an account of these actions for the purpose of rewarding you on that final day of accountability. One effect of this fact is that you have no need of being compensated now for any good you do—your reward will come in the future. And that reward will be according to what is just and fair. Your Judge knows your motives as well as your deeds; He also knows what you do in secret as well as openly.

So as you walk through another day, remember that you are a steward of Yeshua and someday you will give Him a full account of every thought, word, and action. What a difference this should make today and every day! We all have an appointment with the Judge!

Yeshua in Your Worship

Sovereign Judge, I worship You as the One for whom I live and to whom I must give an account. Help me so live today that You will be pleased and I will be rewarded according to what is right. Thank You for saving me from being condemned for my sins. I want to serve You better today.

May 27

Yahweh Wants to Hear What Is on My Heart

Yahweh in the Word

> "Therefore, confess your sins one to another and pray for one another, so that you may be healed" (James 5:16).

The next four devotionals will feature verses about "one another" and the joy of helping other Christians be established in their Christian growth. The writer for today is James, the half-brother of Jesus and the pastor of the church in Jerusalem. He had set the greater part of his letter on instructions and warnings concerning the Christian life. This epistle is packed with practical wisdom.

James urged believers to not only confess their sins to Yahweh but also to involve fellow believers in this confession if they have been affected by these sins. Personal relationships were of vital importance and if a person had sinned in a manner that harmed that relationship, confession was needed to bring healing. Thus James encouraged openness and honesty with one another.

Yahweh in Your Walk

Melva and Ruth were members of my Bible study group. However, something seemed to have happened to their friendship in the last few months. Melva lost interest in her personal relationship with her dear friend. As their teacher, I noticed the difference in their interaction. One day I confronted Melva about her coldness toward other people. She was shocked that I was aware of her change in fellowship.

She began to cry and confessed that she was having an affair with a man in her office and she did not want her friend to find out the truth because her friend was related to this man. Personal confession seemed to help her. We prayed together and claimed God's promise for healing from this sin. Also, we agreed that Melva would need to make some serious changes in her life, such as how to avoid this man who caused the affair to begin.

The repentant woman took my advice and also confessed her sin to her friend. What a change came about when these two believers prayed for one another! The openness and honesty, as well as acceptance and forgiveness, brought healing to their relationship. They seemed to care more about their friendship than ever before. This kind of confession needs to happen anytime a person sins against Yahweh and His people.

Yahweh in Your Worship

Yahweh, I know the condition of my spiritual heart is important to You. When I consider my personal sins and Your desire for me to confess, I need to follow Your wishes. Help me to recognize any healing that needs to take place in my church family and my friends. Lead me to do as You command when Your Spirit convicts me to be obedient.

May 28

Yahweh Wants Me to Give Friendly Greetings to Others

Yahweh in the Word

> "Greet one another with a holy kiss. All the churches of Christ send you greetings" (Romans 16:16).

As the apostle Paul closed his letter to the Romans, he publicly commended those who had helped and encouraged him in the work of the gospel. He not only greeted them by name, but he also expressed his gratitude for what they had done. This verse shows that Paul was a friend-maker as well as a soul-winner.

He mentions eight others who were with him in Corinth and sent their greetings (vv. 21-23). The fact that Paul had friends in the Lord and appreciated them is important for us to learn. Some saints may choose to live alone, but most of us need one another to help us grow in our Christian walk. Not all the people were faithful to Paul. Some, for selfish reasons, were dividing the churches by teaching false doctrine. These people were probably the same Judaizers who had given Paul trouble in other churches. However, friends were important to this servant of Yahweh.

Yahweh in Your Walk

What is so hard about smiling and greeting a guest or a friend? **I believe the church greeters are some of the most important servants in the church.** The way they make a stranger feel when entering your fellowship is so vital to the worship.

My daughter and I were on vacation and decided to visit a local church on Sunday morning. You won't believe this… but not one person greeted us during the whole time we were on their property!! The feeling that we weren't welcome was very real to me. How could this experience happen to us? The answer is simple. The people did not care about us. What if we had been needing prayer or salvation? I thought about how Paul greeted and expressed appreciation to all the people who ministered to him. A sadness came over me as we departed that church.

I determined to become a greeter when we returned home and have found such satisfaction in hugging and expressing thanks to the people who enter our building. A special joy is mine in greeting the bus filled with senior adults. Many of these people have not been touched all week. My goal is to make sure they know how much we love them. A "holy kiss" is often involved in the greeting. Yes, I even greet the old men with a cheek-kiss!

Yahweh in Your Worship

LORD, help me to have a loving smile and greeting for everyone I meet. May I be faithful to encourage others to focus more on the new guests when they attend our fellowship.

May 29

Yahweh Cares About My Attitude Toward Others

Yahweh in the Word

> *"And be kind and compassionate to one another, forgiving one another, just as God also forgave you in Christ" (Ephesians 4:32).*

A basic Christian principle is to have an attitude of courtesy, care, and concern for others. Happy relationships are possible when a Christian models a Christ-like spirit of neighborly love. Just the opposite is true when people fuss and fight, usually over insignificant things. **The most important issue is not what others have done to us, but what Christ has done for us.**

Paul apparently wrote this letter to several churches in Asia Minor. These new Christ-followers were having a problem with unity. The apostle includes a practical instruction in chapter 4 on the fundamental thought about unity: one body and one Spirit, one hope, one Lord, one faith, one baptism, and one God and Father of all. He includes some exhortations on what to avoid in order to have the desired unity in the church. Don't you recall from your past how some church members were constantly upset about something? They were not serious about building unity.

Yahweh in Your Walk

Forgiveness is difficult for many people. The saying, "I will forgive, but I won't forget" is silly. How often do we see this attitude expressed between people who need to forgive for good? For example, Bill and Fred were brothers who lived in our community. They were raised on a big farm with a loving father. Each boy worked hard to help keep the farm successful. They each dreamed of the day when the land they were plowing would be theirs. However, when their dad died, trouble destroyed the relationship these sons had possessed. The father's legal will gave more land to one son and a less profitable farm to the other son. Bill became angry and walked out of the inheritance meeting; he refused to speak to Fred for the next 40 years.

Bill finally made an effort to forgive his brother. His decision was not easy. A sermon had made him rethink his actions years ago. His pastor offered words of comfort and help about the importance of forgiveness. Bill called Fred and scheduled a meeting. Each brother expressed sadness over the wasted years and they embraced one another in forgiveness. The rest of the story is that Fred included in his will a prosperous farm for Bill in memory of their father. You can forgive and forget!!

Yahweh in Your Worship

Yahweh, I love You and know that I must also love my neighbor. Your Word encourages me to pray and trust You for answers. Some people are just hard to forgive. However, I know that You will guide me to be a forgiver and follow Your example on the cross.

May 30

Yahweh Wants Me to Help Others through Songs

Yahweh in the Word

"Let the word of Christ dwell in you richly in all wisdom, teaching and admonishing one another in psalms and hymns and spiritual songs, singing with grace in your hearts to the Lord " (Colossians 3:16 NKJV).

Paul advised his friends who heard this letter to be concerned about others more than about themselves. One means of expressing this concern was through "teaching and admonishing one another." To teach a person means to give instruction, while admonish means to caution against wrongdoing—one is positive, the other is more negative. Believers need both.

Yahweh in Your Walk

Have you noticed how Yahweh uses songs to help you? I recall many times when a musical message from a soloist or choir gave me just the lift I needed to keep on keeping on. Likewise, there have been occasions when other songs reminded me of the reality of spiritual warfare, helping me be on guard against Satan's deceit.

Notice how Paul covers a wide range of the various types of music: "psalms and hymns and spiritual songs." He goes on to encourage us to use this way of ministering to one another as we participate by "singing with grace" in our hearts. **Only in heaven will we realize the tremendous good that came to us and others through these kinds of songs.**

We have dear friends whose primary means of serving Yahweh through many years has been through songs. Hugh and Carolyn Brooks were, at one time, on the faculty at Penn State University where they taught courses in recreation. Both of them are talented musicians who learned to combine singing with recreation. They developed a group of 10 talented young performers in 1976 known as "Re-Creation." Their ministry has been primarily to the patients in many military veterans care centers throughout America. In fact, since the beginning, Re-Creation has now done over 10,000 shows in all 50 states. Many types of songs are used, mainly patriotic and religious. Hugh wrote much of the music used by this enthusiastic group.

Recently, I asked Hugh, now retired, about his twenty years with Re-Creation. He said, "We have learned through these years that there are many kinds of recreation that are beneficial, but the most helpful and re-creative is worship." As an outstanding preacher and singer in his own right, he is an authority on this subject. He and Carolyn continue to serve Yahweh in many ways.

Yahweh in Your Worship

Thank You for great, inspiring, and instructive songs. Help me participate in the ministry of sharing these means of re-creation with others. I bless You for giving the talent of music.

May 31

Yahweh Calls Upon Me to Carry Others' Burdens

Yahweh in the Word

> *"Brothers, if someone is caught in any wrongdoing, you who are spiritual should restore such a person with a gentle sprit, watching out for yourselves so you also won't be tempted. Carry one another's burdens; in this way you will fulfill the law of Christ" (Galatians 6:1-2).*

The apostle Paul comes to the conclusion of his letter to the Galatians with an appeal for them to help bear one another's burdens. His concern seems to be for someone who has been "caught" doing something wrong. This guilty person needs forgiveness and restoration. All this fulfills Christ's law which is to love one another as He has loved us.

Yahweh in Your Walk

Today is the final devotional in this series of "one anothers." Many more could be considered, in fact there are at least 27 such statements in the New Testament. Sixteen of these are from Paul's letters. He was a strong advocate for believers to offer a helping hand to others. Some we have not examined are: "Show family affection to **one another** with brotherly love. Outdo **one another** in showing honor" (Romans 12:10). "Therefore accept **one another**, just as the Messiah also accepted you, to the glory of God" (Romans 15:7). "Be kind and compassionate to **one another**, forgiving **one another**, just as God also forgave you in Christ" (Ephesians 4:32). "Pray for **one another**" (James 5:16). "Encourage **one another**" (1 Thessalonians 4:18).

My friend David Seay is a fine example of how we should bear one another's burdens. His nephew, Chris, lives in West Texas and has struggled for years with various addictions. His family had tried in vain to help him and basically gave up. However, David knew the difference Christ could make in this young man, so he prayed often for him and reached out with compassion. Recently, David made a special trip from Nashville to Amarillo just to meet with Chris, who brought his girlfriend along. As a result of David's witness, Chris received Jesus and has begun a new life as a committed Christian. The young lady also made a new dedication of herself to follow Jesus! David sent them new Bibles and is staying in touch to help them grow.

We are all sent to help people like Chris. The question we must face is: Are we willing to be persistent in our efforts to see Yahweh make a difference in those who have stumbled beneath the load of life? And **will we give the time, money, and effort in paying the price to be of help?** The answer is: Yes, we will do this if we have the love of Jesus controlling our decisions.

Yahweh in Your Worship

Gracious Yahweh, You came to my aid and rescued me when I could not help myself. Now guide me to pass on to other needy persons that same compassion and love. Make me aware of those whom you would have me to help for Your glory.

June 1

Yahweh Tsidkenu Provides Righteousness for Me

Yahweh in the Word

> "The days are coming—this is the LORD's declaration—when I will raise up a Righteous Branch of David. He will reign wisely as king and administer justice and righteousness in the land. In His days Judah will be saved, and Israel will dwell securely. This is what He will be named: Yahweh Our Righteousness (Yahweh Tsidkenu, pronounced tsid-KAY-nu)" (Jeremiah 23:5-6).

Notice the words "righteous" and "righteousness" in these verses. The Hebrew root of these words means "to be straight" and implies truthfulness, moral uprightness, integrity, and faithfulness. Righteousness is a basic aspect of Yahweh's character. He is righteous and always acts in a righteous manner. The "Righteous Branch" mentioned above refers to Jesus (Yeshua) who was a descendant of David. As Jesus said, He and the Father are one, in the sense of being of the same divine nature. Thus, here the name Yahweh Tsidkenu (I AM the One Who Is Righteousness) is given to Him.

Yahweh in Your Walk

We all face difficult questions, many of which begin with "how." For example: How can I be successful? How can I overcome bad habits? How can I improve my health? And on and on the list can be. **But the most significant and life altering question is: How can a sinner like me have a meaningful relationship with Yahweh?** What must I do to avoid the penalty for my sins which is eternal separation from God?

The answer to this question is found in these good news words from the apostle Paul: "God proves His own love for us in that while we were still sinners Christ died for us… since we have now been declared righteous by His blood, we will be saved through Him from wrath" (Romans 5:8-9). What a wonderful truth—"we (believers) have now been declared righteous by His blood." **Sinners are saved by grace through faith—they are declared righteous by Yahweh Tsidkenu.**

As you begin this new month and walk through this new day, lay hold of the amazing fact that, because of what Yeshua did for you on the cross, you are righteous in Yahweh's sight. You have no sin debt to pay, no fear of separation from Him. Hallelujah (which means Praise to Yahweh)!

Yahweh in Your Worship

"Jesus paid it all; all to Him I owe. Sin had left a crimson stain; He washed it white as snow. And when before the throne I stand in Him complete, 'Jesus died my soul to save,' my lips shall still repeat." Thank You, Yahweh Tsidkenu, for providing the righteousness I need, but can never produce. Help me learn to appreciate the wonder of this grace gift. Use me to pass on this truth to others. I want to become involved in sharing the good news of Your provision for our sin to those who have never heard the gospel.

June 2

Yahweh Tsidkenu Works His Righteousness in Me

Yahweh in the Word

> *"If you know that He is righteous, you know this as well: Everyone who does what is right has been born of Him"* (1 John 2:29).

The person who lives a righteous life—does what is right—must have a righteous nature. Only Yahweh has a perfectly righteous nature. Thus in order to live a righteous life we must share Yahweh's nature. This miracle occurs when we are born again—"born of Him." We then become partakers of the divine nature. Or as the Scripture declares, "Christ lives in me" (Galatians 2:20).

Yahweh in Your Walk

Yesterday's study helped us understand the truth that when we receive Yeshua by faith, Yahweh declares us to be righteous—totally forgiven for all sin. But we need more than forgiveness for the past, we need the desire and power to live a righteous life from now on.

Suppose, for example, that you were found guilty of a very serious crime and were sentenced to die. But for some unexplainable reason the judge gave you a pardon and set you free. That would be extremely good news. However, as you walk out of prison, you have been forgiven for your crime, but you would be the same person you were before—with the same unlawful nature. What you need is more than a pardon, you need a new heart, a new nature—one that practices righteous actions. Otherwise, you would continue being a law-breaker.

Because Yahweh Tsidkenu knows this and loves us, He supplies not only the right standing we need before Him, He also imparts to us His own righteous nature which enables us to live a righteous life. Thus **we have both a righteous position and a righteous disposition!** Yahweh Tsidkenu meets all our need for righteousness.

Yahweh in Your Worship

Seize this day as a day of righteousness by offering yourself, just as you are, to be completely controlled by Yahweh Tsidkenu. Here is a prayer I offer each morning:

"Master, I want this day to be a day of Your control; to know the lordship of Your love triumphant in my soul, and all my longings all my cares upon that love to roll. I want to know Your fellowship more fully all the way and in its bright reality to walk with You this day; losing my life that in Your life God's will shall be my stay. I want to prove as Spirit taught the power of Jesus' Name, as victors did who by Your blood once fought and overcame. O Master make these wants to be unto fulfillment brought, and day by day unto Yourself lead captive every thought. Then shall at evensong be praise for all that God has wrought." Amen.

Perhaps this could become one of your prayers of commitment.

June 3

Yahweh Takes Pleasure in Me

Yahweh in the Word

> "Yahweh your God is among you, a warrior who saves. He will rejoice over you with gladness. He will bring you quietness with His love. He will delight in you with shouts of joy" (Zephaniah 3: 17).

Zephaniah was God's prophet to the people of Judah before they fell to their enemy. He gave a forceful warning of impending judgment because of their sins. But He concludes his message with this promise to the remnant of Yahweh's people who would repent and return to Him. Notice in this verse the expressions of forgiveness and restoration along with the gladness and shouts of joy coming from Yahweh.

Yahweh in Your Walk

Let's take a brief walk through the amazing truths found in these four statements regarding Yahweh's unconditional love for all His children.

1. Yahweh is among us as a warrior who saves. We are never alone as we engage our enemies. He is always present to assist us in each battle, and He guarantees us ultimate victory.
2. Yahweh rejoices over us with gladness. In spite of our shortcomings and failures, He loves us as we are and finds much pleasure in us as His redeemed children.
3. Yahweh will bring quietness with His love, that is, He quietens our fears as we remember how much He loves us.
4. Yahweh finds such delight in us as His children that He shouts with joy.

What a remarkable expression of Yahweh's absolute goodness, mercy, and love. **The pleasure and delight He finds in us is beyond our comprehension, especially when we consider how unworthy we are.** And yet, He loves us as a good father loves his children—in spite of their faults.

Surely we must walk through this day with a renewed sense of value to our Father. If we bring such pleasure to Him, surely we can find the good in ourselves that He finds. **Let's celebrate this relationship of joy, knowing that Yahweh is with us, delivering us, quieting us, and shouting with delightful joy over us.**

Yahweh in Your Worship

O Yahweh, how amazing is Your love for me. Help me to see myself as Your child, created by You and for You. Enable me to find the reason for rejoicing over me that You find. I do worship and adore You. I stand amazed at Your unconditional love for me. Use me to share Your love with those I will be with today.

June 4

Yahweh Gives My Final Home a New Name

Yahweh in the Word

> "You will be called by a new name that Yahweh's mouth will announce. You will be a glorious crown in Yahweh's hand, and a royal diadem in the palm of your God. You will no longer be called Deserted, and your land will not be called Desolate; instead you will be called My Delight is in Her, and your land Married; for Yahweh delights in you and your land will be married. For as a young man marries a young woman, so your sons will marry you; and as a groom rejoices over his bride, so your God will rejoice over you" (Isaiah 62:2b-5).

The prophet Isaiah uses the image of the joy of marriage to describe the future for Yahweh's people. Their condition will be changed from feeling deserted and desolate to one of being Yahweh's delight and cause for rejoicing. One Old Testament scholar says of this passage, "There is no finer statement of the Lord's personal concern for His people in all the Old Testament."

Yahweh in Your Walk

Jack DeVore was a personal friend and associate; we served together on a church staff in Arizona. His favorite gospel song was "Beulah Land," which was sung at his funeral. The scriptural basis for these great lyrics comes from the words of today's Bible text. You will notice the words "married" or "marries" or "marry" occur several times. The Hebrew word for married is **beulah**. Thus Beulah Land refers to that new place Yahweh has prepared for His people where His relationship with us will have the intimacy of marriage.

Here is one verse and the chorus of the song:

> I'm kind of homesick for a country to which I've never been before;
> No sad goodbyes will ever be spoken, and time won't matter anymore.
> Beulah land, I'm longing for you, And some day, on thee I'll stand,
> There my home shall be eternal, Beulah land, sweet Beulah land.

What a beautiful metaphor of the glories of heaven. As you walk through this day, remember that this is your destiny. **Yahweh has a new name for the place He has prepared for you—no longer a place like this world where at times you feel deserted and desolate. Rather, Married Land where Yahweh rejoices over us, as a groom rejoices over his bride.**

Yahweh in Your Worship

Thank You Yahweh for the assurance of heaven. But even more, thank You for the intimate relationship I have with You now. Help me seize this new day with joy and excitement over all You are doing in and through me. I praise You for all the good You prepare for Your people. Make me aware of any person I meet today who needs to hear this good news, and speak through me of Your amazing love and eternal provision for them.

June 5

Yahweh Hears My Morning Prayers

Yahweh in the Word

"At daybreak Yahweh, You hear my voice; at daybreak I plead my case to You and watch expectantly… let all who take refuge in You rejoice; let them shout for joy forever. May You shelter them and may those who love Your name boast about You. For You, Lord, bless the righteous one; You surround him with favor like a shield " (Psalm 5:3-12).

David wrote this prayer at a time when he was being verbally attacked by his enemies. In spite of such unfair criticism he chose to focus on the goodness of Yahweh and express his confidence in His protection and favor.

Yahweh in Your Walk

I am what is known as an "early riser." On most mornings as I walk down the lane of our front yard to retrieve the morning paper, the sun is just emerging in the eastern sky. I find much pleasure in singing these words from an old hymn:

> When morning guilds the skies, my heart awaking cries; May Jesus Christ be praised!
> Alike at work or prayer, to Jesus I repair; May Jesus Christ be praised!
> The night becomes as day when from the heart we say, May Jesus Christ be praised!
> The powers of darkness fear, when this sweet song they hear: May Jesus Christ be praised!
> Be this while life is mine, my canticle divine: May Jesus Christ be praised!
> Be this the eternal song through all the ages long; May Jesus Christ be praised!

What a great way to begin the day! You can choose to start off each day with prayers of praise and adoration, or focusing on how bad you feel, or grumbling about some mistreatment you may have received. Refuse those kinds of negative thoughts. Make the choice to rejoice! Remember that Yahweh is with you, to bless and help you through the day. **Lift up your spirit as you lift up your voice with shouts of joy to Him. He is worthy of this—and you are capable of this.**

Recently, I saw these words printed on a coffee cup: "I would enjoy the day more if it started later!" Perhaps the best solution to this problem is to go to bed earlier. Let me challenge you to take control of the way you begin each day. Set your alarm to go off earlier than others in your family normally get up. Arise while it is quiet and spend the first 30 minutes or more in private meditation, prayer, and worship. You will be very pleasantly surprised at how much better your entire day will be. Try it, you'll like it!

Yahweh in Your Worship

Yahweh, I need Your help to begin each day with a quiet, uninterrupted time of worship and adoration of You. Thank You for always being present—at whatever time I call upon You.

June 6

Yahweh Calls Me to Decide to Serve Him Daily

Yahweh in the Word

> "Choose for yourselves today the one you will serve... As for me and my family, we will serve Yahweh" (Joshua 24:15 NKJV)

Joshua included this challenge in his farewell speech to the people he led. They had driven out several people groups who worshiped and served various idols. He called on them to make a clear choice about which god they would worship and serve.

Yahweh in Your Walk

Today is the anniversary of D-Day in Europe. On June 6, 1944 more than 150,000 Allied forces landed on the beaches of France to begin their invasion of that Nazi-held territory. Many of these troops lost their lives in this bold attack which proved to be a turning point in World War II. All these soldiers made a personal decision to participate in this dangerous endeavor. Historians state that the meaning of D-Day is "a day on which something important is planned or expected to happen."

This being the case, there is a sense in which every day is a D-Day for us—a day on which we make a decision to worship and serve Yahweh or not. Joshua was himself a military leader; he was Yahweh's choice to lead the Israelites in their conquest of the land which Yahweh had promised to give Abraham many years earlier. As Joshua prepared to die, he left his people with a call to follow the example of him and his family in committing themselves to worship and serve Yahweh rather than the false gods of their enemies.

Perhaps you can recall a specific time in your life when you made a deliberate decision to become a follower of Jesus—an initial commitment to trust Him as your personal Savior and Lord—that was your D-Day. However, as you have discovered, that significant life-changing choice needs to be repeated **every day**—once in a lifetime is not enough, this must become a day-by-day fresh surrender to Him. We recommend that you form the habit of making this new choice the first thing upon awakening each day—before leaving your bed. **Simply and sincerely offer yourself—body, mind, spirit, to the One you have chosen to worship and serve that day**. You will never regret such a disciplined act of worship.

Yahweh in Your Worship

Thank You, Yahweh, for preserving for me the example of Joshua. I want to be like him as Your intentional worshiper and servant. You alone are worthy of such devotion. I praise You and thank You for making Yourself known to me. Help me this day to make You known to others by my words of testimony and my life of devoted service to You. May others see Your life on display in all my words and deeds.

June 7

Yahweh Helps Me Lie Down in Peace and Sleep

Yahweh in the Word

> *"You have put more joy in my heart than they have when their grain and new wine abound. I will both lie down and sleep in peace, for You alone, Yahweh, make me live in safety" (Psalm 4:7-8).*

Yesterday we considered a song of David concerning prayer at daybreak. Today's psalm is another by David, but this time he speaks of lying down and sleeping. Both morning and evening, and all the time in between are appropriate times for celebrating Yahweh's comforting presence—He never leaves us alone.

Yahweh in Your Walk

When I was a small child my mother would come to my bed with me to "tuck me in and hear my prayers." The first bedtime prayer I can remember was: "Now I lay me down to sleep, I pray the Lord my soul to keep. If I should die before I wake, I pray the Lord my soul to take. Amen" Later, she taught me "The Lord's Prayer," and then to pray in my own words.

That habit of praying at bedtime has stayed with me all through these many years. Now, as part of this prayer time, I quote David's words from the text for today's devotional: "I will both lie down and sleep in peace, for You alone, Yahweh, make me live in safety." I find much comfort in the words of this simple prayer. **Yahweh is the only One who provides the safety I need in order to sleep in peace.** This goes back to my first prayer, "I pray the Lord my soul to keep."

These prayers are our ways of committing ourselves to Yahweh for His safekeeping. We believe that He not only hears us but also gives the protection and care we need. The apostle Paul referred to this same trust when he wrote these words to young Timothy: "I know whom I have believed and am persuaded that He is able to keep what I have committed to Him until that Day" (2 Timothy 1:12). Such confident trust enables us to lie down in peace and sleep.

I recommend this practice of bedtime praying. Of course you will want to expand your prayers beyond these simple models, including a time of thanksgiving for the blessings of the day, intercessory prayers for family members, friends, and other concerns. But always include the commitment of yourself into Yahweh's keeping.

Yahweh in Your Worship

Yes, O Yahweh, I do commit myself, my family, my vocation, friends, and all I possess to Your eternal care and keeping. Thank You for Your faithfulness in protecting us from the enemy. Our times are always in Your good hands. Help me be a strong witness to others of the peace I find in the assurance of Your unfailing presence.

June 8

Yahweh Listens to Me All Through the Night

Yahweh in the Word

> "Yahweh, I remember Your name in the night, and I obey Your instruction" (Psalm 119:55).

The psalmist was pleased to know that when he was sleepless, he could recall Yahweh's name and what this name meant to him. Perhaps the instruction he obeyed was similar to that given to Joshua by Moses, "This book of instruction must not depart from your mouth; you are to recite it day and night so that you may carefully observe everything written in it" (Joshua 1:8). Whether during the day or night, one's relationship to Yahweh controls both thoughts and actions.

Yahweh in Your Walk

Most of us have various kinds of sleeping problems. For some, insomnia becomes a serious matter, while for others it is more of a nuisance. Whatever your sleep pattern may be, these words from the psalmist offer wise counsel. Since Yahweh never sleeps (Psalm 121:4), He is available to us at all hours of the day and night. Apparently, David took advantage of this for he wrote, "When I think of You as I lie on my bed, I meditate on You during the night watches because You are my helper; I will rejoice in the shadow of Your wings" (Psalm 63:6-7).

Consider some practical ways to redeem time spent during periods of sleeplessness.

1. Do as the psalmist said in our text—Remember Yahweh's name. As we are learning in these devotionals, **His name is Yahweh, which means, "I AM."** Earlier we pointed out this can be extended to read, "I AM whatever you need in order to become all I desire for you to be." I have often awakened during the night with thoughts of anxiety—I think about "what ifs." Such as What if my plans do not work out or What if I'm not able to do what I think I should or on and on. . . just general worries. But I have learned to replace these kinds of thoughts with thoughts about Yahweh—His greatness and goodness, the promises He has made, etc. I remember His name and what comfort that brings to me as I "rejoice in the shadow of Your wings."
2. How about spending some of this sleepless time praying for others and their needs. Notice the psalmist said, "I obey Your instruction." He has instructed us to pray one for another; here's a good time to do just that. **As you lie there in the stillness of the night, what an excellent opportunity for intercessory prayer.** I often begin going over the list of persons I want to pray for and before long I'm fast asleep. Good sleeping pill!
3. Review Scriptures you have memorized or are working on. Psalm 23 works well for me.

Yahweh in Your Worship

Let these suggestions help you redeem more time for worship, day and night. Seize the opportunity for intercessory prayer when you are sleepless. Ask Yahweh to remind you of those who need your special prayers at that time.

June 9

Yahweh Teaches Me to Seize the Opportunities of Each Day

Yahweh in the Word

> *"Yahweh will be your confidence and will keep your foot from a snare. When it is in your power don't withhold good from the one it belongs to. Don't say to your neighbor, 'Go away! Come back later. I'll give it tomorrow'—when it is there with you" (Proverbs 3:26-28).*

The Book of Proverbs is known as the wisdom book of the Bible. Yahweh inspired the writer (probably Solomon) to record numerous "short sayings based on long experience." This text for today is a good example of such wisdom. Here Yahweh affirms the importance of being diligent to reach out to a needy person at the time of their need, not procrastinating.

Yahweh in Your Walk

Think carefully about this truth: **You will never have another day exactly like this one—never have the exact same opportunities to worship and serve God by reaching out to help others.** So, I challenge you is to seize this day by being sensitive and alert to all it has to offer. You will never pass through this day again.

Stephen Grellet (1773-1855) came to America as a missionary from France. He is credited with composing these very thought provoking words:

> I expect to pass through this world but once. Any good, therefore, that I can do or any kindness I can show to any fellow creature, let me do it now. Let me not defer or neglect it for I shall not pass the way again.

The principle idea of *carpe diem* ("seize the day") is that of being diligent and alert to opportunities that come your way, then grasping those once-in-a-lifetime chances to act on them. Here's an example: As I was writing these words on my computer, my phone rang. A solicitor named Rick offered to install in our house a security system at a very low cost. Since I am not interested in his product, I could have just hung up the phone or rudely scolded him for disturbing me. Instead, I recognized this as a once-in-a-lifetime opportunity to speak a blessing to this stranger. So, I politely thanked him for the call, told him I was not interested, then said, "I want to give you something" and quoted the blessing found in Numbers 6:22-27 which I memorized many years ago. I doubt if Rick has ever had this kind of response to his calls!

That opportunity came once in a lifetime to me, because **I will never pass this way again**. The same is true of countless opportunities that come every day. Seize the privilege of speaking kind words to your family members, now, while you have them with you. Take advantage of giving help to neighbors, friends, fellow-workers, or whoever Yahweh brings across your path.

Yahweh in Your Worship

Thank You for this reminder of the importance of living this day to its full potential. I trust You to make me aware of the needs in others I will have the privilege of meeting today.

June 10

Yahweh Removes My Transgressions from Me

Yahweh in the Word

> *"As far as the east is from the west so far has He removed our transgressions from us. As a father has compassion on his children, so Yahweh has compassion on those who fear Him" (Psalm 103:12-13)*

The 103rd Psalm is a beautiful celebration of "The Forgiving God." Numerous references are made to Yahweh's mercy, forgiveness, and compassion toward His children. In our text the psalmist calls on the facts of geography to emphasize the completeness of Yahweh's forgiveness. He removes our transgressions as far as the east is from the west—endless.

Yahweh in Your Walk

Most of us have trouble with forgiveness. First, we find it difficult to truly forgive those who have wronged us in some serious manner; we tend to carry a grudge against them. Secondly, we have trouble believing that Yahweh actually forgives us our sins against Him; surely He remembers our rebellious ways, those many times when we have disobeyed Him.

However, God's Word is clear in declaring that we who have experienced His forgiveness due to the sacrifice of our Lord Jesus on the cross must believe this good news and extend the same forgiveness to others. **We forgive because we have been forgiven.** Although we sometimes struggle with this truth, the more we learn about Yahweh's forgiveness the easier such mercy is accepted and passed on.

Notice our text for today declares our transgressions are removed as far as the east is from the west. This metaphor indicates the unlimited, endless extent of forgiveness, because there is no point on earth where east and west meet. If we start going west and continue on, we never come to the end of west—same is true going east. However, if Yahweh's forgiveness was as far as the north is from the south that would mean limited forgiveness. You can go north until north ends at the North Pole, then you begin going south! The psalmist knew his geography!

So, as you walk through this day, and every day, find comfort in knowing the completeness of Yahweh's forgiveness—and be gracious to extend that same mercy to all those who wrong you. Remember also, that this divine kind of forgiveness is available even if it is never claimed. We must share the good news of Yahweh's mercy to those who have never asked for it. And, likewise, our forgiveness of those who transgress against us is there—whether claimed by others or not. In other words, we never have to decide whether we will forgive someone or not. We have the reservoir of Yahweh's mercy ready to pour out on whoever needs it.

Yahweh in Your Worship

Today I seize this truth about forgiveness O Yahweh. How unlimited is Your mercy and kindness to me. And I claim that same grace to reach out to those who have wronged me.

June 11

Yahweh Wants to Give His Strength to Me

Yahweh in the Word

> "The eyes of Yahweh roam throughout the earth to show Himself strong for those whose hearts are completely His" (2 Chronicles 16:9).

King Asa of Judah seemed to forget how Yahweh had given him victory in the past over his enemies. So he resorted to his own scheme of bribing a pagan king to help him defeat his current enemy, the king of Israel. Although his strategy worked, Yahweh sent His prophet Hanani to scold Asa for not trusting Him for the victory. Our text is a portion of the message Hanani gave to Asa. Rather than be repentant for his mistake, Asa became angry with Hanani and put the prophet in prison.

Yahweh in Your Walk

The psalmist declared, "Yahweh is my strength and my song; He has become my salvation" (Psalm 118:14). Here is the testimony of a person who recognized his need of strength beyond himself. He found in Yahweh the strength he lacked. Our text indicates that Yahweh searches for those who need His strength and He is faithful to provide all that strength. As the apostle Paul said, "I am able to do all things through Him who strengthens me" (Philippians 4:13).

You probably can identify with those who sense their own weakness, but can you likewise testify of Yahweh supplying all the strength you need? Sometimes we are tempted to despair because of how weak we feel. Perhaps you are dealing with some issue and you just lack the strength to do anything about resolving it. Take heart, most believers will find themselves in a similar situation.

Referring to Paul again, he learned a very important lesson about his own personal weakness. Listen to his testimony: "Therefore, so that I would not exalt myself, a thorn in the flesh was given to me, a messenger of Satan to torment me so I would not exalt myself. Concerning this, I pleaded with the Lord three times to take it away from me. But He said to me, 'My grace is sufficient for you, for power is perfected in weakness.' Therefore, I will most gladly boast all the more about my weaknesses, so that Christ's power may reside in me. So I take pleasure in weaknesses, insults, catastrophes, persecutions, and in pressures, because of Christ. For when I am weak, then I am strong" (2 Corinthians 12:9-10). How about that? Paul discovered that contrary to his weakness being a handicap, it actually resulted in more strength because he relied more on Yeshua for His strength!

When you feel too weak to overcome something that tests your faith, give thanks that you are driven to depend more on Yahweh and His strength. Such a "thorn in the flesh" is actually a blessing. Affirm the words of Paul, "When I am weak, then I am strong."

Yahweh in Your Worship

Yahweh I want my heart to be completely Yours. Thank You for giving all the strength I need in order to be all You would have me be.

June 12

Yahweh Advises Me to Guard My Heart

Yahweh in the Word

> *"Guard your heart above all else, for it is the source of life" (Proverbs 4:23).*

King Solomon wrote most of the proverbs found in the Bible. He was known as the wisest man of his time. The advice he gave others was well worth hearing and heeding. However, toward the end of his life, he failed to follow his own advice. We have the same opportunity to follow the ways of wisdom. Our heart is the inner person we are; here is where life decisions are made.

Yahweh in Your Walk

Perhaps no other word in the Bible is as all inclusive as the term ***heart***. This word refers to the center of the physical, mental, and spiritual life of persons. Our heart includes our will, mind, conscience, emotions, and for believers is the dwelling place of the Holy Spirit and the Lord Jesus. Consider a few biblical statements regarding the heart that speak of its importance:

> "As a man thinks in his heart, so is he" (Proverbs 23:7 KJV).
> "The mouth speaks from the overflow of the heart" (Matthew 12:34).
> "Each person should do as he has decided in his heart" (2 Corinthians 9:7)
> "Love the Lord your God with all your heart…." (Mark 12:30).
> "Man does not see what Yahweh sees, for man sees what is visible, but Yahweh sees the heart" (1Samuel 16:7).
> "You will seek Me and find Me when you search for Me with all your heart" (Jeremiah 29:13).
> "I will give you a new heart and put a new spirit within you; I will remove your heart of stone and give you a heart of flesh" (Ezekiel 36:26).

Can you see just from these few references how important it is to "guard your heart above all else"? Our responsibility is to make certain nothing unclean is permitted to enter our heart. This means we must avoid looking at pictures, books, movies, videos, etc. that tend to corrupt our heart and lead to thoughts that grieve the Holy Spirit. **On the positive side we must seek to fill our heart with Yahweh's Word, as well as information that is wholesome and pleasing to Yahweh.** The psalmist said, "I have treasured Your word in my heart so that I may not sin against You" (Psalm 119:1). Apart from Yahweh's help we cannot guard our heart and keep it clean. We must echo the psalmist's words, "God, create a clean heart for me and renew a steadfast spirit within me" (Psalm 51:10).

Yahweh in Your Worship

I bow myself before You, Holy Yahweh. Take control of my heart and teach me to be diligent in guarding it against all evil. I trust You to fill my heart with love for You and all others. May I always have a heart filled with love for You and all others.

June 13

Yahweh Gives Me a Love Song to Sing

Yahweh in the Word

> "My love is mine and I am his... I am my love's and my love is mine... I belong to my love, and his desire is for me" *(Song of Songs 2:16; 6:3; 7:10).*

The Song of Songs, also known as The Song of Solomon, was probably written by King Solomon as the first verse states. We are told that he was the prolific writer of 3,000 proverbs and 1,005 songs in addition to writing about plants, animal life, birds, reptiles, and fish. And people came from everywhere to listen to his wisdom (1Kings 4:32-34). Our text comes from a vivid description of romantic love between Solomon and one of his many wives.

Yahweh in Your Walk

The love between a husband and his wife is the theme of this remarkable and unique book of the Bible. **Romantic love is God's gift to us and should be celebrated as a pure and holy expression of human affection.** The descriptions of sensual intimacy found herein are paralleled in the love relationship between Yahweh and His people. This love is possessive as our text suggests—He is mine and I am His. George Wade Robinson (1838-1877) was an Irish writer of poems and hymns. He was inspired by reading the Song of Solomon to compose a well-known and loved hymn containing these words:

> His forever, only His; Who the Lord and me shall part?
> Ah, with what a rest of bliss, Christ can fill the loving heart!
> Heav'n and earth may fade and flee, first born light in gloom decline;
> But while God and I shall be, I am His, and He is mine.

Yahweh gave King Solomon a love song to sing. As His beloved children we also are given a love song to sing. We sing of romantic love, as did Solomon, when we experience the intimacy of marriage. **Husbands and wives have every reason to celebrate their love for one another, and to enjoy to the fullest the expression of that love in sexual pleasure.** All this is Yahweh's gift and is to be received with gratitude and experienced in a manner pleasing to Him.

We also have a different kind of love song to sing as we relate personally to our Lord Jesus and to one another in the fellowship of believers. The apostle Paul, more than other biblical writers, compared marital love to that of Christ for His church. He said, "Husbands love your wives, just as Christ loved the church and gave Himself for her" (Ephesians 5:25).

Yahweh in Your Worship

Thank You, Lord Yahweh, for loving me with an everlasting love; help me pass that same love on to my family, church, and those outside Your kingdom. I celebrate Your love for me.

June 14

Yahweh Wants Me to Look Forward to Heaven

Yahweh in the Word

"Precious in the sight of Yahweh is the death of His saints" (Psalm 116:15)

Yahweh places great value on His people passing from this life to be with Him in Heaven.

Yahweh in Your Walk

Fear is a natural response to that which is unknown. For this reason many people fear their own death. However, Yahweh has "turned on the light" regarding what lies beyond the grave. The death of Jesus, followed by His resurrection, ascension, and appearing again to His followers, goes a long way in removing any anxiety we may have about our own departure from this life. **Many other statements from the Bible add to our assurance that what happens to believers after physical death is far better than this side of that inevitable experience.**

Our biblical text today is a good example of this help. Yahweh, who knows all things, looks upon the death of His people as a precious, valuable experience—for them and for Him. One of the earliest biblical descriptions of the true meaning of death is found in this account of Abraham's passing: "He took his last breath and died at a ripe old age, old and contented, and he was gathered to his people" (Genesis 25:8). This same phrase—"was gathered to his people"—is used to describe the death of Isaac, Jacob, Moses, and Aaron. For each of these, as well as for all Yahweh's people, death is literally a home going. The apostle Paul knew this and wrote, "For me living is Christ and dying is gain" (Philippians 1:21).

On March 1, 1981, D. Martyn Lloyd-Jones, well-known Bible scholar, was on his deathbed. He had served as the pastor of London's Westminster Chapel for 49 years. Although he had lost his voice due to his illness, he wrote these words on a piece of paper: "Do not hold me back from glory." This fine servant of Yahweh realized the fact that for a Christian "the best is always yet to be." Life in this world is merely a brief preparation for what lies ahead.

There is an interesting monument in Valladolid, Spain, where Christopher Columbus died in 1506. This monument features a lion destroying one of the Latin words that had been part of Spain's motto for centuries, "Ne Plus Ultra," which means "No More Beyond." Travelers there assumed that Spain was the end of the earth. The lion tore away the word "Ne" or "no," making the motto read, "Plus Ultra," there is indeed more beyond, as Columbus discovered. In the same sense Plus Ultra applies to death for a Christian—there is more beyond, and it's the best.

Yahweh in Your Worship

Eternal Yahweh, I worship You as the Giver of life eternal. Thank You for removing from me the fear of death. I look forward to being with You, face-to-face forever. Use me today to help others prepare to meet You.

June 15

Yahweh Makes This a Special Day for Me

Yahweh in the Word

> "This is the day Yahweh has made; let us rejoice and be glad in it" (Psalm 118:24).

The psalmist chose to celebrate the present day as a gift from Yahweh—a day created by Him for the psalmist to use in a joyful manner.

Yahweh in Your Walk

What are you expecting from this day? **Regardless of what may happen, you can make the choice to rejoice and be glad, simply because you know that Yahweh made this day as a gift to you.** Here's an example of this positive attitude: An elderly Christian woman had come to live in a retirement center. The attendant who welcomed her began to describe her new room as he pushed her wheelchair down a corridor. The woman said, "O I know I will just love my new place!" The attendant said, "But you haven't seen your room yet." She replied, "That has nothing to do with it. Happiness is something you decide on ahead of time. Whether I like my room or not doesn't depend on how the furniture is arranged. It's how I arrange my mind." Well said!

Let's consider some facts about this new day Yahweh has given you. Perhaps these will help you arrange your mind as you walk forward today.

1. Today you have the pleasure of choosing to rejoice and be glad for Yahweh's gift of life.
2. Today you will experience many of life's extras—blessings that are not essential to life, such as seeing colors in nature, smelling pleasant fragrances, hearing melodious sounds, tasting delicious foods, and touching objects that feel soft and warm.
3. Today you will have opportunities to relate to others and be an encouragement to them.
4. Today you can commune with Yahweh through worship and prayers for His kingdom to come and His will to be done.
5. Today you can celebrate the gift of eternal life, knowing that the best is yet to come.

> This is the day Yahweh has made; He calls the hours His own;
> Let heaven rejoice, let earth be glad, and praise surround the throne.—Watts

Yahweh in Your Worship

Gracious Yahweh, I seize this once-in-a-lifetime opportunity to experience all You have for me in this new day which You have made just for me. I look forward to walking with You through the pleasures and privileges You have prepared for me. Help me be alert to all the reasons for worshiping You as we journey together. May this be a day for celebrating Your eternal life in my experiences here and now.

June 16

Yahweh Invites Me to Seek Him

Yahweh in the Word

> "Seek Yahweh while He may be found; call to Him while He is near. Let the wicked one abandon his way and the sinful one his thought; let him return to Yahweh, so He may have compassion on him, and to our God, for He will freely forgive" (Isaiah 55:6-7).

We find many invitations in the Bible from Yahweh; He continually reaches out to welcome all who seek a meaningful relationship with Him. His promise is to respond to all seekers with compassion and forgiveness.

Yahweh in Your Walk

Yahweh is unique among all the so-called gods of this world. A study of world religions confirms this truth. His uniqueness is that, unlike these other false gods, He takes the initiative in reaching out to us; He comes to us with His offer of forgiveness and reconciliation. The invitation in our text for today is a clear example of this.

Consider the experience of a man named Saul of Tarsus. We first meet him in the book of Acts where he guards the clothing of those who stoned to death a man named Stephen, one of Jesus' disciples (Acts 7:58-59). The next time we read of Saul he is on his way to the city of Damascus, with the intention of arresting other believers. This young man was a dedicated terrorist as far as Christians were concerned; becoming a follower of Jesus was totally unthinkable to him. And yet, Yeshua took the initiative to intervene in Saul's life. In Acts 9 we read of the amazing conversion experience of this most unlikely candidate. Apart from Yeshua reaching out to Saul and offering him a new way of life, he would never have been saved.

What about your own experience of becoming a believer? You probably did not have a Damascus Road encounter like Saul, but are you aware of Yahweh's initiative in awakening you to your need of Him? You may think that you began this process called salvation, but the truth is—He reached out to you first. And His invitation calls you to turn from your ways of rebellion against Him and receive His compassion and forgiveness. What an amazing miracle!

Think about His invitation to seek Him **while** He may be found, and to call on Him **while** He is near. Now He is available, but that will not always be true. The time may come when this invitation is no longer valid. **If you have not responded, now is the time to accept His offer**. You may have family members or friends who need your encouragement to hear and receive His promised forgiveness and compassion. Pray about reaching out to them in His appointed way.

Yahweh in Your Worship

Thank You for including me in Your work of saving sinners. Your mercy and grace have made possible my restoration to You. I worship You with praise, thanksgiving, and the offer of myself to be Your witness today. Make me aware of those in my circle of acquaintance whom You are seeking to redeem. Give me Your compassion to share this good news of Your salvation.

June 17

Yahweh's Thoughts and Ways Are Far Beyond My Understanding

Yahweh in the Word

> *"For My thoughts are not your thoughts and your ways are not My ways. This is Yahweh's declaration. For as the heaven is higher than earth, so My ways are higher than your ways, and My thoughts than your thoughts (Isaiah 55:8-9).*

Yahweh speaks through Isaiah His prophet to remind readers that His thoughts and ways are infinitely higher and greater than theirs. All humankind has limits of thought and understanding; Yahweh is infinite.

Yahweh in Your Walk

As you walk through this and every day, you will be confronted with mysteries beyond your comprehension. As a pastor, I have had many occasions when people asked me questions I could not answer. For example, the mystery of the Trinity—how can Yahweh be one God, but three persons—Father, Son, and Holy Spirit? Or other matters, hard to figure out—such as all the wonders of creation; how and when did Yahweh create all things?

Some persons have an attitude that insists on a plausible explanation of all mysteries. They basically say, "If I can't understand it, I won't believe it." On the other hand is the individual who said to me, "I don't have to comprehend all about God. In fact, I want to worship a God who is so great that I cannot grasp all His thoughts and actions." And this is true of Yahweh—as He declared through Isaiah, His thoughts and ways are as far beyond ours as the heavens are higher than the earth.

Having the faith to accept what cannot be explained is part of our human experience. Something as simple as eating food requires faith. We do not know if our meals are safe from toxic elements, yet we consume them without question. Think of the mystery of the internet—who of us can explain how this means of communication works, yet we enjoy using it. My point is that we do not have to understand how something works before we use it. The same is true in the spiritual realm—who can comprehend Yahweh and all His wondrous works? However, by faith, we learn to receive His gifts and be blessed by them.

The term *inscrutable* means incomprehensible, mysterious, beyond understanding. Charles Swindoll, a well-known Christian leader once gave this good advice about dealing with facts beyond our ability to explain: **"Don't try to unscrew the inscrutable!"** Well spoken. We should seek to understand what is within our comprehension, and leave the rest to Yahweh.

Yahweh in Your Worship

Thank You, Yahweh, for being so great and wondrous. And thank You for coming down to our level through Your Son that we might know more about You. I enjoy what I do understand and entrust to You, by faith, all the mysteries of life that I cannot explain. Today, I will walk through this day with a sense of wonder and awe because of Your greatness and goodness.

June 18

My Disappointments Are Sometimes Yahweh's Appointments for Me

Yahweh in the Word

> "Lord, if You had been here, my brother would not have died" (John 11:21, 32).

Both Martha and her sister Mary made this same statement to Jesus regarding the death of their brother Lazarus. Jesus had deliberately waited to arrive four days after Lazarus' death in order to demonstrate His power over death. These sisters were unaware of what He would do.

Yahweh in Your Walk

We all experience disappointments in life—certain things we expected to happen don't turn out like we hoped they would, and we are left feeling disappointed. Martha and Mary sent for Jesus in time for Him to arrive and heal their brother Lazarus before he died. When Jesus did not appear until it was too late, they were disappointed. However, to their surprise and pleasure, Jesus called Lazarus back from the dead and restored him to them. What appeared to be a sad **disappointment** proved to be Yeshua's divine **appointment**.

I read the testimony of an airline pilot who was scheduled to fly a certain plane. At the last minute he was informed that another pilot had been chosen to take his place—he was very disappointed, and even angry that this had happened. Later that day he heard that the plane had been hijacked by terrorists and crashed, killing everyone on board. Then he realized that Yahweh had spared his life that he might be a witness of His providence.

Can you think of times when your disappointments have turned out to be good? If we begin each day by committing that day to Yahweh, we will often discover that His plans are far better than ours, and when some of our plans do not work out, it is because He has something better in mind for us. **So, as you walk through each day, watch for the good that often comes from disappointments.** Ask Yahweh to teach you what He has in store that is better than you planned.

One Monday morning I went to my office and found a note on my desk that I was to meet with my manager at a given time. I assumed he wanted an update on several conferences I had been leading in other states. To my surprise, my meeting was with him and a person from the personnel department. They handed me a paper showing my early retirement benefits—I had just been fired! What a shock; what a disappointment! However, I found out later that Yahweh had other plans for me that proved to be much better than I ever expected. This apparent loss was part of His appointment for my promotion. **Keep looking beyond your disappointments; Yahweh's ways are always better than your ways.**

Yahweh in Your Worship

How grateful I am, O Yahweh, that You have plans for me that are far better than I can imagine. Teach me to always trust You to work Your best through all my life experiences. Use me today as a witness of Your goodness and faithfulness. Forgive me when I have failed to recognize Your hand at work in my affairs. Thank You for keeping Your promise to always guide me.

June 19

Yahweh Has Me Nearer My Home Today

Yahweh in the Word

> "For we know that if our temporary, earthly dwelling is destroyed, we have a building from God, an eternal dwelling in the heavens, not made with hands... we are confident and satisfied to be out of the body and at home with the Lord. Therefore, whether we are at home or away, we make it our aim to be pleasing to Him" (2 Corinthians 5:1, 8-9).

Paul wanted his readers to find comfort in the fact that life in this body is temporary; this temporary dwelling place must die. He went on to assure them that Yahweh has prepared an eternal, permanent home with Him. Our purpose then is to please Him in every way.

Yahweh in Your Walk

I recently read about an older Christian who was greeted this way by a friend, "It's good to see that you are still in the land of the living!" He replied, "Oh, I'm not in the land of the living; I'm actually in the land of the dying, but I look forward someday to being in the land of the living, when I'm in heaven." Isn't that an interesting and accurate statement? We all are in the land of the dying because everyone here must eventually die, and we are getting closer to that appointment every day. Thus, the land of the living is not here but in heaven.

Too often we think of this life as being the main event, and we must get all we can while we can. Actually, this life is more like a warm-up in preparation for the main event. Such a truth can have a large effect upon our sense of values. Rather than laying up treasures and pleasures here, we ought to be concerned about laying up treasures in heaven, just as our Lord said, "Don't collect for yourselves treasures on earth, where moth and rust destroy and where thieves break in and steal. But collect for yourselves treasures in heaven, where neither moth nor rust destroys, and where thieves don't break in and steal. For where your treasure is there you heart will be also" (Matthew 6:19-21). Where are your best treasures being kept?

In the light of these truths about heaven, I try not to think of myself as getting older, rather of getting nearer—just as these lines from an old gospel song declare:

> One sweetly solemn thought comes to me o'er and o'er; I am nearer to my home today than I've ever been before.
> Nearer my Father's house, where the many mansions be; nearer the great white throne, nearer the crystal sea.
> Nearer the bound of life where we lay our burdens down; nearer leaving the cross, nearer gaining the crown.—Phoebe Cary 1824-1871

Yahweh in Your Worship

Gracious Lord, I look forward to that day when I will worship You with all Your children in heaven. Help me prepare for that by being Your faithful servant and witness today.

June 20

Yeshua Wants Me to Repent

Yeshua in the Word

> *"From then on Jesus (Yeshua) began to preach, 'Repent because the kingdom of heaven has come near'" (Matthew 4:17).*

Both Jesus and John the Baptist began their public ministries with the same message—calling upon their hearers to repent, declaring that the kingdom of heaven was near and available.

Yeshua in Your Walk

Do you often think of your need for repentance? Most Christians know that a person must repent and believe the gospel message in order to be saved. However, the need for repentance continues as long as we live in this world because we continue to sin after our conversion. The word *repent* literally means "to change your way of thinking." For example, before we are saved we may think we are capable of managing our own life without God. We must change that way of independent thinking in order to humble ourselves before Him and seek His mercy and grace. But there are other areas of our life where a change in thinking needs to occur. This fact is the reason for our ongoing need of repentance. Whenever we sin, we must also repent and confess.

The classic biblical illustration of the meaning of repentance is found in the story of the Prodigal Son (Luke 15:11-31). The attitude or way of thinking shown by both sons reveals much about the true nature of repentance and the lack of it. The younger son who left his family and went to a far country was helped to repent by coming to the end of his independence—wanting to eat with the hogs he was hired to feed. His change in thinking is seen in his return home with a confession of sin on his lips.

The older brother also needed to change his way of thinking about his brother and their father. But the story ends with no indication of repentance on his part. Both sons were guilty of sin, one found forgiveness through repentance and confession; the other remained alienated from his family as he hardened his heart.

The psalmist gave us a great example to follow when he prayed, "Search me, God, and know my heart; test me and know my concerns. See if there is any offensive way in me; lead me in the everlasting way" (Psalm 139:23-24). Why not offer that kind of prayer for yourself on a regular basis? You may have sinful attitudes that need repentance, confession, and the claim of forgiveness and cleansing. **Never assume that your need of repentance is over; Yahweh will lead you to repent as needed when you daily commit yourself to His leading.**

Yeshua in Your Worship

O Yeshua, Lord of my life, I come before Your throne to offer the sacrifices of praise and thanksgiving. How merciful and kind You are to me. Make me aware of any way of thinking that displeases You; show me Your ways and lead me there. Let the words of my mouth and the meditation of my heart be acceptable in Your sight, my Lord and my Redeemer.

June 21

Yahweh Wants Me to Be Disciplined as I Run Life's Race

Yahweh in the Word

> "Don't you know that the runners in a stadium all race, but only one receives the prize? Run in such a way to win the prize. Now everyone who competes exercises self-control in everything. However, they do it to receive a crown that will face away, but we a crown that will never fade away. Therefore I do not run like one who runs aimlessly or box like one beating the air. Instead, I discipline my body and bring it under strict control, so that after preaching to others, I myself will not be disqualified" (1 Corinthians 9:24-27).

Paul often used athletic events as illustrations of the demands for living a disciplined Christian life. Here he appeals for his readers to keep their bodies under strict control in order to finish the race of life successfully and receive an eternal reward.

Yahweh in Your Walk

Several years ago my friend Rodney Whaley and his team of sled dogs participated in the annual Iditarod Trail Race in Alaska. This race covers a 1,049-mile route from Anchorage to Nome. In 2011, a record time was set by John Baker, who covered the entire route in 8 days, 19 hours, 46 minutes, and 39 seconds. These "mushers," as they are called, give serious time to preparing for this grueling race against both time and the elements. They are disciplined both physically and mentally in order to endure this most rigorous challenge.

Rodney also disciplines himself for a far more significant and challenging race than the Iditarod, and that is the race called The Christian Life. He chooses to give priority to this kind of discipline because he knows the ultimate reward is one that is unfading and eternal. Included in the final biblical message of the apostle Paul are these words regarding the reward he anticipated: "I have fought the good fight, I have finished the race, I have kept the faith. There is reserved for me in the future the crown of righteousness, which the Lord, the righteous Judge, will give me on that day, and not only to me, but to all those who have loved His appearing" (2 Timothy 4:7-8).

Are you a disciplined disciple of Yeshua? What actions will you take today to control your body, mind, and spirit for His sake? **Today would be an excellent time to begin following those disciplines that can help produce a godly lifestyle.** Included in these practices should be such matters as: a plan of daily Bible reading and study, Scripture memorization, private worship, intercessory prayer, and planned ways of serving the Lord by helping others. As you consider these basic disciplines, you may offer excuses for not having enough time or some other way out, but **the truth is—if you really want to do these things, you will find a way.** Remember, you are preparing to meet Yeshua; will you receive an eternal, unfading reward from Him?

Yahweh in Your Worship

I do love You and sincerely want to please You in all I am and do. Help me be more disciplined.

June 22

Yahweh's Ultimate Plan for Me Is to Make Me a Christ-like Person

Yahweh in the Word

> "We all, with unveiled faces, are looking as in a mirror at the glory of the Lord and are being transformed into the same image from glory to glory; this is from the Lord who is the Spirit" (2 Corinthians 3:18).

These words of the apostle Paul refer to a miraculous transformation which the Holy Spirit seeks to accomplish in every person who believes in Jesus and sincerely seeks to conform to Yahweh's purpose.

Yahweh in Your Walk

If you are a serious follower of Jesus who regularly opens the Bible and allows the Holy Spirit to teach you, then **you are not the same person you were a year ago**. You may not be conscious of any significant change, but this and other biblical texts reveal the fact that Yahweh's plan is for you and all believers to progressively become more and more like His Son. You are being "transformed" into His image. The word "transformed" is the same as "transfigured" in the accounts of Jesus' transfiguration (Matthew 17:2). It describes a change on the outside that comes from within. Our English word ***metamorphosis*** is a transliteration of this Greek term. Metamorphosis is the process whereby an insect changes from a larva into a pupa and then into a mature insect—a change that comes from within. **The Holy Spirit is working within you to change you outwardly. Your attitude and actions will reflect this transformation.**

Each time you are exposed to Yahweh's truth in the Bible, the Holy Spirit works to make a gradual change in your way of thinking. He also uses your life experiences to help you become more Christ-like, more loving, kind, patient, and faithful. As you pray, acknowledge this work of grace, claiming Yahweh's transforming work. One of my favorite songs expresses this.

> O to be like Thee! Blessed Redeemer, this is my constant longing and prayer;
> Gladly I'll forfeit all of earth's treasure, Jesus, Thy perfect likeness to wear.
> O to be like Thee! Full of compassion, loving, forgiving, tender and kind;
> Helping the helpless, cheering the fainting, seeking the wand'ring sinner to find.
> O to be like Thee! While I am pleading, pour out Thy Spirit, fill with Thy love;
> Make me a temple meet for Thy dwelling, fit me for life and heaven above.
> O to be like Thee! O to be like Thee, Blessed Redeemer, pure as Thou art!
> Come in Thy sweetness, come in Thy fullness—stamp Thine own image deep on my heart.
> —Thomas Obadiah Chisholm (1806-1860)

Yahweh in Your Worship

Holy Father, how amazing that Your plan is for me to become Christ-like. I worship You and yield myself to Your control this day. I long to exhibit those beautiful virtues that only Your Spirit can produce through me. Thank You for Your patience with me.

June 23

Yahweh Wants Me to Be a Good Citizen

Yahweh in the Word

> "Submit to every human authority because of the Lord, whether to the Emperor as the supreme authority or to governors as those sent out by him to punish those who do what is evil and to praise those who do what is good. For it is God's will that you silence the ignorance of foolish people by doing good. As God's slaves, live as free people, but don't use your freedom as a way to conceal evil. Honor everyone. Love the brotherhood. Fear God. Honor the Emperor" (1 Peter 2:13-17).

Evidence shows that the apostle Peter wrote this letter while he was in Rome. At this time Christians were being persecuted by the Roman government, led by the emperor Nero. Peter wrote to encourage believers who were suffering for their faith. The words in this text call on them to submit to the government in spite of its corruption.

Yahweh in Your Walk

Would you consider yourself to be a good citizen? If every citizen performed civic duties as you do, would this be a better or worse nation? Various biblical references call on you to be a good citizen. For example, Paul wrote: "Everyone must submit to the governing authorities, for there is no authority except from God, and those that exist are instituted by God.... For government is God's servant for your good. But if you do wrong, be afraid, because it does not carry the sword for no reason" (Romans 13:1-4).

Let's consider some ways you can be the good citizen Yahweh wants you to be. First, pray for those who are leaders in government. Again, Paul wrote to Timothy: "First of all, then I urge that petitions, prayers, intercession, and thanksgivings be made for everyone, for kings and all those who are in authority, so that we may lead a tranquil and quiet life in all godliness and dignity. This is good, and it pleases God our Savior, who wants everyone to be saved and to come to the knowledge of the truth" (1 Timothy 2:1-4). Your prayers invite Yahweh to influence political leaders in their lifestyles and decisions. **Many are quick to criticize such leaders, but how many are serious about praying for them?** Which do you think will make the most difference?

Second, be a registered voter and participate in every election—locally and nationally. This means you will want to be well informed about issues and candidates. **Learn about what is at stake and vote for those whom you believe will represent you best.** Always give preference to those candidates who have strong Christian reputations and will seek to uphold biblical standards, regardless of political party affiliations. Stand strong for justice and righteousness.

Finally, be willing to be involved in political life as Yahweh leads you. He calls you to be salt and light—making a difference by your example and influence. Get involved; be His witness.

Yahweh in Your Worship

Yahweh, You are my sovereign King. I choose to honor and serve You in all I do.

June 24

Yahweh Has Given Me Abilities to Use for Him

Yahweh in the Word

> "Yahweh also spoke to Moses: 'Look, I have appointed by name Bezalel son of Uri, son of Hur, of the tribe of Judah. I have filled him with God's Spirit, with wisdom, understanding, and ability in every craft to design artistic works in gold, silver, and bronze, to cut gemstones for mounting, and to carve wood for work in every craft'" (Exodus 31:1-5).

Yahweh commanded Moses to make a special worship center for His people. He gave specific details for each part of this amazing portable tabernacle and all its furnishings. Bezalel was just one of the craftsmen whom Yahweh gifted for this amazing work.

Yahweh in Your Walk

Do you look with amazement at the finished work of various craftsmen? When I see what artists, woodcarvers, sculptors, workers with needle and thread, and other artisans do, I am impressed with their ability and say, "How can they do that?" When other gifted persons perform music or ballet or feats of acrobatics, I stand in wonder at such skill. What amazing talents some people have! Where did they get these impressive abilities?

Our Scripture text for today tells of how Yahweh declared to Moses that He was giving various skills to different workers so they could produce what was needed for the new tabernacle. He made clear that their abilities came directly as gifts from Him. Is this not a revelation to us about how all persons obtain their skills? **Yahweh decides who has certain abilities to be used in accomplishing His purposes.**

Think about yourself for a moment. What abilities, skills, talents, etc., do you possess? What is it you can do, and enjoy doing, that many others cannot do? Where did you get these special interests and why do you have them? These questions deserve careful thought and proper answers. As Paul asked the Corinthian Christians, "What do you have that you didn't receive? (1 Corinthians 4:7). No matter what special talents you have, the ultimate source is Yahweh's gifts to you. **He gave you the ability, the desire to develop the ability, and the strength and wisdom to use the ability—it all comes from Him!**

So what does all this mean in a practical way? **First**, you should be humble about your abilities; you do not deserve credit for them—they are gifts to you. **Second**, remember who gave them to you? Be thankful to Yahweh as the Source of all you have that is good. **Third**, be willing to use whatever skills you have for Him and His kingdom. Your talents were not given to you to make you rich or famous or admired; He is the One to be honored by all you can do. Be a good steward. **Seek ways to use your God-given skills in a way that advances His kingdom.**

Yahweh in Your Worship

Thank You, Lord of life, for all You have given me. I come to lay these gifts on Your altar as a sacrifice of thanksgiving. I know that apart from Your help I can do nothing. Get honor from me.

June 25

Yahweh's Name Is Magnificent

Yahweh in the Word

> "Yahweh, our Lord, how magnificent is Your name throughout the earth....
> Yahweh, our Lord, how magnificent is Your name throughout the earth!"
> (Psalm 8:1, 9).

This psalm of David is a hymn of celebration that focuses attention on the greatness and glory of Yahweh. This masterpiece of praise begins and ends with the same statement about His magnificence.

Yahweh in Your Walk

In biblical times a person's name often told something about them. For example Moses' name means "drawn out"—since he was drawn out of the river where his mother placed him in a basket. Abraham's name means "father of nations," and so he was. Jacob ("cheater") had his name changed to Israel ("prince of God"). Many other examples could be given. Yahweh revealed His name, which means "I AM" to Moses at a burning bush in the desert. He wanted Moses to know that as he sought to lead the Israelites out of Egypt, through the wilderness and up to the land of promise, Yahweh would be with him and provide for every need.

Although Yahweh has numerous terms in combination to His name, as you have discovered in these devotionals, His name is Yahweh (I AM), which communicates to us that He is all we need to become all He wants us to be. His reply to whatever we need is always the same: "I AM."

Yahweh also has many titles that describe Him, such as God, Father, Lord, Almighty, Redeemer, Master, Teacher, Savior, King of kings, etc. But He has just one single name—Yahweh. **You will find many books written on the names (plural) of God, but the truth is—He has one name and many titles, not many names.** The same is true of us. For example, I have one name—James Earl Harvey, but many titles, such as son, father, husband, pastor, teacher, author.

There are more than 500 occurrences in the Bible of the term "name" referring to Yahweh. Each time you could substitute His actual name to make the meaning clearer, such as in our text for today, "Yahweh, our Lord, how magnificent is Your name (Yahweh) throughout the earth!" I suggest you start doing this to make the statements more meaningful. Again, "Our Father in heaven, hallowed be Your name (Yahweh)." His name is magnificent indeed. As He said through Isaiah the prophet, "My people will know My name; therefore they will know on that day that I am He who says: Here I am" (Isaiah 52:6).

Yahweh in Your Worship

Holy Yahweh, thank You for revealing Your sacred name to me. Now I can worship You with greater understanding of who You are. Today I celebrate Your magnificence as the One who has not only created me but also redeemed me and given Yourself to me. I know I can do all that pleases You because You live in me and provide everything I need. Thank You. I trust You to use me to make known to others the truth about Your wonderful name.

June 26

Yahweh Makes Me More than a Conqueror

Yahweh in the Word

> *"Yet in all these things we are more than conquerors through Him who loved us" (Romans 8:37).*

Paul has just given a list of various challenges that may come to believers, such as affliction, anguish, persecutions, famine, danger, sword, and even death. Then he declares that because of God's presence and power, all who trust in Him are enabled to overcome these difficulties.

Yahweh in Your Walk

Our text for today has an interesting phrase: "we are more than conquerors." We know that to conquer something is to overcome it, but how can we be **more** than conquerors? One suggestion is that when a Roman army overcame their enemy, they forced the conquered people to be not only prisoners but also slaves who served them. In a similar manner Paul is saying that those who follow Jesus not only overcome problems but are actually served by these various threats.

When I read this I think of Joni Eareckson Tada who was 18 years-old when she became paralyzed from her shoulders down due to a diving accident. For several years she was very bitter and depressed over this severe disability. But through her walk with Yahweh, she has become more than a conqueror, writing over 40 books to encourage others who struggle with handicaps. She also learned to be an artist by holding a brush in her teeth; and she founded an organization called "Joni and Friends" to help others, and travels widely giving her testimony. In 2010 she was diagnosed with breast cancer, but continues overcoming and inspiring others. These trials could easily have overcome her, however, she has learned to be more than a conqueror through Christ.

Another example is Fanny Crosby who became blind shortly after her birth due to a physician's error. She went on to write more than 8,000 gospel songs and hymns and was known as the "Queen of Gospel Song Writers." On one occasion she was asked if she wished she had normal vision. She replied that her blindness was a gift from God. Here is another example of a person becoming more than a conqueror.

Perhaps you have experienced some kind of trial—some happening that was a threat to your desire to live a normal life. The testimony of persons like Paul, Joni, and Fanny can encourage you to look differently at your difficulties—as you find the courage and power to overcome these challenges through dependence upon Jesus, your testimony can be an encouragement to others.

Yahweh in Your Worship

Thank You, Yahweh, that You are far greater than any problem I face. I choose to worship You as the One who enables me to become more than a conqueror. Help me use this victory to give honor and glory to You. I claim Your strength and wisdom today in dealing with every challenge. Teach me to be a help to others as they struggle with issues beyond their control. I offer myself to You as a witness to Your power to overcome all that hinders true peace of mind.

June 27

Yeshua Gives Me an Abundant Life

Yeshua in the Word

> *"A thief comes only to steal and to kill and to destroy. I have come so that they may have life and have it in abundance" (John 10:10).*

Jesus speaks here about those who are His sheep. As the Good Shepherd He protects His sheep from the enemy (Satan) who seeks to steal, kill, and destroy them. The Good Shepherd has come to provide a life that is secure, satisfying, and abundant in provisions.

Yeshua in Your Walk

The word translated "abundance" in our text literally means "an exceeding measure, above the ordinary." The life that Jesus came to give His followers is more than an improved life, more than a fuller life, more than a more enjoyable life; **He came to give us a new life, one that abounds in love, joy, and peace**. Thom Rainer says it like this: "Deep inside the heart of every Christian is a desire to break out of the shell of the common and to be a part of something miraculous.… People need to know that the normal Christian life is one of victories and even miracles. As one preacher said, 'Christians must forever depart from the sameness, the lameness, and the tameness of their daily routine and experience the authentic abundant Christian life.'"

The New Testament speaks of an abundance of grace (Romans 5:17), an abundance of mercy (1 Peter 1:3), and an abundance of joy (2 Corinthians 8:2). All these are parts of the abundant life Jesus gives to all who trust Him as Savior and submit to Him as Lord. Abundance means overflowing, more than can be contained, and that which abounds. The psalmist spoke of this in the Twenty-Third Psalm when he wrote: "my cup runs over." As benefactors of this kind of life, we are able to give an effective witness regarding the difference Yeshua makes in us.

This kind of super-sufficiency is intended to be the experience of the normal Christian life. If you are not enjoying this special quality of life, you need to examine your personal relationship with Yeshua. **The abundant life is actually His life being lived out in our bodies**. Every believer has Christ living within, seeking to be seen without. When His Spirit is in control of us, His life overflows like an artesian well.

Yeshua in Your Worship

Allow me to suggest a simple discipline that can bring you nearer to the abundant life Jesus came to give you: Pause right now. Relax as you close your eyes in a mood of prayer. Begin your prayer by thanking Yeshua for His presence; spend a few moments worshiping Him with words of praise and adoration. Now claim by faith His promise of an abundant life. Meditate on how this life abounds in peace, joy, and fellowship with Him. Ask Him to be in complete control of you—your body, mind, and spirit. Present yourself as a living sacrifice to Him; thank Him for receiving you and keeping you as His very own sheep. Repeat this discipline every day, adding to it more expressions of worship and submission to Him. You will experience His abundance!

June 28

Yahweh Helps Me to Let Go of Past Hurts

Yahweh in the Word

> "One thing I do: Forgetting what is behind and reaching forward to what is ahead, I pursue as my goal the prize promised by God's heavenly call in Christ Jesus. Therefore, all who are mature should think this way (Philippians 3:13-15).

The apostle Paul gave this testimony to his readers in the city of Philippi. They remembered that when he and Silas first came to their city they had been arrested, beaten, and imprisoned (Acts 16:12-23). Now he chooses to forget these past grievances and move forward to the ultimate prize of being in heaven. He exhorts them to do the same as evidence of being mature in faith.

Yahweh in Your Walk

Recently, a friend called to "unload" on me, telling me of all the bad things she had endured in her present church fellowship. As I listened to this "poor me" testimony, I thought of these words from Paul. If anyone ever had a good reason to complain about being mistreated, he would head the list. And yet, Paul chose to take the "high road" and focus, not on past disappointments, but on future blessings.

Today you face the same choice—you can whine about all the bad things that have happened in your past, or you can focus on all the good—now and forever. Which will you choose? When Paul said he was "forgetting what is behind," he did not mean that he could simply erase past events from his memory. He was saying that he refused to go back in his mind and re-live these hurts. The fact is—you cannot change the past; it's done, over, never to be affected by present thoughts or actions. So, let it go! Move on to those things where you can make a difference—today and tomorrow.

Paul calls you to always be "reaching forward to what is ahead." I think of my friend Gerald Stow who has had more than his share of trouble—such as the typical criticisms he received, first as a pastor, then as the leader of a denominational agency, plus several bouts with cancer. And yet, I have never heard him complain. Rather, he celebrates each day as a new opportunity to press on to what is ahead. What a blessing to be his friend; he inspires all who know him because of his positive outlook on life.

How about your reputation? Do your friends think of you as the president of the "Poor Me Club" or as a mature believer who chooses to let go of pain and focus on gain? Join Paul in this "one thing I do" commitment—be positive, be hopeful, be thankful, be mature.

Yahweh in Your Worship

Gracious Lord, You have been so good to me. I worship You as the Giver of all that is good—even the gift of being able to forget past wrongs and focus on future blessings. Help me be an example of a person who is forgiving and forgetting—just as You have done toward me. Today, I choose to celebrate Your favors by worshiping You in spirit and in truth.

June 29

Yahweh Gives Me Hope

Yahweh in the Word

> "Praise the God and Father of our Lord Jesus Christ. According to His great mercy, He has given us a new birth into a living hope through the resurrection of Jesus Christ from the dead and into an inheritance that is imperishable, uncorrupted, and unfading, kept in heaven for you" (1 Peter 1:3-4).

The apostle Peter sent this letter to fellow believers who had been scattered from their homes due to persecution. He offered comfort to them by reminding them of the "living hope" they had been given through the resurrection of Jesus. In Him they had a permanent inheritance of a home in heaven—something persecution could not take from them.

Yahweh in Your Walk

When I was first asked to consider serving as the interim pastor of the **Little Hope Baptist Church,** I thought someone was playing a joke on me—surely no church would have that name! However, after serving there as an interim on two different occasions, my wife and I came to love the dear people of this fellowship—originally named for the Little Hope community where it was founded many years ago. These saints made us feel so loved and appreciated.

Thoughts of changing the church's name began surfacing during my last interim there. On an Easter service, I read the text for our devotion today. As I came to the words "living hope," I paused to say, "Wouldn't that be a good name for this church?" Later, the members voted to re-name their fellowship, **Living Hope Baptist Church**. Today this family of faith is seeing strong growth, a new enlarged worship and fellowship structure, with many new members.

Think about the living hope you have—the assurance of life abundant and everlasting—all because of the life, death, burial, resurrection, ascension and return of the Lord Jesus. Regardless of your circumstances, this hope is secure; nothing can ever take it from you. You have an inheritance in heaven that is "imperishable, uncorrupted, and unfading." Recently, I saw a sign which read: Hope means **H**old **O**n **P**ain **E**nds! I like that. Whatever pain you may experience in this life—physically, mentally, spiritually, or otherwise—will ultimately end. All your present discomfort is temporary—the best is always yet to be!

At one time you may have had little hope, but now, in Jesus, you have living hope! How thankful to have such a blessed assurance. **Now, seek to be a good steward of such comforting truth as you reach out to those who have no hope.**

Yahweh in Your Worship

I worship You, O Yahweh, giver of all hope. Thank You for delivering me from all fear of the future. I rest in Your promise of an eternal inheritance with You. Help me to be actively seeking to communicate this good news to others. I pray for opportunities to be a bold witness of You.

June 30

Yahweh Assures Me of His Love

Yahweh in the Word

> *"'I have loved you,' says Yahweh" (Malachi 1:2).*

The name of this last prophetic voice of the Old Testament is Malachi, a name meaning "My messenger." He was sent to remind Yahweh's people of His unchanging love for them, in spite of their rebellion and disobedience toward Him.

Yahweh in Your Walk

Can you recall times when you have felt completely unworthy of Yahweh's love for you? Perhaps you even doubted if He actually did love you due to your behavior or attitude. Such feelings are typical for those who believe that Yahweh is holy and righteous. We wonder: How could a holy God love someone as unholy as I? Malachi was sent by Yahweh to point out His displeasure with His people, but also assure them of His mercy, forgiveness, and love. His first words through His prophet were, "I have loved you." Yahweh anticipated His people responding to this affirmation of divine love by asking, "How have You loved us?" (1:2).

The remainder of Malachi's message expresses Yahweh's answer to this question. First, He tells His people to **look back**—their history reveals His love because He chose them and has blessed them in many special ways. Then, He calls on them to **look up**—His love is clearly expressed in the fact that He sent Malachi to warn them of the consequences of their sins. Finally, He asks them to **look ahead**—the book ends with a promise of the future "day of the Lord," when all that's wrong will be made right.

We can learn valuable lessons from these ancient words. Yahweh's unchanging love for us can be discovered by His actions on our behalf in the past, present, and future. Whenever you are tempted to doubt His love for you, pause and think of His goodness to you in so many ways—most notably, His gift of life through His Son, the Lord Jesus. He is the living love of Yahweh in your past, present, and future. As the apostle John declared, "This is how we have come to know love: He laid down His life for us" (1 John 3:16). These words speak primarily of the cross; however, Yeshua continues laying down His life for us presently as He intercedes for us in heaven, and as He prepares for His return for us in the future. **Does Yahweh love you? YES!**

This book of Malachi is of special interest concerning these devotionals that focus on "Yahweh." Malachi repeats the name Yahweh 46 times in the 55 verses of his book—more frequently than any other Old Testament writer. His favorite term is Yahweh Sabaoth—"the LORD of hosts" (24 times). These facts serve as a clear reminder to us of the prominence of this special, holy name.

Yahweh in Your Worship

Thank You, gracious Yahweh, for giving me this reassurance of Your great love for me. Help me to prove my love for You through heart-felt worship as well as obedience to Your commands. I long to serve You with greater zeal and commitment, and to be Your witness to others.

July 1
Yahweh Is Always Present with Me

Yahweh in the Word

> *"The perimeter of the city will be six miles, and the name of the city from that day on will be: Yahweh Is There" (Ezekiel 48:35).*

The prophet Ezekiel was with Yahweh's people in Babylon where they had been taken captive due to their disobedience to Him. His role was to offer hope to these prisoners, so far from their homeland. He uses the statement, "Then they shall know that I am Yahweh" over 60 times indicating the purpose for their captivity. Verse 35 is the last one in the book of Ezekiel. Yahweh offered assurance to His people that He had a future for them including the fact that He would always be with them—their ultimate residence would be a city named Yahweh Shammah (I AM present). Thirty-three years later in 538 B.C. King Cyrus issued a decree permitting them to return to their homeland. More than 40,000 exiles accepted his offer.

Yahweh in Your Walk

Yahweh Shammah (pronounced YAH-way SHAUM-mah) is the fifth combination we will consider in this series. In one sense this is the most significant of all these terms. I say that because unless He is present with us none of the other attributes will make any difference to us. **How comforting and reassuring to know that Yahweh is always with us**. As the psalmist declared, "Even though I go through the darkest valley, I fear no danger, for You are with me; Your rod and Your staff—they comfort me" (Psalm 23:4).

What an incredible truth—Yahweh, the sovereign God of the entire universe promises to always be with you! Could anything be more amazing than this? How could you ever fear whatever challenging life experiences may come? **As you consider overcoming obstacles remember—you can't but He can. Put your trust in Him and move forward with the assurance of His victorious power.**

So as you walk through this day, remember that Yahweh is present with you. **You know this is true, not because you have some feeling that He is near, but because you believe His promise.** Yeshua said, "Remember, I am with you always, to the end of the age" (Matthew 28:20). Moses gave these words to Yahweh's people, "It is Yahweh your God who goes with you; He will not leave you or forsake you" (Deuteronomy 31:6).

Yahweh in Your Worship

If you are like most Christians, you often offer a prayer like this, "Dear Lord, please be **with** me today," or "Please be **with** me in my job." Have you ever considered this kind of prayer to be unnecessary? In fact it is contrary to faith. If we believe Yahweh's promises, we know He is always **with** us. A much better prayer would be, "Thank You that You are with me now and always. I claim the wonderful promise of Your continual presence with me. Help me to become more aware of Your unfailing presence and of the difference You can make in all I am and do.

July 2

Yahweh's Presence Gives Me All the Power I Need

Yahweh in the Word

> *"You will receive power when the Holy Spirit has come upon you, and you will be My witnesses in Jerusalem, in all Judea and Samaria, and to the ends of the earth" (Acts 1:8).*

These are the words of Jesus to those first disciples. The book of Acts is the incredible story of what these simple fishermen, along with other untrained, ordinary men and women, were able to accomplish following their being filled with the Holy Spirit. This same Spirit of Yahweh is given to every believer at the moment of their new birth. In fact, He is the new nature that becomes a part of us. The Holy Spirit is the One who is with us always—the same as Yahweh Shammah.

Yahweh in Your Walk

My cousin, Mike Laufer, has always been rather timid and shy. When we were younger and attended family events, he would be very quiet and reserved while others were talking and being engaged in various activities. His tendency to be withdrawn was probably one reason he did not marry until he was much older than the rest of us. His wife, Fay, is just the opposite of him, very outgoing, talkative, and social in nature. She has been very good for Mike; they make an effective team of workers for Yahweh.

Several years ago, they felt Yahweh leading them to volunteer as missionaries to help serve refugees in Greece. As part of their preparation they were trained to share their faith and give witness to these homeless people who were mostly Muslim in their beliefs. Sometime later, on one of their stateside visits, Mike's wife told me how bold and vocal Mike had become as he witnessed to these refugees. As I thought about this remarkable change in him, I realized this was the work of the Holy Spirit working through His servant. He had empowered this disciple, who was timid by nature, to speak freely.

One expression of Yahweh's power is found in the word "boldness." Some form of this term occurs nine times in Acts, referring to speech that is clear, confident, and unhindered. Repeatedly, these unschooled men and women who are described in this missionary book gave confident witness regarding their reception of new life in Christ. Even when they stood before courts of law, they were fearless in their testimonies of what they had experienced as followers of Jesus. When threatened with beatings and imprisonment, they were bold as they affirmed their refusal to cease speaking in His name. **As we yield to the control of Yahweh Shammah, He will produce this same freedom of speech in us.** We, too, will disregard personal safety as we speak clearly and confidently of His saving, transforming power.

Yahweh in Your Worship

I worship You, O Yahweh Shammah. I'm so thankful to know You are always with me. I choose to seize this day of opportunities to be Your confident witness. Make me sensitive to each person I meet today, and give a clear expression of Your love and truth through all I do and say.

July 3

Yahweh Shammah Is Constantly at Work in Me

Yahweh in the Word

> *"For it is God who is working in you, enabling you both to desire and to work out His good purpose" (Philippians 2:13).*

Here is a truly remarkable truth. According to this and other biblical references, **Yahweh is not only present with us and in us but He also is working in us!** Think about this: Yahweh, the One who created and upholds all things by His mighty power, actually lives in us by His Spirit, and—is actively at work in each of us! Such a truth amazes me! I confess that I cannot comprehend all that this means, but I claim this incredible blessing by faith. Now, the question is—what is He up to in us? What is He working to accomplish?

Yahweh in Your Walk

A man began attending the worship services where I was the pastor. One Sunday he came forward in the invitation time and told me he wanted to accept Jesus as his Savior. Later I asked him to tell me about this decision. His words were, "Preacher, I don't know what happened, but somethin' got to workin' on me, and I knew I needed the Lord."

I was pleased to be able to tell him that the Holy Spirit was the One workin' on him. Paul talks about this when he says, "I am sure of this, that He who started a good work in you will carry it on to completion until the day of Christ Jesus" (Philippians 1:6). **Yahweh lives in us and does His work in us by the Holy Spirit. This work includes conviction about our need of a Savior, plus all else needed for our growth and service.**

Our friends, Ron and Regena Burrow, accompanied us on a missions trip to the Philippines. This was their first time to participate in planned personal evangelism. As we visited many poor Filipinos in their flimsy huts both Ron and Regena were moved with compassion as they reached out to these needy people. It was obvious that Yahweh was doing His work of ministry through them. After returning home, they kept in touch with some of these friends to help them more.

As you walk through this day, carry some object with you—like a small battery—to remind you of the power of Yahweh at work in you continuously. Again, Paul writing about the maturity needed by all believers said, "I labor for this striving with His strength that works powerfully in me" (Colossians 1:29). The terms he used for "strength that works" are from the root word meaning *energy*. Yahweh is literally energizing us by His resident Spirit that we may become mature in faith and serve with power. Today when you see or feel this battery or other object you carry, offer a prayer of thanks for Yahweh Shammah and His activity in you.

Yahweh in Your Worship

Yahweh Shammah, thank You for Your presence at work in me and in all Your people today. I am trusting You to perform whatever is needed to cause me to become the witness I should be.

July 4

Yahweh Is My Source of True Freedom

Yahweh in the Word

> "The Spirit of the Lord God is on Me, because the LORD (Yahweh) has anointed Me to bring good news to the poor. He has sent Me to heal the brokenhearted, to proclaim liberty to the captives and freedom to the prisoners; to proclaim the year of Yahweh's favor, and the day of our God's vengeance; to comfort all who mourn..." (Isaiah 61:1-2).

Jesus began His public ministry by going to His hometown synagogue on a Sabbath day and reading these words from the prophet Isaiah. Afterwards He said, "Today as you listen, this Scripture has been fulfilled" (Luke 4:16-19). In other words, He was claiming to be the One Isaiah wrote about, some 700 years earlier. Included in this prophecy is the promise of freedom from the bondage of sin.

Yahweh in Your Walk

Today we Americans celebrate our liberty as a nation. The Declaration of Independence was signed on July 4, 1776. We certainly have much to be thankful for as we enjoy all the freedoms guaranteed by this historic event. Pause today and meditate on all the sacrifices that have been made by fellow Americans for the preservation of this freedom during these past years. How blessed we are to live without fear of persecution for basic human rights.

However, **a more significant freedom is available to all persons of all nations and all generations—the liberty offered by Yahweh to all believers through His Son, our Lord Jesus Christ.** Surely this is "good news to the poor" and "liberty to the captives."

The worst bondage is to be enslaved to sin and its consequences. **Apart from a personal relationship to Jesus, every person lives as a spiritual prisoner to sin.** But Yahweh sent His Son to set us free. He said, "Everyone who commits sin is a slave of sin... if the Son sets you free, you really will be free" (John 8:34-36). Here is the source of real freedom. By paying our debt to sin, the Lord Jesus offers us release from bondage to both the power and practice of sin. We become free in Him to live abundantly.

Walk through this day in the freedom Yahweh supplies. Claim by faith His liberating presence as well as His power to overcome sinful thoughts, words, and actions. And be a witness of this freedom to those you relate to—at home, school, work, and play. **No other cause is more worthy of our participation and support than this.**

Yahweh in Your Worship

How truly grateful I am O Yahweh for the freedom You have given me. Thank You that I can seize all the opportunities I have to live at liberty today. I want to extend this same liberty to everyone I meet. Make me aware of those You bring to my path to hear this good news. Teach me to pray effectively for those in other countries who have never heard this liberating truth. Thank You for sending Your missionaries to the ends of the earth that all may know You.

July 5

Yahweh Sometimes Says No to Me

Yahweh in the Word

> *"At that time I begged Yahweh… Please let me cross over and see the beautiful land on the other side of the Jordan… but Yahweh was angry with me… and said, 'That's enough! Do not speak to Me again about this matter'"* (Deuteronomy 3:23-26).

These are the sad words of Moses as he asked Yahweh to allow him to enter the Promised Land. However, Moses forfeited that privilege by his earlier disobedience. Yahweh denied Moses' request and used Joshua to be the new leader who would take His people to their new homeland.

Yahweh in Your Walk

The Bible records several noteworthy occasions when Yahweh said no to requests from His finest servants. One example is the time recorded by the apostle Paul, "…a thorn in the flesh was given to me so I would not exalt myself. Concerning this, I pleaded with the Lord three times to take it away from me. But He said to me, 'My grace is sufficient for you, for power is perfected in weakness'" (2 Corinthians 12:7-9). Earlier the most significant denial came to our Lord Jesus as He offered this prayer two times just before enduring the cross, "My Father! If it is possible, let this cup pass from Me. Yet not as I will, but as You will" (Matthew 26:39).

In both of these instances Yahweh refused the initial request made of Him because something better came as the result of His denial. Paul became stronger as he was forced to depend more on the Lord. And Jesus became our all-sufficient Redeemer because He went on to endure the cross. We must remember these examples of Yahweh's plans for us being better than ours.

Here is a valuable lesson for us. **Sometimes Yahweh's answer to our requests of Him is no. Not because He wants to withhold His blessing, but because He has something better in store for us—better than what we asked.** What this means is that we should always follow the example of Jesus when He added these important words to His request: "Not as I will, but as You will." Our confidence is in Yahweh's best plan for us, not in our plan for ourselves. He knows us and our actual needs better than we know ourselves.

You may remember an old radio and TV show entitled, "Father Knows Best." These three words remind us of an important biblical truth—**our heavenly Father always knows what is best for His children. And more importantly, gives them what is best.**

Yahweh in Your Worship

Thank You, Yahweh, that there are times when You deny my requests of You because You know my needs much better than I. Teach me to thank You and praise You when Your answers are not what I desire. Help me remember that sometimes my disappointments are actually Your divine appointments for me. Use me to help others understand this important truth so they can discover the benefit of trusting Your answers to their prayers.

July 6

Yeshua Calls Me to Follow Him

Yeshua in the Word

> *"As He (Yeshua) was walking along the Sea of Galilee, He saw two brothers, Simon, who was called Peter, and his brother Andrew. They were casting a net into the sea, since they were fishermen. 'Follow Me,' He told them, 'and I will make you fish for people!'"* (Matt. 4:18-19).

You may remember that "Yeshua" is Jesus' name in Hebrew, meaning "Yahweh is salvation." As He began His public ministry, Yeshua called 12 men to be His disciples (later known as apostles). His invitation to each man was simply, "Follow Me." And His promise was to train them to become "fishers of men." In other words, these who chose to follow Yeshua would enlist others to follow Him—from one generation to the next, till the end of time. Following Him basically meant to so believe in Him and trust Him that they would obey Him.

Yeshua in Your Walk

As you progress through each day, do you ever think of yourself as being a disciple of Jesus, one who follows Him? Just as surely as He called Peter and Andrew, and the other 10 first disciples, to follow Him—He calls you! **Yeshua wants you to trust Him to the extent that you willingly seek to obey Him in all things.**

This is one reason Bible study is so essential to discipleship, especially the study of Jesus' life and teachings. Every day we should be reading something Jesus said or did—that is, read the Gospels. As we read these most significant facts, we must also be committed to following what they tell us to do or be.

I remember a woman who became a follower of Jesus after a very worldly lifestyle—she had been a bartender in a local club. One day she told me she wanted to talk to me about a problem she was having. She had read where Jesus said when we pray, we should go into our closet, close the door, and pray to the Father in secret (Matthew 6:6 KJV). She took these words literally and said she found it very crowded and stuffy, kneeling down to pray among all her shoes and clothes in there! How relieved she was when I explained what Jesus meant about praying privately.

If only we all were more concerned about keeping Jesus' teachings! **How about beginning a plan of selecting one of Jesus' commands or instructions and focus for one week on seeking to follow Him in that manner, and then go to another teaching for the next week, and so on.** This kind of serious obedience can literally transform any person. One caution: depend on Him, not yourself, for the power and persistence to keep this discipline going.

Yeshua in Your Worship

Lord Yeshua, I do want to be Your devoted follower. You are indeed, "Yahweh is salvation" and I worship You as the One I choose to follow for the rest of my life. I praise You for calling me to follow You. I gladly seize this day for Your glory in all I think and say and do.

July 7

Yahweh Will Guide Me

Yahweh in the Word

> "Trust in Yahweh with all your heart, and do not rely on your own understanding; think about Him in all your ways, and He will guide you on the right paths" (Proverbs 3:5-6).

The wise writer of the Book of Proverbs offers this sound advice to his son (v. 1). **Trusting in Yahweh means to make the choice to rely on Him and His promises.** On the negative side he says, "do not rely on your own understanding." There is nothing wrong with trying to understand our life experiences—just do not make the mistake of depending on such understanding. This means, do not demand that you understand something before moving forward with trust in Yahweh. We can trust Him when we may not understand Him or His ways. **The promise we can count on is that Yahweh will guide us in the right way we should go.**

Yahweh in Your Walk

This text has been of great help to me. I first discovered these words as a college student. My student pastor recommended the discipline of scripture memory and suggested a plan of memorizing key Bible verses that I followed for many years. One of the passages was Proverbs 3:5-6. Many times since then I have found these words to be of sound advice.

The first application of these wise words came as I struggled with deciding on my life vocation. As a college freshman I enrolled in the School of Engineering, thinking that would be a good career for me. However, during my sophomore year I began doubting my decision. As I struggled with knowing what to do, I remembered the text of today's devotional. I realized that I was relying too much on my "own understanding" rather than simply trusting Yahweh. **When I decided to trust Him with all my heart and think about Him in all my ways, His guidance gradually became clear to me.** His plan for me was to be a preacher/teacher, and I have followed that path for over 50 years. (His plan for you will be perfectly suited to you.)

Since that time there have been many occasions when I wasn't sure about which way to go. But I have learned to place more faith in His guidance than in my own understanding. I still try to understand many things about life, but I know that I must not rely on figuring them out for myself. I strongly recommend that you memorize this key Bible passage and begin claiming its promise for yourself. As I look back across these many years of life experiences, I can see much evidence of Yahweh's faithful guidance.

Yahweh in Your Worship

Let these words of Fanny Crosby be the guide for your worship: "All the way my Savior leads me; what have I to ask beside? Can I doubt His tender mercy, who thro' life has been my Guide? Heavenly peace, divinest comfort, here by faith in Him to dwell! For I know whate'er befall me, Jesus doeth all things well." Yahweh, I thank You for promising to be my Guide through life. Teach me to trust You with all my heart.

July 8

Yahweh Gives Me All the Strength I Need

Yahweh in the Word

> *"Do you not know? Have you not heard? Yahweh is the everlasting God, the Creator of the whole earth. He never grows faint or weary; there is no limit to His understanding. He gives strength to the weary and strengthens the powerless. Youth may faint and grow weary, and young men stumble and fall, but those who trust in Yahweh will renew their strength; they will soar on wings like eagles; they will run and not grow weary; they will walk and not faint" (Isaiah 40:28-31).*

Here is one of the great passages of the Bible regarding Yahweh's gift of strength to all who need it. He helps all who put their trust in Him, regardless of their circumstances. Whether our need is for soaring like eagles or running a race or simply walking, Yahweh gives the strength.

Yahweh in Your Walk

The sport of running keeps gaining adherents. I see cars with small stickers on the rear window reading "13.1" or "26.2" referring to half and full marathon races. Recently another driver had this sign "0.0"—a non-runner! Do you know about the Comrades Marathon held annually in South Africa? This oldest ultra-marathon, covering 56 miles, began in 1921. Bruce Fordyce dominated this race in the 1980s winning it nine times between 1981 and 1990. His best time was 5 hours 24 minutes and 7 seconds! What amazing strength and endurance!

The Bible has numerous references to the fact that our life experience is much like running a race. Consider this admonition from the apostle Paul: "Don't you know that the runners in a stadium all race, but only one receives the prize? Run in such a way to win the prize (1 Corinthians 9:24). And the writer of Hebrews advised, "Let us run with endurance the race that lies before us, keeping our eyes on Jesus, the source and perfecter of our faith…." (Hebrews 12:1-2). **Life is like a marathon; we must keep pressing on and not give up.**

Endurance is the supreme requirement for completing any race. All runners are at some time tempted to give up and quit before crossing the finish line. Christians are especially susceptible to Satan's suggestions that we drop out before the end. Here is where Yahweh wants to make a difference for each of us. When we remember how Yeshua refused to give up, enduring to the end, we are encouraged by His noble example. And the apostle Paul declared, "One thing I do: Forgetting what is behind and reaching forward to what is ahead, I pursue as my goal the prize promised by God's heavenly call in Christ Jesus" (Philippians 3:13-14). **We must claim Yahweh's promise to give power to the weary and powerless, and finish the race—one step at a time.**

Yahweh in Your Worship

I bow in thanksgiving and praise before You, O Yahweh. You are the strength I need and do not have in myself. Enable me today to seize every chance I have to be strong in You.

July 9

Yahweh's Requirements of Me Are Very Clear

Yahweh in the Word

> *"Mankind, He has told you what is good and what it is Yahweh requires of you: to act justly, to love faithfulness, and to walk humbly with your God" (Micah 6:8).*

Micah's name means "Who is like Yahweh?" He was called to be Yahweh's prophet to His people in Judah. His ministry was one of giving a warning of impending judgment because the people practiced injustice and had turned from Yahweh to the worship of idols. However, he also offered them hope in the person of a future Ruler who would bring peace.

Yahweh in Your Walk

I have taught college classes for many years. One lesson I have learned is that in every class there are students who have difficulty following instructions. For example, I give guidelines regarding term papers; these include such matters as the assigned subject and the minimum number of pages to be written. Invariably, some students ignore these requirements and "do their own thing." When they see their grade, they are surprised that I counted off for not following the stated requirements.

Yahweh wants us to know exactly what He expects of us as His people. Through His prophets He has repeatedly made these requirements clear. **Notice how our text for today expresses these three which Micah calls "good."**

1. **"To act justly."** We are to treat others fairly, according to Yahweh's standard of what is right. If we cheat others or lie to them or take advantage of them, we grieve Yahweh's Spirit. Our Lord said, "Whatever you did to one of the least of these brothers of Mine, you did for Me" (Matthew 25:40).
2. **"To love faithfulness."** The Hebrew word for "faithfulness" here is sometimes translated "kindness" or "mercy" and expresses Yahweh's way of dealing graciously with us. We are to be faithful in showing these same virtues as we relate to all others.
3. **"To walk humbly with your God."** Walking with God refers to a close intimate relationship with Him. Only the truly humble person can do this—the one who has an awareness of his own unworthiness and thus submits to Yahweh's provision and control.

Knowing these requirements is important, however, fulfilling them is something far more significant. The people of Micah's day found themselves incapable of living up to this high standard. The same is true of us unless we learn to depend upon the indwelling Holy Spirit to bear this Yahweh-like fruit through us.

Yahweh in Your Worship

Righteous Yahweh, thank You that what You require of us, You produce in us by Your Spirit.

July 10

Yahweh Wants to Teach Me to Wait For Him

Yahweh in the Word

> *"Wait for Yahweh; be strong and courageous. Wait for Yahweh"* (Psalm 27:14).

In order to appreciate the message of this last verse of the psalm, we must read the entire chapter. Notice the previous affirmations: "Yahweh is my light and my salvation… the stronghold of my life… He will conceal me in His shelter… set me on high on a rock… hear my voice when I call… Yahweh cares for me… I am certain I will see Yahweh's goodness." All these express the psalmist's confidence that Yahweh will meet his every need. However, the last verse acknowledges the fact that he must "wait for Yahweh" to act—and be patient. All this happens in His time.

Yahweh in Your Walk

Most of us struggle with being patient; we want what we want when we want it. Unfortunately, this is often not Yahweh's way of dealing with our requests of Him. The truth is—if He answered all our prayers immediately, we would soon think we were god and He was our servant. His delays are for our benefit; **He wants to teach us to be patient and wait for Him to act in His time. His delays remind us that He is in control, not us.**

Listen to David's testimony: "I waited patiently for Yahweh, and He turned to me and heard my cry for help. He brought me up from a desolate pit, out of the muddy clay, and set my feet on a rock, making my steps secure" (Psalm 40:1-2). His prayer was answered, but in Yahweh's time, not his. He needed to learn to wait patiently. Our text begins and ends with a call for us to "Wait for Yahweh," but in between these calls are the words "be strong and courageous." **While we wait, we must be strong in faith—believing Yahweh hears and answers, and courageous—in dealing with whatever circumstances we face.**

My friend had lost his job and needed employment to provide for his family. He asked Yahweh to guide him as he searched for work. But nothing happened to encourage him. Finally, after what seemed a prolonged delay, a position opened, and it was better than he expected. His testimony was that Yahweh taught him valuable lessons as he waited. We also must learn to wait for His answers—and be strong and courageous.

Remember that life with Yahweh is a journey, not an event. We are on a journey of learning, with Him as our teacher. Ask Him to teach you what He would have you learn from every situation.

Yahweh in Your Worship

Yahweh, I praise You that my times are in Your hands. Thank You for the valuable lessons You teach me as I wait patiently. You are the potter; I am the clay. Mold me according to Your will. Use me to share these valuable truths with others who may need patience before You.

July 11

Yahweh Provides Healing for My Sin

Yahweh in the Word

> *"I am broken by the brokenness of my dear people. I mourn; horror has taken hold of me. Is there no balm in Gilead? Is there no physician there? So why has the healing of my dear people not come about? (Jeremiah 8:22).*

The prophet Jeremiah was deeply grieved over the sins of his people. In spite of Yahweh's warnings, they continued to rebel against Him. Gilead was an area just east of the Jordan River near Galilee. Medicinal balms to aid in healing were found there.

Yahweh in Your Walk

The news media is mostly about bad news. So much violence and lawlessness abounds in our nation and world. All this evil makes us wonder if a solution can ever be found. Is there not some way to bring healing to this sick world? Jeremiah asked a similar question in our text for today. He was familiar with the healing balms found in the region of Gilead, and he asked if a similar remedy for the sins of his people could be found. An old spiritual song deals with this same issue and points to Yahweh's answer:

> Sometimes I feel discouraged, and think my work's in vain,
> But then the Holy Spirit revives my soul again.
> There is a balm in Gilead to make the wounded whole;
> There is a balm in Gilead to heal the sin-sick soul.

We know what this "balm in Gilead" is—the blood of Jesus has purchased forgiveness and cleansing from all sin. Moreover, through Him all humankind can be delivered from the old sinful human nature and become a new creation in Christ Jesus. Listen to this good news from Paul's writing: "Therefore if anyone is in Christ, he is a new creation; old things have passed away, and look, new things have come" (2 Corinthians 5:17). **The only permanent cure for the ills of our world is found in this new nature that comes from trusting Yeshua for a new life. He is the true "balm of Gilead."**

I have a friend who began life, as so many have, going the wrong way. He was rebellious as a child, into drugs and stealing as a youth, then spent several years in prison. But there he heard the gospel and was converted. When he was released from prison, he had also been released spiritually from his old evil nature—he was a new creation! Now he is working to reach others who are like he used to be—spiritually dead in sin. What a change! This kind of transformation is the ultimate and permanent cure for all the ills of our world.

Yahweh in Your Worship

I seize this day as an opportunity to walk with You, O Yahweh. You are my life and health; I worship You and praise You as the One who has brought wholeness to me. Thank You.

July 12

Yahweh Has His Hand upon Me

Yahweh in the Word

> *"Ezra came to Jerusalem in the fifth month, during the seventh year of the king. He began the journey from Babylon on the first day of the first month and arrived in Jerusalem on the first day of the fifth month since the gracious hand of his God was on him. Now Ezra had determined in his heart to study the law of Yahweh, obey it, and teach its statutes and ordinances in Israel"* (Ezra 7:8-10).

Ezra was a scribe, which means he was an expert in Yahweh's law. He was allowed to lead a large group of Jewish exiles in Babylon back to Jerusalem to seek a restoration of obedience to Yahweh's law, given through Moses. His journey was 900 miles over a period of four months.

Yahweh in Your Walk

We find at least four verses in the book of Ezra which read, "The hand of Yahweh was upon him." The meaning of that simple phrase is that Yahweh was with Ezra, blessing him, guiding him, and using him to make a difference for the kingdom of God. One evidence of such favor is found in these words from our text: "Ezra had determined in his heart to study the law of Yahweh, obey it, and teach its statutes and ordinances in Israel." When we learn that Ezra's name is a shortened form of a name meaning "Yahweh is my help," we understand why this man was so successful in his service to Yahweh's people.

Would you like to have Yahweh's hand upon you? Would you like to know that He is using you to make a difference in the lives of other people—all for His glory and the advancement of His kingdom in this world? I can assure you that this is Yahweh's desire concerning you. His holy hand reaches out to bless you and make you a blessing to others. How can this become a reality? Simply by following the example of this humble man of God. **First,** determine in your heart to study His word for the purpose of obeying all it teaches you to be and do. Be a hearer, reader, and serious student of the Bible. Be diligent to do this, not just for knowledge and information, but to know more about Yahweh and His will for you. **Second,** add to this, as did Ezra, the sharing (teaching) of biblical truth to others. In other words, pass on what you learn to those Yahweh brings across your path—maybe family members, co-workers, neighbors, friends—anyone. **You can be certain that Yahweh's mighty hand will be upon you for this worthy purpose. He will be faithful to enable you to serve Him effectively, just as did Ezra.**

Yahweh in Your Worship

Yahweh, You know me completely. You know and understand my weaknesses and fears as well as the potential You made me to fulfill. I choose to seize the opportunity to follow the noble example of Ezra by being more committed to the study of Your word each day. Help me to obey all Your commands as I should. Use me to help others know You and Your truth more fully. Thank You for placing Your hand upon me.

July 13

Yahweh Had a Purpose for Me before I Was Conceived

Yahweh in the Word

> "The word of Yahweh came to me: 'I chose you before I formed you in the womb; I set you apart before you were born. I appointed you a prophet to the nations'" (Jeremiah 1:4-5).

Jeremiah begins his book of prophecy with a testimony of how Yahweh called him to this awesome task. These words from Yahweh speak powerfully to us of His knowledge of us and of His sovereign plan for us even before we are conceived in our mother's womb.

Yahweh in Your Walk

Do you have a sense of purpose for your life? Have you considered the possibility that Yahweh created you for a special reason? One of the most widely read books in recent years is **The Purpose-Driven Life: What on Earth Am I Here for?** by pastor Rick Warren. Such popularity speaks clearly of the fact that most people are interested in this important subject. Warren states: "You cannot fulfill God's purpose for your life while focusing on your own plans." Just the possibility that you were created by Yahweh for His purpose is such an inspiring thought. Think of how Jeremiah was helped by this amazing news.

The question we must address is: **Since we were made by Yahweh for His purpose, how can we discover what that purpose is?** Again we listen to His word to Jeremiah, "Yahweh is His name, says this, 'Call to Me and I will answer you and tell you great and incomprehensible things you do not know'" (Jeremiah 33:2-3). The encouraging truth is—**Yahweh wants us to know and understand and fulfill His purpose for creating us.** And, as we seek the revelation of His reason, He will show us all we need to know in His timing. In other words, we do not need to know everything at once—just one step at a time.

A young man came to me wanting help in discovering God's will for his life. I asked him if he was willing to meet with me to study the Bible, pray, and learn more about the Christian life. He was reluctant to follow this kind of discipline; his interest was in knowing what special purpose God had for him—some vocation that would be exciting. When I insisted on beginning with the development of the kind of godly man God could use, he was not interested. Too often we are all like that; we want to see the big picture now.

Yahweh's purpose for all of us begins with the same requirement—become the kind of person He can use. As we focus on this process of character building, He will unfold more and more of His plan for us. Our role is to patiently, persistently add little by little to godliness in pursuing His will. All this is a walk of faith, believing, as the psalmist said, "My times are in Your hands."

Yahweh in Your Worship

Thank You, heavenly Father, that You have a purpose for my life that is worthy of my pursuit. Help me to discover what You want to reveal to me today. Give me the patience to keep on track. I choose to seize opportunities You will give me to follow You each day.

July 14

Yahweh Wants Me to Be Transformed

Yahweh in the Word

> "Therefore, brothers, by the mercies of God, I urge you to present your bodies as a living sacrifice, holy and pleasing to God, this is your spiritual worship. Do not be conformed to this age, but be transformed by the renewing of your mind, so that you may discern what is the good, pleasing, and perfect will of God" (Romans 12:1-2).

Worship in Old Testament times often involved the sacrificing of some animal as an offering to Yahweh. The apostle Paul is urging his readers to worship Him by presenting themselves, body and spirit, as a living sacrifice. He goes on to encourage them to not be molded by this present age, but to be changed by a new way of thinking, thus perceiving God's good, pleasing, and perfect will.

Yahweh in Your Walk

One of nature's most amazing creatures is the butterfly. For instance, the monarch butterfly can travel 3,000 miles on its migration from North America to Central America and end up on the same tree its parents or even grandparents landed on a generation or two before—guided by a brain the size of a pinhead! It all begins with a caterpillar that builds a chrysalis around itself, and then releases a chemical that slowly changes it into a beautiful butterfly. This process is known as metamorphosis, a word meaning "change in form."

The apostle Paul used the same term to describe the "change in form" a Christian experiences by the "renewing of your mind." Rather than letting this world and its false standards "squeeze" us into its ways, we can literally be "transformed" by choosing a new way of thinking. Paul's immediate application of this new outlook is found in the verse 3 following his appeal: "For by the grace given to me, I tell everyone among you not to think of himself more highly than he should think. Instead, think sensibly, as God has distributed a measure of faith to each one."

The world's way of thinking encourages us to think highly of ourselves in the sense of being proud and boastful of our accomplishments. **God's new way of thinking causes us to recognize that whatever we are and do in a commendable manner, is actually the result of His gifts to us.** Thus all the praise belongs to Him, not to us. **We find our sense of significance, not in what we accomplish, but in the fact of His love for us and His work of grace in us.** Therefore, we are transformed from our old way to a new way of thinking about ourselves and of His goodness. **All this change is a part of our spiritual worship, as we give ourselves as living sacrifices to Him.**

Yahweh in Your Worship

Thank You, Yahweh, for Your transforming power. I worship You for changing me from a self-centered person to one controlled by You. I want to seize every opportunity this day to demonstrate that Your will is the best way for everyone to journey through this life.

July 15

Yahweh's Mercy to Me Is New Every Morning

Yahweh in the Word

"Because of Yahweh's faithful love we do not perish, for His mercies never end. They are new every morning; great is Your faithfulness" (Lamentations 3:22-23).

The prophet Jeremiah was subjected to much sorrow. He witnessed the final days of Yahweh's people in Judah before being carried away as captives to Babylon. As the author of Lamentations he expressed his deep grief over the sins of his people which led to their fall to the Babylonians, followed by years in exile. However, in the midst of such sadness, the prophet offers hope as he speaks eloquently of Yahweh's unfailing mercy and compassion.

Yahweh in Your Walk

Several years ago I was invited to speak at the Homecoming Day celebration of a small country church where I had served as their interim pastor. The subject I chose was "Some Things Never Change." In my introduction I mentioned the fact that many changes had occurred in them and in me since my tenure as their pastor years before. Then I went on to point to several very important things that never change, such as Yahweh, His word, His truth, and His mercy toward us. The thrust of my message was **that these unchanging realities are the foundations upon which we can build a strong life, plus an unshakeable hope for the future.**

Jeremiah gave his hearers the same message. Notice these solid facts: Yahweh's faithful love, unending mercies that are new every morning, and Yahweh's great faithfulness. Because of these unchanging, reliable facts, "we do not perish." Here is the firm basis for our hope—not our feeble efforts at serving Yahweh, but His unfailing faithfulness to be forever merciful to us.

One of my favorite hymns, "Great Is Thy Faithfulness," was written by Thomas Obadiah Chisholm (1866-1960) and is based on our text for today. The first stanza has these memorable lines: "Great is Thy faithfulness, O God my Father, there is no shadow of turning with Thee; Thou changest not, Thy compassions they fail not; as Thou hast been Thou forever wilt be." When Chisholm was nearing the end of his earthly life he wrote: "My income has not been large at any time due to impaired health in the earlier years which has followed me on until now. Although I must not fail to record here the unfailing faithfulness of a covenant-keeping God and that He has given me many wonderful displays of His providing care, for which I am filled with astonishing gratefulness."

As you walk through this new day, be aware of the unfailing mercies of Yahweh that are new and refreshing every morning. His faithfulness enables you to be more faithful to Him.

Yahweh in Your Worship

Great is Your faithfulness to be merciful to me, O Yahweh. Therefore, I offer praise and gratitude to You. Thank You for Your faithful love for me and for all others who need Your mercy. Use me today as a witness of Your great and changeless goodness.

July 16

Yahweh Always Provides for Me a Way to Escape Temptation

Yahweh in the Word

> *"No temptation has overtaken you except what is common to humanity. God is faithful, and He will not allow you to be tempted beyond what you are able, but with the temptation He will also provide a way of escape so that you are able to bear it" (1 Corinthians 10:13).*

These words of promise from the apostle Paul are very encouraging to you. Although Yahweh allows you to be tempted to sin, He promises to guard you from any temptation that is more than you can resist, and also provides a "way of escape" so you can avoid yielding to the temptation.

Yahweh in Your Walk

Satan, the master deceiver is behind every temptation. You can learn much about his evil strategy from the first temptation in Genesis 3:1-7. The serpent was the devil in disguise; he led Eve to doubt Yahweh's word and to believe a lie. Satan always seeks to make disobeying Yahweh more appealing than obeying Him. Every temptation you face has its source in Satan's deceit; the Bible declares that Satan is a liar and the father of all lies.

You are not immune to temptation but Yahweh has given you a clear example of how to overcome temptation. Consider the example of Jesus' temptations in the wilderness (Luke 4:1-13). First, we notice that when these temptations came, He is described as being "full of the Holy Spirit," which indicates that Satan may attack when you are at your peak spiritually; he goes after the strong as well as the weak. Next, each of three temptations were aimed at self-gratification—hunger after prolonged fasting, worldly power and importance, and self-glorification. The key to Jesus' success in resisting all of Satan's appeals is found in the fact that He responded each time by quoting some appropriate Scripture—He relied on "the sword of the Spirit," which is the word of God (Ephesians 6:17).

Here, then, is the proven strategy for dealing with temptation: **Ask Yahweh to show you statements from His word that fit your areas of greatest vulnerability; memorize these powerful words and use them whenever the tempter attacks—be prepared in advance!** One example—if you are often tempted to love this world and all it offers, use these words to defend yourself: "Do not love the world or the things that belong to the world. If anyone loves the world, love for the Father is not in him. For everything that belongs to the world—the lust of the flesh, the lust of the eyes, and the pride in one's lifestyle—is not from the Father, but is from the world. And the world with its lust is passing away, but the one who does God's will remains forever" (1John 2:15-17). Commit these powerful words to memory and quote them to the adversary when he attacks. Your faith in Yahweh's truth will give you victory. (See 1 Jn. 5:4-5).

Yahweh in Your Worship

Yahweh, You invite me to come before Your throne of grace to receive help in times of need. I need the victory over temptation that only You can give. Thank You for Your strong Word.

July 17

Yahweh Is My Personal Teacher

Yahweh in the Word

> "Make Your ways known to me, Yahweh; teach me Your paths. Guide me in Your truth and teach me, for You are the God of my salvation; I wait for You all day long… Yahweh is good and upright; therefore He shows sinners the way. He leads the humble in what is right and teaches them His way" (Psalm 25:4-5, 8-9).

The psalmist acknowledged his need of knowing Yahweh's ways for him to live. Thus he asked Yahweh to be his teacher. He went on to affirm his confidence that Yahweh would indeed teach him all he needed to know.

Yahweh in Your Walk

My wife and I are finding much pleasure in spending time with Aden, our first great-grandchild. Each time we are with him, he seems to be learning something new. As we all know learning is a life-long adventure. From the time of our birth we are engaged in learning something new—learning to walk, feed ourselves, talk, obey parents, and on and on the process goes. However, good learning requires a good teacher. Fortunately our great-grandson has good parents who are giving the strong, patient training he needs.

The same need for learning is found in the spiritual realm—learning the ways of Yahweh. The psalmist recognized the importance of being instructed in the ways of living that would be pleasing to Yahweh. He was encouraged to know that this vital need would be faithfully met if he would become a humble, teachable learner. **As you think about yourself in this matter of being taught by Yahweh, can you truthfully say that you are open to receive divine instruction?** Do you have a real longing to learn more about pleasing Yahweh as well as serving Him more effectively? These are basic qualifications for being taught by Him. Make certain you are ready and willing to learn.

Jesus knew that all His followers would need personal instruction, thus He made this interesting promise: "It is for your benefit that I go away, because if I don't go away the Counselor will not come to you. If I go, I will send Him to you… When the Spirit of truth comes, He will guide you into all truth" (John 16:7, 13). **The Holy Spirit is Yahweh's gift of a personal teacher to every believer.** How significant this divine instructor is always present with us, continually guiding us into all truth. When we are reading the Word of God or listening to some gifted human teacher or going through some life-experience, the Holy Spirit is working to help us.

Yahweh in Your Worship

Spirit of the living God, I claim Your ministry of guiding me into all the truth I need to learn. Thank You for Your constant presence and faithful instruction. Help me be the learner I need to be. Direct me in the ways of righteousness and truth for Your honor and glory. I long to be a doer of the word and not just a student. I claim Your power to put into practice what You teach me.

July 18

Yahweh Enables Me to Rejoice in My Times of Trouble

Yahweh in the Word

> "We also rejoice in our afflictions, because we know that affliction produces endurance, endurance produces proven character, and proven character produces hope. This hope will not disappoint us, because God's love has been poured out in our hearts through the Holy Spirit who was given to us" (Romans 5:3-5).

Here is Paul's testimony of how he learned to handle the many trials he experienced as a follower of Jesus. Unlike most people who complain about their sufferings, Paul knew that Yahweh worked through these difficulties to bring about good results in his life.

Yahweh in Your Walk

How do you respond to difficulties that come to you, especially unexpected trials? If you are like most people, you may wonder why God is allowing this to happen to you, and you may feel sorry for yourself and complain to others and even to Yahweh. As one of my friends says, "You consider yourself to be the president of the "Poor-Me" Club.

But what should be the response of believers to personal trouble? Here is where Paul and other biblical persons give us the right answers. Paul made the choice to rejoice. He could do this because he knew about the good results that would come through these tough experiences. Notice the process he identifies in this Scripture text.

1. **Affliction produces endurance**. The term "affliction" refers to those situations that bring pressure and stress to us. One authority defines affliction as "the sufferings due to the pressure of unpleasant circumstances." Yahweh works through these kinds of experiences to produce endurance in us. Endurance means that virtue of putting up with unpleasant circumstances patiently, without complaining—the person who keeps on keeping on in a spirit of meekness.

2. **Endurance produces proven character.** The word translated "character" means to be tested and proven. Here is the idea of metal being passed through the heat of flames and coming out better, because all its impurities have been consumed. A person of good character is someone who has "gone through the fires of adversity" and come out stronger than before.

3. **Proven character produces hope**. Hope means the confident expectation of what is certain to be. Paul says that this kind of hope "will not disappoint us because God's love has been poured out in our hearts through the Holy Spirit who was given to us." **The ultimate result of this entire process is a better person with a stronger confidence in Yahweh and His promises.**

Yahweh in Your Worship

I bow in worship before You because Your Word assures me that my trials are for my good. Thank You for being with me in every hardship, and working through it to make me a better person. Forgive me when I have complained to You about the way You seek to build me up.

July 19

Yahweh Comforts Me So I Can Comfort Others

Yahweh in the Word

> "Praise the God and Father of our Lord Jesus Christ, the Father of mercies and the God of all comfort. He comforts us in all our affliction, so that we may be able to comfort those who are in any kind of affliction, through the comfort we ourselves receive from God" (2 Cor. 1:3-4).

The apostle Paul began his letter to the Corinthians with an expression of praise to Yahweh for His ministry of comfort to them. He goes on to remind his readers that one result of such comfort is that they are now equipped to pass that comfort on to others who need it.

Yahweh in Your Walk

As you walk through this day, you will probably meet someone who needs words of comfort. They may be facing some kind of difficulty similar to what you have encountered in the past. Be alert to the fact that Yahweh may have arranged this opportunity for you to pass on to them His words of comfort to you. An old statement of truth goes like this: "Every blessing from God comes to you on its way to someone else." Seek to be Yahweh's channel of blessing every day. This ministry of comfort can easily occur as you simply share helpful biblical truths.

Your testimony of how Yahweh has helped you through various trials is more powerful than you realize. You are a steward of His favor toward you; seek to be faithful to share your experience with others. Memorizing Bible verses that have helped you will enable you to have these truths ready to pass on. Consider pursuing this kind of comfort through messages you can send to those you hear about, whether acquaintances or not. Yahweh will lead you as you offer yourself to Him.

When I think of our devotional text, I remember hearing a daily radio broadcast in our home when I was a child. This gospel song was the theme of that program:

> Out in the highways and byways of life, many are weary and sad.
> Carry the sunshine where darkness is rife, making the sorrowing glad.
> Tell the sweet story of Christ and His love; tell of His power to forgive.
> Others will trust Him if only you prove true every moment you live.
> **Give as 'twas given to you in your need;** love as the Master loved you.
> Be to the helpless a helper indeed; unto your mission be true.
> Make me a blessing; make me a blessing. Out of my life may Jesus shine.
> Make me a blessing, O Savior I pray. Make me a blessing to someone today.
> Ira B. Wilson (1880-1950)

Yahweh in Your Worship

God of all comfort, thank You for comforting me in times of trial. Help me to be Your instrument to share that same comfort with others. Keep me alert to Your appointments.

July 20

Yahweh Is a God of Restoration for Me

Yahweh in the Word

> *"I will restore to you the years that the swarming locust has eaten… You shall eat in plenty and be satisfied, and praise the name of Yahweh your God, who has dealt wondrously with you… Then you shall know that I am in the midst of Israel, and that I am Yahweh your God and there is no other"* (Joel 2:25-27 NKJV).

The prophet Joel brought this message from Yahweh to His people who had experienced the loss of their crops due to an invasion of locusts. Yahweh had sent these devouring insects, hoping to awaken His people to their sins and their need for repentance. His promise was to restore their losses and thereby prove to them His presence as the only true God.

Yahweh in Your Walk

My friend, George Stringer, recently sent me some interesting pictures via email. He found an old tractor that was no longer usable—all rusty and in sad disrepair, which he determined to restore to its original condition. The pictures showed the tractor when he found it, then other photos of the process of disassembly, cleaning, repairing, repainting, and reassembly—a long, tedious work of restoration. George finds much pleasure in restoring anything to its original condition.

Rebuilding this old tractor reminds me of the way **Yahweh finds delight in taking a person whose usefulness has been marred by sin, and accomplishing His amazing work of restoring them once more to the productive person He planned for them to be**. A poet said it this way:

> 'Twas battered and scarred. And the auctioneer thought it hardly worth his while
> To waste his time on the old violin but he held it up with a smile.
> "What am I bid, good people," he cried. "Who starts the bidding for me?"
> "One dollar, one dollar, Do I hear two? Two dollars, who makes it three?"
> But no, from the room far back a gray bearded man came forward and picked up the bow.
> Then wiping the dust from the old violin and tightening up the strings,
> He played a melody, pure and sweet as sweet as the angel sings.
> The music ceased and the auctioneer with a voice that was quiet and low.
> Said "What now am I bid for this old violin?" As he held it aloft with its' bow.
> "One thousand, one thousand, Do I hear two? Two thousand, who makes it three?"
> Three thousand once, three thousand twice. Going and gone," said he.
> The audience cheered, but some of them cried, "We just don't understand.
> What changed its' worth?" Swift came the reply, "The Touch of the Master's Hand."

Yahweh in Your Worship

Thank You, Yahweh, for Your touch of restoration upon me. I bless You for making such a difference in me. Only You can work such a miracle and I worship You for being so gracious and good. Use me as an effective witness of Your transforming power.

July 21

Yeshua Brings Healing to Me by His Touch

Yeshua in the Word

> "Then a man with a serious skin disease came to Him and on his knees begged Him: 'If You are willing, You can make me clean.' Moved with compassion, Jesus reached out His hand and touched him. 'I am willing.' He told him. 'Be made clean.' Immediately the disease left him, and he was healed" (Mark 1:40-42).

The gospel accounts record numerous occasions when Yeshua reached out to individuals who needed His healing touch. Often, like this leper, these persons were outcasts due to their illness. His compassion motivated Him to extend both healing and restoration.

Yeshua in Your Walk

Have you discovered **the ministry of touch**? **Your hands symbolize your life in an interesting manner.** I grew up in a farming community where we spoke of "harvest hands." The Navy uses the term, "All hands on deck." And the Bible speaks of our need of having "clean hands and a pure heart." These sayings do not refer to our actual hands, but use the word "hand" to denote our life—the person we are. **There can be, therefore, a ministry performed by reaching out our hand and touching another person.** For example, when I pray for someone, I place my hand on their shoulder or hold their hand in mine. Often, when I am in a group of believers and someone leads a prayer, I lay my hand on the shoulder of a person next to me—just to communicate compassion and to extend a blessing to them.

We see many examples in the gospels of this ministry of touch as performed by Jesus. He could have brought healing by simply speaking a word, but instead, He often reached out His hand to express the extension of Himself to another person. Yesterday, we looked at a portion of an old poem sometimes called "The Touch of the Master's Hand." Here's the rest of that composition:

> And many a man with life out of tune all battered and bruised by sin
> Is auctioned cheap to a thoughtless crowd much like that old violin.
> A mess of pottage, a glass of wine, a game, and he travels on.
> He is going once, he is going twice, he is going and almost gone.
> But the Master comes, and the foolish crowd never can quite understand
> The worth of a soul and the change that is wrought by the touch of the Master's hand.
> by Myra Brooks Welch

Let Him touch you, and bring His complete restoration. Then share with others the good news of His powerful touch.

Yeshua in Your Worship

Gracious Yeshua, I worship You with the sacrifices of praise and thanksgiving. Your compassionate touch has made all the difference for me. As I walk through this day, use me to reach out and touch others in Your name. Help me be a channel of Your love.

July 22

Yahweh Sends His Angel to Help Me

Yahweh in the Word

> "The Angel of Yahweh encamps around those who fear Him and rescues them" (Psalm 34:7).

There are numerous references in this psalm to the protection and deliverance Yahweh provided for the writer (David). "Those who fear Him" means those who know Yahweh and have a deep respect and reverence for Him.

Yahweh in Your Walk

Have you ever had what could be labeled a "close call"? That is, you came close to having a serious accident, but didn't? Or perhaps you had an accident that was almost fatal, but wasn't? If so, you probably considered yourself to be very "lucky." I contend that there is no such thing as luck. In fact, I would spell luck as **LORD**. Yahweh is not only with us constantly but also He provides protection and care for us.

One expression of His care is what may be labeled "guardian angels." **In our Scripture text for today the psalmist, who had many "close calls," declares that "the Angel of Yahweh encamps around those who fear Him and rescues them."** David knew this to be true from his own experiences. Who are these mysterious creatures called angels? The term translated *angel* in both Old and New Testament means messenger. Notice the word *evangelist* is built on the word angel. An evangelist is a messenger of good news. Much of the work of angels in the Bible was to convey some message from Yahweh. Many angel appearances happened at the birth of Christ and there are some 70 references to angels in the Revelation, as they gave special messages to the apostle John.

Angels also have a ministry of deliverance, such as Peter being set free from prison (Acts 12:4), and many other instances. Recently I read the testimony of a pastor in Wales who, many years ago, was traveling by horseback, carrying a large sum of money from one church to another. Robbers knew of his mission and were waiting to ambush him. As he rode along another rider on a white horse joined him. When the pastor greeted him, he did not reply and remained silent as they rode past the robbers who remained in hiding due to two horsemen rather than one. After passing them, the rider on the white horse vanished leaving the pastor alone; then he realized that this companion had been an angel sent by God.

Sometimes angels assume human form, as this horseman, while other times they are invisible. The author of Hebrews declares that believers have sometimes shown hospitality to angels without knowing it (Hebrews 13:2). **Just be aware and thankful that Yahweh sends angels to protect those who worship Him.** One of these heavenly messengers is assigned to you.

Yahweh in Your Worship

Thank You, Yahweh, for sending Your angel to protect me. I worship You as my defender, deliverer and Lord. As I learn more about Your care for me, I love You more and more.

July 23

Yeshua Wants Me to Practice Loving People

Yeshua in the Word

"But the fruit of the Spirit is love…" (Galatians 5:22).

Yahweh is so good to His children! Before Jesus ascended back to heaven, He assured the believers that a Comforter would come. Along with His presence would be nine qualities to help believers become more Christ-like. These inward traits are called, "The Fruit of the Spirit." **For the next nine days each devotional will feature one expression of this fruit.** These virtues are like individual parts of one fruit and find expression in the lives of Spirit-controlled individuals.

Love heads the list and is the most God-like quality. Paul reminded his readers that love is the greatest (1 Corinthians 13:13). A good word to describe this trait is "selflessness." All the rest of the fruit is really an outgrowth of love. Divine love for others is another way of describing this fruit. This love is that which has its source in Yahweh. The greatest expression of God's love is seen at Calvary. Yeshua talked about the fruit of the Spirit in John 15. And fruit is what He wants in our lives, as He states in this passage—fruit, more fruit, and much fruit. Although this love is God's gift to us (Romans 5:5), we must cultivate and pray for opportunities to grow in love (Philippians 1:9). **When a person practices this kind of love, he experiences joy—that inward peace and sufficiency that is not affected by outward circumstances**. You have this love in your heart and life if you are a believer.

Paul also names some sins in chapter 5:19-21 that stand in contrast to love and should be avoided, such as: sexual immorality, moral impurity, promiscuity, idolatry, sorcery, hatreds, strife, jealousy, outbursts of anger, selfish ambitions, dissensions, factions, envy, drunkenness, carousing, and anything similar. All these are contrary to Yahweh's love.

Yeshua in Your Walk

Seminary life was difficult enough without having a baby added to the stress. Jim and I worked jobs and pastored a church in Oklahoma on the weekends. So I questioned God's decision to add a baby to our family. "How can we do this, Lord?" These thoughts were my reasoning until our son was born. My husband and I were busy students and rarely spent time together. However, God had His plan in place for us. The day that James Mark Harvey was born introduced a new kind of love for me. Words cannot express the love I instantly felt for this tiny baby. Little did we know that our 10-year-old son was serious when he announced to the family that he was going to China and tell people about Jesus. Little did we know that years later our son and his wife, Judy, would serve God on a foreign field and see hundreds of Asians become followers of Jesus. Yes, the Holy Spirit produces a new kind of love and that love means everything to me.

Yeshua in Your Worship

Lord, lead me to love all people like You love them. Show me the individuals I need to meet and "love on." Help me to know more about what is written in Your Word about Your kind of love.

July 24

Yeshua Wants Me to Have Joy in the Midst of Trouble

Yeshua in the Word

> *"But the fruit of the Spirit is… joy" (Galatians 5:22).*

Today our focus is on the word joy. This characteristic always accompanies love. Sometimes people think joy and happiness are the same words. However, happiness is determined by outward circumstances. Paul's letter to the Philippians is an expression of joy. He wrote to his friends from a prison cell in Rome. The Greek word for joy comes from the same root as grace. **A redemptive experience with Christ and the knowledge that a person's sins are forgiven produces joy.** Plus he has assurance that a believer is a child of God and has eternal life. Paul was an outstanding example of joy (Philippians 1:4). This inward peace and sufficiency is not affected by outward circumstances. You can have joy in the midst of trouble. Read a beautiful expression of this character of God as expressed in Zephaniah 3:17. "Yahweh your God is among you, a warrior who saves. He will rejoice over you with gladness. He will bring you quietness with his love. He will delight in you with shouts of joy."

People around us are starving for love, joy, peace, and all the other graces of the Spirit. When they find them in our lives, they know that we have something they lack. **Could your example change their life?**

Yeshua in Your Walk

The Middle Ages was a period of history sometimes called "The Dark Ages." Spiritual and moral darkness had invaded the church. The ethical standards of many Christian leaders were characterized by disgrace, shame, and corruption. And yet, Yahweh still loved His people. A devotional poem about the Lord was written at this time by Bernard of Clairvaux. In his early twenties, he chose the life of a monk and entered a monastery in France. God used this young man's forceful personality and talents to provide leadership for his generation of believers. This poem became a hymn titled, "Jesus, the Very Thought of Thee." One phrase is especially interesting when the situations of his day are recalled. He wrote,

> Jesus, our only joy be Thou, and Thou our prize wilt be;
> Jesus, be Thou our glory now and through eternity.

The joy expressed in these words came from an inward dwelling of the Holy Spirit Who produced spiritual fruit. "The Dark Ages" weren't dark for Bernard.

Yeshua in Your Worship

Yeshua, I want to spend time thanking You for the Holy Spirit's work in my life. Guide me to express appropriate praise for such a special Gift to me. I want to be so filled with the Spirit that His perfect fruit will be shown through me today. May Your joy be expressed through me and passed on to others.

July 25

Yeshua Wants Me to Live a Life of Peace

Yeshua in the Word

> *"But the fruit of the Spirit is… peace" (Galatians 5:22).*

Peace is the most preciousof all gifts and graces of the Holy Spirit. In all of Paul's salutations he uses grace and peace. The order is correct. **Once we experience God's grace, we know His peace.** Some scholars have described this kind of peace as being at ease, a calmness under the skin, a quiet assurance which operates in either war or calm. Yesterday, the fruit studied was joy. Joy may be more exciting, but peace is more comforting. The apostle Paul experienced this kind of peace when he wrote, "And the peace of God which surpasses every thought, will guard your hearts and your minds in Christ Jesus" (Philippians 4:7).

One person described this peace as "God's own calm, restful heart possessing ours and filling us with His divine stillness." A peace like Paul describes cannot be understood. No rational explanation exists for this experience. This spiritual fruit saves us from anxious concerns. Another description of this peace is that it crowds out our anxieties and fills us with such satisfaction that nothing really makes us afraid. A life of peace leads to a life of praise and a life of praise leads back to a life of peace. So now, we have read about love, joy, and peace. These three can change your life and the years you have remaining on your earthly home. Finally, there is no law against these characteristics and no law which will produce them. **You cannot produce any of this fruit by your own effort.** Religion can never give this to you. **Only Christ can give you deep-down peace.**

Yeshua in Your Walk

I witnessed this kind of peace years ago when my father-in-law died from lung cancer. A family death was new to us. Other friends had lost loved ones, but not us. My mother-in-law was beside herself with grief. Her companion of many years was gone. They had spent much time together enjoying their hobbies and old friends. Now, what would she do? Where would she go? We began to pray for her and asked Yahweh to give her peace during these trials. Isn't it interesting that we believers often wait until a crisis to call upon God for help? And our prayer was answered. When I went into her room where she was resting on her bed, I sensed something different about her and thought perhaps the doctor needed to be called. Wrong assessment! She sat up and said, "Something warm just passed over my body. I felt like I was totally covered in something I can't explain." From that moment on, through the days of mourning and decisions, she remained strong and said "God washed over me a peace that is wonderful." Through the years, she shared that experience of the God of peace and brought much comfort to other grieving widows.

Yeshua in Your Worship

Help me, Lord, to understand that You are the source of peace. Lead me to grow in peace by giving myself totally to You. Forgive me for doubting the truths of Your Word. Make me a peace-loving follower of Your guidance.

July 26

Yeshua Wants Me to Be Patient

Yeshua in the Word

"But the fruit of the Spirit is… patience" (Galatians 5:22).

A good definition of the word "patience" is: being steadfastly kind toward people who can and will aggravate or persecute others. The word suggests a slowness to avenge wrongs suffered or a refusal to get even. When the experiences of missionary Paul are recalled, he had many opportunities to lose his patience, but biblical descriptions of his life present an example of patience. One of the characteristics of Yahweh is described as patience. "The Lord does not delay His promise, as some understand delay, but is patient with you, not wanting any to perish, but all to come to repentance" (2 Peter 3:9). Paul also encouraged believers to be patient: "And we exhort you, brother; warn those who are lazy, comfort the discouraged, help the weak, be patient with everyone" (1 Thessalonians 5:14).

One Bible translation uses the word "longsuffering" to describe patience. This meaning suggests courageous endurance without quitting. **The Christian who is longsuffering will not avenge himself or wish difficulties on those who oppose him**. He will be kind and gentle, even with the most offensive individual, and sow goodness where others sow evil. **Human nature can never do this on its own, only the Holy Spirit can.** Therefore, when a person says, "I can't control my patience with my neighbors anymore." **That person doesn't understand the power of the Holy Spirit to provide all the patience you will ever need.**

Yeshua in Your Walk

A woman noticed a small boy looking in her bakery window one morning. He was obviously hungry and poorly clothed for such a cold day. Customers kept her busy and when she did look out the window again, the boy was gone. Each day he returned to the same spot and sometimes stood in the doorway. The owner began to lose her patience with this little nuisance. One cold morning she went outside to confront him and immediately noticed the boy had no socks and wore a warn-out pair of shoes. She invited him into the bakery and gave him some bread and milk, then asked her assistant to watch the shop for a little while. This once impatient woman went to the shoe store and bought the boy a new pair of shoes. His excitement was a joy to watch. He left her and immediately ran down the street. Later that day, he returned to the bakery and said, "Hey, lady, I forgot to thank you for my shoes. Can I ask you a question? Are you God's wife?" "No," she replied smiling, "but I am one of His children." Her patience had demonstrated the fruit of the Spirit to a little boy who had been a pest.

Yeshua in Your Worship

Lord, I claim the Holy Spirit's work in me to produce the patience I will use for You. Help me to be alert to needs around me so that I can make a difference in someone's life. Sometimes I lose my patience with other people and am ashamed of my attitude. Only You can change me and make me become more like You.

July 27

Yeshua Wants Me to Actively Seek Ways to Be Kind to Others

Yeshua in the Word

"But the fruit of the Spirit is… kindness" (Galatians 5:22).

Christian kindness is an action of love that never fails. The Old Testament example of David and Mephibosheth illustrates the attitude we should have toward other people. Following David's victory over Goliath, he became recognized as the leader to command the armies of King Saul. Continued wars prevailed between the two men and lasted even after Saul's death. David grew progressively stronger and Saul's house grew weaker. David's success did not cause him to forget his covenant with his good friend, Jonathan, Saul's son. After David finally triumphed over his enemies, he desired to show kindness to someone from Saul's house. In 2 Samuel 9:1 David asked: "Is there anyone still left of the house of Saul to whom I can show kindness for Jonathan's sake?" He issued a command to find a survivor. The king sought not only to keep a personal promise, but also to be a witness of Yahweh's care and blessing to humankind. He actively sought ways to be kind to others.

Fruit is produced by yielding to the Holy Spirit who indwells us. The Holy Spirit wants to produce fruit, but we must do our part in this process. A believer cannot assume the role of "lone ranger." Other people are involved in your life who need to see the fruit of the Spirit in you.

Yeshua in Your Walk

The apostle Paul wrote to the Colossians (3:12) and said, "Therefore, God's chosen ones, holy, and loved, put on heartfelt compassion, kindness, humility, gentleness, and patience." Kindness is one of the characteristics of God. Every **Christian should care about people who are not experiencing kindness in their world**. Suppose one of the following opportunities for showing kindness occurred in your life, what would you do in each situation? **Can you really choose to make a difference in needs of other people?**

+A young mother in your neighborhood has the flu. Her small children are cared for by out-of-town family members, but she needs help. What act of kindness would you do for her?

+A Care-center calls you about a forgotten patient who has died. No family members can be located. What would you do to show kindness?

+Thomas, a senior adult in your church, can no longer drive his car. He loves to go for drives and to eat in restaurants. How could you make his life more enjoyable?

+A farm family lost all their possessions because of a fire. How could you get involved in helping these people?

Yeshua in Your Worship

Lord, I ask for help in practicing kindness. I want to thank You for the Spirit's work in my life and I need Your help in those areas where I feel out of step with Your plan for my life. May Your kind actions be performed consistently through me. Show me someone today whom I could help by reaching out in Your kindness.

July 28

Yeshua Desires for Me to Reflect His Goodness

Yeshua in the Word

> *"But the fruit of the Spirit is... goodness" (Galatians 5:22).*

The characteristic of goodness is a product of Yahweh's Spirit in us. This fruit will help the world know that Yahweh loves all people and reaches out to meet their greatest needs. Psalm 107 begins like this: "Give thanks to Yahweh, for He is good." The psalm goes on to describe Yahweh's dealings with Israel that are described as "good." Many Bible teachers believe that this psalm was composed after the Israelites returned from 70 years of captivity in Babylon. These former captives were rejoicing in their return to Jerusalem and thanked God for His act of salvation in delivering them from bondage. The whole psalm is a celebration of God's goodness. The writer wanted his people to worship Yahweh because of His goodness. While this characteristic is similar to the goodness of humans, Yahweh's goodness is perfect and complete. And His goodness always leads to truth and righteousness.

Yeshua in Your Walk

An e-mail came to my computer the other day. The attachment included these words:

> *Good morning, this is God.*
> *I will be handling*
> *All of your problems today.*
> *I will not need your help,*
> *So have a good day.*

After reading these words, I began to wonder just how I would live if I had a "good day." Here are some of my thoughts about this:

First, I would begin the day with a quiet time. Reading my Bible and praying would be top priority. Sometimes people wait until evening to have this special time with the Lord. To me, that habit is like going into battle all day, then coming home in the evening to put on your armor!

Then, I would focus on my family. Expressions of love and concern would be spoken. "What can I do for you today?" would be asked. Responding to their reply would be very important. Throughout the day I would look for opportunities to demonstrate goodness to them. Keeping in touch with family is a priority for me. Our daughter, Martha, calls us from North Carolina every day just to see how we are doing. How we love those phone calls! Our son and his wife are missionaries in Singapore. Because of the computer, we can Skype and talk with them, just like they were in the room with us.

Finally to have a good day, I would want to focus on reaching out to help hurting people in my area of ministry. Besides direct involvement, I want to remember their personal needs in prayer.

Yeshua in Your Worship

Yeshua, I ask for help in practicing goodness. **I want the fruit of the Spirit to be clearly demonstrated in my relationships with others.** Guide me today to be intentional in performing some good deed for another person who needs help.

July 29

Yeshua Would Have Me Be Strong in Faith

Yeshua in the Word

"But the fruit of the Spirit is... faith" (Galatians 5:22).

Some translations use "faithfulness" rather than "faith" in this text. The original word can be rendered either way. They actually belong together in the sense that **faith produces faithfulness**. A favorite definition for faith is: a loyalty based on a firm persuasion about my conviction concerning Christ. This characteristic of Yahweh is commanded in Revelation 2:10, "Be faithful until death, and I will give you the crown of life." One of the great descriptions of God in the Bible is that He is faithful. Therefore, His children should be like Him. "Let us hold on to the confession of our hope without wavering for He who promised is faithful" (Hebrews 10:23). Faithfulness for the believer means dependability. Yahweh can count on us. **His Spirit will produce this fruit in us if we will be submissive to Him.**

Our friend Sally Ozment has proven herself a faithful advocate for missions in her local church where she serves as the missions leader and keeps others informed regarding local and global mission activities. In addition she is her state's representative for SBC Missionary Parents Fellowship, a nation-wide organization of parents who have children that have been appointed as career missionaries or for short-term projects. **We admire her dependability in these areas.**

Yeshua in Your Walk

God has been faithful to send us other outstanding examples of people who followed His leadership in the area of faith. Many songs from the past describe this kind of virtue. I remember singing some of the great gospel songs and believing every word. One of my favorite writers was Fanny J. Crosby. She has been called "the queen of hymn writers." Her faithfulness to God was modeled throughout her life, beginning at her birth in 1820, and ending in her home-going in 1915. An eye infection when she was an infant was mistreated by a doctor, resulting in a lifetime of blindness. Her grandmother encouraged young Fanny to memorize entire books of the Bible. The Institution for the Blind in New York provided her education and recognition as a poet. The words from this song mean so much to me:

> All the way my Savior leads me; What have I to ask beside?
> Can I doubt His tender mercies, Who thro' life has been my Guide.
> Heav'nly peace divinest comfort, Here **by faith** in Him to dwell!
> For I know whate'er befall me, Jesus doeth all things well.

Yeshua in Your Worship

Yeshua, help my Christian walk to be different because I have allowed the Holy Spirit to exercise the fruit of faith in my life. Lead me to learn how to be more fruitful as I discover and apply these nine special characteristics in my daily walk. I long to be more like You in every aspect of life.

July 30

Yeshua Wants Me to be Gentle Toward Others

Yeshua in the Word

"The fruit of the Spirit is… gentleness" (Galatians 5:23).

A good definition for gentleness is "a quite sense of adequacy that comes from being controlled by the Holy Spirit." A good example would be a wild horse that has been broken. When Jesus entered Simon Peter's life, this plain fisherman, later nicknamed "the rock," seemed an unlikely person to serve as the Lord's disciple. He often spoke without thinking and was often impatient and impulsive. His denial of Jesus reflects this carnal nature.

Later in his life, difficulties surfaced over prejudice against Gentile people. The word gentleness would not be used to describe this apostle until later in his life. His brother Andrew would certainly display the fruit of gentleness. However, Peter was changed by the love of Jesus and became a communicator of the gospel to the early church. **A gentle person is a teachable person, not a know-it-all.** He learns from the Master teacher. Gentleness means that you will do Yahweh's will, that you are willing to yield your will to His control.

The apostle Peter was the author of 1 and 2 Peter, letters that sought to comfort the persecuted believers with the message of hope of eternal life. Read these two letters and notice the gentleness with which Peter addressed the needs of the people. Is this the same man who cursed and denied knowing Jesus? Yes, the same man, but with a changed heart—a heart of gentleness. We see this change in his advice to wives to have the "imperishable quality of a gentle and quiet spirit, which is very valuable in God's eyes" (1 Peter 3:4).

Yeshua in Your Walk

Many Bible students would agree that the outstanding persons of the Old Testament and New Testament would be Moses and Jesus. How interesting that both are described as being humble, gentle, and meek. We read of Moses, "Now the man Moses was very meek, above all the men which were upon the face of the earth" (Numbers 12:3 KJV). And Jesus declared, "All of you, take up My yoke and learn from Me, because I am gentle and humble in heart, and you will find rest for yourselves" (Matthew 11:29).

These characteristics would not describe what this world considers to be true of great leaders. And yet, here are two of the greatest of all leaders—they were gentle, in the truest sense of the word. **We do well to give high value to these simple virtues and pursue these qualities for ourselves.**

Yeshua in Your Worship

Thank You, Lord, for being the ultimate example of what being gentle means. I claim Your Spirit within me to produce this same virtue. Help me show gentleness in all my dealings with others, especially my family and friends. Use me to encourage gentleness among those who need to learn how to be controlled by Your Spirit.

July 31

Yeshua Wants Me to Have Self-Control

Yeshua in the Word

"But the fruit of the Spirit is… self-control" (Galatians 5:23).

Today's devotional concludes the studies on the fruit of the Spirit. Eight different virtues have been considered and now the ninth focuses on having self-control over thoughts and actions. **First Samuel 26 presents a clear example of mastering self-control.** David had been driven from Israel by King Saul who was terribly angry and jealous. His goal was to hunt down and kill this person who was threatening his power. David and one companion slipped into Saul's camp and stood over the sleeping ruler. The king's spear and canteen were taken as evidence of David's opportunity to kill Saul.

The word "self-control" is used in two other places. (Read Acts 24:25 and 2 Peter 1:6.) A person having this fruit doesn't drift with the current of evil practices; he dares to stand up against them. An interesting fact about these devotionals is that Paul begins with love or selflessness, and closes with self-control. These two virtues make possible the other characteristics.

The work of the Holy Spirit is to make us more like Christ for His glory, not for the praise of men. **As we choose each day to submit to His control and trust His work in us, we become "fruit-bearers" of the Spirit.**

Yeshua in Your Walk

Hebrews 12:1 offers this advice, "Lay aside every weight and sin that so easily ensnares us…." Habits, practices, or attitudes that hinder our spiritual welfare and service for the Lord, must be controlled. **The way to achieve this self-control is to place ourselves under the Holy Spirit's leadership and direction.**

Read the following situations and decide how self-control would make a difference:

> Tom gets so angry at the ballgame that profanity flies from his mouth.
> Sylvia has participated in diet programs for the last 10 years, but is still obese.
> Jimmy's parents are often called to the school because of his temper related problems.
> Helen can be described as a "road-rage" driver.

> Consider your personal answer to the following questions about self-control:

> What area of your life is not lacking in self-control?
> In what ways does your lack of self-control affect Christians and non-Christians?
> What do all expressions of the fruit of the Spirit have in common?
> Which fruit do you find most difficult to exercise?

Yeshua in Your Worship

Thank You, Yeshua, for the opportunity to be fruitful. May Your likeness be seen in my actions and attitude every day.

August 1
Yahweh Is My Personal Shepherd

Yahweh in the Word

> *"The LORD (Yahweh) is my shepherd; there is nothing I lack" (Psalm 23:1).*

Here is another combination of Yahweh's name—Yahweh Rohi (YAH-way ROW-ee), which means "Yahweh is my shepherd." David grew up as a shepherd boy, caring for his father's sheep. Later he wrote this psalm, which has become a favorite for many Bible loving persons. David was very familiar with the tender loving care needed by sheep and provided by a good shepherd. Thus we find multiple references to this intimate relationship of care in these well-known words.

Yahweh in Your Walk

Some Bible students refer to Psalm 23 as the "He-Me Psalm," due to the many times this personal relationship between Yahweh and the psalmist is mentioned. (Read the psalm and see how many of these you can identify.) The wonder-filled result of the Shepherd's care is found in these words of reassurance: "there is nothing I lack." Another way of translating this verse is: "Because Yahweh is my personal shepherd, I will always have everything I need."

There are times, however, when we may feel the need of something we do not have. Our first response should be to make sure we aren't dealing with greed rather than actual need. Many times we think we need something when actually we don't—just a desire for something more than we have. A second possibility we should consider is—perhaps we already have what we want and just aren't aware of it. For example there have been times when I asked Yahweh to give me more patience, or more love for others. The truth is that these virtues are the fruit of the Holy Spirit who lives in me. I already have all the love and patience God could give me, I just need to claim this fruit to be expressed more fully through me.

So, as you walk through today, be thankful for your personal Shepherd and His provisions for all you need. Let Him know that you appreciate all He gives you and trust Him to be in complete control—like a sheep following a good shepherd. Ask Him to remind you to seek His guidance each time you make a significant decision. **If you have appointments with people, always pause beforehand and commit the event to His control.** When happenings come that are beyond your power to understand or to manage, turn to Him for guidance and wisdom to make right decisions. **Think of your day as a journey with the Good Shepherd leading the way, always available when you need His counsel.**

Yahweh in Your Worship

Yahweh Rohi, I rejoice to be in Your loving care today. Thank You for faithfully provided all I need and more. I claim Your help to walk closely with You by being obedient to Your will for me. Keep me from straying from Your fellowship; I want to be close to You. Use me to help other sheep become part of Your flock.

August 2

Yahweh Rohi Gives Me All the Leadership I Need

Yahweh in the Word

> *"Yahweh Rohi… leads me beside quiet waters… leads me along the right paths for His name's sake" (Psalm 23:2-3).*

Shepherds go ahead of their sheep to make sure the way is safe and that the sheep can follow him. Sheep are not able to find their own way as some other animals can do; they must have a shepherd to lead them. In these verses, the psalmist compares himself to a sheep and affirms the personal guidance given by a good shepherd.

Yahweh in Your Walk

When God's Word compares us to sheep, that is not a compliment. Sheep are very apt to stray off from the flock and become helplessly lost. The prophet Isaiah said it right, "We all went astray like sheep; we all have turned to our own way…" (Isaiah 53:6). We all desperately need a good shepherd. And Yahweh Rohi meets this need. He will be faithful to pursue us when we stray from the path of righteousness. And if we stumble and fall, He will tenderly lift us up and place us back on track.

Today you will make many decisions, some are very routine and require little thought and probably have minor consequences. However, other choices may be rather significant. **Sometimes what seems like a small matter has major importance.** For example, think about a time when a rather casual meeting of some new person later proved life-altering. Although you were not aware of this at the time—Yahweh knew, and He was leading you—along the right path. Such experiences remind us of the fact that Yahweh Rohi is actively working to lead us. **Since He is ahead of us as our Shepherd, He knows all about our events for the day. You can trust Him to prepare you for what is coming.**

Years ago, I formed the habit of offering this simple biblical prayer every morning as my feet touch the floor beside my bed, "Yahweh, today my times are in Your hands" (Psalm 31:15). I believe Yahweh takes this commitment seriously and arranges the events of that day in ways far beyond my imagination. **He even turns my disappointments into His-appointments, bringing forth good from situations that may appear bad from my point of view.** He alone can and will give all the leadership we need—every day.

Yahweh in Your Worship

Sing these words as you worship Yahweh Rohi: "He leadeth me! O blessed thought! O words with heavenly comfort fraught! Whate'er I do, where'er I be, still 'tis God's hand that leadeth me." Yes, Yahweh, I worship You as my faithful Shepherd, leading me today and throughout my life. Thank You for Your faithful shepherding of me in the past. Help me remember Your tender mercies as I begin this day with all its challenges and opportunities. I want to actively seize this new segment of time and claim all You have planned for me.

August 3

Yahweh's Presence Removes My Fears

Yahweh in the Word

> "Even when I go through the darkest valley, I fear no danger, for You (Yahweh) are with me; Your rod and Your staff—they comfort me" (Psalm 23:4).

Sometimes shepherds had to lead their sheep through dark valleys in order to find the best pastures. Wolves could hide in these dark places and attack the sheep. However, a good shepherd was skilled at using a short, thick club (staff) to defend his sheep. These sheep had nothing to fear as they passed through danger.

Yahweh in Your Walk

We all experience fear. Some fears are good and keep us from harm. Other fears can be a hindrance and even cause us to shut down. The psalmist gives us the best remedy for those fears that keep us from walking without a sense of peace and security through each day. He confidently declares, "I fear no danger, for Yahweh is with me." **The awareness of His presence as the One who gives leadership along the path of life, as well as protection from whatever causes fear, results in lasting calmness.**

An old gospel song says it this way, "What have I to dread, what have I to fear, leaning on the everlasting arms? I have blessed peace with my Lord so near, leaning on the everlasting arms." Elisha Hoffman wrote these words after reading Deuteronomy 33:27, "God of old is your dwelling place, and underneath are the everlasting arms. He drives out the enemy before you."

All through this day, your Shepherd is not only walking just ahead of you; He lives within you and His strong, everlasting arms will hold you up and protect you from every enemy. How comforting and peace-giving is this truth. When Satan seeks to tempt you to be afraid, remind him of your Shepherd who uses His rod and staff to defend you from your enemies.

Work at memorizing Psalm 23. This precious affirmation of trust will become the sword of the Spirit as you face any fear. Perhaps you can form a habit of driving your car with any source of audio turned off so you can use the quiet time to meditate on the words of this psalm. Then when you lie down to rest at night, again meditate on its words and phrases. These are simple ways of feasting on the riches of Yahweh's truth. Hopefully, you will find this discipline to provide a resource of peace and deliverance from fear.

Yahweh in Your Worship

O Yahweh Rohi, You are with me through every dark valley of life. Therefore I choose not to fear but to trust Your protecting care. Thank You for staying with me always. Through all the life-changes I face, You remain the same. I worship You and seize this day as one of peace and security. Use me to share with others this comforting truth of what fellowship with You can mean to anyone who lives with fear.

August 4

Yahweh Rohi Gives Life in Abundance to Me

Yahweh in the Word

> "Yahweh Rohi… prepares a table before me in the presence of my enemies;
> You anoint my head with oil; my cup overflows" (Psalm 23: 5).

The setting in this powerful psalm changes from the sheep-shepherd motif (vv. 1-4) to that of a host and honored guest (vv. 5-6). However, the theme of a caring intimacy flows through both. Verse five presents the scene of a banquet where the host (Yahweh) has made us welcome by spreading a feast before us, anointing us with oil—a symbol of honor, and the overflowing cup—a vivid picture of abundance.

Yahweh in Your Walk

A friend gave my wife a plaque with these interesting words drawn from Psalm 23:5: "I'm drinking from my saucer 'cause my cup is running over." What a lovely expression of abundance! This theme of a life of abundance is found often in the Bible. One statement of Jesus comes to mind, "I have come so that they may have life and have it in abundance" (John 10:10).

When the psalmist declared, "My cup overflows," he gave a vivid picture of the abundant life given to all believers—a life of abundance. Abundance here refers to a life that receives more blessings than it can contain; there is an overflow. Such is the experience of all who place their trust in Yahweh. Our privilege is to be a channel of blessings to others; we must remember that every blessing that comes to us, comes on its way to someone else. As an old poem states:

> Have you had a kindness shown? Pass it on.
> 'Twas not meant for you alone. Pass it on.
> Let it travel down the years. Let it dry another's tears.
> 'Til in heaven the deed appears. Pass it on.

Consider this same truth found in an interesting figure of speech used by Jesus regarding this abundant life when He made this promise: "If anyone is thirsty, he should come to Me and drink! The one who believes in Me, as the Scripture has said, will have streams of living water flow from deep within him. He said this about the Spirit" (John 7:37-38). We who believe can truthfully say, "My cup overflows, in fact I have a river of living water flowing out of me!" **This abundance is the work of God's Holy Spirit in every Christian. Our task is not to make the river flow, but to keep the channel clear.**

Yahweh in Your Worship

Thank You Yahweh for Your life of abundance in me. How grateful I am for the unfailing supply of blessings You pour out for me and through me for others. May I learn to celebrate this overflow as I seize this day for Your glory and my good. Make me aware of those I meet today who need to discover this abundant life experience. Meet their need through my abundance.

August 5

Yahweh Rohi Pursues Me with His Favor

Yahweh in the Word

> "Only goodness and faithful love will pursue me all the days of my life" (Psalm 23:6a).

The first five verses of this psalm relate to present blessings from Yahweh, verse 6 looks to the future. His goodness and faithful love "pursue" us in the sense of Yahweh always seeking to bring His goodness and faithful love as blessings to us. This favor will surely be ours throughout all our future; we cannot escape these gifts. Regardless of our past sins and failures, Yahweh is never "out to get us" for these mistakes, rather He pursues us throughout our life with both goodness and love for our benefit.

Yahweh in Your Walk

Francis Thompson wrote a classic poem entitled "The Hound of Heaven" in which he portrays God as being like a hunting dog relentlessly pursuing his prey. The poet describes himself as fleeing with rebellion against God, when actually God was after him to bless, not harm him. **We also are the objects of Yahweh's pursuits; His goodness and faithful love are extended to us all the days of our lives.**

As you walk through this day, seek to be more aware of all the expressions of Yahweh's goodness and love. Notice perhaps with new appreciation, those everyday blessings that we so often take for granted. For example, think about the what-ifs of life: what if you were unable to walk, or to see, or to hear, or to taste, or to smell, or to feel by touching, or… on and on. What if you were totally isolated from all others? What if you knew nothing about Yahweh? What if you did not have a Bible? What if no one had taught you to read?

All these are real possibilities. There are many individuals who do **not** have some of these blessings. And yet, do you often think of these as being expressions of Yahweh's goodness and faithful love to you? **Why not take time today to write a list of as many of God's blessings as you can recall?** "Count your many blessings, name them one by one. And it will surprise you what the Lord has done." Pause to give thanks for each of these divine favors. Perhaps Yahweh will lead you to share with others your renewed awareness of His goodness and faithful love as seen in His gifts that we so often take for granted.

How blessed to know that these same grace gifts and more will probably be yours "all the days" of your life. And even if some of these expressions of His favor be lost, due to illness or aging or accident, you will still have His **presence** which is always greater than His **presents**.

Yahweh in Your Worship

Yes, Yahweh, I do know that You are persistently pursuing me in order to bless me. I thank You for always taking the initiative in bestowing Your favor upon me. Make me more aware of this as I seek to seize this day and claim it fully.

August 6

Yahweh's House Will Be My Home Forever

Yahweh in the Word

"I will dwell in the house of Yahweh as long as I live" (Psalm 23:6b)

In verse 5 the psalmist described the pleasures of a banquet at the home of his host. Now, in verse 6 he affirms that this feast occurs in Yahweh's house and this celebration with its abundant provisions will continue forever. There the psalmist will no longer be a temporary guest, but a permanent resident. What a beautiful picture of the eternal abode of believers.

Just as Jesus promised, "In My Father's house are many dwelling places; if not, I would have told you. I am going away to prepare a place for you. If I go away and prepare a place for you, I will come back and receive you to Myself, so that where I am you may be also" (John 14:2-3).

Yahweh in Your Walk

An older Christian friend was nearing his departure after an extended illness. As I sought to comfort him, he said, "Please don't grieve for me; I'm going home, and what a wonderful place that is." **What a difference it makes to know that where we are going after this brief life is "the house of Yahweh."**

We find various biblical descriptions of the beauties of heaven. However, what will make heaven so wonderful will be the presence of Yahweh. **Just to be with Him for all eternity means pleasure beyond our greatest imagination.** Think of all He will explain to you that seemed a mystery in this life. Anticipate having unbroken fellowship, not only with Yahweh but also with all loved ones and friends who have gone before you.

Albert Brumley expressed his assurance of going to heaven in this way:

> This world is not my home, I'm just a passing through. My treasures are laid up somewhere beyond the blue. The angels beckon me from heaven's open door, and I can't feel at home in this world anymore.

As you walk through this day, keep in mind Yahweh's promise of spending eternity with Him in His beautiful home. **Let this awareness of heaven keep you from giving more attention and value than you should to the temporary things of earth.** Remember that the apostle Paul assured us that "the things that are seen are temporary, but the things that are unseen are eternal" (2 Corinthians 4:18).

Yahweh in Your Worship

Forgive me, Yahweh, when I live as if this world was the most important place for me. Help me remember Your promise of a much better place in Your home in heaven. Deliver me from giving too much value to all those things that are temporal, and direct me to treasure that which is eternal.

August 7

Yahweh Will Sometimes Bring Good from My Disappointments

Yahweh in the Word

> "A man's heart plans his way, but Yahweh determines his steps" (Proverbs 16:9).

The writer of Proverbs (probably Solomon) makes this wise observation: A person makes plans according to what he considers to be best. However, Yahweh is sovereign in His control of His people and sometimes brings to pass a better plan ("steps") than they intended.

Yahweh in Your Walk

As you begin this day, you have certain plans regarding expected happenings. However, **you have learned from experience that sometimes your plans change by circumstances beyond your control**. A well-known saying states it this way: "The best laid plans of mice and men often go awry." You can probably testify to this truth from your own life.

The Dayspring Chorale, a traveling high school singing group, arrived at a nursing home for a Thursday concert only to discover they were expected on Friday. They were told they could go ahead and sing, but only for a short time due to a scheduled memorial service for one of the residents. The son of the man who had died heard them sing and asked if they would remain and sing for the service. Their singing of Christian songs brought much comfort and hope to all who came to the memorial. Yahweh used their "mistake" to be a time of needed ministry!

Recently I heard about a friend who had been diagnosed with a very serious illness. I planned to visit him but did not know when or where that might occur. One day as I was leaving my appointment with a physician, I walked down the hallway of the office building and there stood my friend—as if waiting for us to meet! I had plans but Yahweh had better plans, and He directed my steps.

I have learned from many similar experiences that Yahweh's schedule is always best, although often unknown by me in advance. **My dis-appointments have often proved to be His-appointments.** As you begin this and every day, pause to offer a prayer like this from Psalm 31:15 "My times are in Your hands." **You will be surprised at how often Yahweh will guide your steps to something better than you planned.** A Yahweh serendipity!

> Sometimes our plan does not unfold
> The way we thought it would;
> But God is always in control
> To use it for our good!—Sper

Yahweh in Your Worship

Yes, Yahweh, today my times are in Your wise hands. Thank You for all You have planned for me. I praise You in advance for the good appointments You have made.

August 8

Yahweh Teaches Me to Pray for Others

Yahweh in the Word

> "Arise, cry out in the night from the first watch of the night. Pour out your heart like water before Yahweh's presence. Lift up your hands to Him for the lives of your children who are fainting from hunger on the corner of every street" (Lamentations 2:19).

The prophet Jeremiah was probably the writer of this book. He was lamenting the condition of Yahweh's people due to the destruction of Jerusalem and the Temple in 586 B.C. In this text he calls for parents to call upon Yahweh on behalf of their children.

Yahweh in Your Walk

About 30 years ago two women felt called by Yahweh to begin a ministry of prayer for their children as well as the children of others. More mothers joined them and the organization grew and became known as "Mom's in Touch." Presently, this ministry is found in all 50 states and 140 countries around the world. They meet for one hour each week to pray for children in schools. Their goal is for every school in the world to be covered with prayer.

Our text for today is one of the Bible verses "Mom's in Touch" uses as the basis for believing Yahweh hears their prayers and that He answers. Theirs is a ministry of intercessory praying. They are convinced that such praying makes a real difference in the life of each child and of the school they attend. These women come from many different Christian denominations, different racial and ethnic groups—all united by a common belief in Yahweh's promises to hear and answer the prayers of His people.

You may not be a mother but **you are called by Yahweh to join all believers everywhere in the ministry of praying for others**. Hopefully, you have your own list of persons for whom you pray. The Bible urges us to pray for our leaders, both in government and local churches. Our Lord Yeshua mentioned one concern for all His followers to remember in prayer. He said, "Therefore, pray to the Lord of the harvest to send out workers into His harvest" (Luke 10:2).

Listen to this interesting information from the book of Revelation: "Another angel with a gold incense burner, came and stood at the altar. He was given a large amount of incense to offer with the prayers of all the saints on the gold altar in front of the throne. The smoke of the incense, with the prayers of the saints, went up in the presence of God from the angel's hand" (Revelation 8:3-4). **Here is a clear record of the presence in heaven of the prayers of Yahweh's people**. Yes, your prayers for others are important and do make a difference.

Yahweh in Your Worship

Thank You Yahweh for calling me to join all Your children to make a difference in this world by praying for others. Help me be faithful to this important ministry. Today, I want to seize opportunities to pray for those You will bring across my path and in my mind.

August 9

Yahweh Will Remove My Sins from Me

Yahweh in the Word

> "Who is a God like You, removing iniquity and passing over rebellion for the remnant of His inheritance? He does not hold on to His anger forever, because He delights in faithful love. He will again have compassion on us; He will vanquish our iniquities. You will cast all our sins into the depths of the sea" (Micah 7:18-19).

Micah, whose name means "Who is like Yahweh?" was God's prophet, sent with a message of both warning and hope to His people. In these closing verses of his book, Micah offers encouragement to his fellow Jews by looking forward to the future when they would return from captivity in Babylon and be fully restored as Yahweh's chosen nation. This text focuses on His gracious removal of their sin and guilt.

Yahweh in Your Walk

All humankind shares one very serious problem—that is the problem of sin. We were all born with a fallen nature, one that rebels against God. Here is the underlying explanation for our attitudes and actions that result in grief for ourselves and others. Yahweh is fully aware of this human flaw and is committed to bringing a permanent remedy. The message of the gospel is that Yahweh so loved every person that He went to the extreme of sending His Son to show us how we should live, then die to provide deliverance from our sin and guilt—freeing us to experience the new life He provides.

Micah declared good news when he said that Yahweh would "vanquish our iniquities," then "cast all our sins into the depths of the sea." All this is available to us today if we will turn from our rebellion against Yahweh and, by faith, receive the Lord Jesus as our Savior and Lord. As one writer said, "God promises to cast our sins into the depths of the sea. He then puts up a sign saying NO FISHING!" In other words, sin is to be forgiven and forgotten, by both Yahweh and by us. **By faith in Yahweh's promise, we know He forgives. He will not bring up the sins of our past and neither should we.**

An old hymn has these helpful lines, "He breaks the power of cancelled sin and sets the prisoner free." Cancelled sin refers to our sins that have been confessed and forgiven. We must let go of these sins and move on to living in freedom from them. Do not allow Satan to cause you unnecessary grief and guilt by reminding you of your sinful past. Stand up to him by declaring your faith in Yahweh's promise to forgive once and forever.

Yahweh in Your Worship

I choose to seize the truth of forgiven and forgotten sin. Today, Yahweh, I rejoice in Your continuing love and compassion toward me. Thank You for forgiving and forgetting all my sins. I rejoice in the peace that comes from knowing You have removed my sins from me forever. Teach me to overcome my sinful nature and live in the freedom of the new nature in Christ.

August 10

Yahweh Provides Cleansing from All My Sins

Yahweh in the Word

> "On that day a fountain will be opened for the house of David and for the residents of Jerusalem, to wash away sin and impurity… I will say: They are my people, and they will say Yahweh is our God" (Zechariah 13:1, 9b).

The prophet Zechariah was sent by Yahweh to call His people to repent of their sins and return to Him. These who had come back to their homeland after many years in captivity were guilty of worshiping idols and heeding the words of false prophets. Our text is a message of hope for their future, ultimately fulfilled through the sacrifice of Jesus.

Yahweh in Your Walk

William Cowper (1731-1800) was an English poet who wrote many hymns which are sung today. At one time, however, he became so depressed that he spent several years in an institution for the mentally ill. While there he read the words of our text and from that was inspired to write the familiar hymn beginning with these words:

> There is a fountain filled with blood drawn from Emmanuel's veins,
> And sinners plunged beneath that flood, lose all their guilty stains.
>
> …
>
> The dying thief rejoiced to see that fountain in his day;
> And there may I, though vile as he, wash all my sins away.

The apostle John clearly identified this cleansing fountain when he stated: "If we walk in the light as He Himself is in the light, we have fellowship with one another, and the blood of Jesus His Son cleanses us from all sin… If we confess our sins, He is faithful and righteous to forgive us our sins and to cleanse us from all unrighteousness" (1 John 1:7, 9). What good news for us sinners! **Yahweh promises to not only forgive our sins when we confess them but also to completely cleanse us from the defilement of those forgiven sins.**

You will notice from this text that the single condition on our part for forgiveness and cleansing is to "confess our sins." This word **confess** literally means "to agree with," that is, we must agree with what Yahweh says about our sins. **First,** that we alone are responsible for our rebellion against Him, disobeying His commands. **Second,** that these actions are serious and deserving of the punishment of eternal separation from Him. **Third,** we cannot save ourselves from our sins and thus we call upon Him for mercy and pardon. When we confess in this manner, He promises to forgive and cleanse us. All this is possible because Jesus gave His life for us upon the cross—His shed blood became our "cleansing fountain."

Yahweh in Your Worship

Most gracious and merciful Yahweh, I do confess that I have sinned and now claim Your pardon and cleansing. Thank You for being so good to me. I seize this day of opportunities to serve You.

August 11

Yahweh Hears and Answers My Prayers

Yahweh in the Word

> "Yahweh who made heaven and earth, Yahweh who made it to establish it, Yahweh is His name, says this: 'Call to Me and I will answer you and tell you great and incomprehensible things you do not know'" (Jeremiah 33:2-3).

Yahweh spoke these words to Jeremiah in order to remind the prophet who was speaking to him—the One who created all things. A person so great would have no problem answering Jeremiah's requests regarding much smaller matters than creation. Yahweh also promised to reveal to him mysteries beyond the prophet's limited understanding.

Yahweh in Your Walk

The experience of calling upon Yahweh with some specific personal request and receiving an answer is amazing indeed. **To think that someone as great as the sovereign Creator of all things would give attention to our little concerns is incomprehensible indeed.** Allow to share my most recent example of that miracle.

My wife and I went to a local restaurant for lunch. When time came to pay the bill, I could not find my billfold with the credit card I often use. Unfortunately, my wife forgot to bring her purse and I had no cash, so we were in trouble. She stayed at the table while I drove home, looked in vain for my cards, and then returned with one of her cards. All this time I am trying to remember the last time I had this wallet and where I might have left it—nothing came up in my mind. When we returned home, I began a very thorough search after offering a simple prayer like this: "Yahweh, You know where this lost item is, please guide me to locate it."

Later that afternoon, our grandson made an unexpected visit to our home. I told him of my loss and he replied, "I did the same thing several years ago. After searching in vain, I obtained a new driver's license and all the credit cards. However, several months later, I put on an old coat and there was my wallet in the pocket!" When he said that, I went immediately to my clothes closet and found my lost wallet in trousers I wore three days earlier! I breathed a prayer of thanks to Yahweh. I believe He heard my plea and sent His answer by my grandson.

This story is an example of many such answers to prayer regarding relatively small matters. I could likewise relate similar answers to much more significant requests. The point is, **Yahweh does hear and does answer in His own time and manner. Amazing love and kindness!**

Yahweh in Your Worship

Gracious Yahweh, I praise You and thank You for hearing and answering all my prayers—not always when and how I prefer, but in Your time and way which is best. Your love includes and covers every concern we have; I am so grateful for Your involvement. Forgive me when I fail to include You in all I seek to do.

August 12
Yahweh Calls Me to Draw Near to Him

Yahweh in the Word

> "Draw near to God, and He will draw near to you. Cleanse your hands, sinners, and purify your hearts, double-minded people!" (James 4:8).

These words come to us from James, the half-brother of Jesus. He became a believer sometime after the resurrection of Jesus. His letter is one of the earliest writings of the New Testament. In this text he appeals to his readers to seek a close relationship with God by the removal of their sins, becoming single-minded in their devotion to Him.

Yahweh in Your Walk

One of my favorite hymn writers was Fannie Crosby (1820-1915) who composed some 8,000 hymns plus many other works of poetry in spite of being blind since infancy. In one of these works she spoke of her desire to be closer to God:

> I am thine, O Lord, I have heard Thy voice, and it told Thy love to me;
> But I long to rise in the arms of faith, and be closer drawn to Thee.
> Draw me nearer, nearer blessed Lord, to the cross where Thou hast died:
> Draw me nearer, nearer, nearer, blessed Lord, to Thy precious bleeding side.

These words of prayer express the desire of most Christians. **We long to have a closer relationship with our Lord Yeshua. James helps us know that such a nearness to Him is possible if we are willing to turn from our sins and seek His forgiveness and cleansing.** Drawing near to Him means that we must actively seek a closer relationship. In response to such efforts, He will draw near to us. Only one thing prevents a close, intimate fellowship with Yahweh. Isaiah exposed that barrier in these words: "Your iniquities have built barriers between you and your God, and your sins have made Him hide His face from you" (Isaiah 59:2). The moment we repent of our sins, confess them and claim His pardon and cleansing, He removes the barriers and restores the closeness we seek.

Sometimes these sins are unknown to us; we may not recognize the problem. This prayer of David becomes very helpful at such a time: "Search me, God, and know my heart; test me and know my concerns. See if there is any offensive way in me; lead me in the everlasting way" (Psalm 139:23-24). Yahweh will answer such a sincere prayer and bring His conviction for sin to us. The result can be a closer relationship with Him than you have ever known before.

Yahweh in Your Worship

Thank You most merciful and gracious Yahweh for Your willingness and provision for me to have a closer relationship with You. I seize this opportunity to draw near to You for Your glory as well as for my good.

August 13

Yahweh Wants to Use What I Have for His Purposes

Yahweh in the Word

> *"You give them something to eat, He responded… And He asked them, 'How many loaves to you have? Go look.' When they found out they said, 'Five, and two fish.' Then He instructed them to have all the people sit down in groups on the green grass… Then He took the five loaves and the two fish, and looking up to heaven, He blessed and broke the loaves. He kept giving them to His disciples to set before the people. He also divided the two fish among them all. Everyone ate and was filled" (Mark 6:37-43).*

This miracle of feeding more than 5,000 people with five loaves and two fish is the only one found in all four Gospels. Certainly this was a very impressive event.

Yahweh in Your Walk

An old gospel song has this line: "Little is much when God is in it!" The miracle of our text is a good example of this truth. Only in the gospel of John's account of this event do we learn that the five small loaves and two fish comprised the lunch of a young boy who was present. Jesus used that meager beginning to feed a multitude, and had 12 baskets-full left over!

We can learn practical lessons from every miracle Jesus performed. In fact, John called them "sign miracles," meaning each one was like a sign pointing to something greater beyond the actual event. **One clear lesson from this amazing happening is that Jesus can take our small means, multiply them, and accomplish far more than we could.** He is the divine Multiplier! One essential ingredient in this recipe for greatness is that all we have must be place in His hands. He took all five loaves and two fish, leaving the boy with nothing.

We may assume that our talents, possessions, and abilities are too small to make much difference, however, if we turn all these over to Jesus, He makes the little become much! I am thinking of a small boy I knew many years ago. His family was part of the little country church where I was the pastor. They were a rather poor family with very limited means, but they loved Jesus and committed all their children to Him. Today that boy, Greg Idell, is a missionary in Canada serving under the North American Mission Board. He and his family were small in the sight of this world, but Yahweh had plans to use him greatly.

That same truth applies to all of us and to all we possess—Yahweh wants to take the small offering we can bring Him, multiply it, and use it to accomplish far more than we could. How important that we begin our daily walk with a full and complete surrender to Him.

Yahweh in Your Worship

All to Jesus I surrender, all to You I freely give. Thank You Yahweh that my small offering of myself and all I have, plus Your power to multiply, equals greatness. I gladly place my limited possessions into Your unlimited power and plan for me. I worship You as the only true and living God.

August 14

Yahweh Wants to Help Me in Many Ways

Yahweh in the Word

> "Happy is the one whose help is the God of Jacob, whose hope is in Yahweh his God. (Ps.146:5).

When Yahweh is described here as "the God of Jacob," we know He is a God who helps those who desperately need it. Jacob, whose name means "cheater," was often in trouble due to his deceitful ways. And yet, Yahweh was merciful to him and often came to his aid.

Yahweh in Your Walk

You can be sure of one thing today—you are going to need Yahweh's help. No matter what happens, apart from His presence and faithful assistance, you will not do well. The psalmist was aware of his dependence upon Yahweh, and he makes a long list of all the good ways Yahweh helps him. As you read through these provisions, pause to give thanks for each one.

The list begins with the most obvious help—He is the Creator of everything there is. Apart from Him nothing would exist. Even the air we breathe is His gift. Next, Yahweh is forever faithful—you can always count on Him to be the same, yesterday, today, and forever. Also, He reaches out to insure justice for all who are "exploited" (oppressed). Here is the hope mentioned by the psalmist in our text for today. He provides food to satisfy the needs of the hungry; He sets prisoners free, especially those who are in bondage to their sins. Yahweh opens the eyes of the blind (both physically and spiritually) and raises up all who are oppressed (bowed down). He expresses His love to the righteous and His protection to foreigners. Those who are fatherless (orphans) and the widows are helped by Him. Yahweh even helps the wicked by frustrating them (turning his ways upside down). He does this to help the evil person wake up and turn from his wickedness. These are just a few of the many ways Yahweh provides the practical help we need.

What a powerful statement of Yahweh's initiative in reaching out to make a difference for everyone—all who know Him and all who don't. **Yahweh has no favorites; He is concerned for all persons, and offers His life-changing help to them.** These acts of compassion provoke the psalmist to begin this chapter with this appeal to his soul:

"Hallelujah! My soul, praise Yahweh! I will praise Yahweh all my life; I will sing to my God as long as I live." Let this become your response as you meditate upon all the help Yahweh offers you today. **Express your gratitude in your own words of thanksgiving.** As you walk through this day, be mindful of all His provisions for you, from the most basic to the most remarkable. Yes, happy is the one whose help and hope is the God of Jacob."

Yahweh in Your Worship

All praise, glory, thanksgiving, and honor belong to You, Yahweh, my personal helper, redeemer, and friend. I am amazed at Your compassion expressed toward me in so many practical ways. As I walk through each day, help me be more aware of all the help You give.

August 15

Yahweh Has Prepared Great Blessings for Me

Yahweh in the Word

> "But as it is written: 'What eye did not see and ear did not hear, and what never entered the human mind—God prepared this for those who love Him.' Now God has revealed these things to us by the Spirit, for the Spirit searches everything, even the depths of God" (1 Cor. 2:9-10).

The apostle Paul wrote this to believers in the city of Corinth. He is quoting words from Isaiah 52:15 and 64:4. Paul applies this truth to his readers in the sense that none of them could have seen nor heard nor even thought about the amazing salvation plans Yahweh had for them until the Holy Spirit revealed this to them.

Yahweh in Your Walk

Recently our pastor, Darrell Gwaltney, spoke about his humble beginnings, coming from parents who had very meager financial means and limited education. He went on to tell how as a young man he would never have imagined all the fine opportunities for education, travel, and service for the Lord he experienced later. My wife and I have a similar testimony. Growing up in a rather obscure place, we often marvel at the blessings Yahweh has given us—so much more than we could ever have thought possible. He prepared for these opportunities long before they appeared.

All this reminds me of the story of Frances Ridley Havergal, a well-known writer of hymns. When she was eleven years old, she learned that her mother was not going to live long. Fanny, as she was called, refused to believe such a loss would be hers. One of the last things her beloved mother told Frances was, **"Fanny dear, pray God to prepare you for all He is preparing for you."** This became her lifelong prayer. Although Frances suffered from poor health most of her life, she wrote many great hymns before she passed on in 1878 at the age of forty-two. Among these compositions are: "Take My Life and Let It Be," "Lord, Speak to Me That I May Speak," and "Who Is on the Lord's Side?" Carved on her tombstone at her own request is: "The blood of Jesus Christ his Son cleanseth us from all sin" (1 John 1:7).

As you walk through this day, give some time to recalling those unexpected blessings you have experienced in the past by Yahweh's favor. Then commit yourself afresh to whatever He has in store for your remaining time in this world. Claim the Holy Spirit's ministry of revealing these gifts. **Ask Him to prepare you for all He is preparing for you**. When your day comes to be promoted from here to eternity, you will join others who say, "I cannot believe how good Yahweh was to me all along my journey. When I started walking with Him, I would not have believed all the wonderful things He had prepared for me."

Yahweh in Your Worship

Gracious Yahweh, I do love You and worship You as the Giver of every good and perfect gift. Thank You for the amazing opportunities You have planned for me this day and every day. Holy Spirit, help me recognize all those special blessings that come from Father, Son, and Holy Spirit.

August 16

Yeshua Wants Me to Remember Him in the Lord's Supper

Yeshua in the Word

> "For I received from the Lord what I also passed on to you: On the night when He was betrayed, the Lord Jesus took bread, gave thanks, broke it, and said, 'This is My body, which is for you. Do this in remembrance of Me.' In the same way, after supper He also took the cup and said, 'This cup is the new covenant established by My blood. Do this, as often as you drink it, in remembrance of Me.' For as often as you eat this bread and drink the cup, you proclaim the Lord's death until He comes" (1 Corinthians 11:23-26).

These words are the apostle Paul's account of the Lord's Supper. Although Paul was not present for this meaningful event, later he was given these words by Jesus Himself. Notice that two times Yeshua says to do this "in remembrance of Me." Taking the bread and the cup of juice are reminders of His sacrifice on the cross for us.

Yeshua in Your Walk

Several years ago my wife and I visited the Lincoln Memorial in Washington, D.C. We were deeply impressed as we read from his speeches and looked at the monument of him seated in a huge chair. All these things helped us to remember this great U.S. president. Think about another monument. **Yeshua left His own memorial in the form of a simple piece of bread and a cup of juice.** When we look upon these elements we recall His death for our sins. However, unlike other monuments to great people, His has one distinctive difference: **We who believe in Him actually partake of His monument—we eat the bread and drink from the cup.**

When we visit other monuments, we simply look at them. But our Lord's monument requires our participation—eating and drinking these reminders. He deliberately chose this action to symbolize the reality of our having partaken of Him by faith. **As surely as eating and drinking food nourishes us physically, partaking of His body and blood by faith brings spiritual life.**

The ordinance of the Lord's Supper is intended to be a church family event; we join other believers in this solemn celebration. Your involvement in this visual reminder on a regular basis is very important as you recall His supreme love-gift to you. In addition to these times of church fellowship, I also begin each day with my own Lord's Supper by partaking of a cup of coffee and a small piece of bread as I recite these adapted words from an old communion hymn:

> Bread of heaven, on Thee I feed, for Thy flesh is meat indeed;
> Ever may my soul be fed with this true and living bread.
> Day by day with strength supplied, through the life of Him who died.
> Vine of heaven, Thy blood supplies this blest cup of sacrifice;
> Lord, Thy wounds my healing give, to Thy cross I look and live;
> Jesus, may I ever be grafted, rooted, built in Thee. Josiah Conder (1789-1855)

Yeshua in Your Worship

Blessed Savior, I worship You as the atoning sacrifice for my sins.

August 17

Yahweh Owns Me

Yahweh in the Word

> "Don't you know that your body is a sanctuary of the Holy Spirit who is in you, whom you have from God? You are not your own, for you were bought at a price. Therefore glorify God in your body and in your spirit, which belong to God" (1 Corinthians 6:19-20).

Some of the Corinthian Christians failed to understand that because Yahweh purchased them through the sacrifice of His Son, they now belonged to Him, body and spirit. Paul wrote these words to remind them of this fact. He was helping them realize that any form of sexual sin was a sin against the Holy Spirit's sanctuary—their body.

Yahweh in Your Walk

We are sometimes challenged to think about, **"Who am I?"** Certainly this is a vitally important question to answer. We all need a clear sense of identity. However, equally significant is to know, **"Whose am I?"** The question of ownership is one we must all reckon with, especially after we become a follower of Yeshua. Before we believed on Him as our Savior and Lord we were our own person, in fact we may have said to ourselves or to others, "This is my life and I can do with it as I please." And that was true at one time, but since committing ourselves to Him, our ownership has changed. As Paul reminded the Corinthians: "You are not your own, for you were bought at a price."

The readers of Paul's letter were very familiar with slave markets where individuals would be bought and sold. **When Yeshua died upon the cross to pay the penalty for all our sins, He also purchased us from Satan's slave market and set us free to serve Him.** So now, our body and spirit, along with all we possess belongs to Him—our ownership has changed! And this fact changes everything about our lives; we no longer make decisions based on what we want or how we view life, rather what is His will for us.

Yahweh in Your Worship

John Wesley (1703-1791) felt strongly about Yahweh being his new owner, he and wrote this prayer which revealed his complete surrender to Him. Let this be your own expression of worship today.

> I am no longer my own, but yours. Put me to what you will, rank me with whom you will. Put me to doing, put me to suffering. Let me be employed by you or laid aside by you, enabled for you or brought low by you. Let me be full, let me be empty. Let me have all things, let me have nothing. I freely and heartily yield all things to your pleasure and disposal. And now, O Glorious and blessed God, Father, Son, and Holy Spirit, you are mine, and I am yours. So be it. And the covenant which I have made on earth, let it be ratified in heaven. Amen.

(You may want to copy this prayer and keep it where you can find it to use as you worship later.)

August 18

Yahweh's Words Can Make a Powerful Impact Upon Me

Yahweh in the Word

> "'Is not My word like fire'—this is Yahweh's declaration—'and like a hammer that pulverizes rock?'" (Jeremiah 23:29).

One of Jeremiah's tasks as a prophet of Yahweh was to expose false prophets and warn the people to beware of their claims to speak the truth. In contrast to false teachings, Yahweh's word always makes a powerful impact upon its hearers.

Yahweh in Your Walk

As you walk through each day, you are inundated with words—all kinds of words—words from the world's media, entertaining words, conversational words, written words, helpful words, hurtful words, and on and on, but there are some words that can have a greater impact upon you than all others—Yahweh's words. As the prophet declared, Yahweh's word is like fire that consumes and like a hammer that breaks in pieces. These images reveal the powerful effect of the truths found in the Bible.

Think further about these two metaphors. Fire is often used in Scripture to speak of purifying and refining in the sense of burning up the dross and consuming all that is impure. The psalmist declared, "I have treasured Your word in my heart so that I may not sin against You" (Psalm 119:11). **As you examine biblical teachings, the Holy Spirit uses His truth to convict you of sins in your life and leads you to repentance, confession, and cleansing.**

Moreover, the Word is used as a hammer by the Holy Spirit to break down walls of resistance against Yahweh. There are times when your pride may need to be broken by being confronted with truth from His word. When King David had sinned with Bathsheba, Yahweh sent Nathan the prophet to bring conviction for his behavior. Later David wrote these words, "Against You—You alone—I have sinned and done this evil in Your sight… Let me hear joy and gladness; let the bones You have crushed rejoice" (Psalm 51:4, 8). **How very important for you to have a plan of searching the Scriptures daily. By doing this you place a fire and hammer in the hands of the Holy Spirit that He may purify your heart and break down any barriers.**

You are familiar with the translation of the Bible authorized by King James of England and completed in 1611. He also influenced a revised version of The Book of Common Prayer in 1604 which contains this prayer regarding the value of the Bible: "Blessed Lord, who hast caused all holy Scriptures to be written for our learning; grant that we may… hear them, read, mark, learn, and inwardly digest them, that by patience, and comfort of [Your] holy Word, we may embrace and every hold fast the blessed hope of everlasting life." This ancient prayer affirms the authority of Scripture as well as its significant benefit to all who pursue its content.

Yahweh in Your Worship

Thank You, holy Father, for giving me Your Word as a lamp, a light, a fire, and a hammer.

August 19

Yahweh Wants Me to Know that He Is Holy

Yahweh in the Word

> *"Holy, holy, holy is the LORD of Hosts (Yahweh Sabaoth); His glory fills the whole earth" (Isaiah 6:3)*

The prophet Isaiah had a vision in which he saw Yahweh in the temple in heaven with seraphim (angels) standing above Him; they were calling to one another with these solemn words to declare the holiness of Yahweh.

Yahweh in Your Walk

What comes to your mind when you think of the holiness of Yahweh? Perhaps you think of Him as being without sin, perfect in every way. Certainly this is true, but His holiness is far more than that. The term **holy** basically means to be separate, and set apart from all that is unholy. Other terms from this root are sanctified, sanctuary, and saint. Thus when the angels declared that Yahweh is holy (repeated three times to magnify the meaning), they were revealing to Isaiah that Yahweh is separate from all else in creation because of His greatness, righteousness, and majesty—He is therefore to be worshiped and honored by all.

While Reginald Heber (1783-1826) was the bishop of Calcutta, India, he was surrounded by the worship of many false gods. As he contemplated the holiness of the one true God, he was inspired to write what the poet Alfred Lord Tennyson called "The world's greatest hymn."

> Holy, holy, holy! Lord God Almighty! Early in the morning our song shall rise to Thee,
> Holy, holy, holy! merciful and mighty! God in three Persons, blessed Trinity!
> Holy, holy, holy! all the saints adore Thee, casting down their golden crowns around the glassy sea;
> Cherubim and seraphim falling down before Thee, which wert and art and evermore shall be.
> Holy, holy, holy! though the darkness hide Thee, though the eye of sinful man Thy glory may not see.
> Only Thou art holy—there is none beside Thee, perfect in pow'r, in love and purity.
> Holy, holy, holy! Lord God Almighty! All thy works shall praise Thy name in earth and sky and sea!
> Holy, holy, holy! merciful and mighty! God in three Persons, blessed Trinity!

As you sing or say these magnificent words, seek to focus upon the holiness of Yahweh; ask Him to help you comprehend more of the meaning of this truth.

Yahweh in Your Worship

O holy Yahweh, I long to know more of Your greatness, majesty, and love. Help me to worship You with a greater understanding of who You are and all You do in this great universe.

August 20

Yahweh Created Me to Live a Productive Life

Yahweh in the Word

> "The righteous thrive like a palm tree and grow like a cedar tree in Lebanon. Planted in the house of Yahweh, they thrive in the courts of our God. They will still bear fruit in old age, healthy and green, to declare: 'Yahweh is just; He is my rock, and there is no unrighteousness in Him'" (Psalm 92:12-15).

This psalmist compared human life to trees—a palm and a cedar. His point was that persons who have a right relationship with Yahweh continue to thrive and grow and be fruitful even in old age. Their testimony speaks of Yahweh's justice, righteousness, and faithfulness—like a rock.

Yahweh in Your Walk

Yahweh's first words to Adam and Eve were: "Be fruitful…." (Genesis 1:28). His plan was for them to bear children, but also to live productive lives. That original purpose for all humankind has never changed. We all have a divine mission to fulfill, and that mission is to live lives that thrive and grow and bear fruit—even in old age.

Think for a moment about yourself; what evidence can you show that your life, up to now, has produced that which pleases Yahweh and begins to fulfill His purpose for creating you. Surely none of us is satisfied with our achievements; we have all sinned come short of our God-given potential. No one can boast of being all He intended for us to be. However, we can be forgiven for the past and make a fresh start, with Yahweh's help, to become more productive for Him than ever before.

What is the secret of living a fruitful life? The psalmist gave the answer in these words: "**Planted** in the house of Yahweh, they **thrive** in the courts of our God," which is another way of expressing the essential need for a personal relationship with Yahweh—**His life in us is the only means to authentic productivity**. Jesus spoke clearly about this when He said to His disciples, "I am the vine; you are the branches. The one who remains in Me and I in him produces much fruit, because you can do nothing without Me" (John 15:5). **You will not be a fruitful person by simply trying harder to do good; rather, as you make yourself available to Him and trust Him to work in and through you, He will produce the fruit.**

As you begin this new day, filled with opportunities, **seize the day** by offering yourself to Yeshua as His branch; claim the most productive life ever lived—His life, to thrive through you.

Yahweh in Your Worship

Thank You, Holy Father, for creating me to bear much fruit—for Your glory. Today, I choose to depend entirely upon You to work Your wonderful will in and through me. Here am I, use me to be a true blessing to everyone I meet. May Your productive life thrive in me—even in old age!

August 21

Yahweh Warns Me about False Teachers

Yahweh in the Word

> *If there come any unto you, and bring not this doctrine, receive him not into your house, neither bid him Godspeed" (2 John 1:10).*

Although the apostle John is known as the "Apostle of Love," he was aware that false teachers were seeking to lead astray the true followers of Jesus. He advises them to avoid giving hospitality to such evil persons.

Yahweh in Your Walk

You have probably heard the term "wolves in sheep's clothing." **We must recognize that not everyone who gives the appearance of being a true follower of Jesus is actually that way.** In fact today there are many false cults who claim to worship and serve our Lord, but in reality they deny the truth of biblical revelation about Him. The Jesus they claim to know is not the same as the Jesus of the Bible. When these who twist the truth come to us, we must know what to do.

Several months ago I was working in my front yard when a car stopped in my driveway. Two nicely dressed couples were seated in the front and back of the car. One couple got out and approached me with literature in their hands. I recognized them as belonging to a cult who claimed to have special information about Yahweh's kingdom. Before they could speak, I said, "Thank you for coming here today, I want to tell you about Yahweh and the good news of eternal life through His Son, the Lord Jesus Christ." I continued by giving my own testimony of His grace and mercy to me—not giving them a change to say anything. Then I said, "Now, before you go, I want to pray for you." As I reached out my hands to touch them, they quickly backed away, got in their car and left, without ever saying a word! No hospitality here!

The term "Godspeed" in our text means *May God prosper you.* When astronaut John Glenn took off to become the first American to orbit the earth, the ground control leader was quoted as saying, "Godspeed, John Glenn." This blessing is always appropriate for such events, however, as the apostle John warns, not for teachers of false doctrines. Hospitality was not to be extended to these who sought to pervert the truth. When members of religious cults offer to come to your home or engage you in conversation, the safest response is to politely decline their invitation. If, however, you are familiar with their false teachings and have prepared a biblical response, you may be able to enlighten them. Just beware of Satan's attempt to bring confusion and doubt to you. The best defense against erroneous doctrines is to have a firm grasp of the truth, with Scripture references to back up your beliefs. And to avoid contact with those who pervert truth.

Yahweh in Your Worship

Lord God of all truth, thank You for revealing truth to me. Help me to love truth and to love all who may not know the way of truth. Guard me against false teachings; thank You for giving the Spirit of truth to live in me and to guide me into all that honors and pleases You.

August 22

Yahweh Is the Solid Rock on Which I Stand

Yahweh in the Word

> "David spoke the words of this song to Yahweh on the day Yahweh rescued him from the hand of all his enemies and from the hand of Saul. He said, 'Yahweh is my rock, my fortress and my deliverer, my God, my mountain where I seek refuge.'" (2 Samuel 22:1-3).

David wrote this song to celebrate Yahweh's deliverance from his enemies. He found Yahweh to be a solid rock on which he could stand to overcome all adversaries.

Yahweh in Your Walk

You may be familiar with the "Old Man of the Mountain" which was a huge rock formation near Franconia, New Hampshire. This likeness to a man's face was some 40 feet tall and 25 feet wide high up on the side of a mountain. In 1850 Nathaniel Hawthorne wrote a short story based in this amazing rock entitled, ***The Great Stone Face***. This famous profile became the New Hampshire state emblem, appearing on license plates, postage stamps, stationery, and various other items. However, to everyone's disappointment, due to natural causes, the face collapsed on May 3, 2003. Now, only a jagged rock wall remains.

Fortunately, we who trust Yahweh have in Him a solid rock that will never fail. We can say with David, "Yahweh is my rock, my fortress and my deliverer." And long before David, Moses wrote a similar song in which he said, "I will proclaim Yahweh's name. Declare the greatness of our God! The Rock—His work is perfect; all His ways are entirely just. A faithful God, without prejudice, He is righteous and true" (Deuteronomy 32: 3-4).

As you walk through this day, you need a solid foundation for your life, one that will enable you to stand firm in the face of adversity as well as endure the test of time. Everything you can see is actually temporary and will one day be destroyed by the fire of Yahweh's judgment, but He will always be the same yesterday, today and forever. **How comforting and reassuring to know that your hope is built on the Rock that will never collapse—never fail to provide a secure base on which you can stand.**

An Englishman named Edward Mote (1797-1874) wrote more than 150 hymn texts. One of the best known and loved contains these lines from his own testimony:

> My hope is built on nothing less than Jesus blood and righteousness;
> I dare not trust the sweetest frame, but wholly lean on Jesus name.
> On Christ the solid Rock I stand; all other ground is sinking sand;
> All other ground is sinking sand.

Yahweh in Your Worship

O Rock of Ages, I rejoice that You are the eternal foundation for my hope and peace.

August 23

Yeshua Has Chosen You to Be His Bride

Yeshua in the Word

> "Then I heard something like the voice of a vast multitude, like the sound of cascading waters, and like the rumbling of loud thunder, saying, 'Hallelujah, because our Lord God, the Almighty, has begun to reign! Let us be glad, rejoice, and give Him glory, because the marriage of the Lamb has come, and His wife has prepared herself...Those invited to the marriage feast of the Lamb are fortunate!'" (Revelation 19:6-9).

Throughout the Bible Yahweh uses the image of a bride and groom to describe the intimate relationship He desires with His people. Sometimes He accused Israel of being guilty of adultery because they chose to worship idols rather than Him. In today's text the apostle John was given a revelation of a future time when Yeshua (the Lamb) would be married to His bride (the church).

Yeshua in Your Walk

On this date in 1953, my bride and I exchanged our marriage vows. How blessed we have been to have one another for these many years. The intimate companionship we have enjoyed is comparable to the personal relationship we have with Yeshua, one that began even before we were married. My dear wife often speaks of us as being "soul-mates." The love we have for one another is a reflection of the love Christ has for us.

When the apostle Paul gave instructions for the way husbands and wives should relate to one another, he used the metaphor of the relationship between Christ and His bride—the church (Ephesians 5:22-31). His main emphasis was upon the tender love and affectionate care husbands and wives are to have for each other—just as Christ loved us and gave Himself for us.

If you have received Jesus as your Savior and Lord you are a part of the bride of Christ—His church. He desires a spiritual intimacy with you, similar to the physical intimacy between a husband and wife. Such a meaningful personal relationship includes love, loyalty, and devotion. You have His promise to be true and faithful to you—for richer or poorer, in sickness and in health, for better or for worse—and not even physical death can ever separate you from Him. In fact, you are on your way to a great heavenly celebration which the Bible describes as "the marriage feast of the Lamb." **What a glorious future! How important to be preparing.**

And so, as you progress through this and every day, do so with the firm assurance that your most intimate and constant companion is Jesus Christ. He will never leave you and is always present to provide for all your needs. Your life is secure in Him; you have nothing to fear. Live in peace.

Yeshua in Your Worship

Lamb of God, holy Savior and Lord, I bow in humble worship before You. All praise and honor belong to You, the One who gave Yourself for my deliverance from sin. Thank You for setting me free that I may worship and serve You each day. I'm so glad to be a part of Your bride.

August 24

Yahweh Wants Me to Be a Coworker with Other Missionaries

Yahweh in the Word

> "Dear friend, you are showing faithfulness by whatever you do for the brothers, especially when they are strangers. They have testified to your love in front of the church. You will do well to send them on their journey in a manner worthy of God, since they set out for the sake of the Name, accepting nothing from pagans. Therefore, we ought to support such men so that we can be coworkers with the truth" (3 John 5-8).

The apostle John was probably in Ephesus when he wrote this brief epistle to Gaius. He commends the believers who had welcomed traveling missionaries, helping to send them on their journey. Such support allowed them to actually share in the work of these laborers.

Yahweh in Your Walk

How would you like to participate in the ministry of Christian missionaries all over the world? What a privilege to actually share the Good News with those who have never heard it before! The truth is that you and I can do this by helping with the financial support of such frontline workers. Just as the apostle John commended those whom he addressed in our biblical text for today, we can also "be coworkers with the truth."

Can you say that some of your giving includes missionaries serving in places where you can never go? If your church has a plan to give financial support to mission causes, be intentional in giving generously to these worthy needs. **In addition to giving your money, give your prayer support.** Listen to this appeal from a missionary named Paul, "Now I appeal to you, brothers, through our Lord Jesus Christ and through the love the Spirit, to join with me in fervent prayers to God on my behalf" (Romans 15:30). Here is a fervent "appeal"—the word actually means to plead or to beg—for prayer support from other believers. Paul knew what a difference such prayers could make.

Hopefully, you are developing a list of Christian workers for whom you pray daily. You may want to seek to correspond with them so you can be more specific in your praying. Although your motive in this is not what you receive but how you can help, you do have the assurance of being a colaborer with these witnesses. **You are standing beside them, holding up their hands as they reach out to help others. What a good feeling comes from such a partnership!**

Someday in heaven, these missionaries will thank you personally for holding the lifeline as they went out to serve. You were an essential participant in every good work they did. So, remember to give generously and to pray faithfully for those who are laboring in fields where Yahweh has sent them. At the same time, be committed to your own mission field right where you are.

Yahweh in Your Worship

Thank You, Lord of the harvest, for including me in Your team of workers. Help me be faithful to give and to pray in support of those You have sent. And use me as Your missionary today.

August 25

Yeshua Wants Me to Be Childlike

Yeshua in the Word

> "At that time the disciples came to Jesus and said, 'Who is greatest in the kingdom of heaven?' Then he called a child to Him and had him stand among them. 'I assure you,' He said, 'unless you are converted and become like children, you will never enter the kingdom of heaven. Therefore, whoever humbles himself like this child—this one is the greatest in the kingdom of heaven. And whoever welcomes one child like this in My name welcomes Me" (Matt. 18:1-5).

On several occasions the disciples revealed their desire to achieve greatness in the sight of God. Each time Jesus rebuked their erroneous concepts and taught them the way to true greatness. In this instance He used the humble attitude of a child as an example for them to follow.

Yeshua in Your Walk

Byrdie is a 92 year-old woman in our church. Her mind is sharp and her spirit is strong although her body shows signs of aging. She always greets me with a big smile, a warm hug, and a kiss on my cheek. She is a childlike mature adult; her attitude expresses true humility, kindness, and a spirit of working in harmony with other believers. I have never heard critical words from her or any expression of selfishness—wanting things done her way. **I wish everyone in our church had this same humble, unselfish manner. Byrdie inspires me by her example of what it means to be great in the kingdom of heaven.**

How do you measure up when it comes to humility—childlikeness? Do you have a prideful spirit—one that things more highly of oneself than is proper? We all need to develop a balanced attitude about ourselves—not thinking too highly nor too lowly about who we are. We are helped with this by looking at Yeshua. He had the lowliest of births—a manger, and grew up in a rather poor family. He lived the simple life of an itinerant teacher, never accumulating property or wealth; then died as a despised, forsaken criminal. Although He healed countless numbers of people and was unequaled as a teacher, He never became the least bit boastful or proud of who He was or what He did. He is our ultimate example of what it means to have a childlike spirit.

Notice that in our Scripture text for today Jesus said to His disciples, "unless you are converted and become like children, you will never enter the kingdom of heaven." To be converted means to be changed. **We must be changed from proud, self-assertive, arrogant persons—to childlike individuals who humble themselves and place the needs of others ahead of our own.** This is a change we can make with His help. How about making a commitment to Him today that you will seek to move forward toward becoming more humble, more considerate of others, and less prideful—a true childlike mature adult citizen of the kingdom?

Yeshua in Your Worship

Gracious Lord, You said, "Let the little children come to me." Help me become like one of these whom You welcome. Forgive my pridefulness; teach me Your ways of true humility.

August 26

Yahweh Commands that I Be Still from All Fears

Yahweh in the Word

> *"Be still and know that I am God; I will be exalted among the nations. I will be exalted in the earth! Yahweh Sabaoth is with us; the God of Jacob is our refuge" (Psalm 46:10-11, NKJV).*

The mood of this psalm is that of warfare and natural disasters, such as earthquakes and floods. The psalmist gives reassurance to Yahweh's people of His "present help in trouble." Two times he assures his readers with these comforting words: "Yahweh Sabaoth (LORD of hosts) is with us; the God of Jacob is our refuge."

Yahweh in Your Walk

Recently a friend called me to tell of various problems she was dealing with. Her focus was clearly on these difficulties and how distressed she felt about them. As I listened it became obvious that her primary concern was over her inability to get others to act and think like she thought they should—she was frustrated because she could not control others. The ultimate solution to her situation is found in these words from Psalm 46: "Be still and know that I am God."

Regardless of the nature of those things that threaten your peace of mind, the answer is basically the same: **Be still from your fears and remember that your God is Yahweh Sabaoth—the sovereign Lord who controls all things.** Note how this psalm begins: "God is our refuge and strength, a very present help in trouble. Therefore, we will not fear...." Most of the times when you are upset about various matters, the best thing you can do is to calm down, be still from all your anxieties, and remember who Yahweh is.

The psalmist referred here to Yahweh as the God of Jacob. Do you recall the turbulent life this patriarch lived? Because of his deceitfulness he had to flee from his brother Esau and later from his father-in-law Laban. His own sons lied to him about their brother Joseph. His life was filled with trouble, and yet Yahweh chose to use this man to be the father of what became the twelve tribes of Israel (Jacob's new name).

Take heart from the example of Jacob; you have the same God he had. Yahweh can work to enable you to overcome all adversity, just as He did with Jacob. Be still from all your fears and know that Yahweh can and will accomplish His purpose for you. He is your refuge and your strength; a very present help in trouble. Therefore, do not fear—be still and remember who He is.

Yahweh in Your Worship

Almighty Yahweh, You are my refuge and strength, my help in every challenging situation. I worship You for being so good to me. How blest I am to know You and to have You always with me. Forgive me when I resort to my own meager ways of solving my problems. Remind me to continue trusting You and following Your guidance. Use me to help others learn these life-lessons. Make me the bold witness I should be regarding Your deliverance from all fears.

August 27

Yahweh Invites Me to Search for Him

Yahweh in the Word

> *"You will seek Me and find Me when you search for Me with all your heart. I will be found by you—this is Yahweh's declaration" (Jeremiah 29:13-14).*

These words of hope were spoken by Yahweh through His prophet Jeremiah. Yahweh promised to be found by His people when they searched for Him with all their hearts.

Yahweh in Your Walk

Think about this: What are you searching for and hoping to find today? Perhaps your answer includes such things as peace of mind, happiness, prosperity, or other typical things. Can you truthfully say that you are searching for a better understanding of Yahweh—an improved relationship with Him? Hopefully, you will agree that this should be on your list of priorities. The good news is that He promises to reward anyone's whole-hearted quest for Him.

But how should we go about such a search; where can we find Yahweh? **The Scriptures point to two primary sources through which Yahweh reveals Himself.** The first is the world of nature. As Paul wrote to the Romans: "His invisible attributes, that is, His eternal power and divine nature have been clearly seen since the creation of the world, being understood through what He has made" (Romans 1:20). The second source of divine revelation is the Lord Jesus Himself. The apostle John said, "No one has ever seen God. The One and Only Son—the One who is at the Father's side—He has revealed Him" (John 1:18).

The apostle Philip is a good example of someone who longed to know Yahweh better. One day he said to Jesus, "Lord, show us the Father, and that's enough for us." Jesus replied, "Have I been among you all this time without your knowing Me, Philip? The one who has seen Me has seen the Father....Believe Me that I am in the Father and the Father is in Me" (John 14:8-11). We may well envy Philip and the others who saw Jesus in the flesh. They had an advantage over us when it comes to seeing Jesus in the flesh. However, **we can "see" Jesus by reading the first-hand account given by these disciples in the Gospels.**

So if you want to respond positively to Yahweh's invitation to **"search for Me with all your heart," begin by observing more closely the wonders of nature and by being more intentional about your study of the Bible, especially the Gospels.** Commit yourself to reading something Jesus said or did every day. Before you read, ask the Holy Spirit to reveal His truth to you. Pray with the hymn writer who said: "Beyond the sacred page I seek Thee, Lord; my spirit pants for Thee, O Living Word. Show me the truth concealed within Thy Word, and in Thy Book revealed I see the Lord."

Yahweh in Your Worship

Thank You, Holy Yahweh, for making Yourself known to all who seek You. I claim the disclosure of Yourself through nature and through the Word. I long to know You better daily.

August 28

Yahweh Wants Me to Be Deeply Rooted in Him

Yahweh in the Word

> "The man who trusts in Yahweh, whose confidence indeed is Yahweh, is blessed. He will be like a tree planted by water; it sends its roots out toward a stream, it doesn't fear when heat comes, and its foliage remains green. It will not worry in a year of drought or cease producing fruit" (Jeremiah 17: 7-8).

Yahweh spoke these comforting words to His people through the prophet Jeremiah. He compares the person who trusts in Yahweh to a tree with deep roots—a tree that flourishes even when heat and drought are present.

Yahweh in Your Walk

As you approach the driveway leading up to my neighbor's farm house, you find these words on your left inscribed in stone: "Tap Root Farm." On the right side of the drive is the Scripture reference from our text for today: "Jeremiah 17:7-8." Frank and Frances Ingraham moved to this lovely country home in 1961. After a discussion with their three children, they agreed on the name Tap Root Farm and the Scripture verses. They all wanted their new home to be a place of blessing, not only for themselves but also for all who would come their way. And that desire has been abundantly fulfilled.

Through these many years they have continued to trust in Yahweh as they have reached out to many neighbors, friends, and strangers. Much good fruit has come from this godly home. Frank's career has been that of a lawyer, helping many Christian institutions with strong legal counsel. In addition he has taught a Bible class at their local church. He sometimes says, "My love is for the Lord, His land, and His law!" Frances has served alongside as a faithful wife, mother, and homemaker supreme. She loves to preserve and share the good fruits of their large vegetable garden and orchard.

Life has not been easy for the Ingrahams; their only son died as the result of a tractor accident. Other challenges have been encountered, but through it all they have been like trees with deep tap roots, continuing to produce good fruit.

We can all learn lessons for living from this dear family. **If our trust and confidence is in the Lord, we have unseen resources that enable us to be productive for Him even in times of "heat" and "drought."** Our spiritual roots go deep into the One who supplies all we need to be all He would have us be. As you leave Tap Root Farm, you see another biblical promise at the gate: "Behold, I am with you and will keep you wherever you go, and will bring you back to this land; for I will not leave you until I have done what I have spoken to you" (Genesis 28:15).

Yahweh in Your Worship

Gracious Lord, I want my roots to go deeply into Your great reservoir of grace. I do worship You because of Your abundant blessings to me. May I be a good steward of all these riches.

August 29

Yeshua Makes All things New for Me

Yeshua in the Word

> *"Therefore, if anyone is in Christ, he is a new creation; old things have passed away, and look, new things have come" (2 Corinthians 5:17).*

Paul reminds believers in Corinth that because they are united to Jesus Christ, they have experienced an entirely new life. The old, former ways of living have been left behind; a new kind of life has come to them—the very life of Christ.

Yeshua in Your Walk

There is something very attractive about newness—like having a new day or a new opportunity or a new experience. Think about your walk today as being filled with newness as a believer in Christ. Our Scripture text speaks of "new things have come." Look at some of these new things that are revealed by the Bible. Focus on these today rather than old, depressing things.

1. **A New Creation.** When you received Jesus as your Savior, you were given a new life; you were "born again." This new life is actually His life in you. All He is—now is yours.
2. **A New Covenant.** Through the prophets Jeremiah and Ezekiel, Yahweh promised a "new covenant" with His people. "I will make a new covenant with the house of Israel and with the house of Judah... I will put My teaching within them and write it on their hearts. I will be their God, and they will be My people" (Jeremiah 31:31, 33). "I will give you a new heart and put a new spirit within you... I will place My Spirit within you...." (Ezekiel 36:26-27). And Jesus said at the last supper: "This cup is the new covenant established by My blood; it is shed for you" (Luke 22:20). The word covenant describes our relationship with Yahweh—one of grace.
3. **A New Way of Life.** "Therefore we are buried with Him by baptism into death, in order that, just as Christ was raised from the dead by the glory of the Father, so we too may walk in a new way of life" (Romans 6:4). This new life is characterized by a new commandment—"I give you a new command: Love one another. Just as I have loved you...." (John 13:34).
4. **A New Heaven and a New Earth.** The future is bright for all believers; this old world with all its trouble and all its wrongs—such as disease, natural disasters, warfare and violence—will be replaced by a new earth in which all will be restored to its original paradise. "We wait for the new heavens and a new earth, where righteousness will dwell" (2 Peter 3:12-13).
5. **A New Song.** In light of all this newness, we must sing a new song—one of praise and thanksgiving. "He put a new song in my mouth, a hymn of praise to our God" (Psalm 40:2).

Yeshua in Your Worship

I bow in humble adoration to the One who alone makes all things new. How gracious of You to give such blessings today and hope for tomorrow. I do sing a new song—one of thanksgiving.

August 30

Yeshua Saves Me from My Old Way of Living

Yeshua in the Word

> "Therefore, if anyone is in Christ, he is a new creation; old things have passed away, and look, new things have come" (2 Corinthians 5:17).

The apostle Paul is the writer of Scripture who says the most about the old life and the new life. He had experienced such a radical change at his own conversion that he knew the huge difference Christ can make in a person's life.

Yeshua in Your Walk

You have noticed that our Scripture text for today is the same as yesterday when we considered some of the aspects of our new life in Christ. Today we will look at the "old things" that pass away when we receive Jesus as our Savior and Lord.

I recall the testimony of my friend Hughie who was a "rough neck" on an oil well rig near Hobbs, New Mexico. My first encounter with this rugged man was one Sunday morning when he came lumbering down the church aisle during the time for decision to say, "I need God!" That was the beginning of a total transformation for him. I remember the time later when he said to me, "I have had to lose half of my vocabulary since I came to Christ!" **He was an example of someone who discovered how "old things" pass away as we begin walking the path of righteousness.**

Paul explained how this kind of change happens when he wrote: "We know that our old self was crucified with Him in order that sin's dominion over the body may be abolished, so that we may no longer be enslaved to sin, since a person who has died is freed from sin's claims" (Romans 6:6-7). Before we experience the salvation Yeshua gives, we have what Paul calls an "old self." This old human nature, the one we are born with, expresses itself in rebellion against God. Thus we, by nature, follow a lifestyle of self-centeredness and pride; we follow the lusts of the flesh, practicing such things as Paul lists in his letters: "Now the works of the flesh are obvious: sexual immorality, idolatry, sorcery, hatreds, strife, jealousy, outbursts of anger, selfish ambitions, dissensions, factions, envy, drunkenness, carousing, and anything similar" (Galatians 5:19-21). These are some of the "old things" that will pass away as we yield control of our lives to Jesus.

None of us will get rid of all this old life-style quickly or easily. In fact, some of these "works of the flesh" continue to surface from time to time. However, our new nature—the indwelling Holy Spirit—gives victory over these evils as we yield control to Him. His fruit is described as "love, joy, peace, patience, kindness, goodness, faith, gentleness, and self-control" (Galatians 5:22-23).

Yeshua in Your Worship

Holy Spirit, I worship You and thank You for empowering me to live above the old, sinful, selfish ways I used to love. I praise You for Your beautiful life of holiness expressed through me as I yield to You. Use me today as an example of what it means to be a follower of Jesus.

August 31

Yahweh Wants Me to Serve Him through My Occupation

Yahweh in the Word

> *"Luke, the dearly loved physician, and Demas greet you" (Colossians 4: 14).*

The apostle Paul wrote this letter to believers in the city of Colossae. He was in prison at the time of writing. His purpose was to correct the influence of false teachers in that church. He concludes his letter with greetings from several of his coworkers including Luke and Demas.

Yahweh in Your Walk

Do you ever think about your vocation as a means of serving Yahweh? Earlier in this letter to the Colossians, Paul wrote these words to Christian slaves: "Whatever you do, do it enthusiastically, as something done for the Lord and not for men, knowing that you will receive the reward of an inheritance from the Lord. You serve the Lord Christ" (3:23-24). Slavery was a common vocation in those days. Many slaves were more like household servants and were treated well. **The life-principle given here is that whatever we do—to make a living—should be done with whole-heartedness, as to the Lord, and not to some human employer. We must look upon our vocation as way of serving Yahweh, not just a means to get a paycheck.**

Two men are mentioned in our Scripture passage for today. Luke, the one who wrote the Gospel of Luke and the Acts of the Apostles, is identified (only here) as "the dearly loved physician." He obviously used his medical training to assist Paul and others. The other coworker was Demas, who apparently was loyal to Paul at this time. However, later Paul said of him: "Demas has deserted me, because he loved this present world, and has gone to Thessalonica" (2 Timothy 4:10). What a sad commentary on this man who once served the Lord and Paul, but fell away.

This month of August reminds me of another physician who, along with his dear wife, served the Lord as a missionary doctor for 36 years in the nation of Jordan. Dr. August Lovegren and I sing together in the church choir. What a dedicated servant and personal friend. His chosen profession of medical practice has made a great difference in the lives of many Jordanians. As a physician he treated all kinds of medical problems while being a strong witness of his Lord.

What about the tasks you will perform today? Do you perceive the importance of doing whatever you do, as a vocation or avocation, with the kind of dedication that pleases your Lord? He has given you the strength and skill to do your work well; He wants you to serve Him through all you do. Be like Luke and August Lovegren; honor Yahweh through your vocation.

Yahweh in Your Worship

Thank You, dear Lord, for giving me the ability and opportunity to earn a living by my occupation. I dedicate myself and my work to You. Help me be a witness of Your goodness by the way I do my daily tasks—with integrity and enthusiasm—because I do them unto You. I want to be a good steward of all You entrust to my care.

September 1

Yahweh Sabaoth Is Sovereign Over All Creation

Yahweh in the Word

> "The earth and everything in it, the world and its inhabitants, belong to Yahweh; for He laid its foundation on the seas and established it on the rivers…Who is He, the King of glory? The LORD of Hosts (Yahweh Sabaoth), He is the King of glory" (Psalm 24:1-2, 10).

A new combination name for our study of Yahweh is found in this impressive passage: Yahweh Sabaoth (pronounced YAH-way tsa-ba-OAT), meaning I AM the sovereign One. To say that He is sovereign refers to the fact that all things have been created by and for Yahweh and He is in total, absolute control over all creation.

This compound name occurs over 285 times in the Old Testament and is quoted twice in the New Testament. One Bible scholar says, "Sovereignty means that God is in all and over all." Therefore, He alone is worthy to be worshiped and served.

Yahweh in Your Walk

Do you ever have the feeling that many things in this world are out of control? Consider the weather. We hear about global warming and wonder where this could lead. How about the work of terrorists or the possibility of nuclear warfare or many other threats to life as we know it? Each day's news seems to bring new reasons for being fearful.

Should we feel anxious about such matters?

We should have enough concern to participate in reasonable efforts to protect ourselves and others from dangers that appear harmful. However, many of these issues are far beyond our ability to do anything about. What then? Here is where this fact of the sovereignty of God becomes very comforting. **The One who is ultimately and finally in control of all things is Yahweh Sabaoth, nothing happens without His knowledge and permission**. He is the absolute Master of all. And the Bible reveals Him to be merciful and gracious toward His creation.

At times it appears that Satan is in control because there is so much evil in this world. But we know that Yahweh is sovereign over all evil powers; He will not allow Satan to dominate His creation. Even though Satan is very active and causes much trouble, his activities are limited by Yahweh and ultimately righteousness and peace will prevail.

Yahweh in Your Worship

Sovereign Lord, Yahweh Sabaoth, I worship You as the One who created everything and is in control of it. My trust is in Your goodness, mercy, and grace. Thank You for delivering me from all anxiety and doubt. I choose to seize this day and all its opportunities to serve You. Help me share the peace I find in Your sovereignty with those who live in constant fear. Use me as a bold witness of Your promises of protection.

September 2

Yahweh Sabaoth Controls All the Hosts of Creation

Yahweh in the Word

"So the heavens and the earth and all their host were completed" (Genesis 2:1).

Here is the first time the word "host" occurs in the Bible. Included in this term are all stars, planets, solar systems—everything in what we know as space. A similar use of the word is found as Yahweh speaks through his prophet Isaiah: "Who will you compare Me to or who is My equal? Asks the Holy One. Look up and see: who created these? He brings out the starry host by number; He calls all of them by name. Because of His great power and strength, not one of them is missing" (Isaiah 40:25-26). **The Scripture is clear in revealing Yahweh Sabaoth as creator and controller of everything in outer space as well as on this planet earth.**

Yahweh in Your Walk

You can remember being outside on a clear moonless night and looking up to the heavens. What an awesome sight! The stars and lighted planets appear as tiny points of light. Some even seem to be rather near and yet they actually are millions of miles away. The most recent figure regarding the size of this universe is measured by light years (the distance light travels in one year at the speed of 186,000 miles per second). Observable matter (by telescope) is spread over a space of at least 93 billion light years in which there are over 100 billion galaxies with around 70 sextillion stars! Talk about big!

And yet, Yahweh Sabaoth created and controls all this—and more. As the psalmist wrote, "The heavens declare the glory of God, and the sky proclaims the work of His hands. Day after day they pour out speech; night after night they communicate knowledge" (Psalm 19:1-2). What speech do the heavens "pour out"? **The glorious message is that Yahweh Sabaoth planned and made all this vast host of the heavens, and He is in constant and complete control of it all.**

The Hubble Space Telescope was launched from a space shuttle in 1990 and now orbits the earth 353 miles above it, sending thousands of photos and other information. The next venture of this type is called The James Webb Space Telescope, and its orbit will be almost a million miles above the earth—far beyond our moon. Both of these man-made devices will simply reveal the wonder of that which Yahweh made in the beginning. Human achievements such as these seem very insignificant compared to the wonders from Yahweh's hands.

Yahweh in Your Worship

All nature is a visible witness to Your greatness and majesty O Yahweh Sabaoth. I seize this day as one given to me that I might join all Your creation in worshiping You. My worship is enriched the better I know You and the wonders of Your amazing creation. Help me point out these wonders to others that they may join me in honoring You for all You have done and are doing in this universe.

September 3

Yahweh Sabaoth Rules Over All the Angels

Yahweh in the Word

> "The Angel of Yahweh encamps around those who fear Him, and rescues them" (Psalm 34:7).

All the angels are among the hosts that are controlled by Yahweh. Some form of the word *angel* occurs more than 300 times in 34 of the 66 Bible books. The terms **hosts** and **angels** often occur together as an indication of the multitude of these special servants of Yahweh. The primary function of angles is to worship Yahweh and do whatever He commands. He is sovereign over both holy and fallen angels, such as Lucifer (Satan). Satan's evil works are by Yahweh's permission; He not only controls evil He also works to bring good from it.

Yahweh in Your Walk

Do you recall times when you have had a "close call"? You almost had an accident, but didn't. Recently, I read about a man who was supposed to be in one of the New York City Trade Towers on 9/11, but missed his ride and thus his life was spared. Another story was about a person who failed to make a connection on a plane that later crashed and all were killed. For a reason beyond our understanding, Yahweh chooses to protect some from these kinds of tragedies. Those who survive do so for a divinely planned purpose.

Unknown to us are the many instances when angels have protected us from injury or illness. The text for today speaks of the ministry of angels to us. Another biblical reference to this favor is: "He will give His angels orders concerning you, to protect you in all your ways" (Psalm 91:11). Add to this another quote regarding angels: "Are they not all ministering spirits sent out to serve those who are going to inherit salvation?" (Hebrews 1:14).

How comforting to know that as you walk through this day, Yahweh Sabaoth sends His angels to protect you and serve you in various ways. These unseen spiritual care-givers will make a huge difference for you. As the chorus of an old song declares, "All night, all day—angels watchin' over me, my Lord."

Unfortunately, we also find fallen angels mentioned in God's Word. Lucifer apparently was once a holy, ruling angel who rebelled against Yahweh, taking a large number of fellow angels with him. However, we are assured that they all remain under Yahweh's control and will eventually be cast into hell. Do not live in fear of these creatures.

Yahweh in Your Worship

Yahweh Sabaoth, I seize this day with the assurance of Your protection and care. Thank You for those angels that will minister to me today. I worship You as the One who provides for all my needs. Only You are aware of all the times when I need Your divine help in overcoming dangers. Make me more aware of Your deliverance from harmful situations. And use me to serve Your purpose for preserving my life.

September 4

Yahweh Sabaoth Is Sovereign Over All the Earth and Its Inhabitants

Yahweh in the Word

"His (Yahweh's) dominion is an everlasting dominion and His kingdom is from generation to generation. All the inhabitants of the earth are counted as nothing and He does what He wants with the army of heaven and the inhabitants of the earth. There is no one who can hold back His hand or say to Him, 'What have You done?'" (Daniel 4:34-35).

How interesting that these words came from a pagan ruler, Nebuchadnezzar, king of Babylon. He used the term "dominion" to include everything in heaven and on earth. And he came to this conclusion after observing Yahweh's amazing control over both people and animal life. He became very eloquent as he expressed the truth he had discovered about Yahweh.

Another ruler who came to this same awareness of Yahweh's sovereignty was Hezekiah, king of Judah. The Assyrian army of 185,000 soldiers threatened to overcome the city of Jerusalem. Hezekiah offered this simple prayer of desperation: "Yahweh Sabaoth, God of Israel, who is enthroned above the cherubim… save us from his hand so that all the kingdoms of the earth may know that You are Yahweh—You alone" (Isaiah 37:16, 20). During the night an angel was sent from Yahweh and destroyed all 185,000 enemy soldiers! What an amazing revelation of Yahweh's sovereignty!

Yahweh in Your Walk

Martin Luther, the leader of the Protestant Reformation during the 16th century, often found himself in trouble with church authorities. Out of his experiences he wrote a classic hymn in 1529 based on Psalm 46. The song became known as "The Battle Hymn of the Reformation." In our hymnals it appears as "A Mighty Fortress Is Our God." Notice this second stanza: "Did we in our own strength confide, our striving would be losing. Were not the right man on our side, the man of God's own choosing. Dost ask who that may be? Christ Jesus, it is He—**Lord Sabaoth** His name, from age to age the same, and He must win the battle."

How reassuring to know that as you walk through this day, no matter what challenges you may face, because Yahweh Sabaoth is on your side, you have nothing to fear. He has all authority in heaven and on earth. He loves you with an everlasting love and has promised to deliver you from all evil. Praise His sovereign name!

Yahweh in Your Worship

From age to age, You are the same Yahweh Sabaoth—Ruler of heaven and earth and all within them. Today I seize this glorious truth and rest from every fear. All glory and praise belong to You. History reveals how often various human authorities have risen to power, only to be cast down and proven helpless. You alone are the eternal, unchanging Sovereign over all creation. Help me be a better witness of this truth about You. I join all creation in worshiping You as the ultimate King of all kings and Lord of all lords.

September 5

Yahweh Is Greater Than All Other Persons and Powers

Yahweh in the Word

> *"David became more and more powerful, and the LORD God of hosts (Yahweh Elohim Sabaoth) was with him" (2 Samuel 5:10).*

We find a most interesting and helpful combination in this verse. The literal meaning of Yahweh Elohim Sabaoth is "I AM the God of hosts." **Elohim** is the first word for God in the Bible. Genesis 1:1 states, "In the beginning God (Elohim) created the heavens and the earth." **Elohim** is actually a plural noun which in this case refers to the plural nature of Yahweh—He is Father, Son, and Holy Spirit; three persons, yet one in nature and purpose. We cannot comprehend this mystery called the Trinity, yet by faith, we know Yahweh in this manner. David became the strong leader he needed to be because Yahweh Elohim Sabaoth was with him.

This threefold combination occurs 16 times in the Old Testament. These words form the most awesome of all the biblical expressions of sovereign power and authority. More clearly than any other combination, these three express the absolute, unequaled, sovereignty of Yahweh—infinitely supreme over all other persons and powers.

Yahweh in Your Walk

Several years ago when I was working through these various combinations of Yahweh's name, this one became especially meaningful to me. I noticed that the first letters of Yahweh Elohim Sabaoth spell **YES**. This bold term of affirmation took on new meaning as I meditated on its practical application. **You probably identify with me when I confess that there are times when I feel very inadequate to be or do what I know Yahweh wants of me.** I say to myself: Can I do this? Can I be all Yahweh expects me to be? Can I make a difference in this world? Can I fulfill the mission in life He has appointed for me?

The resounding answer to all these questions about personal adequacy is found in **Y**ahweh **E**lohim **S**abaoth who has promised always to be with us. **So, YES, we can—do whatever He wants; YES, we can—be all He wants. YES! YES! YES!** The apostle Paul expressed the same truth when he declared, "I am able to do all things through Him who strengthens me" (Philippians 4:13). As you walk through this day with all its opportunities, claim this same sufficiency.

Yahweh in Your Worship

Today I seize this day for Your glory, Yahweh Elohim Sabaoth. I know that You are with me constantly and I claim all the resources of Your wisdom, power, and love. Thank You for making a difference in me and through me—now and always. Forgive me for those times when I have focused on my limitations rather than Your promised power available to me. I long to be a more effective witness regarding Your greatness, goodness, and readiness to use all who will place their trust in You.

September 6

I Am Yahweh's Special Treasure

Yahweh in the Word

> *"They will be Mine, says Yahweh Sabaoth, a special possession on the day I am preparing. I will have compassion on them as a man has compassion on his son who serves him" (Malachi 3:17).*

The term *Yahweh Sabaoth* (LORD of Hosts) occurs 24 times in the brief Book of Malachi. Thus the Old Testament closes with a very strong affirmation of Yahweh's sovereignty. This reference (3:17) is of particular interest. The words "special possession" translate the Hebrew word **segullah** which refers to a personal treasure of supreme value. Yahweh is saying that His people are His special treasure—He values them above all other treasures. Because of this He promises to have compassion on them as their Father. (See also September 22.)

Yahweh in Your Walk

If you were asked, "What is your greatest treasure on this earth?" how would you answer? You might need some time to think about this. We all have various possessions, but which one do we value the most? I would reply by mentioning, of course, my family members. But then I would tell of some 50 volumes of personal journals in which I have written our family history. These books contain the records of more than 50 years of Yahweh's dealings with us. If these were to be lost, we would have no way of replacing them.

If someone asked Yahweh about His most valued possession, He would reply, "My people are My most valued possession, My **segullah**." You and I are included in this special treasure. How blessed are we to be so valued. Just as we will protect our treasures, so does Yahweh Sabaoth. **This truth reminds us that, with the Sovereign Ruler of this universe watching constantly over us, we have no reason to ever be anxious about anything.**

A wise leader has said, "What matters most in life is not **who** you are but **whose** you are." Yahweh assures us that we are His; as His children we belong to Him. But not only His possession, His most treasured possession! We know this is true because of the extreme sacrifice He made to make us His own. "God's love was revealed among us in this way: God sent His one and Only Son into the world so that we might live through Him" (1 John 4:9). As Paul declared, "You are not your own, for you were bought at a price. Therefore glorify God in your body" (1 Corinthians 6:20). We are Yahweh's prized, purchased possession—His segullah! So, let's live like Yahweh's segullahs!

Yahweh in Your Worship

O Yahweh Sabaoth, supreme Ruler over the entire universe, how blessed I am to belong to You. As Your special treasure I worship and adore You. Today I want to live as Your child should live. Help me to remember Whose I am and Whom I represent in this world. I bring myself to You today—Your special possession. Use me to bring others to know You and also become Your treasure.

September 7

Yahweh Will Never Fail to Watch Over Me

Yahweh in the Word

> *"Yahweh will not allow your foot to slip; your Protector will not slumber. Indeed the Protector of Israel does not slumber or sleep" (Psalm 121:3)*

The psalmist celebrates the security of Yahweh's people. He is faithful as their Protector to give constant diligent care.

Yahweh in Your Walk

You have heard of people who "went to sleep on the job" in the sense of failing to do what was expected of them. One biblical example of this is the account of Jesus and His disciples going to Gethsemane, their customary place of prayer. There Jesus asked Peter, James, and John to go farther with Him and to watch and pray. He alone went even farther into this garden as He agonized in prayer to His Father. When He returned He found all the disciples sleeping, and said, "So, couldn't you stay awake with Me one hour? Stay awake and pray, so that you won't enter into temptation. The spirit is willing, but the flesh is weak." The same thing happened two more times. (Matthew 26:36-46).

How comforting to know that the One who promises to watch over us never sleeps; He is wide awake, caring for all our needs 24-7. As one song puts it: "He never sleeps, He never slumbers. He watches me both night and day." It is in this truth that we find the cure for our human tendency to worry. Worry is a form of fear, the fear that our needs or the needs of others we care about will not be met. One observer said, "If worry worked it would be worth it, but it won't."

Rather than resort to worry, which is natural for those who do not know Yahweh, we should commit our cares to Him and rest in His promises. One promise that helps me deal with any kind of fear is "Do not fear, for I am with you; do not be afraid, for I am your God. I will strengthen you; I will help you; I will hold on to you with My righteous right hand" (Isaiah 41:10).

I have read that there are 365 times in the Bible when "Fear not" occurs. I haven't tried to count these for myself, but I know that even if there was only one, that would be enough to give much assurance of Yahweh's constant care of His people. Rejoice in your sleepless Keeper!

Yahweh in Your Worship

O most blessed Yahweh, how I do worship and praise You for Your faithful and continuous care of me as well as of all Your children. Thank You that I can go forth to seize every opportunity this day affords for honoring You. I rejoice in the freedom from fear that You provide. Help me to be awake and diligent to be Your faithful witness today.

September 8

Yahweh Recognizes the Value of Friendship

Yahweh in the Word

> *"Two are better than one because they have a good reward for their efforts. For if either falls, his companion can lift him up; but pity the one who falls without another to lift him up" (Ecclesiastes 4:9-10).*

Most of the statements in the book of Ecclesiastes reflect a humanistic view of life. While the Hebrew word for God (Elohim) occurs some forty times, no mention of God's name (Yahweh) is found. However, we do find sound counsel regarding many aspects of life in this book which Yahweh has included in His inspired Word. Our text for today is an example of this. Yahweh affirms the value of friendship. **None of us should face life alone; we need the companionship of others—"two are better than one" for many reasons.**

Yahweh in Your Walk

Every Christian needs at least one other trusted person to whom he or she can be accountable. In my most recent pastorate I identified three men who had experience in leading congregations. We became close friends and served as a leadership team for the church. We met regularly for prayer and planning. Our agreement was to be mutually accountable to one another. I told them that if they ever noticed that something I said or did was the least bit out of line, they were responsible to bring that to my attention when we all met together; they agreed to the same accountability.

One writer has pointed out our need of having someone who "has our back" in the sense of alerting us to any sneak attack of Satan. He said, "Even when we have carefully put on the whole armor of God described by the apostle Paul, there is no protection for our back! We need someone in our lives to whom we have given permission to diligently watch our backs." Here is wise counsel. None of us can be constantly alert to every approach of our enemy.

Do you have one or more Christian friends with whom you can share mutual accountability? Think about developing such a relationship. The writer of Proverbs alluded to the value of friendship in these words: "Iron sharpens iron, and one man sharpens another" (Proverbs 27:17). You will become a better follower of Jesus if you submit yourself to the evaluation of another disciple. Encourage this friend to be truthful with you about your conduct, lifestyle, habits, mannerisms, and stewardship. Agree to be mutually responsible in all areas of life. Both of you will profit from such openness and frank assessment. Then spend time praying together regarding any weaknesses you find; be candid, refusing to take offense.

Yahweh in Your Worship

Yahweh, I treasure the friends You have given me. Help us make the most of this precious relationship. Teach us to be true worshipers of You and obedient servants in every way. I consider Your friendship to be of greatest value to me; show me what You see I need to change.

September 9

Yahweh Calls Me to Grow Spiritually

Yahweh in the Word

> *"Make every effort to supplement your faith with goodness, goodness with knowledge, knowledge with self-control, self-control with endurance, endurance with godliness, godliness with brotherly affection, and brotherly affection with love. For if these qualities are yours and are increasing, they will keep you from being useless or unfruitful in the knowledge of our Lord Jesus Christ" (2 Peter 1:5-8).*

Simon Peter knew from experience the importance of growing stronger spiritually. After his own failure to be faithful to Jesus, he was a strong advocate for the need for developing in faith. This text presents eight spiritual virtues needed by every follower of Jesus—the "Ladder of Faith."

Yahweh in Your Walk

You may remember that as a child you took pride in measuring your height to see how much you had grown since the last measurement. Growth is a natural experience both physically and mentally, as well as spiritually. Hopefully, as you look back in your experience as a Christian, you can see areas of positive growth. The apostle Peter lists eight terms that describe where such development is needed.

Take a few minutes to examine yourself regarding each of these eight virtues. Notice how each one builds upon or supplements the previous one. *Faith* is the foundation of all the rest. You grow in faith by gaining understanding of the object of your faith—Yahweh and His promises. Add to this growing faith increased *goodness*—reflecting more of the goodness of Yeshua. To goodness add *knowledge* in the sense of knowing better how to show goodness. *Self-control* is gained as you have the knowledge to depend more fully on the Holy Spirit to take control. Such self-control must increase in *endurance* as you learn to keep on keeping on with a godly life style. Supplement such *godliness* with *affection* for all others, especially in the family of faith. And this affection must grow into authentic Christian *love*—a commitment to seek the welfare of others, even at your own sacrifice.

Notice two additional truths mentioned by Peter. First, "make every effort" to grow in these areas. He uses this same combination of words again in verse 10 and chapter 3:14. The meaning is to be diligent about these matters. **We must work at growing in all these areas of Christian character. Growth will not happen without diligent effort.** The second truth is a reminder that such growth will prevent us from becoming "useless or unfruitful." Peter remembered how he was useless to Jesus when he yielded to the temptation to deny ever knowing Him. We never stand still in our spiritual growth; we either become stronger and thus more useful, or weaker and unfruitful. Make the commitment to be diligently seeking to mature in all these areas of growth.

Yahweh in Your Worship

Gracious Yahweh, I long to be more like You in every way. Thank You for Your help as I grow.

September 10

Yahweh Wants Me to Honor Him with All My Possessions

Yahweh in the Word

> *"Honor Yahweh with your possessions and with the first produce of your entire harvest; then your barns will be completely filled, and your vats will overflow with new wine" (Proverbs 3:9-10).*

These words were written to readers who lived in an agricultural society; they were farmers, shepherds, or growers of various kinds of fruits, nuts, and vegetables. The appeal of this proverb is for a person to use all possessions in a way that honors Yahweh.

Yahweh in Your Walk

The biblical view of life sees Yahweh as the creator and therefore the owner of all things. As the psalmist wrote: "The earth and everything in it, the world and its inhabitants belong to Yahweh, for He laid its foundation on the seas and established it on the rivers" (Psalm 24:1-2). **None of us actually owns anything; we are just temporary possessors of whatever we have.** As one person has truthfully observed: "All we own is what we take with us when we die."

The biblical view of life sees humankind as stewards or managers. Whatever material wealth we have belongs to Yahweh who has entrusted us with it while we live in this world. At the end of life we must give an account to the Owner; He will ask, What did you do with what I gave you?

When my wife and I were newly married, our pastor challenged us to begin honoring Yahweh with our financial possessions by becoming tithers (giving the first tenth of our gross income through our church). We practiced this for several years, then realized we were just returning to Yahweh what was already His (the first tenth) and not giving any of what was ours. So we began increasing our giving from 10% to 11% for one year. The next year we moved up to 12%, and so on until we were above 20%. Our testimony agrees with the promise of our text today—Yahweh has blessed and prospered us far beyond anything we expected—no debt and an abundance of more than we need.

Our motive is not to give in order to gain in return. We have simply attempted to be good stewards of what was entrusted to us. And we know that stewardship includes all our possessions, not just financial gain. We want to honor Yahweh with all we have from Him. We long to hear Him say, Well done, good and faithful stewards.

Yahweh in Your Worship

Sovereign Yahweh, You are the owner and giver of all I possess. I want to seize every opportunity You give me to be a good and faithful manager of what is Yours. Thank You for entrusting so much to my care. I claim Your guidance and wisdom as I seek to become a better steward of Yours. Forgive me when I forget that my role in life is as manager, not owner. I long to bring pleasure to You as a faithful steward.

September 11

Yahweh Wants Me to Know Him Intimately

Yahweh in the Word

> "Let us strive to know Yahweh. His appearance is as sure as the dawn. He will come to us like the rain, like the spring showers that water the land… For I desire loyalty and not sacrifice, the knowledge of God rather than burnt offerings" (Hosea 6:3,6).

The prophet Hosea was sent by Yahweh to call His people to abandon their idols and cease their unjust treatment of one another. Through Hosea's marriage to an unworthy woman, Yahweh sought to reveal His great love toward His undeserving children. What Yahweh desired more than all their empty worship and meaningless sacrifices was for them to know Him in an intimate manner, as a husband knows his wife.

Yahweh in Your Walk

We may think of eternal life as meaning to live forever. But this is not the biblical concept. There is a sense in which everyone will live forever—either in heaven or in hell. **The eternal life Jesus came to give is a different kind of life, a quality of life unknown before.** He defined such life in these words taken from His longest recorded prayer, offered shortly before He went to the cross: "Father, the hour has come. Glorify Your Son so that the Son may glorify You, for You gave Him authority over all flesh; so He may give eternal life to all You have given Him. This is eternal life: that they may know You, the only true God, and the One You have sent—Jesus Christ" (John 17:1-3).

Eternal life is the result of a personal knowledge of Yahweh and His Son Yeshua. **Nothing is more important than this intimate relationship—not sacrifices, nor service, nor performance of religious rituals.** Our ultimate purpose for life is to know Yahweh, His Son Yeshua, and to make them known to others. I like the way this song by Graham Kendrick expresses this truth:

> All I once held dear built my life upon. All this world reveres, and wars to own.
> All I once thought gain I have counted loss, spent and worthless now, compared to this—
> Knowing You, Jesus, knowing You, there is no greater thing. You're my all, You're the best, You're my joy, my righteousness and I love You, Lord.
> Now my heart's desire is to know You more, to be found in You and known as Yours.
> To possess by faith what I could not earn, all surpassing gift of righteousness.

So, "let us strive to know Yahweh." The only way this happens is to be a serious, consistent student of His Word. Each time you open the Bible, ask Him to reveal Himself to You. He will!

Yahweh in Your Worship

I worship You as Father, Son, and Holy Spirit. Thank You for making Yourself known to me. Help me know You better every day. I seize the opportunities for learning more about You.

September 12
Yahweh Wants Me to Learn to Praise Him

Yahweh in the Word

> *"Let everything that breathes praise Yahweh. Hallelujah!" (Psalm 150:6)*

The book of Psalms ends with these challenging words. You will want to read this brief chapter to appreciate this devotional. Notice it begins and ends with the word "Hallelujah" which means ***praise Yahweh*** (Hallel means ***praise***, and jah is the shortened form of ***Yahweh***.)

Yahweh in Your Walk

One of the dominant themes of the Bible, especially the Psalms, is that of praising Yahweh. To praise Him means to respond to His revelation of Himself and His works with expressions of gratitude and celebration of His worth, His majesty, His greatness, His goodness, and His marvelous works. The Hebrew title of the book of Psalms is "Hallel," meaning ***praise***. This final chapter helps us understand the nature of praise.

First, **<u>where</u> are we to praise Him?** Verse 1 declares: "Praise God in His sanctuary. Praise Him in His mighty heavens." His "sanctuary" would include the entire universe which is His home. The "mighty heavens" may refer to all His creation. The point of these expressions is that Yahweh is to be praised everywhere! **As you walk through each day, make a special effort to express your own praise to Yahweh wherever you are.** Such praise can be spoken orally or silently.

Second, **<u>why</u> are we to praise Him?** Verse 2 commands: "Praise Him for His powerful acts; praise Him for His abundant greatness." His acts of creation, His provision for us, His deliverance of us from our sins, His work of reconciling us to Himself, His revelation of Himself to us—all these powerful works deserve praise. Again, as you go about every day, lift up your heart to praise Yahweh for all His many gifts to you and to all others.

Third, **<u>how</u> are we to praise Him?** Verses 3-5 mention the various musical instruments and actions used in Hebrew worship: trumpet, harp, lyre, tambourine, flute, strings, cymbals, and dance. Praise can be expressed through whatever means we choose to honor Him. **If you play a musical instrument, use that as a means of praise to Him.**

Finally, **<u>who</u> is to praise Him?** Verse 6 calls for "everything that breathes" to participate in praise. Certainly this includes all living persons—like you and me. Let's give more attention to this vitally important expression of worship—both privately and with others. He alone is worthy!

Yahweh in Your Worship

Hallelujah! I offer my sincere gratitude for all You are, all You do, and all You mean to me. Help me to express more fully and more often the praise I feel in my heart toward You. Make me a witness of Your greatness by praising You more often, as I worship You alone and with others.

September 13

Yahweh Helps Me to Forgive Others

Yahweh in the Word

> "Therefore, God's chosen ones, holy and loved, put on heartfelt compassion, kindness, humility, gentleness, and patience, accepting one another and forgiving one another if anyone has a complaint against another. Just as the Lord has forgiven you, so you must also forgive" (Colossians 3:12-13).

These words from Paul's letter to believers in Colossae apply to us just as well as to them. What he describes here is the character and attitude of Jesus. We are to be like Him in all these virtues which build strong relationships among Christians. Notice that our forgiveness of others grows out of His forgiveness of us.

Yahweh in Your Walk

You have probably heard of Corrie ten Boom, a Dutch Christian, who helped many Jews escape arrest during World War II. Later she was arrested and sent to a concentration camp where she witnessed many atrocities at the hands of German soldiers. Her sister along with some 50,000 other women died in this camp. In her book, *The Hiding Place*, she tells of her struggle with forgiving those who wronged her along with many others. Later she wrote that those who chose to forgive their enemies were able to rebuild their lives much better than those who remained unforgiving. She was able, after the war, to share her testimony in more than 60 countries. She believed God spared her life so she could be a witness of His love and mercy.

You probably could tell of some mistreatment by another person. **Have you been willing to forgive and move on, leaving all resentment behind?** Yahweh wants to help us do this by reminding us of His forgiveness of our many sins against Him. **We can choose to forgive because we have experienced His forgiveness, but even more—we have His Spirit living in us and enabling us to practice forgiveness.**

Those who choose not to forgive and carry a grudge against another, suffer more than the offender. **An attitude of bitterness and resentment actually poisons a person's spirit and causes unnecessary pain.** If this describes you, ask Yahweh for His help—claiming His mercy and grace to be expressed through you. You may need to contact the person who wronged you and seek reconciliation with them. Sometimes an offender is not aware of the grief their actions have caused. All this needs to be resolved and put away—by the grace of the Lord Jesus.

Yahweh in Your Worship

Merciful Savior, thank You for Your complete and final forgiveness for all my sins. I worship You as my Redeemer and Lord. Help me to be forgiving of those who have wronged me, and guide me to assure them of that forgiveness. May Your love and grace be expressed to them through me, now and always. Use me to help others experience Your forgiveness and learn how to pass that mercy on.

September 14

Yahweh Supplies Everything I Need by Giving Me Himself

Yahweh in the Word

> *"The entire fullness of God's nature dwells bodily in Christ, and you have been filled by Him, who is the head over every ruler and authority"* (Colossians 2:9-10).

False teachers were trying to convince Colossian Christians that they needed more than to believe in Christ in order to fulfill what God required of them—such things as circumcision and keeping various religious laws. The apostle Paul wrote this letter to correct this and other erroneous teachings. He said, "You have been filled (completed) by Him." He is all you need.

Yahweh in Your Walk

If you pour water into a glass until it is full, there is no room for more water—it's filled. In a similar manner, when a person receives Jesus by faith, He fills all the room that person has for Him. And He who fills us is Himself the "entire fullness of God's nature." **In other words, we are filled with Yahweh's fullness!** What a blessed condition to experience!

If we find ourselves longing for more than we have, we simply have not claimed what is already ours. In Him we are **complete**—in every way. We have **complete** deliverance from sin and guilt, **complete** provisions for all our spiritual and emotional needs, **complete** assurance of life everlasting, **complete** power to do whatever we need in order to please Him, **complete** victory over Satan, our old nature, and this world, **complete** purpose for life and service, and on and on we could go. **There is literally no room for more of Yahweh than we already have.**

I heard about a rather poor European family who saved their money for years so they could come to America. When they boarded the ship, they brought a small amount of food which they carefully rationed each day. After three days their small son complained of not having enough to eat, so the father gave him a nickel to buy an ice cream cone at the ship's galley. After a long time, the boy returned with a big smile on his face. "Where have you been?" asked the concerned father. "In the galley, eating three ice cream cones and a steak dinner!" he replied. "All that for a nickel?" "Oh no, the food is free," the boy replied. "It comes with the ticket."

Yahweh provides all the spiritual riches we need when we receive His gift of eternal life. All we have to do is to claim what is rightfully ours in Christ. It all comes with the ticket! But like this poor family, we sometimes fail to understand what we have been given in His Son by Yahweh. Here is where the study of God's Word makes such a difference; there we learn of the riches of grace in Christ Jesus. And we discover the way of actually claiming what is ours.

Yahweh in Your Worship

O Yahweh, giver of everything I need, and more. I worship You with praise and gratitude filling my heart. Teach me to appropriate all the riches You have given Me. You are my ultimate treasure. I bless You for being so generous to me. Now, use me to share this good news with others. Help me be as generous toward them as You are toward me.

September 15

Yahweh Is Giving Me Spiritual Renewal Every Day

Yahweh in the Word

> *"Therefore we do not give up. Even though our outer person is being destroyed, our inner person is being renewed day by day. For our momentary light affliction is producing for us an absolutely incomparable eternal weight of glory. So we do not focus on what is seen, but on what is unseen. For what is seen is temporary, but what is unseen is eternal"* (2 Corinthians 4:16-18).

The apostle Paul reminds his readers in Corinth of all the trials he and his missionary team had endured (vv. 7-15). But they were not discouraged to the point of giving up. Instead, they focused attention on the unseen spiritual renewal they were experiencing through these troubles.

Yahweh in Your Walk

What do you see when you look in a mirror? As we age, we see a general loss of various features we would like to keep, such as smooth skin, bright eyes, firm muscles, thick hair, etc. However, we know that this "clay jar" (v. 7) we live in is slowly fading away. As Paul declared, "Our outer person is being destroyed." **If our physical appearance is our primary focus, all this deterioration can be very depressing—we are losing the battle!** No matter how many "lifts" a person may have, the inevitable physical "fall" will occur.

So what should we do as followers of Jesus? The apostle's advice is: Do not give up! **Do not focus on the temporary things that are seen, rather focus on the eternal unseen values in life.** And when you experience affliction, remember that Yahweh uses our trials to produce in us the maturity of character and faith we all need—these are the things that really matter—not our outward appearance.

Women go to a beauty shop or hair salon to become more attractive. And we men are pleased at the result. But have you ever thought of **God's Beauty Shop**? Just as women endure all kinds of unpleasant treatments in order to look better, Yahweh uses various life-experiences to improve us spiritually. James puts it like this: "Consider it a great joy, my brothers, whenever you experience various trials, knowing that the testing of your faith produces endurance. But endurance must do its complete work, so that you may be mature and complete, lacking nothing" (James 1:2-4). Dealing with trouble is part of growing up as a Christian. Learn from it!

As you walk through this day with Yahweh, be willing for Him to work on your inner person by allowing various trials to come your way. Thank Him that He is using these difficulties to produce results that, though unseen, are of eternal significance. Let Him bring spiritual renewal inside your deteriorating body—in His time and His way. Each day He wants to make new the real person you are—for His glory.

Yahweh in Your Worship

Holy Spirit, I joyfully submit to Your work to make me the person who brings glory to Yahweh. Thank You for bringing spiritual renewal to me every day. I long to be more like Yeshua.

September 16

Yahweh Has Spared My Life to Serve His Good Purpose

Yahweh in the Word

> "And now for a little while grace has been shown from Yahweh our God, to leave us a remnant to escape, and to give us a peg in His holy place, that our God may enlighten our eyes and give us a measure of revival in our bondage… to revive us, to repair the house of our God, to rebuild its ruins, and to give us a wall in Judah and Jerusalem" (Ezra 9:8-9).

Ezra was a Hebrew scribe who returned to Jerusalem with other Jews from exile in Babylon. His major contribution was to restore the reading of Scripture and various aspects of worship. These words in our text express his belief that Yahweh had spared a small number (a remnant) of His people in order to rebuild the temple, establish worship, and return to obedience to His word.

Yahweh in Your Walk

Think for a moment about people you know, family and friends, who are no longer with you in this world; they have departed this life, some when rather young. **Have you ever wondered why Yahweh has let you live this long?** Perhaps He has a special purpose for you to fulfill before He calls you home. He has left you as a remnant of His grace for His special plan.

Recently I read an interesting story of how those who first cleared farmland for cultivation would often leave one tree standing in the middle of the field. That tree was left to provide shade for animals that would occupy that field—a "remnant tree." The apostle Paul referred to himself as a Hebrew who had been spared by Yahweh to be a part of a "remnant chosen by grace" (Romans 11:5) to declare the gospel to both Jews and Gentiles.

Yahweh has chosen to spare your life in order for you to fulfill a special purpose. You are to be His witness to your family, your friends, and others. In addition He has other specific tasks for you to perform. Here are some practical suggestions for making this happen:

1. Thank Yahweh every day for giving you another day to serve His purpose in creating you and for allowing you the years you have lived.
2. Ask Yahweh to help you discover more about the work He wants to accomplish through you.
3. Present yourself daily to become His ambassador, His laborer, His witness, and His servant.
4. Celebrate the fact that you are special to Yahweh and that He has placed you where you are for His good purpose.

Yahweh in Your Worship

Gracious Yahweh, I do not fully understand why You have chosen to spare my life these years. But I want each remaining day to be a blessing to You and a fulfillment of Your purpose for me. Help me seize this day of opportunities for honoring You.

September 17

My Baptism Honors Yeshua

Yeshua in the Word

> *"We were buried with Him by baptism into death, in order that, just as Christ was raised from the dead by the glory of the Father, so we too may walk in a new way of life. For if we have been joined with Him in the likeness of His death, we will certainly also be in the likeness of His resurrection"* (Romans 6:4-5).

New Testament baptism is the immersion in water of a believer in Christ. This act is a public affirmation that the person being baptized has trusted Yeshua as his or her personal Savior and Lord. The water is a symbol of a grave, thus the death, burial, and resurrection of Jesus is pictured, but also the person being baptized affirms his belief that he has died to an old way of sinful living and been buried with Him and is now raised from death to a new life with Christ.

Yeshua in Your Walk

Adoniram Judson (1788-1850) went to Burma as a missionary, along with his devoted wife Ann. They were faithful witnesses for several years before seeing the first Burmese man come to faith in Christ. Judson recorded this prayer on that occasion: "Oh, may it prove the beginning of a series of baptisms in the Burman Empire which shall continue in uninterrupted succession to the end of time." By the time Judson died there were more than 7,000 Burmese who had become believers. He wrote a baptism hymn with these words:

> Come, Holy Spirit, Dove divine, on these baptismal waters shine,
> And teach our hearts, in highest strain, to praise the Lamb for sinners slain.
> We sink beneath the water's face, and thank Thee for Thy saving grace;
> We die to sin and seek a grave with Thee, beneath the yielding wave.
> And as we rise with Thee to live, O let the Holy Spirit give
> The sealing unction from above, the joy of life, the fire of love.

As you walk through this day, recall your own baptism experience. Remember that you are spiritually dead to your old carnal nature and alive to the life of Christ who, by His Spirit, lives in you. Seek to be a faithful representative of Yeshua by your attitude and actions. Be a witness of the One who died for you and rose again to be your resurrection life.

If you have not been baptized by immersion, seek to fulfill this important aspect of your decision to follow the Lord Jesus. Immersion in water is the only form of baptism that symbolizes these basic teachings of the new life in Christ. You do not want to miss this biblical way of giving a public witness of your commitment to Him.

Yeshua in Your Worship

Thank you, Lord, for Your baptism as an example for me to follow. I worship You as my Savior and Master. Help me today to seize every opportunity to share Your life with others.

September 18

Yahweh Is Working All Things Together for My Good

Yahweh in the Word

> "We know that all things work together for the good of those who love God: those who are called according to His purpose" (Romans 8:28).

The promise of this verse is that Yahweh is at work through all of life's experiences to bring about His good purpose for all who love Him.

Yahweh in Your Walk

Each day finds you walking through experiences that may bring unexpected challenges. Some are pleasant and enjoyable, others cause heartache and grief. **If you love Yahweh and have placed yourself in His care, you can know for certain that He will work through all your life experiences for your good and His glory.**

Several years ago I came across these comforting words written by Alan Redpath (1907-1989). He was a British evangelist, pastor and author. During his later years he suffered a severe stroke.

> This I Know:
>
> There is nothing—no circumstance, no trouble, no testing that can ever touch me until,
> First of all, it has come past God and past Christ, right through to me.
> If it has come that far, it has come with a great purpose,
>   which I may not understand at the moment, but, as I refuse to become panicky,
> as I lift up my eyes to Him and accept it as coming from the throne of God
> for some great purpose of blessing for my own heart, no sorrow will ever disturb me,
> no trial will ever disarm me, no circumstance will ever cause me to fret—for I shall
>   rest in the joy of who my Lord is!

These beautiful words reflect the truth of our Scripture text for today. Yahweh is sovereign over all things. Nothing occurs without His permission. And because He is love, everything He allows must be for a good purpose. Paul had learned this through his experiences as a devoted follower of Jesus. You may also arrive at this firm conclusion regarding your life. Your part is to continue being a person who loves Yahweh, and who proves that love by seeking to obey Him in all things. Begin forming the habit of starting every day with an intentional commitment to Him of yourself and all you have. Affirm your love and gratitude for Him. Thank Him at the beginning of every day that He will be faithful to use all that happens that day for your good.

Yahweh in Your Worship

O Yahweh, I do worship and adore You for Your goodness to me. Thank You for the blest assurance that whatever happens to me will be controlled by You to help me grow to become more like You. Help me be a witness of Your greatness and goodness to those around me today. Deliver me from anxious feelings when things seem to go wrong; I know You are always there.

September 19

Yeshua Wants to Be the Author of My Life Story

Yeshua in the Word

> "Therefore we also, since we are surrounded by so great a cloud of witnesses, let us lay aside every weight and the sin which so easily ensnares us, and let us run with endurance the race that is set before us, looking unto Jesus, the **author** and finisher of our faith, who for the joy that was set before Him endured the cross, despising the shame, and has sat down at the right hand of the throne of God" (Hebrews 12:1-2 NKJV).

The writer of Hebrews challenged his readers to learn from the "Heroes of the Faith" listed in Chapter 11. He appealed for them to be like track athletes who lay aside any garment that would impede their performance and to run with endurance the race of life, always looking to Jesus for an example.

Yeshua in Your Walk

I read an interesting story about Steve Saint. His father, missionary pilot Nate Saint, was killed in 1956, along with four other missionaries, by the Waodani tribe in Ecuador. Steve was just a four-year-old lad when this tragedy occurred. Years later, as an adult, Steve returned to Ecuador and became friends with Mincaye, one of the natives who killed his father. This miracle of forgiveness was possible because of successful efforts to evangelize this tribe. Steve's motto is: "Let God Write Your Story." He says, "You have a lot of people… who want to write their own story and have God be their editor when [it] goes wrong. I decided long ago to let God write my story." When Steve was in a serious accident in 2012, he said to his family, "Let's let God write this chapter too." His trust in God has enabled him to move toward recovery.

What if you followed Steve's example and turned the writing of your life-story over to Yeshua? Notice in our Scripture text for today this phrase: "looking unto Jesus, the **author** and finisher of our faith." Who could be a better author of your life-story than Jesus? Why not begin your walk through this and every day with a simple prayer like this: "Lord Jesus, Your love for me is beyond measure and You know far better than I what is best for me. Therefore, I trust You to compose and fulfill Your planned experiences for me today. I thank You in advance for Your faithfulness to guide me through the exciting adventure of this chapter of our life together."

If you choose this approach to life, you can be certain that unexpected happenings will occur, and some may be painful—just like Steve's accident. But you can likewise be certain that Yeshua is in control and will bring you safely through as a better person. **Your history will become His-story!** What better way could you spend your days in this brief sojourn below?

Yeshua in Your Worship

Most gracious and merciful Lord, I bow before Your throne to offer praise and thanksgiving to You. How amazing that Your love and care are so great for me. Thank You for being willing to be the Author and finisher of my brief life-story. I gladly submit everything to Your control.

September 20

Yahweh Wants Me to Build Strong Relationships with Others

Yahweh in the Word

> "When David had finished speaking with Saul, Jonathan committed himself to David, and loved him as much as he loved himself… Jonathan made a covenant with David because he loved him as much as himself… Jonathan once again swore to David in his love for him, because he loved him as he loved himself" (1 Samuel 18:1-3; 20:17).

Here are three references to Jonathan's love for his friend David. There was an unusually strong bond of love that made their relationship very special. Jonathan was King Saul's son while David came from a rather poor family. Also, Saul became very jealous of David due to his popularity with the people. So, this friendship had to overcome significant barriers that only mutual love and affection could achieve.

Yahweh in Your Walk

Today I heard a pastor say, **"Rectangles destroy relationships."** These words seemed strange and even meaningless until he clarified what he meant. He used "rectangles" to refer to various kinds of rectangular shaped screens that appear on many kinds of electronic equipment, such as TVs, video game devices, smart phones, computers, etc. The point he was making is that many people allow these "rectangles" to interfere with face-to-face communication, and thus, interrupt and even destroy the development of relationships that depend on interacting with one another.

    Recently two young adults came to visit me and my wife. As we sat down together and began conversing, I noticed that they both had what appeared to be a smart phone in their hands. During our rather brief visit, they both looked repeatedly at their phones rather than focus on our conversation. Later, I went to a restaurant and again, two younger adults sat across from one another in a booth, gazing at their phones. I thought to myself, what a shame to waste this opportunity to communicate directly with one another. How sad to see them miss out on building a better relationship. Suppose they had spent those minutes talking and listening to one another.

    Of course, David and Jonathan were never tempted to be distracted by electronic "rectangles," rather, they obviously spent valuable time developing a special friendship. What about you? Examine yourself at this point. **There is a real danger of spending hours with another person, watching television or movies, and only minutes actually getting to know one another.** Real friendships do not happen quickly nor easily. They demand intentional, focused interaction with another person. You are familiar with the slogan: "Don't text and drive." Why not apply that to times with another person? How about: **"Don't let rectangles destroy your relationships"**?

Yahweh in Your Worship

Thank You, Yahweh, that You never let distractions interfere with Your attentiveness to me. You always have time and attention to give to me. Help me be more focused on whoever I am with, just as You give undivided attention to me.

September 21

Yahweh Wants Me to Learn to Communicate the Gospel

Yahweh in the Word

> "For everyone who calls on the name of the Lord will be saved. How can they call on Him they have not believed in? And how can they believe without hearing about Him? And how can they hear without a preacher? And how can they preach unless they are sent?" (Romans 10:14-15).

The apostle Paul was among the first believers to be sent out as missionaries. He had a passion to share the good news with those who had never heard it. He also challenged churches to be missional in the sense of focusing their efforts on unreached people groups.

Yahweh in Your Walk

As you progress through this day, you will probably come in contact with persons who have never called upon Jesus for salvation. Part of the reason for this is the fact that no one has ever explained the gospel message to them—at least in a way they could understand it. **All who have believed must see themselves as obligated to share the message of life with those who have not believed—all of us are missionaries, sent by Yeshua to communicate the gospel.**

In 1814 a man named Thomas Gallaudet graduated from a seminary, intending to become a preacher. Soon he met a nine-year-old hearing impaired girl named Alice. His desire to communicate the gospel to her lead him to refine and develop a system known as "signing" for the deaf. Later, he established the American School for the Deaf with a curriculum that included the gospel message.

Here is an example of how one man learned to share God's truth in a unique manner. As Paul asked, "How can they believe without hearing about Him?" Have you learned to share the basic facts of the message of salvation? Suppose some family member or friend or neighbor or co-worker who knows you claim to be a Christian, asked you to explain to them how to be saved? Could you do that? If not, why not take the time to learn the basic Bible plan of salvation. Perhaps you could ask a friend who practices sharing his or her faith to help you.

In addition to learning the biblical steps to being saved, we must learn ways of overcoming the barriers people have for not believing. Ask Yahweh to lead you to reach out to unsaved persons through what is sometimes called "friendship evangelism." This approach begins by becoming a personal friend with a lost person—sharing life experiences together; letting the person know you are genuinely interested in him or her. Then when the time is right, you share your testimony of what knowing Christ means to you—in a natural, non-threatening manner. Be intentional.

Yahweh in Your Worship

Thank You, Lord of salvation, for sending Your chosen witnesses to me. Now help me pass on to others what I have learned and experienced. Help me be more intentional about reaching out to the unsaved around me. In addition, use me to give and pray so others can be missionaries where I can never go. Yahweh, I want to be involved in sending and going to share the good news.

September 22

Yahweh Has Given Me Many Special Titles

Yahweh in the Word

> "They will be Mine, says Yahweh Sabaoth, a special possession on the day I am preparing. I will have compassion on them as a man has compassion of his son who serves him" (Malachi 3:17).

Yahweh spoke these meaningful words through Malachi, His prophet. He refers to a future "day of the Lord" when all His people will be with Him forever. All this will occur because of Yahweh's compassion for His own. (See September 6.)

Yahweh in Your Walk

Have you ever thought about all the various titles you have that identify who you are? For example my titles include: son, father, husband, Christian, believer, disciple, teacher, pastor, and on the list goes. You, likewise, could make a similar list. In previous devotionals we have considered some of the many titles used in the Bible to describe Yahweh, such as God, Father, Redeemer, Lord, Master, King of kings, Lord of lords, Savior, Teacher, and on and on.

Think today about some of the titles Yahweh has given you. For example in this devotional text is the term "special treasure" (in Hebrew: ***segullah***). Here is a clear reference to the high regard Yahweh has for you, and all His chosen ones. Out of His entire creation you are one of His most highly valued possessions! As we learned earlier, you are the "apple of His eye."

Now consider other terms the Scriptures use to describe you. As a believer, you are a saint (holy one), servant of Yahweh, co-laborer with Christ, His ambassador, His child, part of the bride of Christ, a member of His body on earth, a joint-heir with Christ, His witness, salt of the earth, light of the world, His friend, beloved, first-born, priest, and many other wonderful expressions. **Each of these terms speaks eloquently of how important you are to Yahweh.**

Suppose you were told today that you had been given some big promotion at work, or received an unexpected important recognition—how would you feel? Probably very good! Your self-esteem would get a big boost and your level of motivation for doing more and better would likewise be raised to new heights! Let's imagine a little further—suppose you heard Yahweh's voice telling you that you were His special treasure—a person whom He values highly. How about that? Truth is—this is exactly what He tells you over and over and over again in His word. Just believe it and begin acting more appropriately for someone who is a "child of the King."

Yahweh in Your Worship

Gracious and loving heavenly Father, Lord of all creation, thank You for setting Your divine affection upon me. I confess that I am totally unworthy and unfit to be Your special treasure, but You have chosen me because of Your mercy and grace. Therefore, I celebrate who You have made me to be, and I walk through this day knowing who I am in Your sight. I seize this opportunity to worship You and to rejoice in Your goodness to me. Help me share this good news with others today, especially those who suffer from a poor self-image.

September 23

Yahweh Wants Me to Have True Riches

Yahweh in the Word

> "Instruct those who are rich in the present age not to be arrogant or to set their hope on the uncertainty of wealth, but on God, who richly provides us with all things to enjoy. Instruct them to do what is good, to be rich in good works, to be generous, willing to share, storing up for themselves a good reserve for the age to come, so that they may take hold of life that is real" (1 Timothy 6:17-19).

Paul concludes his first letter to young Timothy with these words of wise counsel. Notice the term "instruct" occurs twice. Timothy is told to teach those of his church who are financially rich not to be proud of their wealth nor to place their trust in money but rather to become rich in good works by using wealth to help needy persons, thus making preparation for "the age to come."

Yahweh in Your Walk

The Scriptures reveal an interesting fact about riches—**there are riches on earth**, which we may enjoy for a short time—**and there are treasures in heaven**, which may bring pleasure forever. Jesus spoke of both kinds when He said, "Don't collect for yourselves treasures on earth where moth and rust destroy and where thieves break in and steal. But collect for yourselves treasures in heaven, where neither moth nor rust destroys, and where thieves don't break in and steal. For where your treasure is, there your heart will be also" (Matthew 6:19-21).

We know how to accumulate riches on earth—by earning money, saving, and keeping what we get. These earthly treasures are very uncertain—they can be lost or stolen, but those riches laid up in heaven are everlasting. **Yahweh wants us to have true riches, the kind that cannot be lost and can be enjoyed forever.** One way to lay up treasures in heaven is to lay them down on earth—in the sense of giving our wealth to help others. Notice how Paul spoke in our text for today about being rich in good works by being generous and willing to share with others. Other passages speak of being rich in faith, in hope, and in love. These are those true riches that can never be lost and will be enjoyed in heaven forever.

I read of an overseas missionary who was approached by robbers who wanted all his money. He gave them the few dollars he carried on him, then said, "Most of my riches are in heaven; I sent them on ahead of me. There's where you can find them." Yes, Yahweh wants you to have true riches. In fact, Paul said it like this: "You know the grace of our Lord Jesus Christ: though He was rich, for your sake He became poor, so that by His poverty you might become rich" (2 Corinthians 8:9). Through the sacrifice of Jesus, we are rich in those treasures in heaven that last.

Yahweh in Your Worship

Thank You Lord for helping me learn the meaning of true wealth. Surely Your presence with me is my greatest treasure. I long to be more generous with the resources You give me to pass on to others. Teach me the best use of my financial wealth as I seek to lay up treasures in heaven.

September 24

Yeshua (Jesus) Wants His People to Maintain their Love for Him

Yeshua in the Word

> *"You have abandoned the love you had at first" (Revelation 2:4).*

The focus of these devotionals for the next seven days will be the seven churches in the Book of Revelation. We begin with first century Ephesus which was an important seaport of Asia Minor. This city was one of the great cities of the ancient world. It was noted for its wealth, culture, commerce, politics, religion and corruptness. The worship of the goddess Artemis attracted many people to this area. Yeshua began His letter to them by commending the life and conduct of the faithful church members in this wicked city.

However, the Ephesian believers had one tragic flaw—they had lost a passionate love for Christ. They probably were doctrinally correct and busy in Christian activity, but lacking their initial purpose. The members did much to benefit themselves and their community but they were acting out of the wrong motives. Work for God must be motivated by love for God or it will not last.

Jesus issued a warning that contained three commands. First, the Ephesian Christians were to remember how they once loved Jesus. Second, they were to repent of their coldness, and finally, they were to do as they had done at first, that is, stand against false teachers and their sinful lifestyles. Each of the seven churches closes with the phrase, "Anyone who has an ear should listen to what the Spirit says to the churches." This letter concluded with a promise to the overcomer. **Such a victor is the person, who by faith, shares in Christ's victory in the Christian life for eternity.**

Yeshua in Your Walk

Through the years numerous religious groups or sects have formed. Many denominations began as a sect, then evolved into churches. Some of these small groups have ceased to exist. For the next seven devotionals, seven of these little known groups, will be presented. **One common thread connects each sect—they lost their first love.** For example, in 1881, Claas Epp, a leader of the Mennonite Brethren, announced that he was meeting Elijah in the skies and proceed with him to heaven. He proclaimed that Christ was to appear on March 8, 1889. Later Epp claimed to be a "son of Christ." His followers remained faithful to this confused man, and continued to follow him until the fall of 1902 when they almost starved to death. Their continual "waiting" for Jesus caused them to cease working and taking care of their family needs. The sect died out because the focus was removed from Christ to Claas Epp. Jesus calls all believers to affirm and maintain their love for Him.

Yeshua in Your Worship

Yeshua, help me to maintain a close fellowship with You through prayer and Bible study. Lead me to remember to express the significance of Your appearance and message to John. Guide me to accept the fact that I do not know the future, but to trust You who not only knows it, but controls it.

September 25

Yeshua Wants His People to Be Faithful to Him

Yeshua in the Word

> *"Don't be afraid of what you are about to suffer… Be faithful until death, and I will give you the crown of life" (Revelation 2:10).*

The church in Smyrna struggled against two hostile forces—a Jewish population strongly opposed to Christianity, and a non-Jewish population strongly loyal to Rome who supported emperor worship. Jesus introduced Himself as the One who was dead and came to life. He knew that the church was going through difficult times. Smyrna was called the "crown of Asia." The city was located about 25 miles north of Ephesus. Temples to Cybele, Apollo, Asclepius, and Aphrodite lined the streets. The heathen splendor that surrounded the Christians could have smothered the church out of existence, but the idol worshippers failed.

Another factor working against the church was the great centers of Caesar worship. Emperor worship had become compulsory under Domitian. Once a year a Roman citizen was required to burn a pinch of incense on the altar to the godhead of Caesar. This act was a test of a person's political loyalty. Everyone was to say, "Caesar is Lord." The Christians would not participate. Persecution came as a result of this choice. Caesar worship placed the church in great peril. Two words were used in the letter to describe what the Christian had to face—tribulation and poverty.

Yeshua in Your Walk

Another sect that did not remain true to Jesus was the Millerite Movement. This group was started by a man named William Miller. He was a farmer of Low Hampton, New York, and an ardent student of the Bible, especially the "chronological portions." He became convinced that many events had been predicted to occur with a specific time and had already transpired according to chronology. Various passages in Daniel and the Revelation were his favorite Scriptures. His popularity became an interest of many people. Soon there were demands for him to lecture. Thus he began to lecture in 1821 to prove his theories. Crowds became interested and many converts were made among preachers and members of the various denominations. He reasoned that the Lord's return would come on October 22, 1844. His group, now called Adventists, gathered for the return, which did not happen. Most of the believers renounced their faith and returned to what was left of their personal possessions such as farms. Persecution soon followed for the remaining members who believed in the imminent second advent. The Seventh Day Adventist denomination came from the work of William Miller.

Yeshua in Your Worship

Lord, help me to endure any persecutions with grace and dignity, and maintain a Christ-like goodness even though opposition may be provoked. Remind me that You are in perfect control over these decisions made by the churches. Yeshua, I know that persecution comes from Satan, not You. **You alone give me the courage and grace I need to deal with opposition.**

September 26

Yeshua Rejects Compromising with False Teachers

Yeshua in the Word

"You have some there who hold to the teaching of Balaam" (Revelation 2:14)

Pergamum was a sophisticated city, a center of Greek culture and education, with a 200,000 volume library. But it was also the center of four cults, and it rivaled Ephesus in its worship of idols. Some people referred to this city as "where that great throne of Satan is located." Jesus commended the church at Pergamum for their faithfulness while enduring persecution, yet among the membership were people whose practices were extremely displeasing to God.

Pergamum, like Smyrna, was a center of Caesar worship. Therefore, to be a Christian in that city was to enter a danger zone, or as Jesus said, "where Satan dwells." The believer had to make a choice to be primarily loyal to Christ, and at the same time live under earthly authority. It was not easy to be a Christian. The temptation to compromise one's allegiance to Christ in favor of earthly powers and thus gain momentary relief from persecution became a reality. One martyr is mentioned by name. He is Antipas. He was a faithful witness for Christ and died for his faith. Despite their faithfulness, some members were holding to the teaching of Balaam and were eating meat offered to idols and practicing sexual immorality. Unbelievers cannot experience the eternal reward of living in God's Kingdom. The message came to these people to repent. The letter ends with a promise of the "white stone" bearing an unknown name. God will give us a new name and a new heart. However, **believers must stay the course and remain faithful until the end of time.**

Yeshua in Your Walk

Another little known sect ceased to exist because they did not maintain their love for Christ. In the early American revival period, the doctrine of perfectionism began to run wild. Charles G. Finney was a supporter of that theory. Following his emotional conversion in 1818, he reportedly said, "So far as I could see, I was in a state in which I did not sin." His ministry as a holiness preacher was identified as hostile toward luxury, personal adornment, and other "worldly" practices. He followers became known as a Perfectionist sect. One characteristic of their belief was the "second blessing"—an emotional experience that must follow conversion. The guidance of the Holy Spirit was sought in visions and gifts. They regarded themselves as the true church and refused to interact with any other religious group. Any modern scholarship was opposed by these fundamentalists. A number of dissatisfied members started their own groups such as the Methodist Episcopal Church and the Methodist Protestant Churches. Some of the Perfectionists still exist today.

Yeshua in Your Worship

Yeshua, please forgive me and my church when we compromise with the world. I know that pain is a part of life, but it is never easy to suffer, no matter what the cause. Help me to maintain my faith when suffering comes.

September 27

Yeshua Calls His Church to Keep Doing His Works

Yeshua in the Word

> "But hold onto what you have until I come. The one who is victorious and keeps My works to the end: I will give him authority over the nations—" (Revelation 2:25-26).

Thyatira was a small, working persons' town, an unimportant city and center for trade in making cloth. Lydia had a business in that city. A cult of Caesar existed that called Caesar the son of God. The Christians claimed Jesus was the Son of God. Jesus saw everything going on in the church—both good and bad. **Their works of love at the beginning were demonstrated in service to the needy.** The Lord was pleased with what they had done. At the present time, however, He accused them of being too tolerant and permissive toward evil.

A woman in the church was specifically leading others into evil. Her nickname was Jezebel. She claimed to be a prophetess, having the power and gifts of the Holy Spirit like the prophets of old. Remember how the Jezebel of the Old Testament was a pagan queen of Israel and was considered the most evil woman who ever lived? This fake leader enticed Christians to commit sexual sins. She used her powers to seduce and deceive the believers away from God. Jesus called on her to repent, but she persistently refused. The Lord of the Lampstands threatened Jezebel and her crowd with severe judgment. He then described the "false doctrine" and explained the consequences of such a teaching.

The Lord did not give up on the church. He wanted them to repent. The church was promised the "bright and morning star" by which to chart their course in life. Christ is also called the morning star in 22:16. A morning star appears just before dawn, when the night is coldest and darkest. **When the world is at its worst, Christ will burst onto the scene, revealing evil with His light of truth and bringing His promised reward.**

Yeshua in Your Walk

This part of the devotional continues to look at groups, cults, and sects that have evolved through the years as a result of some particular church leader. Many denominations began as sects, then evolved into churches. The people followed a certain leader, often without questioning the doctrine being taught. **One such sect was called the "Latter Rain Movement."** A revival, characterized by the baptism of the Holy Spirit, began in East Tennessee and North Carolina. Evidence of Spirit baptism was "speaking in other tongues as the Spirit give utterance."

A.J. Tomlinson, the founder and general overseer of the Church of God, took charge of the movement in 1906. Church members from various parts of the country visited these revival meetings. The group became known as the "Outpouring of the Latter Rain." For the next 40 years these churches functioned throughout the United States. Differences on points of doctrine finally divided the believers. Today about 60 congregations exist.

Yeshua in Your Worship

Yeshua, help me to continue to serve You faithfully by growing in love, faith, and acts of service. Make me aware of shortcomings in my life that I may confess these to You. Thank You for Your mercy and forgiveness. Use me to help my church be faithful in doing Your works.

September 28

Yeshua Wants His Church to Be Alive to Him

Yeshua in the Word

> *"You have a reputation for being alive, but you are dead" (Revelation 3:1).*

Sardis was located on a major road and was prosperous commercially. A thriving wool industry helped the economy. The problem with the Sardis church was not heresy, but spiritual death. The city was infested with sin. Yeshua had little to say about this dead church. To Him the city also was dead. He looked at the heart of the church people and found that they were deceased. The Christians were meeting in a lively place, but it was a façade—they were fake. They were urged to obey the Christian truth they had heard when they first believed in Christ, to get back to the basics of the faith. If they did not repent Jesus warned that He would come to them in a sudden and unexpected judgment. **The Lord basically said, "Wake up and come alive!"**

This dead church in a dead city had a few people who remained faithful and consistent in their lives before the Lord. They needed to repent, to confess its deadness, to put away sin, to be filled with the Spirit, to put life and meaning into all the things they were doing. Yeshua made three promises to the disciples who would overcome. First, they could be clothed with holiness, purity, and righteousness if they would leave their former lifestyle. "Clothed in white" means to be set apart for God and made pure. Second, their names would not be blotted out of the book of life. This book symbolizes Yahweh's knowledge of who belongs to him. Third, He would intercede, speaking for them before the Father in heaven. Their part in this process was to show gratitude to Him by doing the kinds of works in their lives that were consistent with what He expected.

Yeshua in Your Walk

The Shaker doctrine was formulated by Ann Lee, a textile worker in Manchester, England. "Mother Ann," in 1758 converted to the "Shaking Quakers." After enduring persecution for noisy worship services, she had a series of revelations, after which she regarded herself as the second incarnation of Christ. She developed an elaborate theology and established celibacy as the cardinal principle of the community. After Mother Ann's death (1784), the Shaker church came under the leadership of Elder Joseph Meacham. The first Shaker community, established at New Lebanon, New York, in 1787 spread through New England and westward into Kentucky, Ohio, and Indiana. By 1826, 18 Shaker villages had been set up in eight states. The Shaker movement reached its height during the 1840s, when about 6,000 members were enrolled in the church. By 1905 only 1,000 members remained. Today one working Shaker village exists at Sabbath Day Lake, near New Gloucester, Maine. Fewer than 10 members serve in this dying church. Doesn't this church remind you of the church at Sardis? They made a lot of noise, but were spiritually dead.

Yeshua in Your Worship

Yeshua, lead me to witness with my life, not just my words. Help me to remain faithful to the truth about You. Help me be continually on guard against false teachers. I want always to be Your witness of biblical truth. Thank You for Your Spirit who guides us into all truth.

September 29

Yeshua Wants Us to Rely on His Promises as We Remain Faithful

Yeshua in the Word

> "Because you have kept My command to endure, I will also keep you from the hour of testing that is going to come over the whole world to test those who live on the earth" (Revelation 3:10).

Every one of these letters in the Revelation is addressed first to a minister, the "angel" of the church, and the message to Philadelphia particularly has a message of encouragement to preachers. This city was located on a high plateau and produced wine along with leather and textile goods. Jesus reserved His greatest tribute for this church. He commended their faithfulness. According to this Scripture, three descriptions of the church at Philadelphia are identified. They were a missionary church, lovers of Yahweh's Word, and a humble, faithful church. For these reasons, no word of reproof was given. In fact, **the Savior gave three wonderful and encouraging promises to these believers: (1) He would take care of their enemies; (2) He would keep them from tribulation; and (3) He would honor them.**

An interesting observation is that Jesus characterized Himself as the Messiah, the Savior God promised to the Jews. Based on what the Lord knew of the people, He made a promise that the door to His kingdom was open to these faithful followers, with an assurance that no human being can undo what God does for us when He saves us and give us His kingdom.

The church was commended for what they had done and needed to "keep on keeping on." This letter concludes with the church being given a new name. **The name of Yahweh and of the New Jerusalem was to be inscribed on them for eternity.**

Yeshua in Your Walk

Little groups of devotees have continued through the years to follow certain powerful leaders. Most of these believers no longer are part of the original plan. For example, "Reconstructionism" was begun by the Jewish Reconstructionist Foundation in 1940. The key leader of this movement was Mordecai M. Kaplan. The goal was to examine Jewish life and follow six or more directives. The most familiar today was the establishment of a homeland for Jews and their culture in Palestine. The training in old Hebrew rituals was to be emphasized. Kaplan was a coeditor of the *Reconstructionist Sabbath Prayer Book* (1945), which among other unorthodoxies, he denied the literal accuracy of the biblical text. As a result, the Union of Orthodox Rabbis of the United States and Canada declared his theories unacceptable. We may wonder what Jesus would have said to this organization?

Yeshua in Your Worship

I want to thank You, Yeshua, for Your promise to accept me and give me eternal security. Teach me to be patiently obedient to You no matter what I face. Help me to be on guard concerning the world around me. Protect my church from becoming worldly. Your Word clearly reveals Your awareness of all that Your church is doing. Guide us to be pleasing in Your sight.

September 30

Yeshua is Displeased with a Lukewarm Heart

Yeshua in the Word

> "So because you are lukewarm, and neither hot nor cold, I am going to vomit you out of My mouth" (Revelation 3:16).

The seventh church in the book of Revelation that Yeshua addressed was the church at Laodicea, the only one of the churches that received no approval from the Lord. They were a lukewarm, foolish, body of believers. Laodicea was famous for its warm springs which provided water for bathing but was utterly unfit for drinking. The city was prosperous from farming, banking, and manufacturing, and most of the citizens focused on this success. However, these same people did not get too excited about their relationship with Jesus or about their worship of Him. The church thought of itself as rich and wealthy; they needed noting. But Jesus saw them as they were. Their indifference was not appealing to Christ. Yet He offered His invitation of love and fellowship to them.

The people were deceived by their riches into a false security. Jesus told the people what He was going to do about their spiritual condition—vomit them out; it was a nauseating condition to Him. He persistently pleaded with them to recognize their spiritual poverty. Verse 20 is the Lord's invitation to be right with Him and do the works that had been neglected. He challenged members of the church to get rid of their self-sufficient attitude.

Yeshua in Your Walk

The religious painting that has impressed me most is titled, "The Light of the World." This work of art was completed in 1845 by the artist Holman Hunt. Public opinion was at first hostile toward Hunt, but the picture of Christ knocking at the door of the human soul, brought him his first public success. The artist continued interpreting religious scenes until his vision failed and he could no longer see his canvas. The appeal of this work is for all Christians to renew their fellowship with Christ. He is seeking us. Mary Slade wrote the words to an old hymn based on that picture. Remember these words?

> Who at my door is standing, patiently drawing near,
> Entrance within demanding, Whose is the voice I hear?
> Sweetly the tones are falling; open the door for me!
> If thou wilt heed My calling, I will abide with thee.

A warning is repeated again as to all seven churches, "He that hath an ear, let him hear."

Yeshua in Your Worship

Yeshua, help me to have a burning heart on fire for You and not to become bland in my worship. Thank You for being patient and persistent with me as I seek to become all You have created me to be. May the door of my heart be constantly open to You when You knock.

October 1

Yahweh Is My Personal Lord and Master

Yahweh in the Word

> *"I said to Yahweh, 'You are my Lord; I have nothing good besides You'"* (Psalm 16:2).

The term ***adonai*** (pronounced a-doe-NAI) is the Hebrew word for "Lord" in this verse. There are some 340 occurrences of this important word in the Old Testament. The meaning is: master, ruler, sovereign one, or owner. When Yahweh and Adonai occur in combination (Adonai Yahweh) they convey the truth that Yahweh is the sovereign master. Although Yahweh Sabaoth (see September 1-5) expresses Yahweh's sovereignty over all things, Adonai Yahweh speaks of a more individual lordship, namely, Yahweh is my personal Lord and Master.

Yahweh in Your Walk

You will find much literature and special conferences today on the subject of "How to Become Successful." Most of this counsel will focus on self-effort. In other words, you are told that if you are to succeed, you must achieve it—"If it is to be, it's up to me." You must believe in yourself, think positively about yourself, and do all you can to promote yourself. While the authentic Christian life demands our best in terms of personal effort, our trust is not in ourselves and in our best work, but in His work in and through us. As the apostle Paul put it, "I labor for this, striving with His strength that works powerfully in me" (Colossians 1:29). Notice the cooperation expressed in these words between "I labor" and "His strength that works powerfully in me." We are always responsible for doing our part to live in a manner that pleases Yahweh, however, we do so with a sense of complete dependence upon Him.

The New Testament reveals Jesus (Yeshua) as our personal Lord (adonai). He is the One who came to live among us, then die for us, and then be raised as our living, reigning Savior and Lord. He has sent His Holy Spirit to live in and work through us for the glory of Yahweh. There is no conflict between Adonai Yahweh and the Lord Jesus and the Holy Spirit; they are the same in nature and purpose. This Trinity is a mystery which we cannot comprehend, but we are able to experience the tremendous benefits it gives.

So as you walk through this day—and every day, claim Adonai Yahweh as your personal Lord who is actively enabling you to become successful in those endeavors that honor Him. Remember that He said, "I am the vine; you are the branches. The one who remains in Me and I in him produces much fruit, because you can do nothing without Me" (John 15:5).

Yahweh in Your Worship

Adonai Yahweh, Lord and Master, I depend totally upon You this day. I want to seize every opportunity to bring honor and glory to You. I join all Your great family in offering praise and thanksgiving for all You are to us today. I believe You are at work in me for Your glory; thank You for all the resources of grace that enable me to be an effective servant of Yours.

October 2

Yahweh Is the One Who Owns Me and All I Possess

Yahweh in the Word

> *"Abram said, 'Lord God (Adonai Yahweh), what can You give me, since I am childless and the heir of my house is Eliezer of Damascus?'" (Genesis 15:2).*

Here is the first occurrence in the Bible of the combination Adonai Yahweh (I AM Lord). Abram used this term to convey his sense of dependence upon Yahweh as His Lord and owner. He was pleading for some evidence that Yahweh's promise to bless all nations though him (Genesis 12:1-3) would come to pass. Yahweh responded with a covenant ceremony in which He repeated His promise (vv. 8-21).

Yahweh in Your Walk

John Wesley (1703-1791) is known as one of the founders of the Methodist Church. Here is a Covenant Prayer which he required all ministers to offer at an annual renewal event:

> I am no longer my own, but Yours.
> Put me to what You will, rank me with whom You will;
> Put me to doing, put me to suffering.
> Let me be employed by You or laid aside by You.
> Enabled by You or brought low by You.
> Let me be full, let me be empty.
> Let me have all things, let me have nothing.
> I freely and heartily yield all things to Your pleasure and disposal.
> And now, O glorious and blessed God, Father, Son, and Holy Spirit,
> You are mine and I am Yours. So be it.
> And the covenant which I have made on earth, let it be ratified in heaven. Amen

Consider making this your prayer as you remember Adonai Yahweh as your Lord and Owner. He will hear and honor this commitment. By acknowledging that He is sovereign over you and all you possess, you place yourself under His control; you literally belong to Him. **This ownership not only refers to His control of you but also His protective care of His possession. He will faithfully guard you and keep the enemy from overpowering you.** You will find lasting security in this assurance.

Yahweh in Your Worship

Blessed Adonai Yahweh, I joyfully submit myself and all I possess to Your divine control. You alone are worthy of such trust and ownership. How grateful I am for the assurance that You can and will do more with me and all I have than I could ever do. As Your possession I have complete confidence in Your continuous deliverance from all evil powers. Thank You for sheltering me from all that would be harmful. You alone are my keeper who preserves me from Satan's attempt to steal me away from You.

October 3

Yahweh Stands Against the Pride of His People

Yahweh in the Word

> *"The Lord God has sworn by Himself—this is the declaration of Yahweh, the God of Hosts: 'I loathe Jacob's pride and hate his citadels, so I will hand over the city and everything in it'" (Amos 6:8).*

Yahweh chose Amos to be His prophet to warn His people of impending judgment. This keeper of sheep spoke boldly as he reminded both Israel and Judah of their sins. Our text has another of the "Lord God" combinations (Adonai Yahweh—I AM Lord). In addition is the term "Yahweh, the God of Hosts." Placing both of these designations for Yahweh together adds weight to what Yahweh said as He pointed to the pride of His people, assuring them of the coming destruction of their capital city in spite of its strong citadels (defensive walls and towers).

Yahweh in Your Walk

Pride is the sin of rebellion against Yahweh—choosing our way rather than His way. The original sin of Adam and Eve was pride. Satan deceived them into thinking they could disobey Yahweh because they knew better about what was good for them than He did. They followed Satan's lies, chose their own way, and fell from Yahweh's favor.

Of all the sins we commit, pride is the most serious. Pride is self-reliance as over against reliance upon Yahweh. **Pride is trusting in one's own judgment rather than that of God.** Yahweh's people had placed their confidence in Jerusalem's defensive walls instead of calling upon God for protection. You will recall how Simon Peter boasted that he would never deny Jesus, saying that even if all the other disciples failed, he would be faithful to death. A short time later, Peter denied three times that he was Jesus' disciple. Peter was trusting proudly in his own loyalty to Jesus—and he failed. The same will happen to us if we depend upon our own strength rather than the power of God's Spirit within us.

As you walk through this new day, beware of expressions of pride. Acknowledge your continuous need of Yahweh's guidance as you make decisions. Make a habit of calling on Him for His strength as you face temptations. Remember—the spirit is often willing, but the flesh is weak. As the writer of Proverbs warns, "Pride comes before destruction, and an arrogant spirit before a fall" (Proverbs 16:18).

Yahweh in Your Worship

"I need Thee every hour, stay Thou nearby. Temptations lose their power when Thou art nigh. I need Thee, O I need Thee; every hour I need Thee! O bless me now, my Savior, I come to Thee." Gracious Lord, I trust You to awaken me to the danger of pride, and deliver me from its power. In my heart I know that I am nothing apart from You; You are the only One worthy of my trust and worship.

October 4

Yahweh Is to Be the Pride of His People

Yahweh in the Word

> *"Yahweh has sworn by the Pride of Jacob" (Amos 8:7).*

Yesterday's devotional focused on Yahweh's warning regarding His people (Jacob) who placed ultimate pride in their fortified city. Notice that in today's reading we find another reference to the "Pride of Jacob." Since Pride is capitalized it must refer to Yahweh Himself—He is the legitimate Pride of His people (Jacob). Here Yahweh is taking an oath by His own authority ("the Pride of Jacob") that He will bring judgment upon His people because they have forsaken Him.

Yahweh in Your Walk

Although pride is most often a sin, there are times when pride is justified and proper. For example, we may speak of how proud we are of our children for some good achievement. Or we may take pride in our favorite sports team because they have performed well. The Hebrew word for "pride" in Amos 8:7 has the meaning of ***excellency.*** Thus we can always properly boast of the excellency of Yahweh, our God; He is the ultimate Pride of His people.

Think about a few expressions of Yahweh's excellency. **The first would be the excellency of His creation. What an amazing universe He has made!** As you walk through this day, take time to notice the wonders of creation—the natural beauty of the heavens and the earth. Just hold a leaf or flower or blade of grass in your hand—amazing! Look at your hand, another testimony of His excellence. Gaze at a person nearby and think of what a miracle of Yahweh's creative power. And consider the fact that each person is unique—a special, hands-on product of Yahweh's work. As the song declares, "Look all the world over, there's no one exactly like me!"

Now consider the excellency of His re-creation, that is, Yahweh's work of re-creating every person who decides to trust the Lord Jesus as personal Savior and Lord. Here is the ultimate achievement of the Pride of Jacob: namely, every redeemed person throughout all the history of humankind. The Pride of Jacob is none other than our Savior, Lord, and King!

As you experience this new day, a day unlike any other, rejoice in Yahweh as the Pride of Jacob. Express your joy through your own words of adoration and praise.

Yahweh in Your Worship

Holy Yahweh, You are not only the Pride of Jacob but also my Pride of Salvation. Today I choose to rejoice in You with thoughts and words of gratitude and praise. How gracious and merciful of You to choose me as Your favored child. I seize this day for Your glory and honor. Keep me mindful of Your worthiness; teach me to boast in You.

October 5

Yahweh Works Through My Troubles for My Good

Yahweh in the Word

> "Then Job replied to Yahweh: "I know that You can do anything and no plan of Yours can be thwarted. You asked, 'Who is this who conceals My counsel with ignorance?' Surely I spoke things I did not understand, things too wonderful for me to know. You said, 'Listen now, and I will speak. When I question you, you will inform Me.' I had heard rumors about You, but now my eyes have seen You. Therefore I take back my words and repent in dust and ashes" (Job 42:1-6).

Yahweh in Your Walk

You probably are familiar with the story of Job. How he was a very prosperous man who was attacked by Satan and lost all his possessions, his children, and the confidence of his friends. The words in our text reveal his attitude following these severe troubles. He was actually grateful for what happened and felt remorse for his lack of understanding of the reason behind his trials. Let it be said to his credit that Job never lost hope; at one time in the midst of all his losses, he said, "Yet He (Yahweh) knows the way I have taken; when He has tested me, I will emerge as pure gold" (23:10). In spite of all he endured, he held on to his confidence in Yahweh, believing the ultimate result of his experiences would be for his welfare.

You also may be aware that pearls are formed due to the wound suffered by an oyster. If a grain of sand gets inside an oyster and thus causes an irritation, the oyster produces a coating around the sand that eventually becomes a beautiful pearl. Something lustrous is created that would not have happened without pain.

In a similar manner to Job and the oyster, Yahweh allows troubles to come to each of us. But He works through these painful experiences to produce better character than would otherwise be possible. **We must learn with Job that troubles are often Yahweh's way of testing us for the sake of making us better.** Therefore, we should see trials not as disheartening troubles but as opportunities to learn more about Yahweh and to become more useful to Him. Perhaps you can identify with Job when he expressed not only confidence in Yahweh but also genuine repentance for words hastily spoken. **He learned, as must we all—no pain, no pearl!** He allows for us to suffer, so that, like Job, we may mature in our understanding of His love.

Yahweh in Your Worship

Blessed Yahweh, my trust is in You to allow only those experiences that will make me be more conformed to Your will and purpose. Forgive me when I doubt Your process of helping me grow in Your likeness. I thank You and praise You that I can seize whatever comes today as Your gift for my benefit and Your glory.

October 6

Yahweh Can Use Nobodies to Be Somebodies

Yahweh in the Word

> "So Yahweh raised up Othniel son of Kenaz, Caleb's youngest brother, as a deliverer to save the Israelites. The Spirit of Yahweh came on him, and he judged Israel. Othniel went out to battle, and Yahweh handed over Cushan-rishathaim king of Aram to him, so that Othniel overpowered him. Then the land was peaceful 40 years, and Othniel son of Kenaz died" (Judges 3:9-11).

Yahweh's people, Israel, due to their disobedience became subject to their enemy. After eight years of slavery, Israel repented and called upon Yahweh to save them. Yahweh responded in mercy as He chose Othniel, the first of a series of judges, to lead them. Very little is said about this man, but the Spirit of Yahweh came upon him and enabled Othniel to bring peace.

Yahweh in Your Walk

I enjoy reading the biographies of individuals who have made a significant contribution to our lives. Most of them came from very humble, obscure beginnings. No one would have guessed these would have great influence. This fact is also seen in many persons described for us in the Bible. Othniel is one example. He became an effective leader of his own people simply because Yahweh chose to raise him up, anoint him with His Spirit, and enable him to overcome the enemy.

The apostle Paul commented on this same truth in these interesting words: "Brothers, consider your calling: Not many are wise from a human perspective, not many powerful, not many of noble birth. Instead, God has chosen what is foolish in the world to shame the wise, and God has chosen what is weak in the world to shame the strong. God has chosen what is insignificant and despised in the world—what is viewed as nothing—to bring to nothing what is viewed as something, so that no one can boast in His presence" (1 Corinthians 1:26-29).

The lesson we learn from this is that Yahweh is the secret of true greatness; none of us can make ourselves useful to Him. Our role is to simply be available to Him. He alone can make nobodies, like us, into somebodies for Him. We also must remember that this world's concept of greatness is not the same an Yahweh's. In Yahweh's sight, the person is greatest who is willing to be a servant, not a famed leader. Think of ways you can be a servant to others today, and then apply yourself to that humble ministry. In so doing you will be truly great in Yahweh's eyes.

Yahweh in Your Worship

Here am I, send me O Yahweh, to be and do all that is pleasing to You. My dependence is upon You to use me for Your purpose in this world. Thank You for Your wisdom in creating me for the tasks You planned for me to do. Today I want to seize every opportunity to honor You. Help me recognize ways of being a servant to others, for Your sake.

October 7

Yahweh's Presence Is the Secret of Success

Yahweh in the Word

> "*Yahweh was with Joseph, and he became a successful man… and Yahweh made everything he did successful*" (Genesis 39:2-3).

The fact that Yahweh was continuously with Joseph is repeated many times in the amazing story of his life. In this text, Joseph is described as being a successful man and everything he did was successful—all because Yahweh was with him.

Yahweh in Your Walk

Today there are numerous books, CDs, DVDs, workshops, conferences, and other events—all in the name of "How to Be Successful." The Bible reveals the ultimate secret of true success in two simple words: ***Yahweh's Presence***. This fact does not discount the importance of personal effort through hard work and the application of proven principles. However, apart from Yahweh's presence and blessing, no person can be successful in the truest sense of that word.

The book of Genesis gives more space to the story of Joseph than to any other person. He is the outstanding biblical example of how a person should respond to adversity in order to gain prosperity. His was an extremely bumpy road to success—filled with **ups** and **downs**. You may recall how his brothers sold him **down** into slavery, then he worked his way **up** to a leader in Egypt, then he was falsely accused by Pharaoh's wife. This resulted in him going **down** to prison where he remained for more than two years. But Yahweh gave him insight into the meaning of dreams which brought about his release and return **up** to prominence as a leader in the government of Egypt.

There he was able to provide for the survival of his entire family when they came searching for food. Later, Joseph was reconciled to his father and brothers—an amazing story of success in spite of numerous hardships.

You also will have your share of trials as you journey through life. Remember Joseph and how he was able to bounce back repeatedly because Yahweh was with him, just as He is with you. **Resolve never to look at adversity as a problem, rather see it as an opportunity to learn, grow, and become a better person.** Keep your eyes on the goal of honoring Yahweh in all you do, not on circumstances that can be discouraging and even lead to defeat. **Hold on; look up; and grow.**

Yahweh in Your Worship

Gracious Yahweh, I praise You for Your promise never to leave nor forsake me. I know that because You are with me I can overcome all that You allow me to endure. Thank You for giving me the grace needed to overcome all adversity.

October 8

Yahweh Invites Me to Meditate on Him and His Ways

Yahweh in the Word

> "How happy is the man who does not follow the advice of the wicked or take the path of sinners or join a group of mockers! Instead, his delight is in Yahweh's instruction and he meditates on it day and night" (Psalm 1:1-2).

The book of Psalms opens with these significant words which promise true happiness to the person who refuses evil influences, but chooses to find great pleasure by meditating on Yahweh's instruction day and night. Many other references can be found in the psalms regarding the value of thoughtful meditation about Yahweh and His truth as revealed in the Scriptures.

Yahweh in Your Walk

The idea of meditation may cause some believers to be skeptical of its practice. Various kinds of mystical meditation are clearly foreign to biblical teachings. Whereas, the kind of meditation recommended by the Bible is an intentional reflection on the attributes of Yahweh and His purpose for His people. Rather than being self-centered, biblical meditation focuses on Him.

Meditation is actually a form of prayer. A person invites Yahweh to guide one's thoughts as he or she contemplates some word or phrase from the Scriptures. Another term for meditation is **rumination.** You may be familiar with the way a cow takes large bites of hay or grain, then later brings that food back up and ruminates or "chews her cud." In a similar manner, one who meditates focuses on some biblical term, "chewing on it" to gain more insight and understanding.

The apostle Paul gave young Timothy this good advice: "Till I come, give attention to reading, to exhortation, to doctrine. Do not neglect the gift that is in you, which was given to you by prophecy with the laying on of the hands of the presbytery. Meditate on these things: give yourself entirely to them, that your progress may be evident to all" (1 Timothy 4:13-15). Much earlier Moses gave young Joshua similar counsel: "This Book of the Law shall not depart from your mouth, but you shall meditate in it day and night, that you may observe to do according to all that is written in it. For then you will make your way prosperous, and then you will have good success" (Joshua 1:8).

Try this discipline if you aren't familiar with meditation. Select some word or phrase, such as "Yahweh is my shepherd," and ask Him to guide your thoughts as you reflect on what each word means and how you can learn from it. Then move on to another chosen truth and repeat the process. Let meditation become a regular part of your fellowship with Yahweh.

Yahweh in Your Worship

Thank You for giving me the capacity to think more deeply about You and Your great truths.

October 9

Yahweh Always Offers Restoration to Me

Yahweh in the Word

> "Brothers, if someone is caught in any wrongdoing, you who are spiritual should restore such a person with a gentle spirit, watching out for yourselves so you also won't be tempted. Carry one another's burdens; in this way you will fulfill the law of Christ" (Galatians 6:1-2).

The apostle Paul wrote this letter to the churches in Galatia in order to correct various false teachings that came to them after Paul's first visit. In chapter 2:11-14 he reports about an incident when he rebuked Peter, along with Barnabas and others for their improper behavior toward Gentiles. This text contains Paul's counsel on how to restore wrongdoers to the fellowship of believers. Here we find help to deal with similar situations today.

Yahweh in Your Walk

Recently I saw a statement that arrested my attention. The more I thought about it, the more I realized its truth. The impressive words were: "Failure is an event, not a person." Have you ever had an experience which left you feeling that you were a failure? I am sure most people have. The truth, from Yahweh's perspective, is that while we may fail to achieve some intended goal, we are never failures ourselves. **Yahweh sees our potential, not just our performance. He knows what you are capable of by His grace; when you experience failure in some venture, Yahweh always offers to restore you and help you learn from your experience.**

Paul and Barnabas took a young man named John Mark on their first missionary journey. For some unexplained reason, after a short time, John left them and returned to his home in Jerusalem (Acts 13:13). Later Barnabas wanted to give him a second chance by taking him on another missionary trip. But Paul refused, causing a division between him and Barnabas (Acts 15:36-41). However, later references reveal that John Mark was restored to Paul and became a trusted associate (Colossians 4:10, 2 Timothy 4:11, Philemon 24). Mark, who was Barnabas' cousin, later wrote the Gospel of Mark proving that though he once experienced failure, he was not a failure himself. He returned to his original commitment to Yahweh and served well.

As Paul advised the Galatians, those who have been guilty of any wrongdoing should be restored to fellowship by believers. And this should always be done with a spirit of gentleness and compassion, being careful not to fall into the same trap. Here is wise counsel for us: Never write off someone who has stumbled in their journey with Christ. Be forgiving and gracious—even with yourself when you fall. **There's no such thing as a person who is a hopeless failure.**

Yahweh in Your Worship

Thank You for those examples in Your Word of persons, like me, who have come short in some life experience, and yet, have been restored by Your mercy. Help me to show the same to others.

October 10

Yahweh Wants Me to Learn to Pay It Forward

Yahweh in the Word

> "So if you consider me a partner, accept him as you would me. And if he has wronged you in any way, or owes you anything, charge that to my account. I, Paul, write this with my own hand: I will repay it—not mention to you that you owe me even your own self" (Philemon 17-19).

The apostle Paul wrote this brief note from Rome where he was in prison. Philemon was a wealthy friend of his, living in Colossae, many miles away. The note was carried by Onesimus, a former slave of Philemon, who apparently had stolen from his master before running away to Rome. There he met Paul and became a believer in Christ. Paul sent him back, requesting a favor from Philemon and reminding him of his indebtedness.

Yahweh in Your Walk

Several years ago I traveled to the nation of Ukraine where I was part of a mission team seeking to share the gospel message with people there. On this journey I remembered how my grandparents had lived in Eastern Europe before migrating to America. The message about Christ came to me as a child because they taught it to my mother who passed it on to me. There is a real sense in which I am indebted to my grandparents for who I am and what I believe today.

Since they died years ago, I can never repay them directly for this tremendous favor. However, by sharing this good news with others, I am paying forward what I owe to them. **This concept of paying forward our debt can be seen in Paul's letter to Philemon.** Since Paul was the one who helped Philemon become a Christian, he was greatly indebted to Paul. But Paul was many miles away in prison; there was no opportunity for Philemon to repay Paul. When Paul sent Philemon's slave Onesimus back to him, Paul asked Philemon to "pay forward" what was owed by forgiving this runaway and receiving him as a brother in Christ.

"Pay It Forward" has become a very popular and widely promoted idea. There is a movie film by this name, a special set-aside "Pay It Forward Day" each spring, books on this subject, and a website—all this to encourage us to reach out to others with impromptu acts of kindness, expressing our sense of indebtedness to others who have done favors for us. Recently, my wife and I were standing in line at a local sandwich shop waiting to pay for our order. When we reached the register, the clerk said, "The gentleman ahead of you has paid your bill." We were shocked because we had never met him. When we found him and thanked him, he said, "No problem, I'm just paying it forward." **Think of ways you might show this kind of favor.**

Yahweh in Your Worship

Oh Yahweh, how often You have blessed me through the generosity of others. Today I want to seize opportunities to pass these blessings on to others. Help me be discerning of ways to do this.

October 11

Yahweh Calls Me to Be His Ambassador

Yahweh in the Word

> *"Everything is from God, who reconciled us to Himself through Christ and gave us the ministry of reconciliation: That is, in Christ, God was reconciling the world to Himself, not counting their trespasses against them, and He has committed the message of reconciliation to us. Therefore, we are ambassadors for Christ, certain that God is appealing through us. We plead on Christ's behalf, 'Be reconciled to God'" (2 Corinthians 5:18-20).*

We learn from this awesome text that Yahweh has called every Christian to a very special ministry—the "ministry of reconciliation." That is, we who have experienced personal reconciliation to Him through Christ are now sent to share this message of reconciliation with others.

Yahweh in Your Walk

Our son, Mark, grew up in a church where he was a member of a boys' missionary organization called Royal Ambassadors. He learned that an ambassador is "one who represents the person of a king in the court of another." Today, he and his wife are missionaries in Singapore where they are putting into practice the basic teachings he learned many years ago.

Although Mark and Judy are career missionaries, all believers share the same call to represent Jesus Christ wherever we are and whatever our vocation may be. We all have the same ministry—the ministry of reconciliation; all have the same message—the message of reconciliation; all have the same title—ambassadors for Christ; all have the same appeal to others—"be reconciled to God." In other words, **all followers of Christ are sent by Him to help others to be brought into a saving relationship with Him.**

Think about some practical ways you can participate in this ministry—how you can actually be an ambassador for Christ. First, and most important, through intercessory prayer. Every day I give time to praying for missionaries and asking Yahweh to use me as His missionary wherever I am that day. Second, by helping build a strong local church where various kinds of mission work goes on. Working with other believers in giving money and sometimes going personally on various kinds of missions outreach. Third, see **yourself as an ambassador for Christ to your family, friends, neighbors, co-workers, and even strangers you meet.** Such an important task is the reason for living in a manner that reflects this holy calling. Being authentic ambassadors means we must demonstrate what kingdom living is all about. Yes, we all must awaken to the fact that this is our calling, our purpose for living in this world.

Yahweh in Your Worship

Thank You, Yahweh, for reconciling me to Yourself, then sending me to be Your ambassador.

October 12

Yahweh Wants Me to Leave a Good Legacy

Yahweh in the Word

> "A good man leaves an inheritance to his grandchildren...." (Proverbs 13:22a).

An inheritance or legacy is that which a person leaves to family members upon his death. The writer of this proverb commended the inheritance which a good man will pass on, not only to his children but beyond them to the next generation—his grandchildren.

Yahweh in Your Walk

The family unit was very significant in biblical culture. A man hoped to have many children and grandchildren, in fact his success was often determined by the size of his immediate family—a large family was sometimes considered a sign of divine favor. As our text suggests, a good father would take care to pass on to his children and grandchildren a good inheritance. This legacy could be measured not only by material wealth but also by the man's good reputation.

Have you given thought to what kind of legacy you will leave? Even if you have no children, you will leave a definite legacy to those who know and remember you. **Let's focus attention on ways of leaving a worthy inheritance to any who may come after we are gone.**

1. **A legacy of material wealth**. Every person should have a legal document known as a will. This instrument enables you to determine the distribution of your belongings at the time of your death. A wise person sees this as an important part of his or her stewardship. Some persons have an estate worth more after they pass on than they did before—due to life insurance or other assets. Be certain that you leave instructions regarding who receives what portion of property.
2. **A legacy of influence**. You probably have more influence upon those who know you than you realize. This legacy is accumulated over a lifetime of conduct and various ways of serving others. Seize opportunities now, while you have the strength to do so, to make worthy contributions to your family and friends. Be an example of what it means to follow Jesus so others will understand the value of such a life. Be intentional about your influence upon others.
3. **A legacy of belief**. Let me encourage you to prepare a clear statement of your beliefs regarding Yahweh and His purpose for life. Write a journal in which your Christian testimony is fully expressed. State your beliefs about the importance of walking with Him by faith and how a person should follow His commands and principles for living. Long after you are gone from this life, this kind of document will continue to be a clear witness for succeeding generations.

Yahweh in Your Worship

Thank You, Lord, for all I have inherited from those who have gone before me. Help me to leave a good legacy to my family and friends for Your sake.

October 13

Yahweh Wants Me to Speak His Blessing Upon Others

Yahweh in the Word

> "When Israel (Jacob) saw Joseph's sons, he said, 'Who are these?' And Joseph said to his father, 'They are my sons God has given me here.' So Jacob said, 'Bring them to me and I will bless them'" (Genesis 48:8-9).

There are several occasions in the Old Testament where we read about a father pronouncing a blessing upon his sons, or in this case, grandsons. The spoken blessing usually had a predictive sense to it—announcing in advance what would occur in those being blest.

Yahweh in Your Walk

I received a note today from a friend, David Seay, who participates in a men's Bible study that I teach each Tuesday morning. He thanked me for sharing this idea of speaking a blessing upon others. This morning as he was out for his morning run, he came upon two women and paused to visit briefly. He found out they are house-parents in a local children's home. Before he left them, he thanked them for their work and proceeded to speak upon them the blessing found in Numbers 6:22-26. He said they were very surprised and pleased.

Several years ago our family enjoyed a vacation together. During our final day, I asked if I could speak a blessing upon them. They agreed and allowed me to place my hands upon their shoulders and pray Yahweh's favor for each of them. Here's another occasion when I practice speaking a blessing. If I receive a phone call from a solicitor wanting to sell me something, rather than hang up or say, "Not interested," I now listen to them, thank them for their call, and offer a spoken blessing (quite a shock to them). Formerly, I would have considered this interruption to be annoying, but now I believe Yahweh is in control of these calls (because I begin each day committing my time to Him) and I see it as an opportunity to serve Him.

When my wife and I are out shopping in a store, the check-out clerk will often say, "Have a nice day." My wife always responds, "And may you have a blessed day." **As you walk through this day, why not think of yourself as a giver of Yahweh's blessings? Ask Him, as you begin the day, to use you to speak His blessing on others.** If a delivery person comes to your door, bless him or her. Or perhaps some food server will assist you—bless that person. As you practice doing this, you will be the one most blessed!

Yahweh in Your Worship

Bless Yahweh, O my soul, and all that is within me. Bless His holy name. Bless Yahweh and forget not all His benefits. He forgives all my sin, heals all my diseases, redeems me from destruction, crowns me with faithful love and compassion, satisfies me with goodness, and renews my youth like an eagle (Ps. 103:1-5). Help me pass these blessings on to others, today.

October 14

Yeshua Is the Bread of Life to Me

Yeshua in the Word

> *"I am the bread of life," Jesus (Yeshua) told them. "No one who comes to Me will ever be hungry, and no one who believes in Me will ever be thirsty again" (John 6:35).*

The day before Jesus made this amazing claim, He fed more than 5,000 people from the five barley loaves and two fish of a boy's lunch. Now the crowd returned for another miracle of feeding. Jesus used this occasion to teach spiritual truth about Himself as the One who could satisfy all their spiritual needs—permanently.

Yeshua in Your Walk

The apostle John includes many acts and teachings of Jesus that are not found in the other Gospels. Among these are His "I Am" claims recorded in the Gospel of John and the Revelation. Jesus' use of these I AMs identifies Him with Yahweh ("I AM") who appeared to Moses in the desert at the burning bush. **For the next ten days we will examine these statements that reveal helpful truths about Yeshua.** Think carefully about each of these, claiming for yourself the specific benefit each one offers.

Today we begin with **"I am the bread of life."** The Bible uses the term "bread" as an expression of all the physical nourishment that is essential to our living. **Just as surely as our body needs bread in order to live, Jesus provides all the spiritual nourishment we require. His promise to us is that if we believe on Him to the extent of receiving Him by faith, we will never lack anything we need spiritually.**

Chapter 6 of John's Gospel reveals more about the Bread of Life than any other portion of Scripture. Jesus refers to Himself as "bread" a total of eleven times in this chapter. The focus of His words is clear and simple: "I am the living bread that came down from heaven. If anyone eats of this bread he will live forever. The bread that I will give for the life of the world is my flesh" (6:51). His instruction is that a person must eat (partake) of Him in order to have spiritual needs satisfied. Another occasion where this truth is expressed is at the Last Supper when Jesus took bread, gave it to the disciples, and said, "Take and eat it; this is My body" (Matthew 26:26).

We partake of this spiritual bread by asking Him to come into our hearts and perform His work of salvation—turning our lives over to Him. Thus Yeshua becomes our Savior and Lord. He goes on day after day supplying the nourishment we need spiritually. His satisfying ministry to us means our spirit never hungers or thirsts again—we have all we need—and more.

Yeshua in Your Worship

Bread of Heaven, on You I feed, for Your life is all the spiritual food and drink I will ever need.

October 15

Yeshua Is the Light of the World to Me

Yeshua in the Word

> "Then Jesus spoke to them again, 'I am the light of the world. Anyone who follows Me will never walk in the darkness but will have the light of life'" (John 8:12).

The occasion when Jesus (Yeshua) spoke these words was when the scribes and Pharisees brought to Him a woman who had been caught committing adultery. They used this situation to test Him, whether He would approve of her being stoned to death, as the law required. But they all left when Jesus suggested that those without sins of their own be the first to cast stones.

Yeshua in Your Walk

Just as physical light overcomes darkness and thus enables a person to see, Jesus came as spiritual light in a dark, sinful world to reveal truth—truth about Yahweh and truth about this world. When these religious leaders, who were ready to stone a sinful woman, saw their own sinfulness, they left her alone. His words were a light that illumined truth in this situation.

Jesus did not say that He came **to shine** the light; He said, "I **am** the light." His life and teachings expose error and illumine truth. **As long as we choose to follow Him by staying in close fellowship with Him, we have the light of His life and will not walk in spiritual darkness.** As He said later, "The one who believes in Me believes not in Me, but in Him who sent Me. And the one who sees Me sees Him who sent Me. I have come as a light into the world so that everyone who believes in Me would not remain in darkness" (John 12:44-46).

How can the world have His light, now that He has returned to heaven? There are two ways, first by the light of His words. As the psalmist declared, "Your word is a lamp for my feet and a light on my path… The revelation of Your words brings light and gives understanding to the inexperienced" (Psalm 119:105,130). His light is also seen by His presence in the lives of His followers to whom He said, "You are the light of the world… let your light shine before men, so that they may see your good works and give glory to your Father in heaven" (Matthew 5:14,16). We who have the light of His life, are to let that light be seen in our character and conduct. We cannot make that light shine, but we can allow His life to be seen in us.

As you walk through this day, think of yourself as a lamp shinning in the darkness of this world. Make certain that your words and actions reflect His light in you. What a privilege and responsibility! You never know who may be watching you, hoping to find evidence of Him.

Yeshua in Your Worship

Light of the world, thank You for coming to reveal truth to me. I worship You as my Lord and my Life. May Your life shine through me today. Use me to lead others out of darkness to You.

October 16

Yeshua Is the Door for Me to Enter His Kingdom

Yeshua in the Word

> "I am the door. If anyone enters by Me, he will be saved and will come in and go out and find pasture. A thief comes only to steal and to kill and to destroy. I have come so that they may have life and have it in abundance" (John 10:9-10).

Chapter 9 of this gospel records the story of Jesus healing a man who was blind from birth. Because He performed this remarkable miracle on the Sabbath Day, the Pharisees doubted the rumor that Jesus was from Yahweh. After they questioned this man and his parents, they threw him out of the synagogue because he also believed Jesus was from God.

Yeshua in Your Walk

Shepherds and their sheep played a large role in the economy where Jesus lived. During the summer a shepherd would lead his flock to the green pastures on various hillsides. At night he would find a pen, called a fold, out in the open, where he could leave his flock until the next morning. This pen was often formed by building a rock wall to enclose an area where the sheep could rest at night. Several flocks might be staying in the same fold, in the care of a "doorkeeper," who made certain the sheep were safe from wolves and thieves. At night the keeper would lie down across the entry (door) of the fold to keep the sheep in and wolves out.

When Yeshua claimed to be the Door of the sheepfold, He revealed the truth that He is the entrance to Yahweh's kingdom. All who believe in Him will enter this eternal kingdom and be protected from Satan, the "thief" whose desire is "to steal and to kill and to destroy" all humankind. The Pharisees closed the door to the blind man; Jesus was the open door for him.

Notice that Jesus further described His role as the Door by promising that all who enter by Him will not only be saved but also have freedom to go in and out and enjoy an abundant life. The original term used for "abundance" means ***beyond the ordinary, overflowing.*** **Yeshua is the door to the eternal, abundant life—life beyond ordinary human life.** He welcomes all who come to Him by faith. An old gospel song has these lines of welcome:

> Whosoever heareth, shout, shout the sound! Spread the blessed tidings all the world around;
> Tell the joyful news wherever man is found, Whosoever will may come.
> Whosoever cometh need not delay; now the door is open, enter while you may;
> Jesus is the true, the only Living Way: whosoever will may come.—
> Philip P. Bliss

Yeshua in Your Worship

Thank You, Lord Yeshua, for being the Door for me to enter Your eternal kingdom.

October 17

Yeshua Cares for Me as My Good Shepherd

Yeshua in the Word

> *"I am the good shepherd. The good shepherd lays down his life for the sheep… I am the good shepherd. I know My own sheep, and they know Me, as the Father knows Me, and I know the Father. I lay down My life for the sheep… My sheep hear My voice, I know them, and they follow Me. I give them eternal life, and they will never perish—ever! No one will snatch them out of My hand. My Father, who has given them to Me, is greater than all. No one is able to snatch them out of the Father's hand. The Father and I are one" (John 10:11, 14-15, 27-30).*

Yesterday's text began this message from Yeshua about His provision for His people, using the metaphor of the relationship between sheep and a good shepherd. He is not only the door for the sheep to enter the safety and abundance of the kingdom, we also see in this text how diligent is His care and protection for His sheep.

Yeshua and Your Walk

This world is filled with dangers that threaten your safety. You can protect yourself from some of these personal enemies; others are beyond your control. Must you live in the fear of somehow being overcome by these threats? **Yeshua assures you that when you place your life in His care, you are safe and secure; He provides all the care and protection you need—both now and eternally.**

However, you may cite examples of believers who have experienced dreadful accidents, illnesses, and brutal attacks. What about them; where was the Good Shepherd when they needed Him so desperately? The truth is—He is always with His sheep; He never forsakes them. Even if some threat seems to prevail against them, He delivers them by being right beside them and taking them safely home to the place He has prepared for them eternally.

We must see this life through the eyes of faith, believing His promise of an abundant life beyond this temporary experience. But while we remain in this life, which is susceptible to various trials and trouble, we can rest assured that the Good Shepherd is present to provide all the loving care we need now and an eternal security in the future. All this happens because of His sacrifice for us. There are five occasions in this tenth chapter of John where Jesus says that He "lays down His life for the sheep." His guarantee is that His sheep will "never perish—ever!" We are safe in His hand, plus being together with Him in the hand of our Father—double security!

Yeshua and Your Worship

Worthy is the Lamb who was slain, to receive all glory, praise, and honor! I bless You, Yeshua, for giving me all the care and protection I will ever need, therefore, I choose to follow You. Thank You for the eternal security I have in You.

October 18

Yeshua Is My Resurrection and Life

Yeshua in the Word

> *"Jesus said to her, 'I am the resurrection and the life. The one who believes in Me, even if he dies, will live. Everyone who lives and believes in Me will never die—ever'" (John 11:25-26).*

Earlier in chapter 11 we read of the miracle Yeshua performed when He raised His friend Lazarus from the dead. The words of this text were spoken to Lazarus' sister Martha. She had just expressed regret that Jesus was not present four days earlier when Lazarus died; she believed Jesus could have healed him at that time and prevented his death. However, Jesus deliberately waited this long to demonstrate His authority over death. He is, in Himself, the resurrection.

Yeshua in Your Walk

The story is told of an old soldier who said, "When I die do not sound 'Taps' over my grave, but 'Reveille,' the morning call, the summons to rise!" How fitting this sound would be for all who know Him, who is the Resurrection and the Life. Numerous biblical references may be found that express this victory over death for all believers. For example, the apostle Paul wrote these comforting words to Timothy: "Our Savior Christ Jesus, has abolished death and has brought life and immortality to light through the gospel" (2 Timothy 1:10).

Although the death of our physical body occurs, our soul and spirit (the real person we are) lives on. Actually, the believer's physical death is a spiritual liberation; we are set free from this tent of clay to receive our new, perfect spiritual body. Again quoting Paul, "This corruptible (human body) must be clothed with incorruptibility, and this mortal (human body) must be clothed with immortality. Now when this corruptible is clothed with incorruptibility, and this mortal is clothed with immortality, the saying that is written will take place: Death has been swallowed up in victory… thanks be to God who gives us the victory through our Lord Jesus Christ!" (1 Corinthians 15:53-57).

As you walk through this day, rejoice in the assurance you have been given that even though your body will die, you will live on eternally. All the limitations imposed by your physical body will be removed and you will be set free. The resurrection of Yeshua guarantees your own resurrection—to be with Him and all His family forever. You will receive a new body that is not subject to the limitations of your present body.

Yeshua and Your Worship

I seize this opportunity to worship You, O Resurrection and Life to me. All praise belongs to You; You are my victory over sin, death, and the grave. I live because You live—thank You. I ask You to use me this day to be an effective witness to others of these great truths. Help me live out Your resurrection life in me.

October 19

Yeshua Is the Way, the Truth, and the Life for Me

Yeshua in the Word

> "'Lord,' Thomas said, 'we don't know where You're going. How can we know the way?' Jesus told him, 'I am the way, the truth, and the life. No one comes to the Father except through Me'" (John 14:5-6).

These revealing words were spoken by Yeshua shortly before He went on trial for His life. His disciples had heard Him saying that He would soon be leaving them and they could not follow Him at this time (13:33). Among the most memorable promises made by Jesus are these words: "I am going away to prepare a place for you. If I go away and prepare a place for you, I will come back and receive you to Myself, so that where I am you may be also. You know the way to where I am going" (John 14:2-4). Thomas had the courage to ask the questions they were all thinking—where are You going; how can we find the way to be with You?

Yeshua in Your Walk

Life is a journey—from your birth, through your earthly pilgrimage, then beyond the grave to eternity. Yeshua came to make this a successful journey—to help you arrive at the most desirable destination—in heaven with Him. Today you will move forward on this journey. You do not know how long the journey on this earth will last, but you can know the way to your ultimate destination. Think about three words from Jesus' promise: **the way, the truth, and the life.**

The Way Several years ago our family enjoyed a vacation in Hawaii. We had read the life story of Charles Lindberg, the famous aviator who was the first to fly solo across the Atlantic Ocean, and wanted to visit his grave at Hana on the island of Maui. When we asked about the best road, we were surprised to find out that there is just one road to Hana—a very crooked, up and down journey. There are many roads on Maui, but just one way to Hana. In a similar manner, there are many paths for you to choose in life, but just one that leads to eternity with Yahweh; that way is Yeshua. This is true because He opened that way by giving Himself as a sacrifice for our sins.

The Truth All the sayings, teachings, and actions of Jesus reveal truth about Yahweh and humankind. But in addition to revealing truth, He is the truth! In the context of our Scripture for today, He is the truth about the way to the Father and the Father's house. You can trust Him.

The Life Yeshua is the **way** to God, the **truth** about God, and the very **life** of God. All these wonderful resources are found in Him and only in Him. If you have, by faith, received Him, you have all these in abundance. You can walk with confidence and peace through this day with Him.

Yeshua in Your Worship

Today, I celebrate the fact that I am on the right path, with knowledge of truth, and alive in You.

October 20

Yeshua Is the Vine that Produces Fruit through Me

Yeshua in the Word

> "I am the true vine, and My Father is the vineyard keeper. Every branch in Me that does not produce fruit He removes, and He prunes every branch that produces fruit, so that it will produce more fruit… I am the vine; you are the branches. The one who remains in Me and I in him produces much fruit, because you can do nothing without Me" (John 15:1, 5).

Grape vineyards were common where Jesus lived. The fruit they produced provided both food and beverage for the people. He used this metaphor to illustrate the essential relationship between Himself and those who claimed to be His followers. The primary truth He sought to convey is that apart from an intimate, continuous relationship with Him, we can produce nothing.

Yeshua in Your Walk

We come to the seventh and final "I AM" of John's Gospel—"I am the true vine." All seven of these illustrate the same basic truth—**you need Yeshua**. Walk through these once again with this truth in mind: You need bread for nourishment, light to see truth, a door to enter the kingdom, a good shepherd to care for you, the resurrection and the life in order to survive death, the way, truth, and life to make heaven your final home, and now—you need Yeshua's strong life flowing through you to be fruitful. **These metaphors all reveal this simple, yet profound truth. As Jesus declares in this text, "you can do nothing without Me."**

What are your specific needs that Jesus meets according to this vine/branch illustration? First, you need a source of life flowing into you—He is that life, like the sap flowing up from the roots and out to the branches and into the fruit; apart from Him you have no life and can bear no fruit. You also need strong support, just as a branch depends on the vine to hold it up; Jesus is the strength of your life. Moreover, you need the nature of the vine to produce the right fruit of that vine. Yeshua produces the fruit of His Spirit, namely: love, joy, peace, patience, kindness, goodness, faith, gentleness, and self-control (see Galatians 5:22-23).

All this focuses on what the vine does for the branch, but what role does the branch play? The branch must remain firmly attached to the vine. As Jesus declared, "Remain in Me." And this strong attachment happens as His words remain in us and we choose to obey Him. Note also that just as the branch needs the vine so also the vine needs the branch. Fruit grows on branches, not on the main vine. And so, we perceive from this metaphor the essential relationship between vine and branch—Yeshua and His follower. He produces the fruit which we display for all to see.

Yeshua in Your Worship

Thank You, Vineyard Keeper of heaven, for including me in Your vineyard. I welcome Your pruning that I may bear more fruit for Your glory. Nourish others through me for Your pleasure.

October 21

Yeshua Is the Beginning and Ending of All Things for Me

Yeshua in the Word

> "'I am the Alpha and the Omega,' says the Lord God, 'the One who is, who was, and who is coming, the Almighty... Don't be afraid! I am the First and the Last, and the Living One. I was dead, but look—I am alive forever and ever, and I hold the keys of death and Hades'" (Revelation 1:8, 17-18).

Alpha and Omega are the first and last letters of the Greek alphabet, the original language of the New Testament. These terms, along with "the First and the Last," are repeated seven times in the Bible beginning with Isaiah 41:1, 44:6, 48:12, plus four times in the Revelation. Each of these occurrences gives a clear message—Yeshua is the One who began all things as Creator and the One who will conclude all things in His time. He is like the bookends of human history.

Yeshua in Your Walk

We have completed the seven I AMs from John's Gospel, now we turn to two more found in the Revelation, also written by the apostle John. When Jesus said, "I am the Alpha," He was referring to the fact that He is the originator of all things. John called Him "the Word" when he wrote this: "In the beginning was the Word, and the Word was with God, and the Word was God. He was with God in the beginning. All things were created through Him, and apart from Him not one thing was created that has been created" (John 1:1-3).

Creation, as we know it, is moving towards a conclusion—an Omega, the end. Yeshua also controls this event. As He declared, "I hold the keys of death and Hades." All these terms speak clearly of Yeshua's sovereignty—He is in absolute control—He holds the keys. But what comes next? What happens after the final judgment that we read about in Revelation 20? The answer is found in these solemn words from the apostle John: "Then I saw a new heaven and a new earth, for the first heaven and the first earth had passed away, and the sea no longer existed. I also saw the Holy City, new Jerusalem, coming down out of heaven from God, prepared like a bride adorned for her husband... Then the One seated on the throne said, 'Look! I am making everything new... I am the Alpha and the Omega, the Beginning and the End" (Revelation 21:1-2, 5-6). A new beginning is on the way, including a new heaven and earth. Now we know why Jesus said, "Don't be afraid!" **We have nothing to fear; He is in absolute control!**

Yeshua in Your Worship

How awesome You are, O Alpha and Omega! You are worthy of all praise, honor, and adoration for You have made all things from the beginning. And You promise to re-create everything, in Your time. Thank You that Your new creation will be without sin and its consequences—a perfect paradise. I look forward to this glorious future. How merciful of You to include me! Use me to help others prepare for this destiny with You.

October 22

Yeshua Is the Divine/Human Redeemer I Need

Yeshua in the Word

> "I, Jesus, have sent My angel to attest these things to you for the churches. I am the Root and the Offspring of David, the Bright Morning Star" (Revelation 22:16).

Here is the only place in the Revelation where Yeshua names Himself—"I, Jesus." And this is the one place in the Bible where He identifies Himself as "the Root and the Offspring of David, the Bright Morning Star."

Yeshua in Your Walk

A root is the unseen source of life for a living plant. Yeshua is the Root of David in the sense of being the One from whom David came forth—was born. This statement reveals the divine nature of Yeshua; He was in the beginning with God and was God. All humankind has Yeshua as its Root. The human nature of Yeshua is seen as He also is the Offspring of David—a human, blood descendant of his. Luke gives the genealogy of Yeshua all the way back to David, then to Adam. **Thus Yeshua is the only person who ever lived being both divine and human—root and offspring—a miraculous union.**

This amazing miracle occurred in order for Him to become an acceptable sacrifice for our sins. His human nature enabled Him to identify with us; His divine nature empowered Him to live a perfect life as well as reveal the true nature of Yahweh to us. How wonderful is the love of God for us! What incredible provision He has made for our salvation. No other person compares to Yeshua—the One who is our salvation.

He also identifies Himself as "the Bright Morning Star." When morning light begins to dawn, one star remains, shining brightly in the eastern sky. This "star" is actually the planet Venus, reflecting the sun's rays, much as our moon. The significance of this so-called star is that it is the first announcement of a new day. Yeshua concludes the Revelation with the promise of a new and better day to come. As we mentioned in yesterday's devotional, **He announced the coming of a "new heaven and a new earth."**

How very appropriate that following this final "I Am" statement, Yeshua offers an invitation: "Both the Spirit and the bride [church] say, 'Come!' Anyone who hears should say, 'Come!' And the one who is thirsty should come. Whoever desires should take the living water as a gift" (v.17). All that Yeshua came to do is summed up in this appeal for everyone to believe His promise of forgiveness and receive by faith His gift of eternal life. Have you done this?

Yeshua in Your Worship

O Root and Offspring, I seize this opportunity to worship You with sincere gratitude. Thank You for preparing a place for me in Your eternal kingdom.

October 23

Yahweh Wants Me to Help the Poor and Needy

Yahweh in the Word

"The righteous considers the cause of the poor" (Proverbs 29:7 NKJV).

There are many Scripture references such as this one which make clear that Yahweh wants His people to reach out to those who cannot help themselves—such as the poor, orphans, and widows. In Bible times these were the individuals who were most vulnerable to unjust treatment.

Yahweh in Your Walk

You have heard the saying, "God helps those who help themselves." The idea behind this is that God will assist those who are willing to work diligently in order to provide for their basic needs. But what about those who cannot help themselves—such as those in poverty due to circumstances beyond their control, or orphans who are too young to help themselves, or widows who live in a culture where they cannot support themselves? Who is responsible to help these?

A clear teaching of Scripture which is often overlooked is that of Yahweh's favor toward those who cannot provide for their own basic needs. One of the first examples of this truth is seen in the Old Testament law that farmers were not to harvest all their crops but leave some for the poor, whether grapes or grain. Also several of Jesus' teachings and parables focused on helping the needy, such as: "When you host a banquet, invite those who are poor, maimed, lame, or blind. And you will be blessed, because they cannot repay you; for you will be repaid at the resurrection of the righteous" (Luke 14:13-14). (How many of us take this command seriously?)

Most churches provide help for the less fortunate, such as an annual offering for world hunger or food, clothing, and lodging during winter months for the homeless. These are all commendable and should be supported with true compassion. However, each of us should have some consistent outreach to those whom Jesus commands us to assist. We do well to examine ourselves to see what personal effort we are making to relieve the suffering of those who cannot help themselves.

Another ministry that falls under this category is that of helping prisoners, their families, and those who are recently released from prison. Fortunately, there are many faith-based organizations that focus on helping all these kinds of needy persons. Let us follow Yahweh's guidance in finding at least one of these opportunities to give hands-on assistance to these on whom Jesus looks with compassion. Ask Him to show you how to become involved.

Yahweh in Your Worship

Thank You, most merciful Savior, for having pity on me as You have faithfully and generously supplied all my need. Help me to pass on to others Your outstretched hand of provision today. And remind me that all I do for the less fortunate I am doing for You—what a privilege!

October 24

Yahweh Wants Me to Know His Special Name

Yahweh in the Word

> *"Those who know Your name trust in You because You have not abandoned those who seek You, Yahweh" (Psalm 9:10).*

The psalmist knew that the name of the only true and living God is Yahweh. This special name reveals truth about Him that makes Him worthy of our trust. We can be certain that He will never abandon those who sincerely seek Him.

Yahweh in Your Walk

Several years ago we wrote a book entitled **What a Difference a Name Makes.** The subtitle for this book is **A Practical Guide for a Study of the Name Yahweh.** Our research led us in a most interesting and helpful discovery of the meaning of this amazing name. When God revealed Himself to Moses at a burning bush in the desert, He said, "Say this to the Israelites: Yahweh, the God of your fathers, the God of Abraham, the God of Isaac, and the God of Jacob, has sent me to you. **This is My name forever; this is how I am to be remembered in every generation**" (Exodus 3:15).

The word *Yahweh* basically means, "**I AM.**" He revealed to Moses that He is the eternal God—who always has been and always will be. Also, Yahweh is His covenant name; He takes the initiative in reaching out to humankind to engage us in His covenant promise—the promise of eternal life through His Son, our Lord Jesus. There are many combinations of this special name, such as Yahweh Yireh, Yahweh Shalom, and Yahweh Sabaoth (which terms you will find in this devotional guide), plus many titles such as Father, Lord, God, Savior, Teacher, Master, etc. However, just as we have one name and many titles, so it is with Yahweh. (The name Jesus is the Greek form of the Hebrew name Yeshua, meaning *Yahweh is salvation*.)

In our Scripture text for today the psalmist stated that we who know the name Yahweh will put our trust in Him. This is true because **His name means that He is all we need in order to become all He wants us to be—He is our complete sufficiency**. When we know this, we trust Him to provide all we need. Thus we are delivered from all our fears, worries, and anxieties—He is the supply for whatever we require, whether salvation from sin, protection from Satan, deliverance from our old nature, daily needs—you name it and He provides it!

Yahweh in Your Worship

Gracious Yahweh, You mean everything to me. I worship You with praise, thanksgiving, and the full surrender of myself to You. Use me to make known Your special name to others. How comforting to know You are always with me and will provide for all my needs. I choose to put all my trust in You. Today I want to walk through life together with You.

October 25

Yahweh Gives Me a Handful of Benefits

Yahweh in the Word

> "My soul, praise Yahweh and all that is within me, praise His holy name. My soul, praise Yahweh, and do not forget all His benefits. He forgives all your sin; He heals all your diseases. He redeems your life from the Pit; He crowns you with faithful love and compassion. He satisfies you with goodness; your youth is renewed like the eagle" (Psalm 103:1-5).

Yahweh is to be praised for His numerous benefits including forgiveness, healing, redemption, love, goodness, and spiritual renewal.

Yahweh in Your Walk

These verses have become especially meaningful to me as I have memorized them, using the four fingers and thumb of my hand to remind me of each of five wonderful benefits coming from Yahweh to me. Often in the night when I am sleepless, I review these blessings, meditating on each one as the basis for thanksgiving and worship.

1. **Forgiveness.** Yahweh is gracious and merciful as He faithfully forgives **all** my sin. Such pardon and removal of guilt brings true and lasting peace.
2. **Healing**. Apart from His healing of **all** my diseases, I would not be alive today. We have all experiences diseases that could have been fatal, but He has touched our bodies and our spirits with His healing power. In addition to physical healing, He has restored me spiritually as well as relationally.
3. **Redemption.** To redeem means to buy back that which has been lost. Yahweh gave His Son to pay the price for bringing me back into His forever family. Otherwise, I would be eternally doomed to the Pit of destruction.
4. **Coronation.** Yahweh's faithful love and compassion extended to me are like a crown of honor, so undeserved and yet so life changing.
5. **Satisfaction and Renewal**. His goodness to me results in a renewal of strength, like an eagle whose old feathers are replaced with new ones to give him new power.

Meditate on each of these amazing benefits. Let each one provoke you to meaningful worship.

Yahweh in Your Worship

I worship You, most gracious Yahweh, for all Your amazing benefits to me. Each of these reminds me of Your goodness and compassion. I rejoice in all Your favors.

October 26

Yahweh Wants Me to Tell of My Conversion

Yahweh in the Word

> *"I was traveling to Damascus under these circumstances.... while on the road at midday, I saw a light from heaven.... and I heard a voice speaking to me... Then I said, 'Who are You, Lord?' And the Lord replied: 'I am Jesus, the One you are persecuting.... I have appeared to you for this purpose, to appoint you as a servant and a witness of what you have seen and of what I will reveal to you'" (Acts 26:12-16).*

As the apostle Paul stood before King Agrippa, he recounted his conversion experience. Here is the second time Paul shared this story in the book of Acts.

Yahweh in Your Walk

When was the most recent time you have told someone about your Christian conversion? You may have been saved as a very young person, and yet your testimony has value as a witness of the saving power of Jesus. Hopefully, you are bold about sharing the good news of this very personal experience. Jesus told Paul that He saved him for the purpose of being a witness of his experience; the same is true for you. If you have never written out your testimony, that would be a good way of preparing to share it. Ask the Lord to give you opportunities to be His witness.

On the eleventh anniversary of his conversion, Charles Wesley (1707-1788) chose to celebrate that event by writing a hymn that has become a classic for believers. Notice his testimony in these words which he originally entitled: "For the Anniversary Day of One's Conversion."

> O for a thousand tongues to sing my great Redeemer's praise,
> The glories of my God and King, the triumphs of His grace!
> My gracious master and my God, assist me to proclaim,
> To spread thro' all the earth abroad the honors of Thy name.
> Jesus! The name that charms our fears, that bids our sorrows cease,
> Tis music in the sinners' ears; tis life, and health, and peace.
> He breaks the power of canceled sin, He sets the prisoner free;
> His blood can make the foulest clean; His blood availed for me.
> He speaks, and listening to His voice, new life the dead receive;
> The mournful, broken hearts rejoice; the humble poor believe.
> Hear Him, ye deaf; His praise, ye dumb, your loosened tongues employ;
> Ye blind, behold your Savior come; and leap, ye lame, for joy.

Yahweh in Your Worship

Gracious Savior, I worship You as my Redeemer, Lord, and friend. Thank You for delivering me from the bondage of sin and death. May my mouth give testimony to Your saving grace today.

October 27

Yahweh Wants Me to Be Like a Fruitful Tree

Yahweh in the Word

> *"He shall be like a tree planted beside streams of water that bears its fruit in season and whose leaf does not wither. Whatever he does prospers"* (Psalms 1:3).

These inspiring words describe the person who delights in Yahweh's instruction, and meditates on it day and night (v.2). This individual will not wither when trials come but will continually prosper.

Yahweh in Your Walk

The first time I met Alan Lyle he was pushing a broom as one of the custodians of our church. He and his wife, Tina, were newly married and seeking to get established in their lives together. My most recent conversation with him was at breakfast some 20 years later. During these years, this devoted couple has served Yahweh as missionaries in Kyrgyzstan, Rome, Italy, and Florida where they now live. (Another member of our church staff helped them get involved in overseas ministry.) I asked Alan what lesson he has learned from these interesting and fruitful years. He replied, "Tina and I have learned to walk with Christ by faith, knowing that we can always trust Him to provide all we need."

When I think of the Lyles, I think of the promise of our devotional text for today. They have learned to trust in Yahweh for all things; they have developed confidence in His guidance and care, and as a result they have grown to be like a fruitful tree with deep roots. Like most missionaries they have known times of "heat" and "drought," and yet they continue to produce fruit—just as Yahweh promised. Actually, Alan is still a custodian, not of a building, but a custodian and caretaker of the gospel. And they have seen lives changed by the gospel message.

You can follow the example of these dear friends. **Rather than seeking your own plans and lifestyle, commit yourself to Yahweh every day, and throughout each day.** His will for you will not be the same as for the Lyles, but will be just as significant. He will produce fruit through you for His glory. He will faithfully provide for all you need, and more. And just as their walk with Him has sometimes challenged their faith to the maximum, so it will be for you. He wants you to learn to walk by faith, not by sight, trusting Him to be your unfailing resource of provisions. As Paul declared, "We do not focus on what is seen, but on what is unseen. For what is seen is temporary, but what is unseen is eternal" (2 Corinthians 4:18).

Yahweh in Your Worship

Thank You, gracious Yahweh, for Your promise to me. I choose to trust You for all I need. My desire is to be fruitful for Your glory. May my tree of life bear much lasting fruit. Use me to share this good news with others today.

October 28

Yeshua Wants Me to Honor Him in Life and in Death

Yeshua in the Word

> "My eager expectation and hope is that I will not be ashamed about anything, but that now as always, with all boldness, Christ will be highly honored in my body, whether by life or by death. For me, living is Christ and dying is gain" (Philippians 1:20-21).

The apostle Paul wrote this brief letter to the church he planted in the city of Philippi. At this time he was in prison in Rome, facing the possibility of execution. However, he believed he would be delivered and continue serving the Lord.

Yeshua in Your Walk

Notice in our text for today that Paul makes two references to his life and death. First, he wanted Yeshua to be honored in his body, "whether by life or by death." Second, for him "living is Christ and dying is gain." We will all have these same two experiences—living and dying. **The possibility of honoring our Lord by the way we live is something we are familiar with, but have you thought about honoring Him by the way you die?**

Jesus made reference to this when he told Peter that the time would come when Peter's death would glorify God: "'I (Jesus) assure you: When you were young, you would tie your belt and walk wherever you wanted. But when you grow old, you will stretch out your hands and someone else will tie you and carry you where you don't want to go.' He said this to signify by **what kind of death he would glorify God**" (John 21:18-19). These words indicate the fact that Jesus knew that Peter would one day be crucified, just as He was. And there is a tradition saying that Peter insisted on being crucified upside down, rather than upright like his Master. He considered himself to be unworthy of dying as his Master had died.

Dying a martyr's death, as Peter did, could easily happen in a way that honors the Lord but what about a more normal manner of dying—can this honor Him? I think of our dear friend, Lois Freeman, who lived a devoted Christian life. The last time we visited her in the hospice care center, she was her usual cheerful self. She knew she was dying and faced that experience with no sense of dread or fear. Rather, she spoke confidently about the joy of seeing her Savior, along with loved ones who had gone on before. She glorified and honored Him by her life and her death; she believed that her death would indeed be much gain.

Are you confident that your death will mean gain for you? Is it possible that Christ will be honored by your passing? Such a reality depends on how you live before that inevitable event.

Yeshua in Your Worship

Thank You, Lord of life, that You give meaning to both life and death. I join other believers in looking forward to being with You eternally. I trust You to arrange my departure in such a way as to honor You.

October 29

Yahweh Wants Me to Pray for His Enemies

Yahweh in the Word

> "See how Your enemies make an uproar; those who hate You have acted arrogantly... Cover their faces with shame so that they will seek Your name Yahweh... May they know that You alone—whose name is Yahweh—are the Most High over all the earth" (Psalm 83:2, 16, 18).

Asaph, the writer of this psalm, was one of the temple musicians appointed by David. Here he offers of prayer on behalf of Yahweh's enemies, asking Him to help them seek Him and know that He rules over all things.

Yahweh in Your Walk

Jesus taught His followers to love their enemies, bless them, do good to them, and pray for them (Matthew 5:44). But **what about Yahweh's enemies, how should we treat them?** Asaph recorded this prayer, known as Psalm 83, in which he answers this question. And this is a valid concern that becomes more relevant as more and more adherents to other religions move into our neighborhoods. Although most of these who come to American are peace-loving and would not consider themselves enemies of Yahweh, the fact remains that in many of their homelands those who claim to be Christians are not welcome and often persecuted. And those of their own religion who convert to Christianity are considered to be worthy of being executed.

How should we who follow Yeshua deal with persons who reject Him as well as His claim to be Lord over all creation? Asaph gives us a proper example in this prayer. Notice how he prays for Yahweh to help them seek His name and know that He, "whose name is Yahweh," is the "Most High over all the earth."

You may have read the testimonies of how this prayer has been answered in recent years. Some authorities in this field of study give encouraging reports about large numbers of individuals from other religions coming to faith in Christ. Our grandson, James, and his wife, Jen, are missionaries to such persons in a major American city. They find that many who were raised in another religion are open to investigate the claims of Christ, and have a desire to know Him.

How can you help with this worthy outreach? **First**, be like Asaph as you join his prayer for all persons to know about Yahweh. Have names on your prayer list of specific persons, such as the leaders of countries where Christianity is forbidden. **Second**, be pro-active in locating those in your neighborhood, workplace, school, and stores who may not know the gospel facts. Seek to form friendships with them in order to show Yahweh's love and compassion. Be His witness.

Yahweh in Your Worship

Thank You, holy Lord, for revealing Yourself to me; now use me to reach others for Your sake.

October 30

Yahweh Allows Me to Stand before Him and Pray

Yahweh in the Word

> "Those of Israelite descent separated themselves from all foreigners, and they stood and confessed their sins and the guilt of their fathers. While they stood in their places, they read from the book of the law of Yahweh their God for a fourth part of the day and spent another fourth part of the day in confession and worship of Yahweh their God.... 'Stand up, Praise Yahweh your God from everlasting to everlasting.' Praise Your glorious name and may it be exalted above all blessing and praise. You alone are Yahweh... You are Yahweh" (Nehemiah 9:2-7).

These words are from the longest prayer recorded in the Bible. Yahweh's people were assembled at the temple in Jerusalem to celebrate their return from many years of captivity in Babylon. This prayer is one of praise to Yahweh for His mercy and faithfulness, as well as a confession of their persistent rebellion against Him. They stood for much of the day to offer themselves to Him.

Yahweh in Your Walk

When you pray, what bodily posture do you find most appropriate? The Bible speaks of persons praying in various positions—kneeling, hands lifted up, sitting, lying down, standing with head bowed or looking up, etc. None of these is prescribed as being the best. The most important factor is the attitude of one's heart—one of humility, repentance, confession, intercession, and praise. **Yahweh promises to hear your prayer regardless of your chosen posture.**

Our Scripture text for today describes a special time when Yahweh's people stood before Him to hear His word, confess their sins, and worship Him. An English newspaper editor, James Montgomery (1771-1854), wrote a hymn based on this text entitled "Stand Up and Bless the Lord." Here are the first and last stanzas:

> Stand up and bless the Lord, ye people of His choice;
> Stand up and bless the Lord your God with heart and soul and voice.
> Stand up and bless the Lord; the Lord your God adore;
> Stand up and bless His glorious name, henceforth forevermore.

You may want to read the entire prayer of Nehemiah 9. Yahweh's people gave much attention to acknowledging their persistent rebellion against Him throughout their history. In contrast was His patient mercy and compassion. They ended their prayer with an appeal for His forgiveness and a renewal of their covenant with Him. Perhaps you can learn from this example as you pray.

Yahweh in Your Worship

O Sovereign Lord, I choose to stand before You as I confess my complete unworthiness of Your mercy and grace. Thank You for Your forgiveness and restoration. I want to serve You today.

October 31

Yahweh Proves His Love for Me

Yahweh in the Word

> "For God so loved the world that He gave His only begotten Son, that whoever believes in Him should not perish but have everlasting life" (John 3:16, NKJV).

These memorable words were first spoken to Nicodemus, a religious leader of the Jews. Jesus wanted him to know that Yahweh's love for him was best demonstrated in the gift of eternal life through His Son—a gift received by believing.

Yahweh in Your Walk

Recently I asked my friend, Lew Lockhart, to tell me his favorite Bible verse. He quickly replied, "John 3:16." I find this very interesting because this verse speaks of the sacrifice of Jesus for the sake of others. Lew is a living example of a similar sacrifice. He was a college student in 1941 when our nation entered World War II. He signed up for what was then known as the Army Air Corp and subsequently flew 171 missions from New Guinea in the South Pacific. When I visit Lew in his home, I see models of the P-40 and P-38 airplanes in which he flew these missions. He is very modest about his fighter pilot career, but very thankful that he survived.

Each time Lew took off in his plane, he was risking his life for the sake of freedom. He is now 94 years-old and very spry and active. We exchange books and other types of literature which we find interesting. I'm inspired by his love of learning at his advanced age. Most of all, I'm grateful for the sacrifice he and many others have made to defend our nation against those enemies who would destroy our freedom. **We owe these men and women a debt we can never repay.**

However, we know that the supreme sacrifice was made by our Savior who willingly laid down His perfect life on the cross for our spiritual freedom from bondage to sin and death. No other action by Yahweh so clearly reveals His great unconditional love for us as this. Lew responded to this love gift as a teenager and knows he has everlasting life.

Do you have a personal testimony of having believed the wonderful message of John 3:16? If so, you know the peace that comes from receiving this precious gift of life everlasting. Our best way to show gratitude for such a blessing is to be a devout worshiper and witness of Yahweh's love. **As you walk through this day, be intentional about sharing your testimony to others who may not know Jesus.** Help them have the same experience of freedom from sin that you enjoy.

Yahweh in Your Worship

Thank You, Lord, for Your great love for me. I gladly receive the gift of eternal life. Teach me to appreciate all that this blessing means, and use me to share this good news with others today. I choose to lay down my life that others may know You.

November 1

Yahweh Is the One Who Made Me as I Am

Yahweh in the Word

> *"Come, let us worship and bow down; let us kneel before the LORD our Maker. For He is our God, and we are the people of His pasture, the sheep under His care" (Psalm 95:6-7).*

"The LORD our Maker (Yahweh Osenu) is another combination term to describe Yahweh. He is the One who created us, Who determined who we would be—all about our DNA, our personality, physical features, and every aspect of our being. Another psalmist declared, "For it was You who created my inward parts; You knit me together in my mother's womb" (Psalm 139:13). If you have ever watched someone do knitting, you know how precise that work can be and that no two knitted items are exactly the same. Yahweh Osenu (pronounced YAH-way o-SAY-noo) formed us just the way we are, before we were born. What a miracle!

Yahweh in Your Walk

Each of us bears some resemblance to our biological parents. Perhaps you have your mother's eyes or your father's nose, etc. But no one looks exactly the same as one's parents. Each of us is unique in form and appearance. Think of the billions of persons in this world right now, how amazing that every person has distinctive features! Even what we call "identical twins" are not truly identical in appearance.

Even more remarkable are the differences in our personalities and mix of talents and various abilities. We have two grandchildren; one showed an interest in music at a very young age, while the other has no talent for music. Why this difference? Yahweh Osenu made them this way. And He chose to do this for His own purposes for these children. The same is true for each of us—and every other person who ever lived or will live. **One way of discovering what you will enjoy doing as a life vocation is to consider what you naturally find pleasure in doing.** How sad to see a person spending the best years of their lives doing what they dislike.

How should these facts affect us? **First, we should be thankful that we are who and what we are**—thankful that Yahweh Osenu determined to make us as we are. And **second, we should seek to become all He made us to be—the best of who we are—for His sake.** A simple motto states it like this: **"I will do the best I can with what I have, where I am, for Jesus' sake today."**

Yahweh in Your Worship

"Look all the world over, there's no one like me… no one exactly like me." Thank You for making me special—just for Your special purpose. Today I want to seize every opportunity to fulfill this grand plan for my life—for Your glory. Help me choose that vocation I am "cut out" to pursue, and to guide others make the same decision.

November 2

Yahweh Requires My Undivided Allegiance

Yahweh in the Word

> "What does Yahweh your God ask of you except to fear Yahweh your God by walking in all His ways, to love Him, and to worship Him with all your heart and all your soul… for Yahweh your God is the God of gods and Lord of lords, the great, mighty, and awesome God" (Deuteronomy 10:12-17).

Moses was preparing Yahweh's people to enter the land He had promised them. Before going in they needed a reminder of who He is and what He expected of them. They had known about all the gods of Egypt and of the people groups surrounding them. Moses made clear that Yahweh was supreme above all false gods and demanded the undivided allegiance of His people.

Yahweh in Your Walk

On the April 8, 1966 cover of ***Time*** magazine was this bold question: "Is God Dead?" Inside was the lead article which quoted several so-called religious authorities who were questioning the existence of God. Centuries earlier a former shepherd who encountered God personally gave a powerful answer to that question. Moses boldly asserted that not only was Yahweh very much alive but He also demanded unconditional loyalty from His people.

As you walk through this day of life, remember who Yahweh is—"the God of gods and Lord of lords, the great, mighty, and awesome God." He is, in fact, the only true and living God. All other gods who make this claim are simply the imagination of the hearts and minds of people. Remember also what Yahweh requires of you—reverence (fear), obedience (walking in all His ways), love, and whole-hearted worship. **You can choose to give Him this kind of undivided allegiance.** Surely Yahweh, as your Creator, Redeemer, Provider, Care-giver, and loyal Friend deserves this kind of devotion—and more.

My wife and have a dear friend, Florrie Anne Lawton, who is an example to us of a person who has given undivided allegiance to Yahweh all through her life. As a young woman she dedicated herself to serving Him. After graduating from a seminary, she felt led to pursue a career in helping preschoolers and their parents. For more than 60 years she has been totally involved through her service at LifeWay Church Resources as well as her local church in ministering to these precious children. What a legacy she has left in these young hearts—a true servant.

Yahweh in Your Worship

O sovereign, supreme, God of gods and Lord of all lords, I do worship You this day. Yahweh, You are worthy of all praise and adoration. I bring myself before You as an offering, claiming Your guidance and help as I seek to give You the honor You deserve. Thank You for choosing me to know You and walk in all Your ways today.

November 3

Yahweh Supplies the Springs of Salvation for Me

Yahweh in the Word

> "Indeed, God is my salvation; I will trust Him and not be afraid, for Yahweh, Yahweh is my strength and my song. He has become my salvation. You will joyfully draw water from the springs of salvation, and on that day you will say: 'Give thanks to Yahweh; proclaim His name! Celebrate His works among the peoples. Declare that His name is exalted'" (Isaiah 12:2-4).

The prophet Isaiah composed this beautiful song of praise as he was inspired to describe how those whom Yahweh redeems will worship Him. Notice the terms "salvation," "strength," and "song." These all come as a result of joyfully drawing water from the springs of salvation. One interpreter says, "Yahweh is the well; faith is the rope and bucket; joy is the result!"

Yahweh in Your Walk

There are several biblical references that compare salvation to a well or spring or river of water. In portions of Bible lands water was scarce, which meant the sources of water were of great value. You may recall the conversation Jesus had with a woman at a well in Samaria. When He spoke to her of "living water," she asked where she could get this kind of water. Jesus replied, "Everyone who drinks from this water (in the well) will get thirsty again. But whoever drinks from the water that I will give him will never get thirsty again—ever! In fact, the water I will give him will become a well of water springing up within him for eternal life" (John 4:13-14).

Of course Jesus was not speaking of natural water but of Himself as the Water of Life. On another occasion He returned to this same image and said, "If anyone is thirsty, he should come to Me and drink! The one who believes in Me, as the Scripture has said, will have streams of living water flow from deep within him" (John 7:37-38).

We used to live in New Mexico where there were many artesian wells. These are sources of water that once tapped will flow naturally without being pumped. **Every person who by faith receives Yeshua (Jesus) has an artesian well of life springing up from within—the very life of Yahweh satisfying eternally that person's spiritual thirst, and flowing out to quench the thirsts of others!** We are to be like a pipeline for that constant supply of refreshment. What a difference we can make in this world of thirsty people.

Yahweh in Your Worship

Isaiah promised that all who know Yahweh will "Give thanks to Yahweh… Celebrate His works… Declare that His name is exalted!" Here is our call to worship Him as our Water of Life, springing up like an artesian well. Never running dry, but continually quenching our thirst for life. (Try turning the words of our text into your personal prayer of worship and thanksgiving.)

November 4

Yahweh Made This Day Especially for Me

Yahweh in the Word

> "This is the day Yahweh has made; let us rejoice and be glad in it" (Psalm 118:24).

The setting for this song of praise and thanksgiving is a time of trouble for the writer. If you read the entire chapter, you notice several references to his personal enemies. However, he was able to overcome them and emerge victorious. When he speaks of "this is the day" in our text, he means this is the day of victory, thus there is rejoicing and gladness.

Yahweh in Your Walk

Every day we choose our attitude regarding life experiences; this is one of our freedoms as persons created in the image of Yahweh. We can choose to be positive and focus on what is good or we can decide to dwell on thoughts that are basically negative. Here are words from Charles R. Swindoll that have been a great help to me in this regard:

> The longer I live, the more I realize the impact of attitude on life. Attitude, to me is more important than facts. It is more important than the past, than education, than money, than circumstances, than failures, than successes, than what other people think or say or do. It is more important than appearance, giftedness or skill. It will make or break a company… a church… a home. The remarkable thing is we have a choice every day regarding the attitude we will embrace for that day. We cannot change our past… we cannot change the fact that people will act in a certain way. We cannot change the inevitable. The only thing we can do is play on the one string we have, and that is our attitude. I am convinced that life is ten percent what happens to us and ninety percent how we react to it. And so it is that we are in charge of our attitudes.

The psalmist chose not to give way to self-pity and a spirit of revenge toward his enemies, rather to focus on Yahweh's blessings. **As you walk through this day, you likewise can choose to have a positive attitude.** An old song has these lines: "You've got to accentuate the positive; eliminate the negative; latch on to the affirmative, and don't mess with Mister-in-between." So, join this psalmist in declaring that this day has been made by Yahweh—just for me—and I have decided to rejoice and be glad in it!

Yahweh in Your Worship

Thank You, Yahweh, for giving me this newly created day with all its opportunities for walking with You, worshiping You, and serving You. I want to find joy and gladness in all that happens. Make me aware of those around me who need help with their attitude. Use me to share with them the secret of being positive because of Your favor. May I be a good example to my family and friends of someone who chooses to focus on the good side of life.

November 5

Yahweh Will Never Abandon Me

Yahweh in the Word

> *"Yahweh will not abandon His people, because of His great name and because He has determined to make you His own people" (1 Samuel 12:22).*

These are the words of Samuel just before he anointed Saul as Israel's first king. He reminded the people that their desire to have a king like other nations was not Yahweh's best plan for them. However, Samuel went on to assure the people that Yahweh would be merciful and not forsake them because of their bad choice. He would do this because of who He is—as His "great name" Yahweh reveals—I AM. And He would continue to form them into a special nation as He had promised Abraham and others.

Yahweh in Your Walk

There are many very religious people in this world who live in the fear that if they do wrong their god will forsake them; their security is dependent on what they do. If they do more good works than bad, they have a chance of going to some kind of paradise after they die. Otherwise, they have no hope. Samuel assured the people of Israel that Yahweh was not like this. Because of who He is, Yahweh keeps His promises even if His people do not.

Much earlier Moses spoke these words of assurance to Yahweh's people: "It is Yahweh your God who goes with you; He will not leave you or forsake you" (Deuteronomy 31:6). And the writer of Hebrews echoed the same promise to his readers in Hebrews 13:5, "He Himself has said, 'I will never leave you nor forsake you.'"

How comforting to know that as you walk through each day, Yahweh is with you and working in you, not because you are good but because He is. He must be true to His nature which is to be unchanging in His faithfulness to His promises. As Samuel said, "He has determined to make you His own people." This amazing plan has never ceased to be Yahweh's purpose; He is faithfully pursuing His goal of redeeming a new people for Himself. And we can always count on Him to stay with this divine plan.

Critics of this kind of teaching will say, "O you believe that because you claim to be saved, you can live any way you please and still go to heaven when you die." My answer is, "Yes, a Christian can live any way he wants to and still go to heaven—because he wants to live the kind of life that pleases the Lord." Yahweh's promise not to abandon us does not free us from the responsibility to keep His commandments.

Yahweh in Your Worship

I thank You Yahweh for the comfort I find in knowing that You will never abandon Me.

November 6

Yahweh Will Always Be Merciful to Me

Yahweh in the Word

> *"Then Jacob said, 'God of my father Abraham and God of my father Isaac, Yahweh who said to me, 'Go back to your land and to your family, and I will cause you to prosper,' I am unworthy of all the kindness (mercy) and faithfulness You have shown Your servant… Please rescue me from the hand of my brother Esau, for I am afraid of him; otherwise he may come and attack me, the mothers and their children'" (Genesis 32:9-11).*

Jacob cheated his brother Esau out of the blessing which he deserved as the first-born son of his father Isaac. Because of this Jacob fled to another country to escape Esau's wrath. Many years later Yahweh instructed Jacob to return to his home. As the time neared for him to face Esau again, he offered the prayer of our text for today. Jacob acknowledged his complete unworthiness of Yahweh's mercy, and pleads for Him to intervene. Sure enough, when the brothers met, Yahweh had caused Esau to be merciful, forgiving Jacob completely.

Yahweh in Your Walk

The Hebrew word for "kindness (mercy)" in our text is **chesed**, meaning "Yahweh's enduring love." Jacob discovered to his amazement that Yahweh treated him with such mercy, in spite of his total unworthiness. He was a man who had shown no mercy to his brother and yet Yahweh was merciful to him. The reunion of Jacob and Esau was peaceful; in fact, Esau refused Jacob's many gifts of appeasement. Instead he treated this brother with kindness, as he ran to meet him with a warm embrace.

Here is a great example of the way Yahweh always deals with us. None of us deserves the least of Yahweh's favors because we have all rebelled against Him at various times. **What we actually deserve for our many sins is Yahweh's wrath and punishment, but He remains full of mercy towards us.**

This interesting story reminds us of another example of mercy found in the New Testament account of the "Prodigal Son." You recall how this rebellious son demanded his inheritance, left home, and wasted all he had in a sinful lifestyle. When he "came to himself" and realized the error of his ways, he returned home expecting to be treated like a hired servant. He said to his father, just as Jacob said to Yahweh, "I am unworthy…" However, to his surprise his father showed mercy and welcomed him with a celebration (Luke 15:11-32).

Yahweh in Your Worship

"I will sing of the mercies of the Lord forever, I will sing." Yahweh, I want to seize opportunities this day to praise You for Your faithful mercies to me. Use me to share this good news with other sinners who, like me, could never merit the least of Your favors.

November 7

Yahweh Commends the Humble Person

Yahweh in the Word

> "Moses was a very humble man, more so than any man on the face of the earth... Listen to what I say: If there is a prophet among you from Yahweh, I make Myself known to him in a vision; I speak with him in a dream. Not so with My servant Moses; he is faithful in all My household. I speak with him directly, openly, and not in riddles; he sees the form of Yahweh" (Numbers 12: 3, 6-8).

While we may not think of Moses, the powerful leader of Israel, as being humble, Yahweh said he was more humble than any man on earth. So when Miriam and Aaron, Moses' brother and sister were critical of Moses, Yahweh gave the testimony of our text about him. Moreover, they were severely reproved by Yahweh for speaking against their brother (vv. 8-16).

Yahweh in Your Walk

Genuine humility is a character trait that is seen as commendable in Scriptures. Consider these words of wisdom: "Better to be lowly of spirit with the humble than to divide the plunder with the proud" (Proverbs 16:19). "All of you clothe yourselves with humility toward one another because God resists the proud but gives grace to the humble. Humble yourselves, therefore, under the mighty hand of God, so that He may exalt you at the proper time" (1 Peter 5:5-6).

Humility is not considered an admirable nor desirable trait by the world in which we live. On the contrary, the person who promotes himself and takes pride in himself is the one this culture commends. Why this radical difference in values? The answer lies in the true meaning of humility. As one interpreter says, **"Humility does not mean thinking less of oneself, it means thinking of oneself less!"** That is, humility is an attitude of trust in Yahweh, more than trusting in oneself.

Moses was a very strong leader, however, his heart was yielded to Yahweh's control; he saw himself not as being better than others, but simply a lowly sheep herder whom Yahweh chose to use for His purpose. In a similar manner, we must remember that apart from Yahweh, we are nothing but unworthy rebels against Him. **As you walk through this day, let Yahweh know that you are trusting Him, not yourself, to guide in all your decisions and to use you for His purposes.** Be fully submissive to Him in all things; always ask His Spirit to direct your paths.

Yahweh in Your Worship

Yahweh, Lord of heaven and earth, I choose to submit myself to Your sovereign control. How thankful I am that You hear my prayer and always answer according to what is best for me. Help me to seize every opportunity that comes my way for honoring You today. Teach me to be the humble servant of others in all my relationships.

November 8

Yahweh Strengthens Me with His Joy

Yahweh in the Word

> "Today is holy to Yahweh. Do not grieve because the joy of Yahweh is your strength… then all the people began to eat and drink, send portions, and have a great celebration, because they had understood the words that were explained to them" (Nehemiah 8:10-12).

The occasion for out text is the gathering of exiles who had returned from captivity in Babylon. Ezra the scribe and Nehemiah the governor, along with other leaders, read and explained Yahweh's Word to the people. When they heard and understood His promises, they began a celebration lasting seven days. They had a new strength for worshiping and serving Yahweh.

Yahweh in Your Walk

You can remember times when you have rejoiced over some good news; you felt like having a celebration. The word gospel means "good news," in fact it is the best good news we sinners will ever hear. Think about the content of this good news and the joy it brings when we understand it.

> Good news: Yahweh loves you in spite of your sin and complete unworthiness.
> Good news: Yahweh sent His Son to be the atoning sacrifice for your sins.
> Good news: Yahweh gives His Holy Spirit to convict you of your need for Yeshua.
> Good news: Yahweh enables you by His grace to repent and believe the Good News.
> Good news: Yahweh imparts to you the Holy Spirit to give you new life and power.
> Good news: Yahweh promises eternal life to you as you believe in and receive Yeshua.
> Good news: Yahweh sends you to tell others of this new life and how they can have it.

As you think about each of these joy-filled truths, you will experience new spiritual strength that will enable you to worship and serve Yahweh more effectively. I recall how this has been proven over and over in various persons I have seen discover these gospel truths. I remember the glow on the face of a man who discovered this message after spending several years in prison for crimes he had committed. He went on to establish a ministry to other prisoners and their families. At times he faced opposition, but the strength he had from his joy in Yahweh enabled him to keep on keeping on.

You will have times of discouragement as you seek to follow Yahweh. Satan, your enemy, will make certain this happens. He will remind you of your sinful past, your present weakness, and seek to rob you of the power you need to be faithful. Resist him by focusing not on yourself, but upon Yahweh and the good news listed above. Claim by faith the strength that is yours from joy.

Yahweh in Your Worship

Celebrate the joy of salvation. Worship in the strength this joy gives.

November 9

Yahweh Is to Be Praised by Everyone, Everywhere

Yahweh in the Word

> "Praise Yahweh, all nations! Glorify Him, all peoples! For His faithful love to us is great; Yahweh's faithfulness endures forever. Praise Yahweh! (Psalm 117)

This psalm is the shortest of all 150 psalms, and yet its breadth includes all people of all nations and its length is forever—the shortest, but broadest and longest. What an amazing composition!

Yahweh in Your Walk

You are a part of "all peoples" who are told by the psalmist to "Praise Yahweh." Will you do that today; will you intentionally offer your heartfelt praise to Him? To praise Him means to express to Yahweh the fact that you value Him more highly than all else, so you exalt Him with your own words of adoration and admiration. **Praise is the essence of authentic worship, the purest expression of honor and blessing.**

Why not pause just now and offer a sacrifice of praise to Yahweh. He alone is worthy of your praise as your one and only God. Create your own song of praise to Him; that will be a unique praise offering that has never been expressed to Him before—it's your love song to Yahweh.

Notice the reason given by this psalmist for praising Yahweh—"His faithful love to us is great." The words "faithful love" translate a beautiful Hebrew word meaning **covenant loyalty**. Yahweh is God's covenant name—the I AM of the burning bush. His new covenant is one of mercy and grace whereby He provides salvation from sin and its consequences for all who come to Jesus by faith, claiming His offer of forgiveness and eternal life. Yahweh is to be praised because He is faithful to this covenant of grace.

Sometimes you may not feel like praising Yahweh; perhaps various problems have so burdened you that praise is not naturally forthcoming. But listen to these words from David, "I will praise You **every day**" (Psalm 145:2). You and your life situation changes from day to day, but Yahweh remains the same—His "faithfulness endures forever." **So, everyday—good or bad—you can faithfully offer praise to Him for His unchanging goodness, mercy, and love**. Again, spend a few minutes offering praise to Him for who He is, and all He has done, is doing, and will do to bless you. Remember, He is the same yesterday, today, and forever!

Yahweh in Your Worship

Yes, Yahweh, I join all people who know You in offering sincere, heartfelt praise and adoration to You. You alone are worthy of such honor. You are the source of every good and perfect gift—thank You. You are the sustainer of all creation—thank You. I do praise You! Help me to encourage others to worship You with praise.

November 10

Yahweh Wants Me to Be Devoted to Doing Good

Yahweh in the Word

> "This saying is trustworthy. I want you to insist on these things, so that those who have believed God might be careful to devote themselves to good works. These are good and profitable for everyone... And our people must also learn to devote themselves to good works for cases of urgent need, so that they will not be unfruitful" (Titus 3:8, 14).

Titus was one of the apostle Paul's young coworkers. Paul left him on the island of Crete to set up a group of churches there. He wrote a brief letter to him with instructions regarding this work. One theme he addresses repeatedly in this short epistle is that of good works as evidence of being a true follower of Jesus (2:6, 14; 3:1, 8, 14).

Yahweh in Your Walk

The apostle Paul was careful to teach the basic truths about how a person is saved from the consequences of sin. In this letter to Titus, he states this essential doctrine in these words: "He saved us—not by works of righteousness that we had done, but according to His mercy, through the washing of regeneration and renewal by the Holy Spirit. He poured out this Spirit on us abundantly through Jesus Christ our Savior, so that having been justified by His grace, we may become heirs with the hope of eternal life" (3:4-7). You will notice his insistence that salvation is "not by works of righteousness that we had done."

What then is the place of good works if not to earn Yahweh's favor? The apostle declares that good works are the result of salvation—the proof of a new life—not the means of obtaining it. His challenge to us is found in the words ***devote yourself to good works***. The meaning is that we who have experienced Yahweh's salvation are to demonstrate what this salvation means by giving ourselves to doing good to others. I am thinking now of John and Kay, a senior adult couple in our church, who are devoted to doing good for other seniors. They give large amounts of their time and energy to visit these older friends, take them to doctor appointments, bring them to church events, plan special outings for them, ask prayer for their needs, and on and on I could go. No one could question their experience of salvation—just observe their faithful service.

Let me ask you to examine yourself at this point—**what evidence do you give of knowing the Lord Jesus by following His example of going about doing good?** As you think back over the past week, what good works have you done? Perhaps you need to get serious about allowing the Holy Spirit to do His work of loving people in practical ways through you. I like the way this saying puts it: **"As Christians we should do all the good we can, to all the people we can, in all the ways as we can, for as long as we can!"**

Yahweh in Your Worship

I worship You for all the good You have done for me. Help me pass on to others all these blessings. Make me a blessing to them as I reach out with Your love.

November 11

Yahweh Desires for All Wars to Cease

Yahweh in the Word

> "Yahweh will settle disputes among the nations and provide arbitration for many peoples. They will turn their swords into plows and their spears into pruning knives. Nations will not take up the sword against other nations, and they will never again train for war" (Isaiah 2:4).

These words from the prophet Isaiah describe the "last days" when Yahweh will bring about a lasting peace for all people; there will be no more wars.

Yahweh in Your Walk

November 11th was originally known as Armistice Day. On November 11, 1918, near the end of World War I, a ceasefire was observed on the eleventh hour of the eleventh day of the eleventh month. At that time, millions of people around the world participated in a time of silence as they thought about the terrible cost of war as World War I came to an end. It was hoped by many that the "Great War," as it was known, would become the war that would end all wars. Unfortunately, that did not happen, and it was followed by another world war, plus many smaller military conflicts—right up to the present time.

Later, November 11th was designated as Veterans Day to honor all Americans who have served or are serving in the Armed Forces. (Memorial Day in May honors all who have died in the line of duty.) **We can be justly proud of all men and women who have served us so we can enjoy all the benefits of freedom.** However, warfare and all its violence has never been part of Yahweh's perfect will for His creation. All such conflict is the result of sin.

Yahweh's purpose for universal peace will be fulfilled when He returns and establishes a new earth wherein dwells peace—as our text for today describes. Meanwhile, we are called to be peacemakers—beginning in our own families, neighborhoods, churches, and extended relationships. As our Lord declared, "The peacemakers are blessed, for they will be called sons of God" (Matthew 5:9). The ministry of peacemaking involves helping to resolve conflict between individuals and groups, as well as refusing to seek revenge when wronged. Yahweh is a God of peace through reconciliation. **When we become involved where peacemaking is needed, we are behaving as Yahweh's sons and daughters.**

Yahweh in Your Worship

I seize this opportunity to offer the sacrifice of praise to You, O Yahweh, God of peace. May You be known as the only solution to the sin problems of this world. Thank You for Your work to reconcile all creation to Yourself in harmony and peace. Use me as Your ambassador to a world that desperately needs to know Your love and forgiveness. Help me extend Your peace to others today.

November 12

Yahweh Is My Stronghold in Times of Trouble

Yahweh in the Word

> *"Yahweh is good, a stronghold in the day of distress; He cares for those who take refuge in Him" (Nahum 1:7).*

The prophet Nahum, whose name means "comfort," is the only person with this name in the Old Testament. He was sent by Yahweh to pronounce judgment upon the Assyrians and their capital city Nineveh. This wicked nation was causing much trouble for Yahweh's people in Israel and Judah. Our text offered great hope in a "day of distress" for all who put their trust in Yahweh.

Yahweh in Your Walk

I believe very strongly in Yahweh's control of our times. So often I have read some word in the Bible at just the right time—the time I needed it most. Perhaps this devotional is coming to you at such a time. You may be facing some situation where you need the comfort found in the words of this text. If not now, at some point in time you will need the kind of assurance offered here.

As I read the promise given through Nahum, I think of the words of a favorite old hymn:

> Rock of Ages, cleft for me, let me hide myself in Thee;
> Let the water and the blood, from Thy wounded side which flowed,
> Be of sin the double cure, save from wrath and make me pure.

An English author, Augustus Toplady, wrote these words in 1776; they have been called the "best known, best loved, and most widely useful" hymn in the English language. The reason for such a noteworthy reputation is the fact that most people find themselves needing this kind of comfort. **We all need a place of refuge, like a cleft in a great rock, where we are secure till the storm passes**. Notice how this text speaks of Yahweh being both good and caring for all who flee to Him for help.

Since we cannot run to Yahweh physically, how can we go to Him for shelter? Simply by calling upon Him, and claiming His protection and care. Here is where His promises we have memorized make such a difference. There are times when I cannot sleep due to some troubling thoughts. I find comfort and peace by quoting Isaiah 41:10 and other similar words of promise.

Yahweh in Your Worship

Good and caring Yahweh, I praise and worship You for always being there as my Rock of refuge. I choose to take refuge in You when I face trouble beyond my control. You are My only secure and unchanging stronghold in times of distress. Thank You for always being One who is for me, regardless of my unworthiness. Help me today to be Your witness to others in trouble.

November 13

Yahweh Invites Me to Come Boldly to His Throne of Grace

Yahweh in the Word

> "Therefore let us approach the throne of grace with boldness, so that we may receive mercy and find grace to help us at the proper time" (Hebrews 4:16).

The verses just prior to this one speak of the fact that as believers we have a "great high priest" in heaven who sympathizes with our weaknesses and has been tempted in every way that we have been tempted—"Jesus the Son of God." Because of this, we can come before Yahweh in prayer with all confidence ("boldness") that we will receive all the mercy and grace we need.

Yahweh in Your Walk

How interesting that the throne in heaven from which Yahweh rules this world is here described as a "throne of grace." And that we are invited by Him to come before this throne to receive both mercy and grace—to help us in every time of need. Rather than approach Yahweh with a sense of fear that He will not welcome us due to our total unworthiness, we can come with "boldness." This term comes from two Greek words meaning "to speak confidently without fear." That is, we can come before Yahweh in our prayers without any concern that we will be rejected by Him, rather we are assured that He promises to hear us and give us all the mercy and grace we need.

Mercy means that Yahweh forgives our sins and withholds the punishment we deserve. Grace means that Yahweh gives the help we do not deserve. How these truths encourage us to pray with absolute confidence that our prayers are heard and answered. Notice also the phrase "help us at the proper time." Another translation could read "timely help," meaning we will receive the mercy and grace we need just at the time we most need them.

Yahweh is pleased when we come before Him in prayer and remind Him of the promise of this text. As one person said, "God has never, ever, broken a single promise He has spoken." As you walk through this day, take time to respond to His invitation and claim His promise. You will discover the joy of receiving His gracious and merciful help—just at the time you need it.

Yahweh in Your Worship

Thank You, gracious Yahweh, for Your promise of mercy and grace. You know how I need the help only You can give. I worship You as my faithful provider. Teach me to approach Your throne with confidence. I seize this opportunity to express my heartfelt worship of You; You deserve all the honor, praise, and worship I can ever give. Help me be a worshiper throughout this day as I become aware of Your presence with me. Your throne of grace is always open to me and I choose to abide in this amazing place of acceptance and help. Surely now is the "proper time" for me to receive the help of Your mercy and grace. Use me to share this truth with those I meet today who need the encouragement of these truths.

November 14

Yahweh Wants Me to Have Faith in Him

Yahweh in the Word

"Jesus replied to them, 'Have faith in God'" (Mark 11:22).

These simple words were spoken by Jesus to His disciples. Earlier they had seen evidence of a miracle He performed—the withered fig tree. When they marveled at His power over nature, He responded with this brief challenge: "Have faith in God."

Yahweh in Your Walk

We all have faith, and we exercise that faith many times each day. For example, we sit in a chair, believing it will support us; we eat food, believing it to be nourishing; we send mail, believing it will be delivered. Hopefully, you pray, believing Yahweh will hear and answer. At times we may wish we had more faith. However, notice that Jesus did not say, "Have **more** faith"—just "have faith in God." The size of our faith is not the main issue, rather, the size of the object of our faith.

Stuart Briscoe is an excellent interpreter and teacher of biblical truth. He writes, "Faith is only as valid as its object. You could have tremendous faith in very thin ice and drown… You could have very little faith in very thick ice and be perfectly secure." We are to have faith (however small) in God (unlimited power) in order to see great results. In other words, we do not need to "work up a stronger faith." Rather, **we need to grow in our understanding and confidence in the proper object of our faith, which is Yahweh and all He has promised.**

My friend shared this testimony with me: "For a long time I prayed that God would give me more faith, and nothing seemed to change. Then one day I read this in Romans 10:17, 'So then faith comes from what is heard, and what is heard comes from the word of God.' I began reading the Bible more diligently, seeking to know more about the Lord, and my faith has been growing ever since." This makes good sense—the better we know any person who is trustworthy, the more we trust them. Getting better acquainted with Yahweh and His promises will enable us to trust Him more in every situation.

Again, it is not the size of your faith that makes a difference, but this size of the object of your faith; let this be Yahweh, the eternal, sovereign, all-sufficient Master and Lord of this universe. Place your confidence in Him and you will never be disappointed.

Yahweh in Your Worship

Thank You, Yahweh, that You enable me to have faith in You and in Your wonderful promises. Today, I want to seize every opportunity to trust You to provide for every need of mine. You are Yahweh Yireh, the One who faithfully supplies everything I need to be complete. Help me to know You better that I may trust You more. Reveal Yourself more fully through Your Word.

November 15

Yeshua Calls Me His Friend

Yeshua in the Word

> "This is My command: Love one another as I have loved you. No one has greater love than this, that someone would lay down his life for his friends. You are My friends if you do what I command you." (John 15:13).

Jesus spoke these words to His disciples shortly before He was arrested and taken to His cross. The Bible has many commands, most of them from Yahweh or one of His servants. However, only one command is presented by Jesus as "My command." Through Moses, Yahweh gave the command to love others as you love yourself, but Jesus changed that command to: "Love one another **as I have loved you.**" Being His friend has one simple requirement: "Do what I command you."

Yeshua in Your Walk

One of the most highly valued relationships in life is that of friendship. Recently I asked my Bible study class to define friendship. Here are some of the terms they gave me to write on a whiteboard: loyalty, trustworthiness, faithfulness, love, compassion, reliability, and helpfulness. Perhaps you can think of others. But the point is—a friend is someone who genuinely loves you and is present when you need him or her. I am sure you have discovered that some who seem to be your friends, do not pass the reliability test; when you need them, they aren't there. How good to have real friends who are consistently faithful.

But what about friendship with Yahweh? How amazing that this is even possible—to be the friend of God! Only one person in the Old Testament is described by Yahweh as being His friend, "But you Israel, My servant, Jacob, whom I have chosen, the descendant of Abraham, My friend" (Isaiah 41:8). The book of James confirms this when we find, "Abraham believed God, and it was credited to him for righteousness, and he was called God's friend" (James 2:23). What a special relationship existed between Yahweh and Abraham.

The good news is—you can be the friend of Yeshua. Just as Jesus spoke of His friendship with His disciples, the same can be true for you. All you have to do is keep His command to love others as He loves you—a self-sacrificing, loyal love. How can you do this? You can't—with your own resources. But you can if you allow Him to express His love through you. The fruit (product) of the Spirit of Christ is love. As the apostle John declared, "We have come to know and to believe the love that God has for us. God is love, and the one who remains in love remains in God, and God remains in him" (1 John 4:16).

Yeshua in Your Worship

How gracious of You, Lord Yeshua, to welcome me as Your friend. Help me love others with the same self-sacrificing love You have shown to me. I trust You for the power to obey You.

November 16

Yahweh Is Always Near Me

Yahweh in the Word

> "'Am I a God who is only near'—this is Yahweh's declaration—'and not a God who is far away? Can a man hide himself in secret places where I cannot see him?'—Yahweh's declaration. 'Do not I fill the heavens and the earth?'—Yahweh's declaration" (Jeremiah 23:23-24).

The prophet Jeremiah was fulfilling his role as Yahweh's messenger as he wrote these interesting words. He wanted his people to know that in contrast to false gods, Yahweh is both immanent (near) and transcendent (far away). **His presence with us and knowledge of us are complete.**

Yahweh in Your Walk

My friend told me about an interesting conversation he had with his two young sons. They had misbehaved and he asked them if they wanted him to tell either God or Santa Claus about what they had done. The five-year-old replied, "God already knows because He knows everything; so please don't tell Santa!" We smile at this humorous statement, but this boy knew the truth about Yahweh—He knows everything. And one reason for this total knowledge is His presence everywhere.

There have been times when I would have preferred Yahweh not to know everything about what I do—those times when I did wrong. However, most of the time I am comforted by the awareness of His continuous presence. I agree with the song writer, Barbara Fowler Gaultney, who wrote a lovely song with these words in the chorus

> I've seen it in the lightning, heard it in the thunder, and felt it in the rain.
> My Lord is near me all the time; my Lord is near me all the time.

The psalmist celebrated the omnipresence of Yahweh in these memorable words: "Where can I go to escape Your Spirit? Where can I flee from Your presence? If I go up to heaven, You are there; if I make my bed in Sheol, You are there. If I live at the eastern horizon or settle at the western limits, even there Your hand will lead me; Your right hand will hold on to me. If I say, 'Surely the darkness will hide me, and the light around me will be night'—even the darkness is not dark to You. The night shines like the day; darkness and light are alike to You" (Psalm 139:7-12). **Yes, Yahweh is always near you. What a good and comforting truth.**

Yahweh in Your Worship

Thank You, ever present Yahweh, that I do not have to go to some special temple to be in Your presence. You are always nearer than the breath I breathe; You are with me, in me, and actively working in and through me. For these truths I worship and adore You. Help me be more aware of Your continuous nearness, and may that nearness keep me walking in the path of righteousness.

November 17

Yeshua Calls Me to His World-Wide Mission

Yeshua in the Word

> "Then He said to them, 'Go into all the world and preach the gospel to the whole creation" (Mark 16:15).

The Gospel of Mark concludes with this version of Yeshua's commission to His disciples. His call is for all believers to be committed to the sharing of the gospel message to all persons everywhere.

Yeshua in Your Walk

On October 2, 1792, twelve ministers from small churches in Kettering, England, met to form the Baptist Missionary Society. They were convinced that God was leading them to make an attempt to declare the gospel to the unconverted masses of people in India. One of these men was William Carey who was sent the following year to begin this missionary venture. Carey suggested they adopt this slogan: "Expect great things from God; attempt great things for God." The also chose a scripture text for this work: "Enlarge the site of your tent, and let your tent curtains be stretched out; do not hold back; lengthen your ropes, and drive your pegs deep. For you will spread out to the right and to the left and your descendants will dispossess nations and inhabit the desolate cities… Yahweh of hosts is your Redeemer; He is called the God of all the earth" (Isaiah 54:2-3, 5). Today this missionary society has more than 350 workers in 40 countries. The vision Yahweh gave to these humble men with limited means is being fulfilled.

Do you envision yourself as participating in Jesus' commission to take His gospel to all humankind? Perhaps you think this kind of work is just for those who have a special calling. **The truth is—all believers are called and sent to be on mission for our Lord.** Our first mission field is our family members. Beyond this will include our neighbors, schoolmates, work associates, members of various organizations where we belong. Perhaps you will participate in church mission activities. But first, you must see yourself as being called and sent to such outreach efforts.

One of my friends is limited to her house as far as physical activities are concerned. But she is a serious missionary through intercessory prayer for missionaries, plus generous giving to support mission work. In addition, when someone comes to her house, such as a repairman or deliveryman, she seeks to be a personal witness to them. She also uses her telephone to contact prospects for her church. She is definitely "on mission" for Jesus. **Ask Him to show you how you can also fulfill your role in reaching the unreached with His good news. Then do it!**

Yeshua in Your Worship

Thank You, Lord, for including me in Your global mission plan. Help me awaken to Your call.

November 18

Yahweh Wants Me to Be Unashamed of My Commitment to Him

Yahweh in the Word

> "For I am not ashamed of the gospel, because it is God's power for salvation to everyone who believes, first to the Jew, and also to the Greek. For in it God's righteousness is revealed from faith to faith, just as it is written: 'The righteous will live by faith'" (Romans 1:16-17).

Here is Paul's testimony of his confidence in the gospel message. He knows that all people who have faith in the gospel message will be counted righteous before Yahweh.

Yahweh in Your Walk

The following affirmation was found in the room of an African man in Rwanda who was killed in 1980 because he refused to renounce his faith in Christ:

Fellowship of the Unashamed

> "I am part of the fellowship of the unashamed. I have the Holy Spirit power. The die has been cast. I have stepped over the line. The decision has been made—I am a disciple of His. I won't look back, let up, slow down, back away, or be still. My past is redeemed, my present makes sense, my future is secure. I'm finished and done with low living, sight walking, smooth knees, colorless dreams, tame visions, worldly-talking, cheap giving, and dwarfed goals.
>
> I no longer need pre-eminence, prosperity, position, promotions, plaudits, or popularity. I don't have to be right, first, tops, recognized, praised, regarded, or rewarded. I now live by faith, lean on His presence, walk by patience, am lifted by prayer, and I labor with power.
>
> My face is set, my gait is fast, my goal is heaven, my road is narrow, my way is rough, my companions are few, my Guide is reliable, my mission is clear. I cannot be bought, compromised, detoured, hired away, turned back, diluted, or delayed. I will not flinch in the face of sacrifice, hesitate in the presence of the enemy, pander at the pool of popularity, or meander in the maze of mediocrity. I won't give up, shut up, let up, until I have stayed up, stored up, prayed up, paid up, give up till I drop, preach till all know, and work till He stops me. And when He comes my banner will be clear!"
>
> —Dr. Bob Moorehead from *Words Aptly Spoken*

Yahweh in Your Worship

Today, O Yahweh, I want to seize every opportunity to worship and serve You. Thank You for Your strong and faithful commitment to me. Help me to never be ashamed of You nor Your Word. Teach me to walk always in Your path of righteousness. I love You and Praise You. I join the "Fellowship of the Unashamed" that I may be a better witness of You and Your grace.

November 19

Yahweh Wants Me to Learn to Be a Thankful Person

Yahweh in the Word

> "Give thanks in everything for this is God's will for you in Christ Jesus" (1 Thessalonians 5: 18).

The apostle Paul wrote often about the importance of not only being a thankful person but actually expressing that gratitude by **giving thanks** in everything. He assures them that such actions fulfill God's will for them.

Yahweh in Your Walk

These next few devotionals will focus your attention on the subject of thanksgiving. Today's devotional thought is a personal testimony that I want to share. When I left my family home to become an engineering student at the University of Oklahoma, I was a very young, immature Christian—not a real disciple of Jesus. One day I was lying on my dorm bed, reading a class textbook, when two older students came to my room inviting me to attend "noonday" meetings at the Baptist Student Union, near the campus. (One of these men, Von Worten, later became a missionary to Indonesia. Our friendship has continued across these many years; our sons are now missionaries in that area. Another student was Buddy Morris who became, with his wife May, a missionary to Singapore.) Since this was my first invitation to any campus activity, I decided to accept. As I look back, that was Yahweh's appointment for me.

I remember how friendly the leaders and students were in those daily meetings. Soon I became more involved with Bible studies and campus ministry opportunities—leading to a commitment to vocational Christian ministry. I was married the following year and my bride joined me in these exciting disciple-making experiences. We have now been married for over 60 years and served together in numerous pastorates, mission trips, opportunities to write for publication, and so many other privileges. We would not have even dreamed that Yahweh would so bless us.

Just today I received a letter telling about a new approach to this campus ministry at OU called "Paradigm." I quote, "A paradigm refers to a person's frame of mind/worldview, which includes personal beliefs, attitudes, and perspectives on life. A person's paradigm shapes who they become as a person and will help chart the direction of their beliefs, perspectives, and values. We want students to reorient their lives around Jesus Christ and let Him change them from inside out." You can learn more about this ministry at www.paradigmnorman.com.

So today I am very thankful for that moment in time when these young men came to my room with an invitation to join their fellowship of believers—one simple outreach of love that Yahweh used to change the entire direction of my life, and later of our family.

Yahweh in Your Worship

Here am I Lord, send me—wherever You would have me go to make Your eternal difference.

November 20

Yahweh Wants Me to Praise Him with My Song

Yahweh in the Word

> "Yahweh is my strength and my shield; my heart trusts in Him, and I am helped. Therefore my heart rejoices, and I praise Him with my song" (Psalm 28:7).

Apparently, David wrote this psalm when he was being threatened by his enemies. He called upon Yahweh for help and was heard by Him. As the result of answered prayer, David extolls Yahweh for His help.

Yahweh in Your Walk

During this Thanksgiving season, we are reminded to give thanks for our many blessings. How appropriate to participate with others in expressing gratitude to the One from whom all blessings flow. Most of our thanks-giving comes by the words we speak. We have a family custom of having a few grains of corn on our plates as we sit down for our special Thanksgiving dinner. These are a reminder to us of the sparse meal our forefathers had those early days when these pilgrims first came to America. Often we will ask each person at the table to share what they are most thankful for—a very meaningful experience.

But have you considered the possibility of praising and thanking Yahweh with your very own song? Some might say, "I can't sing that well," or "You don't want to hear me sing!" **How about composing a song of praise that you will sing (maybe when alone!) just for Yahweh?** Let the words be your own expressions of gratitude to Him—no need of rhyme or rhythm, just express your thoughts. This personal, original declaration of gratitude from your heart could become a very meaningful time of worship for you.

David was known as the "Sweet-singer of Israel" due to his many recorded songs. He is also a fine example to us of how Yahweh wants to be worshiped by His people—by their own songs of praise. To give you an idea of what to sing, look at David's example in our Scripture text for today. He speaks of Yahweh being his "strength" and "shield." He goes on to say how this "helped" him and caused his heart to rejoice. All these terms accurately reflect the benefits you may also have received from calling upon Yahweh in times of need. Perhaps you will use these words to help you get started with composing your own special song. My experience has proven that once I get started with such a song, I have no trouble coming up with more words and expressions of worship. Give it a try—you'll like it. And **Yahweh will be pleased to hear your song.**

Yahweh in Your Worship

How grateful I am, O Yahweh, to have so much for which to give thanks at this and every season of life. Help me be more specific as I express gratitude to You. Make me aware of blessings.

November 21

Yeshua Invites Me to Become a Lifelong Learner

Yeshua in the Word

> *"Come to Me, all of you who are weary and burdened and I will give you rest. All of you, take up My yoke and learn from Me, because I am gentle and humble in heart, and you will find rest for yourselves. For My yoke is easy and My burden is light" (Matthew 11:28-30).*

Jesus (Yeshua) gives this invitation to all who choose to follow Him. He promises true spiritual rest from the burdens of sin as we become learners from Him.

Yeshua in Your Walk

As we continue these meditations on a Thanksgiving theme, join me in giving thanks to Yahweh that He has created us with the capacity to be a learner all the days of our lives in this world. From the time of our birth till our departure we have a continual need for learning, and we have the God-given capacity for learning (unless mental illness prevents it). The challenge we need is that of always, at every age, being intentional about learning—that is, looking deliberately to Yeshua for His instructions through all of our daily life experiences.

The most encouraging fact about lifelong learning as a follower of Yeshua is found in this promise which He made shortly before leaving His twelve apostles: "I have spoken these things to you while I remain with you. But the Counselor, the Holy Spirit—the Father will send Him in My name—will teach you all things and remind you of everything I have told you" (John 14:25-26). Think of what this means—**we have a resident Teacher with us all the time, One who uses all the events in our lives to teach us the life-lessons we so desperately need to learn.**

Let's make an important application of this truth. When you face unpleasant circumstances that are beyond your control, the normal human response is to have feelings of resentment and self-pity—the "poor me; why is this happening to me?" syndrome. But as a disciple of Yeshua your thought should be: "Thank You, Lord that You are in control of this situation; help me learn the valuable life-lessons that are available only through this experience." Do you see the difference there is in these two contrasting attitudes? Only you can choose which way to respond.

Here is a worthy challenge for you: Commit yourself every day to being a lifelong learner, with the Holy Spirit as your personal Teacher. **Approach each new situation, whether it seems good or bad, with the prayer for Him to show you the truths He wants you to learn.**

Yeshua in Your Worship

Yes, Yeshua, I do thank You for creating me with the capacity to learn. I trust You to work through all that happens today for my growth as Your servant. I wait upon You as my Teacher and Friend. Help me be a strong witness to others regarding the joy of being a lifelong learner.

November 22

Yahweh Loves Me and Draws Me to Himself

Yahweh in the Word

> "Yahweh has appeared of old to me, saying 'Yes, I have loved you with an everlasting love; therefore with lovingkindness I have drawn you'" (Jeremiah 33:3 NKJV).

Here is the testimony of Yahweh's people. He appeared to them at the beginning of their history—the call of Abraham—to assure them of His everlasting love. He took the initiative in reaching out and drawing them to Himself that He might bless them and make them a blessing to all people.

Yahweh in Your Walk

As you pause these days to think of reasons to be thankful, here is another special gift: **Yahweh has such a strong, everlasting love for you that He has chosen to draw you to Himself.** Jesus referred to this same blessing when He said, "As for Me, if I am lifted up from the earth I will draw all people to Myself" (John 12:22). This drawing refers to Yahweh's initiative in seeking to attract you to be reconciled to Him through faith in Jesus, and then to live in intimate fellowship with Him. He has loved you and drawn you into His forever family.

Many believers can testify of a specific time when they sensed this spiritual drawing power at work on their behalf. Perhaps you can recall a similar feeling of strong attraction, like that of a powerful magnet, pulling you into a relationship of trust and love with Yahweh. The term "lovingkindness" in our text for today refers to Yahweh's mercy and grace being expressed toward us. When Jesus spoke of being "lifted up from the earth," He was referring to His death on the cross. Of all the gracious acts of Yahweh, none is as impressive as His willingness to go to the extreme of giving His only Son as a sin offering on our behalf. As Jesus said, "Greater love has no man than this, that a man lay down his life for His friends. You are My friends" (John 15:13-14).

Notice in our text the term "everlasting love." Yahweh's love for us never ends because His love is unconditional—this means that His love for us is not dependent upon our merit or our love in return. His love depends solely upon Him and His eternal compassion toward us. And this is the kind of love He longs to express to and through us to others. If we love others with this same unconditional love, they too will be drawn to Him. **When you thank Him for the wonder of these truths, ask Him to pass this on to others through you as you walk through this day.**

Yahweh in Your Worship

"I stand amazed in the presence of Jesus the Nazarene and wonder how He could love me, a sinner condemned unclean. How marvelous, how wonderful is my Savior's love for me!" Yes, Yahweh, I worship You and thank You for Your everlasting love that has drawn me to You.

November 23

Yahweh Wants Me to Achieve True Greatness

Yahweh in the Word

> "Whoever wants to be great among you must be your servant, and whoever wants to be first among you must be a slave to all. For even the Son of Man did not come to be served but to serve and to give His life—a ransom for many" (Mark 10:43).

Brothers James and John were disciples of Jesus. On one occasion they came to Jesus with a personal request, "Allow us to sit at Your right and at Your left in Your glory" (v.37). These two places were the first and second places of highest honor, next to the ruler who sat between them. Jesus responded with a clear statement about the meaning of true greatness in His kingdom. Notice that He did not reprove them for their ambition; rather helped them know the truth.

Yahweh in Your Walk

In 1968 Martin Luther King Jr. included in his sermon the words from our Scripture text for today. He went on to say, "Everybody can be great, because everybody can serve. You don't have to have a college degree to serve. You don't have to make your subject and your verb agree to serve. You don't have to know about Plato and Aristotle to serve.... You only need a heart full of grace, a soul generated by love."

"Everybody can be great." These words of Dr. King are true. In fact, **Jesus wants everyone to be great—in the sense of true greatness.** Notice in our Scripture text for today the words "servant" and "slave." When Jesus spoke these words, a servant (from which our word *deacon* comes) was a person who waited on tables and did other necessary kinds of work. A slave occupied a lower position than a servant; a slave had no rights and did whatever his master ordered him to do. Neither of these would have been considered a desirable role; they were at the bottom of the social order. And yet Jesus, who was worthy of all honor and of being served, identified Himself as a servant—He came to serve, even to the point of giving His life on a cross. On another occasion He said, "I am among you as the One who serves" (Luke 22:27).

As you consider reasons for being thankful, here's one you may not have thought about before: **Be thankful for the possibility of becoming truly great by choosing to be a servant of others.** What a blessing; what a gift from Yahweh—becoming great in His sight! Why not begin today to find practical ways of serving others—first in your family, then neighborhood, workplace, church, and wherever you are. Humble yourself, like Jesus, and meet others' needs.

Yahweh in Your Worship

Yahweh, Lord of Hosts, I worship You as my Master and King. I am willing to serve You by helping others today. Make me aware of needs that I can meet. Thank You for this opportunity to make a difference in the lives of others. I want to do this as an expression of love for You.

November 24

Yahweh Delivers Me from Envying Others

Yahweh in the Word

> *"Do not be agitated by evildoers; do not envy those who do wrong. For they wither quickly like grass and wilt like tender green plants" (Psalm 37:1-2).*

The psalmist (probably David) advises his readers not to become upset and have feelings of envy when they see evildoers enjoy what seems to be prosperity. Their apparent success is short-lived for they will soon fade and pass away.

Yahweh in Your Walk

During this thanksgiving season you may be tempted to notice the apparent prosperity of those who do not honor the Lord by their lifestyles—such as some popular entertainers, wealthy professional athletes, and other notables. Thoughts of envy may occupy your mind when you wonder why you aren't so fortunate. The psalmist addressed this mistaken response to the prosperity of others when he wrote Psalm 37. He offers wise counsel of how we should deal with such thoughts. Notice four steps that lead to a correct mindset from this helpful chapter:

1. **"Trust in Yahweh and do what is good, dwell in the land and live securely"** (v. 3). Envy is often the result of personal discontent. As believers our trust is not in material wealth or social recognition but in Yahweh and all He faithfully supplies. We have all we need and more in Him.
2. **"Take delight in Yahweh, and He will give you your heart's desires"** (v. 4). When you find delight in Yahweh, your heart desires to know Him better and to live to please Him. He will honor these desires by revealing more of Himself to you and guiding you in His ways.
3. **"Commit your way to Yahweh; trust in Him, and He will act, making your righteousness shine like the dawn, your justice like the noonday"** (vv. 5-6). Place yourself and all your plans in His hands, trusting Him to take action on your behalf. His light will shine through your life.
4. **"Be silent before Yahweh and wait expectantly for Him; do not be agitated by one who prospers in his way, by the man who carries out evil plans"** (v. 7). To be silent before Yahweh means to wait patiently for Him to act. You are not upset by evil doers who seem to prosper because you know the ultimate result of their deeds. Yahweh's way is everlasting.

Take time today to meditate on these four steps to peace of mind—why not memorize them and let them feed your heart in a positive manner? Thank Yahweh for these valuable truths.

Yahweh in Your Worship

I do seize this opportunity to thank You, Yahweh, for giving me these wise instructions.

November 25

Yeshua Asks Me to Pray for More Workers in His Harvest

Yeshua in the Word

> "Then Jesus went to all the towns and villages, teaching in their synagogues, preaching the good news of the kingdom, and healing every disease and every sickness. When He saw the crowds, He felt compassion for them, because they were weary and worn out, like sheep without a shepherd. Then He said to His disciples, 'The harvest is abundant, but the workers are few. Therefore, pray to the Lord of the harvest to send out workers into His harvest'" (Matt. 9:35-38).

These words of Jesus (Yeshua) reveal His concern for sharing the good news with everyone. Since He could not do this by Himself, He appealed for His followers to pray for more helpers, and to join Him themselves. In the passage that follows, we find Jesus calling out 12 disciples by name (10:1-10). These men became the first harvest workers to serve alongside Jesus.

Yeshua in Your Walk

Today you will be in the Lord's harvest field; wherever you find people, He is there to seek and to save the lost. He sends you there as part of His world-wide harvest worker task force. One blessing to be thankful for this special season is that of being involved in reaching others for the kingdom. Let Jesus know you are available as His laborer; what a privilege!

Our Scripture text for today records the only time Jesus gave a specific command to His followers concerning that for which we should pray: "Pray to the Lord of the harvest to send out workers into His harvest." Since we want to obey Him in all things, here is a matter we must take seriously—**praying for more harvest workers.** The purpose for today's devotional is to help you begin obeying this command, if you aren't already doing it.

Allow us to share how we do this. We follow a daily devotional guide entitled "Open Windows," which asks prayer for missionaries on their birthdays. Each day we read these names, praying for them. In addition we ask the Lord of the harvest to send more laborers to work alongside these who are already workers in the harvest fields of the world. You might follow a similar plan or make one of your own. **Just keep asking Yeshua daily to send more workers.**

One word of caution—when you do this, don't be surprised if He sends some of your family members, including you! As we have followed this discipline for years, we have seen our son and his family go to Southeast Asia, and our grandson and his family go to the Kurdish people. Plus we ourselves have been sent on mission trips to many places. He answers your prayer!

Yeshua in Your Worship

Lord of the harvest, I praise You for sending someone to me with the good news. Now I'm asking You to send forth more workers into the harvest fields. Here am I, send me! Thank You!

November 26

Yahweh Wants Me to Pause for Praise During Each Day

Yahweh in the Word

> *"All the earth will worship You and sing praise to You. They will sing praise to Your name"* **Selah** *(Psalm 66:4).*

Psalm 66 is a song of praise and thanksgiving to Yahweh for all His mighty acts. The composer of this song ends with his own testimony of what Yahweh has done for him, and concludes with "May God be praised."

Yahweh in Your Walk

Today we received a birth announcement from friends telling us of the arrival of their baby daughter whom they have named Selah Carol Frohock. This name reminds us of the biblical use of ***selah.*** You have seen this term at the end of our Scripture text for today's devotional. Selah occurs 71 times in the Psalms plus 3 times in the book of Habakkuk. No one knows for certain the exact meaning of Selah. One scholar thinks it is the combination of two Hebrew terms meaning: "to pause" and "to praise." The Amplified Bible translates selah as "to pause and calmly think of that." Since most of the psalms are songs, selah may be a musical notation calling for a pause and contemplation of the truths just sung.

    Perhaps Yahweh included this term in His Word to call for us to pause in our busy lives and calmly think about various truths. For example, there are three occurrences of selah in Psalm 66. Verse 4, our text, reads: "All the earth will worship You and sing praise to You. They will sing praise to Your name." Selah. Verse 7 states: "He rules forever by His might; He keeps His eye on the nations. The rebellious should not exalt themselves." Selah. And verse 15: "I will offer You fatted sheep as burnt offerings, with the fragrant smoke of rams; I will sacrifice oxen with goats." Selah.

    Each of these statements deserves careful thought. They are expressions of worship and praise, affirmation of His sovereignty, and the offering of prescribed sacrifices. **As you walk through this day you will have many occasions to recognize various blessings from Yahweh. Why not let these be a "selah time" for you—a pause for praise experience.** Simply take a few moments to think more carefully than usual about Yahweh's goodness and favor, then express a brief prayer of thanksgiving to Him for some particular gift. Let this become a regular part of your worship every day. We are certain that Selah Carol Frohock's parents will have many occasions for giving thanks to Yahweh for blessing them with this precious daughter. They will have an audible reminder every time they call her name.

Yahweh in Your Worship

Yahweh, I seize this pleasure to worship You with the sacrifice of praise and thanksgiving. **Selah**

November 27

Yahweh Wants Me to Be Like an Eagle

Yahweh in the Word

> "He (Yahweh) satisfies you with goodness; your youth is renewed like the eagle" (Psalm 103:5).

David composed this song of praise for all the great personal benefits that come to those who are worshipers of Yahweh.

Yahweh in Your Walk

I continue to be amazed at the way Yahweh supplies His thoughts for these devotionals. As I sat at the computer and asked Him what He wanted to say on this date, my phone rang. When I answered the caller identified himself as Leon asking me for a donation to an organization doing research on cystic fibrosis. After a brief conversation I told Leon that I wanted to thank him for his call, and then offered him the blessing from Numbers 6:24-26. When I finished he said, "I am also a believer and I want to give you a blessing." He then quoted Psalm 103:1-5. When he came to the text verse for today, I knew this was Yahweh's answer to my prayer.

The eagle is the bird most frequently mentioned in the Bible—in 34 verses. This well-known creature has also been the national bird of the United States since 1782 when it was placed on the great seal of our nation, also appearing on the president's flag, military insignias, and on all $1 bills.

Why is the eagle so prominent in biblical as well as national venues? This majestic bird is known for its strength, courage, and swiftness—as well as for the care it gives to its young. The reference in our text is to the process of renewal an eagle experiences as it matures—new feathers are added as well as a stronger beak and claws. **Thus the message for you is that Yahweh "satisfies you with goodness; your youth is renewed like the eagle."**

As you walk through this new day, be mindful of Yahweh's goodness to you—such as His constant presence, His unchanging love and mercy, His gracious provisions for all your needs, His joy and peace—even in the midst of various trials, His assurance of life abundant and everlasting, His promises that give you hope, His resources of power that enable you to overcome the enemy, His Word that feeds your spirit, and—on and on! All these have the effect of renewing your spiritual youthfulness. So that, even as you age physically, you continue having a strong relationship with Him that makes you young at heart—with a song on your lips, a spring in your step, and a peace that passes all understanding. Be like an eagle! (Thanks for this, Leon!)

Yahweh in Your Worship

O Yahweh, Lord of my life, I do worship and adore You. You are the source of every blessing. Thank You for bringing continual renewal to me, both mentally and spiritually.

November 28

Yahweh Wants Me to Age with Purpose

Yahweh in the Word

"God, You have taught me from my youth, and I still proclaim Your wonderful works. Even when I am old and gray, God, do not abandon me. Then I will proclaim Your power to another generation, Your strength to all who are to come" (Psalm 71:17-18).

The psalmist affirmed his desire to continue being useful to Yahweh even in his older years. His primary concern was to pass on what he had learned about Yahweh's power and strength to the next generation.

Yahweh in Your Walk

Have you given much thought about what old age will mean to you, if you live that long? Some adults dream of retirement years when they will have free time for the things they have always wanted to do, such as travel, play golf, relax, enjoy hobbies, and other pursuits that bring pleasure. While each of these forms of interest can occupy one's time, a serious Christian will have a more mature outlook on the use of the remaining years of life. We must never retire from being useful to Yahweh. He has a meaningful and fruitful purpose for us as long as we live. As one person said, **"If you have a pulse, you have a purpose!"**

While it is often true that as we age we become less physically fit, it shouldn't be that way spiritually. Paul said, "We do not give up. Even though our outer person is being destroyed, our inner person is being renewed day by day... So we do not focus on what is seen, but on what is unseen. For what is seen is temporary, but what is unseen is eternal" (2 Corinthians 4:16, 18). An encouraging truth for us as we age is that **it is possible to become better as the years go by**—better in our outlook on life, a better sense of values, a better relationship with Yahweh and others, and a better worshiper of God. All these truths make aging attractive rather than something to fear and dread.

Years ago I was asked to officiate at the wedding of Mr. Tidwell who was 89 years old at the time. He said to me, "I believe a man should always have something to look forward to." Before he died several years later, his daughter-in-law asked him why he kept studying his Bible so diligently since his time of useful service was practically over. He replied, "I believe that when we get to heaven we will begin where we leave off on earth; I want to have a good start!"

The psalmist said in our text for today, "I will proclaim Your power to another generation, Your strength to all who come." His focus, as he aged, was not on himself and his pleasures but on the contribution he could make to those who followed him. **There is no such thing as retirement from serving Yahweh; as long as we live, He has a purpose for us that demands our best.**

Yahweh in Your Worship

Gracious Lord, thank You for giving me a reason for living as long as I breathe. I offer myself to fulfill that purpose with Your wisdom and strength. Help me grow better as I grow older.

November 29

Yahweh Wants Me to Learn to Wait for Him

Yahweh in the Word

> *"Yahweh is my light and my salvation—whom shall I fear? Yahweh is the stronghold of my life—of whom should I be afraid?.... I am certain that I will see Yahweh's goodness in the land of the living. Wait for Yahweh; be strong and courageous. Wait for Yahweh" (Ps. 27:1, 13-14).*

These words are an affirmation of David's confidence in Yahweh. He was certain that no matter what kind of difficulties he faced, Yahweh would bring him safety through.

Yahweh in Your Walk

The Thanksgiving season is a good time to remember individuals whom Yahweh has used to be a special blessing to you. As we give thanks for such friends, we must mention Jay and Marcia Franks. We first met them as members of the same Sunday School class; our relationship grew from that initial time of fellowship to a strong friendship. As we became better acquainted we recognized that they were among those servants of Yahweh who have a special gift of envisioning what He wants done. Several years ago they challenged us to work with them in planting a new church in our city. Our first meetings were in their home. Later we moved to a private school, then on to purchase the land and buildings of another church that were for sale.

Today this congregation is a thriving fellowship with a new sanctuary, fellowship hall, and offices—all because Yahweh used the Franks to plant a seed. In addition they have envisioned other projects for housing additions, a restaurant, and a downtown hotel. None of these dreams have come to pass as soon as they originally hoped—on each occasion they have learned to wait on Yahweh for His perfect timing. During their times of waiting, other challenges have arisen, such as several bouts with cancer. When we asked them for a favorite Scripture, they mentioned Psalm 27 and said, "In our darkest days we claim this Scripture and it always gets us through."

Have you learned the importance of waiting on Yahweh? We often want our plans to be fulfilled on our time schedule; however, He knows the right timing, the best timing. And in His wisdom, He teaches us to trust Him and wait upon His perfect plans. Think about this: **If God gave us what we want and when we want it, we would soon think we were God, not Him.** Waiting on Him helps us grow in humility and patience—essential virtues for Yahweh's children. So, let us say with the psalmist "But as for me, I trust in You, O Yahweh; I say, 'You are my God; my times are in Your hands'" (Psalm 31:14-15).

Yahweh in Your Worship

I worship You, O Yahweh, because You are my light and my salvation. You deliver me from all my fears. I choose to walk with You and wait for Your purposes to be fulfilled in me. Thank You for Your faithfulness and goodness. Help me be Your witness to those who do not know You.

November 30

Yahweh Wants Me to Grow towards Maturity

Yahweh in the Word

> *"Therefore, leaving the elementary message about the Messiah, let us go on to maturity, not laying again the foundation of repentance from dead works, faith in God, teaching about ritual washings, laying on of hands, the resurrection of the dead, and eternal judgment. And we will do this if God permits" (Hebrews 6:1-3).*

The writer of Hebrews was concerned for the spiritual growth of his readers. Some of them were behaving in an immature manner—not having grown spiritually. So, the writer tells them to stop laying the same foundation over and over, and grow on to maturity.

Yahweh in Your Walk

Can you point to evidence that reveals you to be more spiritually mature than you were one year ago? Another way of stating the same question is: Are you more Christ-like than you were a year ago? Christian maturity is not measured by how well you know the Bible or how often you attend church or how eloquently you can pray or even how many persons you have helped come to Christ as their Savior. All these personal achievements have their place, but they are not indicators of maturity. There is a fundamental difference between Christian works and maturity.

For example, I have two apple trees in my orchard; they have been developing for several years but this year, for the first time, they have produced many apples—they have reached maturity. In a similar manner, your new life began with a new birth, followed by years of growing in faith, acquiring knowledge of truth, serving in various ministries—but what about bearing fruit? That is—the fruit of the Spirit—namely love, joy, peace, patience, kindness, goodness, faith, gentleness, and self-control (Galatians 5:22-23). These nine virtues describe the life of Christ; He is the measurement of spiritual maturity. **To be a mature Christian is to be like Christ.**

You may respond to this truth by thinking—this is not possible; I try as hard as I can, but there is no way I can ever be as good as Jesus. You are exactly right! **Christian maturity is not a matter of you doing your best to be like Him; rather, this kind of maturity is Him living His life in and through you.** Your part is not trying harder, rather, yielding yourself to His control and allowing Him to live His life in you. And you can do this! As one teacher has aptly said, "The Christian life is not my old life made over; it is His life taking over." The apostle Paul put the truth in these words, "I am crucified with Christ; nevertheless I live, yet not I but Christ lives in me" (Galatians 2:19-20). As you begin this day, submit to His control; let His life be yours.

Yahweh in Your Worship

Holy Father, thank You for providing a totally new life for me. Teach me to live this life today. Remind me often that You are my life; be in full control of all I think, say, and do.

Yahweh Is the Most High God

Yahweh in the Word

"I will sing about the name of Yahweh the Most High" (Psalm 7:17).

Here is another combination of God's name: Yahweh the Most High (El Elyon, pronounced EL el-YON). We find this expression many times in the Old Testament. Yahweh's people were surrounded by various groups who worshipped many gods. He wanted to make certain that His people knew that Yahweh was the God above all other so-called gods, who were not real gods at all. Yahweh is the only true and living God—Yahweh El Elyon (I AM the Most High God).

Yahweh in Your Walk

Today as you are exposed to various forms of media you may come in contact with the commonly-held belief that there are many real gods that people worship. Or you may meet someone who believes there are many ways to reach the one true God, whoever that may be. Many people believe that all religions are simply different roads which ultimately lead to heaven. They consider conservative Christians to be very narrow-minded and unwilling to compromise their beliefs.

As followers of Yahweh, we look to the Bible as the final authority in all matters regarding truth about Him and the way to a meaningful relationship with Him. God's Word is very clear in its revelation of Yahweh as God, the Father, Son, and Holy Spirit—all expressions of the One true God. Our Lord Jesus (Yeshua) was specific when He stated, "I am the way, the truth, and the life. No one comes to the Father except through Me" (John 14:6). Yeshua is not one of many ways to the true and living God—Yahweh; He is, in fact, the only way.

David begins this seventh psalm with this strong affirmation: "Yahweh my God" (v.1) which he repeats in verse 3, "Yahweh my God." Then he ends the song with our text for today, "I will sing about the name of Yahweh the Most High God" (verse 17)**. As you walk through this day, give your own expression to this same great declaration, either spoken or perhaps in a song you compose.** Such a personal affirmation will bless Him as well as you. You will be joining a vast multitude on earth and in heaven who are proclaiming this glorious truth.

Yahweh in Your Worship

Yes, Yahweh El Elyon, I agree with all who choose to celebrate who You are—the God Most High. You are the only true and living God. Thank You for choosing to make Yourself known to me. My desire is for You to have complete control of all I think, do, and say today. Remind me to share with others the truth of who You are. I want to be a bold witness of the good news regarding eternal life as Your free gift to all who will accept it by faith.

December 2

Yahweh, the Most High God, Delivers Me from All My Enemies

Yahweh in the Word

> *"Abram is blessed by God Most High, Creator of heaven and earth, and I give praise to God Most High who has handed over your enemies to you.... Abram said to the king of Sodom, 'I have raised my hand in an oath to Yahweh God Most High, Creator of heaven and earth....'" (Genesis 14:19-22).*

The first quote in this passage comes from a man named Melchizedek who was the king of Salem. He pronounced this blessing upon Abram because he had overcome all the armies of his enemies. Abram responded by giving praise to Yahweh God Most High (Yahweh El Elyon) who had led him in this series of victories.

Yahweh in Your Walk

Do you have any enemies? There may be persons who have caused you various kinds of problems; perhaps you consider them to be enemies. However, **all followers of the Lord Jesus have a common enemy.** The apostle Paul identified this enemy in these sobering words: "Our battle is not against flesh and blood, but against the world powers of this darkness, against the spiritual forces of evil in the heavens" (Ephesians 6:12). In other words, Satan and all his demons are our real personal enemies. Sometimes these adversaries work through people to attack us, but the real enemy is this supreme evil one—the devil. If we choose to fight against people, we are not dealing with the real enemy who is Satan working through them.

    As you walk through this day, do not be surprised if this sinister adversary attacks you in some subtle manner. We are cautioned in the Bible to be constantly on guard against him. We also are assured that Satan is a defeated enemy and cannot harm us if we take up the armor Yahweh has provided (See Ephesians 6:13-17), and place our trust in Yahweh El Elyon—the One who has already won the battle for us. As we are reminded: "We are more than victorious through Him who loved us" (Romans 8:37). **Yes, Yahweh, the Most High God is on our side, delivering us from all our enemies by His strong right hand.**

    Our Lord Jesus chose to give us the best example of how to deal with Satan. When tempted by this enemy, Jesus responded by quoting Scriptures—three times. This shows us the way to overcome the tempter. **We must hide Yahweh's Word in our hearts and use it as the "Sword of the Spirit."**

Yahweh in Your Worship

O Yahweh, I seize this day of opportunities, knowing You are always with me. Thank You for saving me from every enemy for Your Name's sake. You are my Rock and my Salvation. I stand firm against every foe in Your strong Name—Yahweh El Elyon.

December 3

Yahweh Is Awe-inspiring

Yahweh in the Word

> *"Yahweh, the Most High (Elyon) is awe-inspiring, a great King over all the earth" (Psalm 47:2).*

Psalm 47 is a jubilant song of praise to Yahweh. The writer admonishes worshipers to clap their hands, shout to God, sound trumpets, and sing praise to Him. All this is to be done in celebration of Yahweh Elyon (the Most High God). He is described as the One who subdues nations as the great King over all the earth.

Yahweh in Your Walk

Can you recall times when you have felt a strong sense of awe? My wife and I traveled to Switzerland several years ago with a group led by our friends, Sam and Yvonne Satterfield. On a Sunday morning they took us on a bus high into the Alps where we gathered on a mountainside for a time of worship. The Satterfields had been there numerous times and knew just the place where we would all be awed by the beauty of that remarkable alpine setting. I have a vivid memory of the grandeur of those awesome majestic mountain peaks all around us as we sang "How Great Thou Art." The reading of passages from the Psalms added to our meaningful experience of worship.

And we have had many other awe-some times in view of Yahweh's amazing works of creation.

However, by far **the most impressive acts of Yahweh are found in His deeds in the lives of His people.** Recently I attended the memorial service for an overseas missionary named Alta Lee Lovegren. She and her husband August served for some 36 years as medical missionaries in Jordan. As I listened to friends and family members relate the acts of compassion performed by this couple, I was struck by a sense of awe. Not so much by what they did, but what Yahweh Elyon did whom they served so faithfully. There were countless people in that Arab country who saw Jesus, the Great Physician, in the actions of this dedicated couple.

Wherever you may go today, seize those opportunities to be a faithful representative of Yahweh Elyon. Allow Him to reveal His greatness through your acts of kindness and mercy. Others may not have a sense of awe about you, but you can point them to your awesome Lord. He is the ultimate Source of all that fills us with wonder and amazement.

Yahweh in Your Worship

I do sing for joy to You, most awesome Yahweh. Words are so inadequate to express the gratitude I feel for Your greatness and goodness. How great You are! Help me to be more aware of the evidence of Your presence and power in the persons I will meet today. I trust You to be glorified through all I do this day. **Forgive me for not taking the time each day to see the wonder of Your presence and work in the lives of people around me.**

Yahweh Is My Spiritual Father

Yahweh in the Word

> *"Yahweh, You are our Father, we are the clay and You are the potter; we all are the work of Your hands" (Isaiah 64:8).*

These are the words of Israel, Yahweh's chosen people. The Hebrew word for father is ***avinu*** (pronounced ah-VEN-u). Since all believers are Yahweh's family, we can also address Him as Yahweh Avinu. He has begotten us, both by creating us and by the new birth we received through believing in the Lord Jesus. Notice that this text describes Yahweh not only as our Father but also as the One who formed us, like a potter forms the clay—we are the work of His hands. He shaped us into the person we are—amazing miracle!

Yahweh in Your Walk

Jesus' favorite term for Yahweh is **Father**. He gave us a Model Prayer beginning with "Our Father in heaven." When we think of Yahweh as Father, we are reminded of the personal, intimate relationship we can have with Him. Just as a good human father gives care and attention to his child, so does Yahweh to us.

Give thought today to your own earthly father. Do you recall memories of good times with him? Hopefully, yours was a kind, thoughtful daddy who sought to mold you into the kind of person you should become. **Pause to thank Yahweh for this human example of His personal care for you.** My own dad was a special gift from Yahweh to me; I saw in his treatment of me what true fatherhood is all about. We spent many hours hiking and camping in the great outdoors. I learned from him to have an appreciation for the One who created all the wonders of nature.

Most important is the fact that with Yahweh as our Father, we are a part of His forever family. All believers of all the ages are our brothers and sisters because Yahweh Avinu gave us a spiritual birth into this eternal family. Think of the security this relationship gives. He not only cares for us and is now molding us, like a potter; He also provides for every need we have. And Yahweh knows our needs better than we do. **Walk at peace through this day, assured that your Father watches over you with His loving protection and care.**

Yahweh in Your Worship

Father, I love You because You first loved me and created me according to Your good plan and purpose. Today, I celebrate this truth and want to seize every opportunity to enjoy Your family. Thank You for adopting me into Your forever family. I want Your likeness to be seen in me through attitudes and actions that accurately reflect Your character. Use me to extend Your family by being a bold witness of the Gospel. May the good news of Your eternal love and mercy be communicated clearly through me.

December 5

Yahweh Will Lead Me This Day in the Way that Is Best

Yahweh in the Word

> "He (Yahweh) renews my life; He leads me along the right paths" (Psalm 23:3).

These familiar words from the 23rd Psalm remind us of the way a shepherd leads his sheep in the way that is best for them. David was probably the writer of these words which were written out of his experience as a shepherd boy. He remembered the many times he had led his sheep along still waters and on to the green pastures.

Yahweh in Your Walk

Not far from our house is a railroad track. Several times each day a train passes by. A road crosses the track about one mile away and I can hear the train's horn sounding to warn drivers to give a right of way. Early one morning as the train passed by I thought of how **this was an illustration of the life of a child of Yahweh.**

Just as a train follows a track that has been laid out in advance, so Yahweh has a path for us to follow each day. This path is the way He wants us to follow—for our welfare and for His glory. Also, the train engine reminds me of Yahweh's power, going before me and providing all the strength I need to follow Him. Just as a train gets all its power from the engine, so we have the indwelling resource of His Spirit all along our journey through each day.

The engineer who sits next to the engine is in full control of all that happens—all the starts and stops, all speeding up and slowing down, all turns and signals. He is like the Holy Spirit who gives guidance, including starts, stops, speed ups and slowdowns—to our daily experiences. The engineer also sounds the horn to clear the track of any hindrance, just as Yahweh's Spirit clears the way of whatever may hinder our progress along the path of life.

We are like the boxcars; each of us carries the cargo given us to be used by someone at the end of the line. In our case the cargo is the Good News about eternal life in Yeshua, as well as the outpouring of this life in loving service to others. **So what is our responsibility? Stay attached to the engine! We do this by abiding in Yahweh, keeping in close fellowship with Him by obeying His commands.**

Next time you hear or see a train, let it remind you of these basic truths. **ALL ABOARD!!**

Yahweh in Your Worship

Thank You precious Yahweh for laying out the best track for me today, and clearing the way. Surely you give me all the power and control I ever need. Help me stay attached to You. May the cargo be delivered through me where You have sent it—and right on time!

December 6

Yahweh Loves Me with an Everlasting Love

Yahweh in the Word

> "This is what Yahweh says, 'I have loved you with an everlasting love; therefore, I have continued to extend faithful love to you'" (Jeremiah 31:3).

Yahweh told Jeremiah to write on a scroll His messages to His people. This statement regarding His love is a small portion of those messages. Although much of what Yahweh had to say through Jeremiah had to do with warnings of impending judgment, even that was an expression of Yahweh's everlasting love for His people. If they had heeded those warnings, they would have been spared much suffering. Yahweh was expressing "tough love" to His children. The Hebrew word used here for faithful love is ***chesed***, meaning "enduring love." Yahweh assures His people that the love He has for them is "everlasting" and will not change with time.

Yahweh in Your Walk

Most marriages in our culture occur because two people claim to love one another and plan to spend their remaining years together. However, in a large number of cases, this so-called love doesn't last and a divorce occurs. Human affection is largely an emotion, and emotions are not lasting; they change rather easily and often. One person has described romantic love this way: "Love is a feeling you feel when you feel like you are having a feeling you have never felt before!" And feelings change.

Fortunately for us, Yahweh's love is more than a feeling of affection. His love is an expression of His very nature. Yahweh loves in the sense that He cares for all persons and is committed to provide the best for them, even to the extreme of giving Himself (on a cross) for them. And this love is everlasting, unchanging, and available to everyone.

As you walk through this day, and every day, you do so with the absolute assurance that Yahweh loves you with an everlasting love and He extends this faithful love to you. Let me encourage you to make the choice to believe this truth, and therefore face whatever comes your way with a sense of peace and security.

How about becoming Yahweh's witness of this love to others? Allow Him to love others through you—be His instrument of enduring love in practical ways. Ask Him to show you how you can seize opportunities today to manifest His everlasting love to others—beginning at home.

Yahweh in Your Worship

I celebrate Your love, most merciful Yahweh. How blest I am to know from personal experience that Your love is everlasting. I offer myself this day to be alert to those about me who need love. Use me to express Your love in practical ways; I want to be Your servant wherever I am.

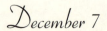

Yahweh Calls for Me to Remember His Acts of Mercy

Yahweh in the Word

> *"Then Moses said to the people, "Remember this day when you came out of Egypt, out of the place of slavery, for Yahweh brought you out of here by the strength of His hand" (Deuteronomy 13:3).*

The Jewish Feast of Passover was a solemn annual celebration that commemorated Yahweh's miraculous deliverance of His people from bondage in Egypt. Moses told the people that the purpose for this observance was to help them remember Yahweh's favor to them. There are many other references in Scripture to the importance of remembering Yahweh's blessings.

Yahweh in Your Walk

Today, December 7, is National Pearl Harbor Remembrance Day. On this date in 1941 the navy and aircraft of the Imperial Japanese Navy staged a surprise attack on the U.S. army and naval base in Honolulu, Hawaii. Huge losses of ships, airplanes, and lives were sustained. As a result the U.S. declared war on Japan and thus began WWII for our nation. This annual memorial day serves to remind us of the importance of being diligent to defend our nation.

Yahweh knows how easy it is for us to forget, even important events. For this reason He has made certain that we have reminders. Perhaps the most significant happening for His people to remember is described in these familiar words of Yeshua, "This do in remembrance of Me" (Luke 22:19). He spoke this during the first Lord's Supper. The elements of bread and the fruit of the vine were symbols of His body and blood which would soon be offered as a sacrifice for all the sins of the world.

I was a young boy during the years of WWII, and I can recall the words, "Remember Pearl Harbor" being repeated often—on public posters, songs, and other media. **For a far more important reason we need the regular reminder of the Lord's Supper to remember the sacrifice of our Lord and Savior.** Let me encourage you to take advantage of every opportunity for observing a communion service with your church family. Such a reminder is needed by all believers, lest we forget our indebtedness to Him who gave Himself in our place. I find the experience of handling the bread and cup to be very helpful in keeping my memory focused on this most vivid revelation of Yahweh's love for me. In fact, I begin each day with a cup (of coffee) and a small piece of bread to obey His command, "This do in remembrance of Me."

Yahweh in Your Worship

Gracious Yahweh, Thank You for giving me a way to remember Your gift of life. I must never forget Your sacrifice in sending Your Son to be my Savior and Lord. Help me be faithful to participate regularly in the Lord's Supper services of my church.

December 8

Yeshua (Jesus) Invites Me to Follow Him

Yeshua in the Word

> "Summoning the crowd along with His disciples, He said to them, 'If anyone wants to be My follower, he must deny himself, take up his cross, and follow Me. For whoever loses his life because of Me and the gospel will save it. For what does it benefit a man to gain the whole world yet lose his life?'" (Mark 8:34-36).

The call to follow Yeshua is found in all four Gospels, a total of twenty-five times. This invitation was Jesus' favorite way to gain disciples. Those who first heard these words came from many varied backgrounds and life-styles, yet the invitation was the same for all.

Yeshua in Your Walk

All of us have chosen to follow someone or something; we are born followers. And to be followers we must meet various criteria. Jesus made clear the requirements for being His follower; these are the most demanding made by any leader. **According to Jesus three words sum up these necessary requirements: deny, die, and obey.**

1. In order to follow Jesus you must *deny* yourself. To deny means to say no. Denying yourself means saying no to yourself. You make a deliberate choice to no longer live your way but His way. This decision is also known as repentance—to change your way of thinking. Rather than make decisions the way your normal human nature would do, you choose His way—self-denial.

2. In order to follow Jesus you must *die* to yourself. The cross meant death to Jesus. To "take up your cross" means that you not only deny yourself but also choose to die to yourself—to self-centered living. Rather than living for yourself, you seek to live for Him. Jesus' promise is that the person who decides to lose his life for His sake will actually be saving real life.

3. In order to *obey* Jesus you must first know His commands and then seek to obey them. On one occasion He said, "I give you a new command: Love one another. Just as I have loved you, you must also love one another" (John 13:34). Obeying this command must become priority in how you treat others. Other commands are found throughout the Gospels. To obey these means you must become a serious student of this biblical material, then seek to conform to all He requires.

As you walk through each day, be seriously committed to following Jesus in all these ways.

Yeshua in Your Worship

Lord Yeshua, thank You for calling me to follow You. I want to seize the opportunity to be Your true disciple this and every day. My dependence is totally upon You for the strength to do this. Teach me to take up my cross daily and faithfully follow You by obeying Your commands.

Yahweh Wants Me to Possess My Possessions

Yahweh in the Word

> "But on Mount Zion there shall be deliverance, and there shall be holiness; the house of Jacob shall possess their possessions" (Obadiah 17, NKJV).

The Book of Obadiah is the shortest of the Old Testament. As one commentator says, "Obadiah is the most minor of the Minor Prophets!" However, this little known servant of Yahweh had an important message for His chosen people. He declared in a few words that Yahweh loved His people and would protect them from their enemies, the Edomites. Their future would be good as His people would rise up and possess what Yahweh had promised them.

Yahweh in Your Walk

I read the sad story of a man who lived in poverty for many years, not knowing that his deceased parents had left a large amount of money for him in a local bank. He had simply failed to claim his inheritance. And yet, this is a picture of many of Yahweh's children who have never claimed their inheritance; they have not possessed their possession. **We are children of the King who has promised great spiritual riches, but these treasures must be claimed by faith.**

Yahweh promised the descendants of Jacob that the day was coming when they would be able to claim what was rightfully theirs. In the final three verses of this brief message from Obadiah, he refers five times to them possessing these promised possessions. Here is Yahweh's message to you: "Exercise your faith by laying claim to all the spiritual riches available to you in Yeshua."

Let's examine some of these riches to see if you have possessed them. First, Yahweh's greatest legacy for His children is His own eternal and abundant life. This life is available to us in Jesus Christ, but we must claim it by welcoming Him into our hearts. **Second,** He has given His own Holy Spirit to live in us, empowering us to be and do all Yahweh has planned for us. By receiving Jesus, we also have His Spirit as a permanent Counselor, Teacher, and Comforter. **Next,** He promises to hear and answer our every prayer, providing everything we need, according to His will. But we must ask in faith. **One more**—the blessed hope of spending eternity with Him and all His family in Heaven.

What does all this mean in a practical sense? If you have truly claimed this rightful inheritance, you now have possessed your possessions. **Begin living like the spiritually wealthy person you are.** Do not ever give in to the "poor me" mentally that so many people have. **You are a child of the King! Live like one by continuing to rejoice in the riches of your inheritance.**

Yahweh in Your Worship

Thank You, Yahweh, for all the riches You have provided for me. Today, I choose to seize this wealth and enjoy it fully. All praise and honor belong to You.

December 10

Yahweh Has a Purpose for Me Living at This Particular Time

Yahweh in the Word

> "Who knows, perhaps you have come to your royal position for such a time as this"(Esther 4:14).

The book of Esther is unique in Scripture. There is no mention of God or prayer in this story of a woman who played a significant role in the history of Yahweh's chosen people. Neither is this book or its main characters mentioned in the New Testament. However, this narrative clearly reveals the divine hand at work behind the scenes. Yahweh had a purpose for this woman in His unfolding plan for His people. She made herself available to Him for fulfilling that purpose.

Yahweh in Your Walk

Do you ever wonder why you are living at this particular time in history? Why has Yahweh chosen to place you where you are and in your unique set of circumstances? Why were you born where you were born? Is there some special reason for you being where you are at this given time? Why are you who you are? All these are legitimate questions—questions worthy of your thought. The ultimate answer to all these queries is the fact that Yahweh is sovereign over all creation. He is the one who decides when we arrive, as well as where, and who we are to be. All these matters are beyond our control. **Our part in Yahweh's scheme of things is to determine to be all He would have us to be—to fulfill His divine will and purpose for our being**.

The words of our text remind me of what David said in Psalm 31:14, words I repeat every morning upon leaving my bed, "But as for me, I trust in You O Yahweh; I say, 'You are my God. My times are in Your hand.'" We never know what a day will bring forth—what situations we will face, some totally unexpected, and even unwanted. What we do know is that Yahweh knows all things, the end from the beginning. **The wisest and safest decision we can make is to place our times in His hands—our experiences in His control.**

There are two different Greek words translated by the English word *time* in the New Testament. One is ***chronos*** meaning time in general; the other is ***kairos*** meaning a moment of opportunity and favor. This second term best describes our living at this "time," this moment of opportunity for fulfilling Yahweh's purpose for us. Just as with Esther, we were born for "such a time" (opportunity) as this. **How exciting to know Yahweh placed us where we are, at this particular time, to be all He needs us to be. Let's go for it!'**

Yahweh in Your Worship

Sovereign Yahweh, You hold all things in Your hands. I trust You to work Your purpose through me today. Help me seize every opportunity to honor You and be Your witness. Show me Your purpose in what happens to me at all times. Forgive my doubts about my life counting for You. Thank You for placing me where I am and creating me to be who I am—for Your purpose.

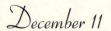

Yahweh Wants Me to Grow Spiritually

Yahweh in the Word

"Grow in the grace and knowledge of our Lord and Savior Jesus Christ. To Him be the glory both now and to the day of eternity" (2 Peter 3:18).

The apostle Peter wrote this second letter to warn believers about false teachers who would seek to lead them astray. His challenge was for them to overcome this departure from truth by growing stronger in their relationship with Jesus, thus giving glory to Him.

Yahweh in Your Walk

Our granddaughter, Jordan, lives a full day's drive away from us. She comes for a visit two or three times a year. Ever since she was just a toddler we have measured her growth in height each time she comes. We keep marks on the wall in our garage to record this progress. Growing taller is natural for her and all children. But far more important than physical growth is her progress in areas that cannot be measured by a ruler. We find greater pleasure as we see her development in character and in knowledge—her mental and spiritual growth.

Simon Peter knew the importance of gaining maturity in the "grace and knowledge of our Lord and Savior Jesus Christ." He had painful memories of the consequences of his own immaturity—that behavior he showed when he denied the Lord. **And so he calls on his readers to grow spiritually and thus overcome the temptation to follow false teachers**.

We know the steps to take for solid physical growth—eating right foods, exercising, getting proper rest, and avoiding diseases. But what are the requirements for spiritual growth? Peter mentions the most important one in these words from his first letter: "Like newborn infants, desire the pure spiritual milk, so that you may grow by it for your salvation, since you have tasted that the Lord is good" (1 Peter 2:2). The Bible provides the "pure spiritual milk" that every Christian needs for growth. **However, we must make the effort to feed on that food.**

How are you measuring up spiritually? Can you—and others—notice signs of growth in this area? I have a friend whose motto is "No Bible, no breakfast." He disciplines himself to spend time in Bible study every morning, before he eats breakfast. Find a system of regular, daily feeding on the Word that works for you, then stay with it—and grow even beyond it. Just going to church and performing various kinds of service will not nourish your spirit.

Yahweh in Your Worship

I bless You, O Bread of Life, for providing all I need to grow in Your grace and knowledge. Help me be more devoted to pursuing spiritual growth. And to do so, not for my pleasure or boasting, but for Your glory, "both now and to the day of eternity."

December 12

Yahweh Uses that Which Is Small

Yahweh in the Word

> "Bethlehem Ephrathah, you are small among the clans of Judah; One will come from you to be ruler over Israel for Me. His origin is from antiquity, from eternity... He will stand and shepherd them in the strength of Yahweh, in the majestic name of Yahweh His God" (Micah 5:2, 4).

The prophet Micah, whose name means "Who is like Yahweh?" wrote these prophetic words about 750 years before the birth of Jesus. Bethlehem was David's hometown, a village located near Jerusalem. Although small, it was the birthplace of Jesus as predicted in this text.

Yahweh in Your Walk

Our culture places a premium on that which is large, whether athletes or schools or armies or arsenals or populations or wealth—if it is large it must be good. Not so in terms of biblical happenings. Yahweh has often chosen that which is small to accomplish huge results. Remember young David, the small shepherd boy who slew the giant Goliath? How about Gideon and his army of 300 men who overcame an enemy numbering thousands? On another occasion a small boy was used by Yahweh to deliver the apostle Paul from almost certain death (Acts 16:23-32). **The biblical evidence is clear that Yahweh often uses that which seems small to accomplish great results.** We could well conclude that one person, plus Yahweh, is always a majority.

What about you, do you see yourself as being rather small in comparison to those who have great wealth, talent, and skills? Have you ever thought to yourself: I will never amount to much; I'm just an ordinary, rather insignificant person? Let me assure you, Yahweh does not see you in that manner. He knows your potential when your small abilities and talents are placed in His mighty hands. When you read the biographies of many people who were used by Yahweh to accomplish great things, you will find that most of them had small beginnings in small places.

Yahweh delights in accomplishing His purposes by using that which the world sees as small. One reason for this is the fact that the credit for such achievements goes to Him rather than the instrument He uses. My wife and I often talk about the small town we came from and how our parents had such small means. We marvel at the opportunities Yahweh has given us, not because we were persons with great potential in ourselves, but because we have sought to be available to Him. We have learned from experience that **Yahweh uses nobodies to become somebodies so that everybody will honor Him.**

Yahweh in Your Worship

O Lord my God, how great Thou art! Apart from You, I am nothing. But by Your grace and power, I can become and perform all that pleases You. I offer myself to You this day. Help me see the large potential in that which appears to be small in myself and in others.

December 13

Yeshua Wants Me to Be Gentle and Humble

Yeshua in the Word

> "All of you, take up My yoke and learn from Me, because I am gentle and humble in heart, and you will find rest for yourselves. For My yoke is easy and My burden is light" (Matthew 11:29-30).

In New Testament times a double "yoke" was often used for training young work animals. An older, larger ox or donkey would be yoked to a smaller animal to train them to pull a plow or cart. Students were also said to be "yoked" to a teacher for the purpose of learning from him. Here Jesus uses this metaphor to invite followers to learn from Him. He described Himself as being a teacher who was "gentle and humble in heart."

Yeshua in Your Walk

Would some friend of yours describe you as being gentle and humble in heart? If not, you have some changes to make if your desire is to be like Jesus. There were times when Jesus displayed anger and strong actions, such as the occasion when He drove the money-changers out of the temple area. His strong rebuke of the scribes and Pharisees is another expression of righteous indignation. These examples show Jesus as a strong person who stood boldly against hypocrisy, however, His basic nature was that of gentleness and humility. What do these virtues mean?

The term translated "gentle" basically refers to a controlled spirit, the opposite of self-assertiveness and self-interest—a person who is meek, mild, and gentle—not in the sense of weakness but of strength under control. Listen to the apostle Paul's use of this word in writing to the Corinthian church: "Now I, Paul, make a personal appeal to you by the gentleness and graciousness of Christ—I who am humble among you in person but bold toward you when absent" (2 Corinthians 10:1). Paul reflected these Christ-like characteristics to the Corinthians.

We are more familiar with the meaning of humility—just the opposite of pride. A humble Christian is one who is dependent on Christ, not seeking to promote himself; a person who is easy to get along with, not set on his own way—one who has strong convictions but is not overbearing. **As you walk through this day, give attention to becoming more like Jesus—more gentle and humble in heart.** Of course, you cannot produce these virtues yourself; they are the fruit of the Holy Spirit. Surrender yourself to Him and let Him live through you.

Yeshua in Your Worship

Blessed Lord Jesus, I worship You for being gentle and humble in heart toward me. Help me seize those opportunities to show these same virtues toward others today. Deliver me from any attitude that does not reflect Your likeness. I long to be more like You in every way. Help me begin this practice with my family members.

December 14

Yahweh Is Always Ready to Guide Me

Yahweh in the Word

> *"Yahweh will always lead you, satisfy you in a parched land, and strengthen your bones. You will be like a watered garden and like a spring whose waters never run dry" (Isaiah 58:11).*

These words from the prophet Isaiah refer to Israel's restoration from captivity in Babylon. Yahweh promises to guide them to a new life of health and prosperity if they will keep His covenant with them. The same promise is available today to all who place their trust in Him.

Yahweh in Your Walk

Many who travel by cars this holiday season will use a device known as a GPS (Global Positioning System) which operates off a satellite. There are always 24 to 32 satellites orbiting the Earth at an altitude of 12,500 miles. A constant signal from at least four of these satellites enables a receiver inside the car to display the best route for a driver to follow. Although these devices are not infallible, they can be very helpful.

All Yahweh's people have a different kind of GPS—**God's Positioning System**! He knows exactly where we are at all times, and the best route in life for us to take. **The wisest decision we can make is to commit our way to Him, trusting Him for His guidance continually.** Here is a good promise to memorize and claim often: "Trust in Yahweh with all your heart, and do not rely on your own understanding; think about Him in all your ways, and He will guide you on the right paths" (Proverbs. 3:5-6).

An interesting episode regarding divine guidance is the familiar story of how the wise men found their way from their home (probably in Babylon or Persia) to the house where the infant Jesus was. Matthew tells us that after they arrived in Jerusalem, they asked, "Where is He who has been born King of the Jews? For we saw His star in the east and have come to worship Him." When King Herod heard about this, he asked the Jewish leaders where the Messiah would be born. They replied, "In Bethlehem of Judah" as was written by the prophet Micah. As the wise men proceeded, the star they had seen in the east led them right to Jesus! (Matthew 2:1-12.) How about that for GPS!

Your experience today regarding Yahweh's guidance may not be as dramatic as the wise men, but if you will claim His promise, He will definitely lead you "in the paths of righteousness for His name's sake" (Psalm 23:3)—not only today but every day.

Yahweh in Your Worship

I joyfully seize this moment in time to give expression to my heartfelt adoration of the One who leads me from day to day. May You, O Yahweh, be exalted and glorified in all the earth.

December 15

Yahweh Wants Me to Be a Coworker with Him

Yahweh in the Word

> "What then is Apollos? And what is Paul? They are servants through whom you believed, and each has the role the Lord has given. I planted, Apollos watered, but God gave the growth. So then neither the one who plants nor the one who waters is anything, but only God who gives the growth. Now the one planting and the one watering are one in purpose, and each will receive his own reward according to his own labor. For we are God's coworkers" (1 Corinthians 3:5-9).

The Corinthian Christians were expressing their spiritual immaturity by causing divisions in the church over who was the most important and therefore favorite leader—Paul, who founded (planted) the church or Apollos, who came later to (water) help the believers grow. Paul rebuked them for this childish behavior (vv. 1-4) and explained in this text the true role that he and Apollos had played in the establishment of this church.

Yahweh in Your Walk

One of my favorite hobbies is vegetable gardening. The most enjoyable part for me is planting the seeds and watching them grow to become productive plants. But sometimes the seeds just won't sprout and come up out of the ground. **Nothing I can do will make the seeds grow.** I can plant and water them, but I can't force them to grow. Only Yahweh can make a seed produce a plant that bears fruit. He has His role and I have mine; we are coworkers.

The same principle applies to kingdom work. We plant the seeds of the gospel by sharing this good news with others, but only Yahweh can make the seeds sprout and grow and produce believers. What a privilege to be a kingdom coworker with Him! Annie Johnson Flint expressed this truth in a thought-provoking poem; here are the words of the first stanza:

> Christ has no hands but our hands to do His work today.
> He has no feet but our feet to lead men in the way.
> He has no tongue but our tongue to tell men how He died.
> He has no help but our help to bring them to His side.

As you walk through this day, watch for opportunities to be a coworker with Yahweh. Ask Him to use your hands, feet, ears, and voice, to help make a difference for others. Seek to be sensitive to ways He may accomplish His work through you. Remember you are a laborer together with Him. Make certain you do your part well, and that He receives all the praise.

Yahweh in Your Worship

O Yahweh, how blessed am I to be a co-laborer with You. Thank You for choosing me to be Your instrument to accomplish Your purpose today. Help me be an effective tool in Your hands.

December 16

Yahweh Promises Me a New Heaven and a New Earth

Yahweh in the Word

"For I will create a new heaven and a new earth; the past events will not be remembered or come to mind. Then be glad and rejoice forever in what I am creating; and I will create Jerusalem to be a joy and its people to be a delight. I will rejoice in Jerusalem and be glad in My people. The sound of weeping and crying will no longer be heard in her" (Isaiah 65:17-19).

These are Yahweh's words to His people concerning their future home. **The promise of a new heaven and new earth is found several times in the Bible. Yahweh's plan is to restore the earth to its original purity and righteousness.** Only He knows when this will happen, but such a reality gives us hope and comfort.

Yahweh in Your Walk

The first chapter of Genesis describes the original creation of the heavens and the earth. Following this amazing miracle, the text says, "God saw all that He had made, and it was very good" (Genesis 1:31). But something tragic happened to spoil the goodness of Yahweh's creation—sin came through the disobedience of Adam and Eve. As the result of their transgression, Yahweh declared, "The ground is cursed because of you" (Genesis 3:17). Immediately, Yahweh began implementing His plan to make a new creation inhabited by a people who had been made truly righteous. Our text for this devotional is a clear expression of this future work of making a totally new heaven and earth.

The apostle John actually saw this miracle and gave his personal testimony: "Then I saw a new heaven and a new earth, the first heaven and the first earth had passed away, and the sea on longer existed... Then the One seated on the throne said, 'Look! I am making everything new'" (Revelation 21:1, 5). Thus the Bible is clear about a future restoration of Yahweh's original creation—one that will be characterized by righteousness and perfection.

How should this truth affect you as you walk through the days and years of your life on this less-than-perfect creation? The apostle Paul helps us answer this significant question as he wrote about his own conclusions in the light of what the future holds for all believers, "I consider that the sufferings of this present time are not worth comparing with the glory that is going to be revealed to us" (Romans 8:18). **We are on our way to a glorious future, one that cannot even be compared to present trials.** As C.S. Lewis wrote, "There are far, far better things ahead than any we leave behind."

Yahweh in Your Worship

Blessed Re-creator of all things, I humble myself before You in absolute amazement of Your plans for the future. Thank You for including me and all Your forever family.

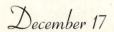

Yahweh Promises Me Ultimate Freedom from All Pain and Tears

Yahweh in the Word

> "Then I heard a loud voice from the throne: 'Look! God's dwelling is with humanity, and He will live with them. They will be His people, and God Himself will be with them and be their God. He will wipe away every tear from their eyes. Death will no longer exist; grief, crying, and pain will exist no longer, because the previous things have passed away'" (Revelation 21:3-4).

The apostle John reported what he heard in the vision given him by Yahweh. Here is a revelation of what will happen in the future—Yahweh will dwell among His people in the new heaven and the new earth (v. 1). He will wipe away all tears by removing the occasion for tears—death, grief, crying, and pain. All these expressions of sorrow will be gone forever.

Yahweh in Your Walk

Today, as every day, you will observe some kind of sorrow—some occasion for the tears of grief. Either through the news media or by personal experience, you will be confronted with the sadness that comes from pain or death. We have learned that this is a part of human life that is very predictable. Our Lord said to His followers, "You will have suffering in this world. Be courageous, I have conquered the world" (John 16:33). This promise applied not only to those original disciples but to all who came later. **This world and this body in which we live have been affected by sin, and sin always brings some kind of pain.**

The good news to us pain-bearers is that the end of all suffering, and the pain and tears that go with it, will come to an end. Our text gives emphasis to the personal care of Yahweh for His people—"He will wipe away every tear from their eyes." We can all remember how when we were hurt our mother comforted and consoled us by taking us in her arms and tenderly wiping away all tears from our eyes as she spoke kind words to us. **Yahweh's promise is that He will remove, not only "every tear" from our eyes but also the cause of our tears—forever.** An old gospel hymn contains these lines:

> I am bound for the Promised Land; I am bound for the Promised Land.
> O who will come and go with me? I am bound for the Promised Land.
> No chilling winds nor poisonous breath can reach that healthful shore;
> sickness and sorrow, pain and death are felt and feared no more (Samuel Stennett).

Remember that today you are one day closer to this place which Yeshua has gone to prepare for you. **Take comfort in the midst of present grief to affirm your assurance that, for a believer in Christ, the best is always yet to be.**

Yahweh in Your Worship

Thank You, Holy Father, for the assurance You give me of the end of all sorrow and grief.

December 18

Yahweh's Timing for Me Is Always Perfect

Yahweh in the Word

> "When the time came to completion, God sent His Son, born of a woman, born under the law, to redeem those under the law, so that we might receive adoption as sons" (Galatians 4:4-5).

Paul wrote these words to believers in the churches to affirm Yahweh's perfect timing in the birth of His Son. As a result of His coming, all who believe in Him become children of God by means of adoption.

Yahweh in Your Walk

One week from today will be Christmas day. You have noticed how commercialized this sacred event has become. So much emphasis on gifts, parties, and even church activities tends to take away from the true meaning of this special time. **Our devotionals for this week will be an attempt to help keep your focus on the real message of Christmas.**

We begin with thoughts about the **timing** of the birth of Jesus. Paul reminded his readers that Yahweh sent His Son "when the time came to completion." Another translation reads: "When the right time came, the time God decided on" (TLB). In other words, **Yahweh brought Jesus into this world at just the right time.** Bible interpreters have pointed to several facts that made this date the right time. For example, for the first time ever there was a system of roadways that made travel much easier throughout the entire Roman Empire. In addition the Greek language was well known in much of the world, aiding in better communication. Also, there was relative peace (Pax Romana) in most areas. All these factors combined to make the birth of Jesus very timely, especially the various missionary journeys to spread this good news. All these matters, and more, combine to affirm Yahweh's wisdom regarding the time of this special event.

What about the timing of events in your life? **Have you ever wondered why certain things happened for you when they did?** If you have placed yourself in Yahweh's hands, you can be certain that He arranges your calendar—the timing of various happenings. So often you will find yourself at a certain place or situation at "just the right time." When you become aware of this, pause and give Him thanks. He is worthy of your gratitude as the time-keeper of your life.

In earlier devotionals we have recommended the practice of beginning every day with this simple prayer of the psalmist: "My **times** are in Your hands" (Psalm 31:15). Such a commitment acknowledges your complete dependence upon Yahweh to arrange the events of that day—for your good and His glory. You can trust Him to be faithful and gracious.

Yahweh in Your Worship

I come before You, Holy Yahweh, to give praise and thanksgiving, especially for Your control.

December 19

Yahweh Gives Me an Example of True Worship

Yahweh in the Word

"Magi from the east came to Jerusalem" (Matthew 2:1).

The place of Jesus' birth was a small village about five miles south of Jerusalem. After He was born, some interesting men came to visit Him. These men were scholarly and known as magi. They were experts in the study of stars, such as astronomy and astrology. The Magi had observed in the heavens an unusual star that was interpreted to be a sign that the Jewish Messiah had been born. The knowledge of such a birth came from Jews who lived in their land, or from the Hebrew Scriptures. God may have given them a special revelation. At any rate, **these Gentiles traveled a great distance to find the Messiah and worship Him.**

Their search brought them to Judea. The assumption that the new "King of the Jews" would have been born in the palace of the capital city, led them to Jerusalem. No one in the city was aware of His birth and their arrival caused much trouble for the whole city. Disappointment or distance did not discourage their efforts to find and worship the Messiah. King Herod was a cruel and crafty man and would not permit anyone, not even his own family, to interfere with his rule or prevent the satisfying of his evil desires. He was troubled at the news of the birth of the new king and wanted him killed. The Wise Men immediately departed for Bethlehem. They located the Messiah in a house with Joseph and Mary. Kingly gifts were presented to the Child, followed by a respectful worship. The mission was accomplished and the magi departed.

Yahweh in Your Walk

Magi were a priestly group in ancient Persia. They are thought to have been followers of Zoroaster, the Persian teacher and prophet. The religion of the magi included astrology, demonology, and magic. (The word magic is derived from the word Magi.) By the first century A.D. the magi were identified with wise men and soothsayers. Thus, the biblical magi who came from the East to worship the infant Jesus were regarded as wise men. In our church Christmas program, we sing about the "Three Kings of the Orient," who followed a guiding star to Bethlehem to pay homage to the newborn Christ Child. They brought with them gold, the gift bestowed on kings, frankincense, used to worship at the altar of God, and myrrh, an embalming agent for the dead.

I am reminded of the three boys who were chosen to be the kings in our church Christmas pageant. Each boy wore a bathrobe and a towel around their heads. You would have thought they were really kings. The choir would sing "We Three Kings of Orient" and the little kings would regally walk down the aisle to their platform position.

Yahweh in Your Worship

Yahweh, provide me opportunities to share what Christ's birth really means to me. **Help me to be faithful to focus on You during these holidays.**

December 20

Yahweh Was In Charge Of Bethlehem

Yahweh in the Word

> *"And Joseph also went up from the town of Nazareth… to Bethlehem, the town of David" (Luke 2:4).*

The imperial decree of Caesar Augustus that all his subjects should enroll for tax purposes, brought May and Joseph to the town of Bethlehem. A prophecy was declared ages before that this place would be the site of the Messiah's birth (Micah 5:2) and Mary's child was born as foretold. The Jewish people were expecting a Messiah. They were looking for a certain person to be born among them whom God would use to deliver them from their enemies. Bethlehem was called the town of David, and Joseph belonged to the house and line of David. Jesse, the father of David, lived in Bethlehem and thus Bethlehem became David's town. The Lord Jesus did not gain any reputation from the place of His birth. The One, who is Bread of life, was born in an obscure hamlet whose name means "the house of bread."

Originally called Aphrah, the town also is referred to as Bethlehem-Judah to distinguish it from another Bethlehem (Joshua 19:15-16) in the territory of the tribe of Zebulun. Bethlehem is first mentioned in the Old Testament as the place where Rachel (wife of the patriarch Jacob) was buried (Genesis 35:19). Thus Jacob saw Bethlehem as a place of death, but the birth of Jesus made the little site a place of life. As a result of His birth, Israel would experience spiritual deliverance and in the future, the establishment of David's throne and kingdom. According to the book of Ruth, the village later became the home of King David's ancestors and of David himself (1 Samuel 17:12). Otherwise the town remained insignificant except for its connection to David.

Yahweh in Your Walk

Yahweh gave a tiny baby to a world torn by strife, poverty, injustice, and greed—just a common gift, yet what far-reaching benefits! Today, the same world has many of the same problems, with one exception—now there is hope for a better life because of Jesus' life, death, burial, resurrection, ascension, and promised return.

As you walk through these days of celebrating Yahweh's gift, take time to meditate on the personal benefits that are now yours in Him. And seek opportunities to share the message of His life with others. Make plans to join others for times of special worship, determine to make a generous financial gift so others may know of Him through an offering for world missions, and seek opportunities to be a witness of the true meaning of Christmas.

Yahweh in Your Worship

Thank You, Yahweh, for a place called Bethlehem. During this season help me understand more than ever the significance of Your gift of the Lord Jesus to me.

December 21

The Search for My Messiah

Yahweh in the Word

"King Herod… asked them where the Messiah would be born" (Matthew 2:4).

When the Magi arrived in Judea, they assumed that the new "king of the Jews" would have been born in the palace of the capital city. These visitors went in search of Him to Jerusalem. Perhaps they marveled that no one in the city was aware of His birth. However, to their credit, they did not allow distance or disappointment to discourage their efforts to find and worship the Messiah. Naturally Herod was troubled at the news of the birth of a new king. He alone wanted to bear the title "King of the Jews." So he quickly gathered the religious leaders and demanded an explanation from them. This group was probably the Jewish Sanhedrin, composed of experts in the Old Testament Scriptures.

The only reason for the king's interest in the situation was to destroy this potential rival to his throne. He responded to Christ in fear and hostility. Three groups of people were involved in this scene. The magi were seeking the King; Herod was opposing the King; and the Jewish priests were ignoring the King. An interesting point here is: the chief priest and scribes did not go to investigate the possibility of this birth. Even the visit of the mysterious Magi from the East was no motivation to find the truth. The king could find no one to help him locate this Messiah.

Yahweh in Your Walk

Every year at this time, local churches, large and small, seek to present a Christmas program and invite the public to attend. This outreach provides an opportunity for people to hear the true meaning of Christmas. Through a combination of music, drama, Scripture readings, and dance, this amazing story is presented. Many church groups write their own program and personalize the entire event. The most impressive scene to me is the visit of the wise men. They usually enter from the back of the church dressed in royal robes and march to the flourish of drums and trumpets. The audience is awed by the processional and a spot light follows these visitors to the front of the church. Then, the Magi go on the stage and one by one remove their crowns and bow before the Christ, the King of kings. Their gifts are presented to the baby Jesus.

One year a small boy on stage saw that Mary was having difficulty opening the gift. He came forward and asked if he could help her. The audience laughed and clapped at this serious decision made by a little boy to help the Christ Child. **This scene leaves me wanting to also bow before the Christ in praise and worship.**

Yahweh in Your Worship

Yahweh, help me focus on worshiping You at this special season that commemorates Your gift. Thank You that I do not need to travel and search for my Messiah; He is here with me.

December 22

Yeshua Goes to Egypt

Yeshua in the Word

> *"So Joseph took the child and his mother during the night and left for Egypt"* (Matt. 2:14).

The visitors from the East presented gifts fit for royalty before returning to their homeland. However, their visit started a chain reaction of events. Joseph, Mary, and Jesus escaped the wrath of Herod by fleeing to Egypt. Herod pretended to want to worship the newborn king when in reality he wanted to destroy the baby. This evil man slaughtered the infant boys, two years of age and under in Bethlehem. This tragedy was understood by Matthew as fulfilment of prophecy.

By now, Joseph was no stranger to receiving guidance through the Lord's angel. He established a pattern of listening and obeying. Yahweh spoke to Joseph in a dream and the little family departed for Egypt. This country lay within the Roman Empire, but outside Herod's jurisdiction. The journey covered about 100 miles. Many Jews lived in this distant place. Herod never felt secure in his position as king. He displayed a character that wanted to destroy any rival. Joseph avoided unnecessary risks and departed under cover of darkness. The child Jesus was called out of Egypt when Herod died and Joseph brought his family back to Israel. The prophecy of Hosea was fulfilled (Hosea 11:1).

Yeshua in Your Walk

Our family decided to spend Christmas in the Sacramento Mountains of New Mexico. A map was used to plan our trip. The car was packed with more than we needed for the vacation week and a cabin was rented near Cloudcroft. Our children, Mark and Martha, found a pine branch that became our tree. We collected items from nature to decorate the tree. Other objects like pine combs and leaves were used around the cabin for decorations. Evening walks in the snow were our favorite times.

One highlight, however, was from God, just for us! The Gemini 7 space program was in effect. These flights were made in 1965—1966. We would stand outside with a transistor radio and listen for news from Houston. All of a sudden we heard the Genesis creation story being read aloud by Lieutenant Colonel Frank Borman. You can imagine our surprise to hear God's Word being read from space. We stopped walking and looked up into the night sky. A tiny light was moving across the heavens and we watched until it disappeared out of sight. **Once again, we discovered that God is everywhere we go and we praised Him.**

Yeshua in Your Worship

Thank You, Father, for accomplishing Your purpose through Jesus, Your Son. Lead me to worship Yeshua every day during this season of celebration.

December 23

Yahweh Places Great Value on All Human Life

Yahweh in the Word

> "He (Herod) gave order to massacre all the male children in and around Bethlehem who were two years old and under in keeping with the time he had learned from the wise men" (Matthew 2:16).

King Herod the Great made a secret request of the magi, who had come from the east. He asked them to report to him where they found the newborn King, and he anxiously awaited their return. However, God directed the wise men and warned them not to revisit Herod. They went home by another route. The king became enraged focusing his anger at this infant boy.

Once again, God intervened to preserve the life of His Son. Mary, Joseph, and Jesus were long gone on their journey to Egypt when Herod's men came searching for the baby boys of Bethlehem. Through the centuries, Bible scholars have tried to guess how many babies were murdered. Perhaps 20 were slain based on the population of Bethlehem at that time. **Today, Christians place great value on human life and oppose any movement that ignores this truth.** Precious infants are born every day and in every color. Who knows but that Yahweh will raise up from these children special teachers of His Word and missionaries to go to the uttermost parts of the world, or godly parents who will rear their children to serve Him.

Yahweh in Your Walk

My favorite vacation site is the Hawaiian Islands. One year, my husband was invited to lead a revival in a local church during the Christmas season. A special event of the week was the retelling of Hawaii's history. Native foods, dances, and costumes were featured. I was introduced to an American Samoan prince. He and his family were living in Oahu while their son attended school. We began visiting and I asked him about his southern Pacific Ocean island. He explained how child sacrifices were once part of their pagan worship. Today, Christians in that same place worship the Son of God and honor their children. During the Christmas pageants on that island, reference is made to King Herod and the Samoan king, who called for children to be murdered. At the close of the revival, this family placed a beautiful lei around my neck and we rejoiced in Yahweh sending His Son into the world.

Yahweh in Your Worship

Yahweh, Your Son is so appreciated and loved. I pray for areas of the world that still abuse their children. Bless the missionaries around the world who will be retelling this wonderful story to all people this season. Provide the guidance needed to reach other people with this good news about a baby boy born in Bethlehem. May I be faithful to Your command to be a witness wherever I am. Make me aware of those nearby who need to know what Christmas is all about.

December 24

Yahweh Promises Hope and Victory for Me

Yahweh in the Word

> *"Bethlehem Ephrathah, you are small among the clans of Judah; One will come from you to be ruler over Israel for Me" (Micah 5:2).*

The Old Testament prophets often proclaimed doom in Judah and then followed that word with a message of hope. Micah's prophecy was given about 600 years before Christ was born. Though verse 1 of Micah is a prediction of danger, verses 2-5 are a prophecy of hope. Following his pronouncement that invaders would insult the king of Israel, Micah declared that the Messiah would be born in Bethlehem, a small town in Judah. Bethlehem means "house of bread." Yahweh often chooses to use little things and make much of them so that He receives the glory. This insignificant location would produce a deliverer who would save His people. The prophet contrasted the failure of the proud kings born in Jerusalem with the triumph of the future Redeemer. He would be a different kind of king and was identified as a member of David's line.

This king would be an ideal ruler. The only hope for Judah lay in the coming Messiah. The prophecy ultimately speaks of Jesus, and we are identified as His flock. **The Christian's hope is founded upon Jesus Christ.** All people must look to Him for peace with God and the peace of God in the world. This prophecy was shared with the Magi by the priests who were in Jerusalem (Matthew 2:1-12).

Yahweh in Your Walk

A Christmas card was once published with the title, "**If Christ Had Not Come.**" The card was presented to a local pastor by a stranger. The pastor, taking a short nap in his study on Christmas Eve, dreamed of a world into which Jesus had never come. No stockings hung on the mantel. No Christmas bells or wreaths of holly, no beautifully decorated Christmas trees, and no Christ to comfort and save us. The pastor walked out into the street, but no church was in view. He came back to his library and every book about the Savior had disappeared. A phone call requested a visit to a poor, dying woman. The pastor could only bow his head and weep in bitter despair. Two days later he conducted her funeral service. No message of consolation and no hope of heaven were available. The man woke-up from his nightmare and began praising Yahweh for His gift. What a difference the birth of baby Jesus had made in his life and message to his congregation. **We can easily agree with this pastor; our lives are radically changed by Him.**

Yahweh in Your Worship

Yahweh, Your gift to me is welcomed and blesses my life every day. I rejoice in the difference You have made in my Christmas celebration. Without Your Son, my heart would be filled with despair. Help me share this good news with others who remain in darkness. Remind me of practical ways I can become involved in getting the gospel message to those who need it.

December 25

Yahweh Wants Us to Keep "The Word" in Christmas

Yahweh in the Word

> *"The Word became flesh and took up residence among us" (John 1:14).*

Merry Christmas, Jesus! The Gospel of John is about Jesus and everywhere in the book Jesus is magnified. Matthew and Luke had already told the birth events in Jesus early life, so John did not go into detail about the angels, the wise men, Bethlehem, and the usual stories. The apostle John chose to go back further in history, back to the "beginning." His record of the incarnation of Jesus was not like a make-believe story. John believed that the Lord came to the earth. He was real and would experience what any human would encounter. The other disciples had personal experiences that convinced them of the reality of the body of Jesus. These men shared their encounter with the Messiah. John points out that the Son of God came in the flesh and was subject to the sin problems of humankind. How was the "Word made flesh?" The miracle of the virgin birth was the beginning (Matthew 1:18).

Yahweh in Your Walk

The season of Advent is a time for celebrations that focus on the expectation and birth of Jesus. One year I challenged my Bible study class to write an Advent devotional book. Each willing person recorded their thoughts about "the Word became flesh." Testimonies by these class members were thrilling to hear. Many had never thought about "the Word" becoming flesh. They just took this verse without much interest. **Advent begins on the fourth Sunday before Christmas and continues to Christmas Eve.** The word, "advent," comes from the Latin *adventus* meaning "arrival."

Various customs are associated with Advent. One that still survives in parts of Europe, notably in Germany, is the hanging of Advent wreaths. These are rings made up of sprigs of evergreens such as holly and ivy, into which are fixed four red candles. Each Sunday of Advent one candle is lit so that by Christmas all four candles are burning. Our church uses this time to decorate for the Christmas season. We call the program the "Hanging of the Greens." The worship service begins with nothing to view except the bare walls in the auditorium. Then throughout the program different items are carried in and used to make the worship center a beautiful place. Appropriate hymns and solos are used to enhance the experience. Different families are selected to light the four candles on the communion table wreath and read the appropriate Scripture passage. "The Word became flesh" is the central message of this meaningful event.

Yahweh in Your Worship

Thank You, Yeshua, that You are the one true Word. Help me to focus on what You have done for me this past year. Give me opportunities to share Your birth announcement with other people during this special time of celebrating Your Advent.

December 26

Yahweh's Name Is to Be Praised

Yahweh in the Word

> "Hallelujah! Give praise, servants of Yahweh; praise the name of Yahweh. Let the name of Yahweh be praised both now and forever. From the rising of the sun to its setting let the name of Yahweh be praised. Yahweh is exalted above all the nations, His glory above the heavens. Who is like Yahweh our God...?" (Psalm 113:1-5).

Several of the psalms begin with "**Hallelujah**," a Hebrew word meaning "praise Yahweh." (***Hallel*** means praise and ***jah*** is the shortened form of Yahweh.) This writer called upon his readers to focus on Yahweh's numerous acts of mercy.

Yahweh in Your Walk

Sometimes we experience an emotional letdown following all the activities and celebrations connected with Christmas. In fact, some persons suffer from the "Christmas blues," due to various psychological responses to this special season. However, **this psalm can help focus our attention on truths that lift our spirits as we recall Yahweh's many favors.**

Notice these words from this chapter that remind us of events associated with the first Christmas: "Yahweh... raises the poor from the dust and lifts the needy... in order to seat them with nobles of His people. He gives the childless woman a household, making her the joyful mother of children" (vv. 7-9). Joseph and Mary were probably among the poor of their day, and yet the birth of Jesus eventually caused this family to be seated among the "nobles" while making Mary the "joyful mother" she became. How gracious of Yahweh to choose this humble family to be the first home of our Savior. Indeed He is worthy of our praises—our Hallelujahs!

During this final week of the year, why not pause to reflect on all the many personal favors Yahweh has bestowed on you. **Spend time praising Him and celebrating what you have discovered about His special name this year.** Notice how this psalmist repeats this phrase three times in these verses: "Praise the name of Yahweh (vv. 1-3)." You may have never understood the significance of this special name before. Remember that our God is Yahweh whose name means "I AM." No other so-called god has this name because only Yahweh is the true and living God who provides everything we need in order to be and do all He plans for us.

Take the wise counsel of the psalmist and give repeated praise to the name of Yahweh.

Yahweh in Your Worship

Hallelujah! I seize this opportunity to express praise to You, most holy and gracious Yahweh. As I recall all Your mercies to me this past year, I humbly thank You for Your kindness. Help me look forward to a new year when knowing and praising Your name will be part of my worship.

December 27

Yahweh Gives Me Talents to Be Used in Serving Him

Yahweh in the Word

> "Moses then said to the Israelites, 'Look, Yahweh has appointed by name Bezalel son of Uri, son of Hur, of the tribe of Judah. He has filled him with God's Spirit, with wisdom, understanding, and ability in every kind of craft to design artistic works in gold, silver, and bronze, to cut gemstones for mounting, and to carve wood for work in every kind of artistic craft'" (Ex. 35:30).

The tabernacle was a very elaborate structure. Much skill was needed to make all the various components of this place for worship. Yahweh gifted a chosen man to lead this special process.

Yahweh in Your Walk

Some of the most beautiful and impressive buildings are places for worship. Many of these are amazing examples of architectural skill. Those who design and erect these structures are artisans whom Yahweh has gifted for this special work. We participated in the process of planning and building a worship center on just one occasion during our years of ministry. Yahweh was faithful to provide the right team of talented builders for this exciting project. One member of this team was also a leader of our church, a friend named Tommy Sanders. He had many years of experience in designing and building various structures. He was like Bezalel in our Scripture text for today—skilled in just the right abilities for this special project.

    There is a sense in which we are all called by Yahweh to be His builders. And He is faithful to give each of us just the right skills, talents, and spiritual gifts needed to do the kind of building He plans for us to do. For example, no task is more important than building a godly home—one where Jesus is honored and served as Lord and Master. Another noteworthy task is that of constructing a business where His purposes are carried out in a manner pleasing to Him. This list can go on and on as every honorable task in life is the result of gifted persons using His abilities.

    Just like Bezalel and Tommy, Yahweh has given you those special skills needed to fulfill His purpose through you. Your role is to develop these abilities and make them available to Him every day. As you are thinking about the New Year, why not make a serious commitment to serve Yahweh in the best possible ways? A simple pledge like this could make a real difference for you and others: **I will do the best I can with what I have, where I am for, Jesus' sake today.** Be sure to keep in mind that doing the best you can means relying on the Lord for the wisdom, strength, and skill you need. Your own "best" is not good enough; His "best" is better!

Yahweh in Your Worship

Thank You, Yahweh, for Your special gifts to me—the abilities to do tasks that are needed in building Your kingdom in this world. I want to be available as Your construction worker today. Without You I can do nothing, but by Your grace I can do all things.

December 28

Yeshua Invites Me to Take Living Water

Yeshua in the Word

> "Both the Spirit and the bride say, 'Come!' Anyone who hears should say, 'Come!' And the one who is thirsty should come. Whoever desires should take the living water as a gift" (Rev. 22:17).

The Revelation concludes with an invitation. All who are thirsty for living water are welcomed to receive it as a gift.

Yeshua in Your Walk

Many churches today are no longer using hymnals—the words to songs are projected on a large screen. While this provides a convenient way for worshipers to follow the lyrics and the leader, there is still an advantage to using hymnals in order to see the names of the hymn writers. Hymn stories have a way of enriching the meaning of the songs being sung. For example, one of the most frequently used invitation hymns is "Just As I Am," written by Charlotte Elliott (1789-1871). In her early thirties she suffered a serious illness that left her weak and depressed. During this time a well-known minister, Dr. Caesar Malan of Switzerland, came to visit her in her home in Brighton, England. When asked if she had peace with God, she replied that there were things in her life she wanted to clean up before becoming a Christian. He replied, "You must come just as you are." She took his wise counsel and trusted the Lord that day.

Some fourteen years later, she remembered his wise counsel and wrote these immortal words:

> Just as I am, without one plea, but that Thy blood was shed for me,
> And that Thou bidd'st me come to Thee, O Lamb of God I come! I come!
> Just as I am, and waiting not to rid my soul of one dark blot,
> To Thee, whose blood can cleanse each spot, O Lamb of God I come! I come!
>
> - - - - -
>
> Just as I am, Thy love unknown hath broken ev'ry barrier down;
> Now to be Thine, yea Thine alone, O Lamb of God I come! I come!
> Just as I am, of that free love the breadth, length, depth, the height to prove,
> Here for a season then above, O Lamb of God I come! I come!

The biblical text for this devotional is the final invitation in the Bible. **You are welcome to receive the free gift of Yeshua's living water.** He made this same offer to the woman at a well in Samaria (John 4:3-26). This living water is Yeshua Himself; He is the water of life that permanently quenches your thirst for life that has meaning and purpose. **Drink of Him daily!**

Yeshua in Your Worship

O Lord Jesus, I do worship You as the only One who can satisfy my thirst for life abundant.

December 29

Yahweh Offers Me His New Covenant

Yahweh in the Word

> *"Look, the days are coming, says Yahweh, when I will make a new covenant with the house of Israel and with the house of Judah... I will put My laws into their minds and write them on their hearts. I will be their God, and they will be My people... I will be merciful to their wrongdoing, and I will never again remember their sins" (Hebrews 8:8-12).*

The writer of Hebrews offers hope to his readers by reminding them of Yahweh's promise through Jeremiah many years earlier (Jeremiah 31:31-34). He goes on to declare that Jesus is the mediator of this new covenant (Hebrews 9:15).

Yahweh in Your Walk

A covenant, in the biblical sense, is an agreement based on promises. The first occurrence of the term ***covenant*** was when Yahweh promised Noah that He would never again destroy life on earth by a flood. The sign of this covenant was a rainbow. Now, each time we see a rainbow, we can be thankful to Him for this important covenant. Later covenants were initiated by Yahweh with Abraham, Moses, and David. Each of these involved a commitment from Yahweh to provide for the needs of His people.

A new covenant was promised through the prophets Jeremiah and Ezekiel. The Scripture text for today's devotional is a basic statement of this covenant. Yahweh promised to write His laws on the minds and hearts of His people. He sealed this covenant with the blood of the Lord Jesus on His cross. At the Last Supper Jesus declared, "This cup is the new covenant established by My blood; it is shed for you" (Luke 22:20). Every time we participate in the Lord's Supper, we commemorate this final and totally adequate covenant.

All this means that as believers we are Yahweh's covenant people—we live in a secure relationship with Him because His covenant is based on His promises and provisions for our needs. This new covenant is one of grace and mercy, and is not dependent upon our faithfulness, rather upon His faithfulness. Our part is to believe and receive His offer of life in place of the death we deserve.

As we look forward to a new year, we do so without the fear that we might somehow fail to obey Yahweh as we should, and thus lose our relationship with Him. He promises us **eternal** life, which means a life that is unending as well as abundant and victorious. Praise Him for His love!

Yahweh in Your Worship

I seize this opportunity to worship You Most gracious Yahweh. You are worthy of all honor, praise, and gratitude. Thank You for including me in Your forever, covenant family of grace.

December 30

Yahweh Will Support Me throughout My Life

Yahweh in the Word

> "Listen to Me, house of Jacob, all the remnant of the house of Israel, who have been sustained from the womb, carried along since birth. I will be the same until your old age, and I will bear you up when you turn gray. I have made you, and I will carry you" (Isaiah 46:3-4).

Yahweh spoke to His people through Isaiah the prophet to assure them of His personal care as long as they live. He promised that just as He provided for their needs from the time of birth, He would continue the same support when they become old.

Yahweh in Your Walk

As another year comes to a close, you can look back and recall Yahweh's faithfulness to provide all you have needed during these months. Think about all the persons He used to help sustain you—family members, friends, doctors and nurses, plus a multitude of people who met your physical needs by producing food, clothing, housing, and on and on the list goes. Working through all these helping hands has been the faithful, sustaining care of Yahweh—He is the ultimate source of all the provisions and providers we enjoy.

When I think of Yahweh working through His chosen servants to meet needs, I remember a dear man and his wife in our church—John and Kay Rush are the leaders of our ministry to senior adults. As I read our Scripture text where Yahweh says, "I will carry you," I think of how the Rushes use both their cars, plus a church bus to literally carry seniors to church, to doctors' appointments and many other activities. Yahweh literally carries His people through John and Kay. And she always has a sack of goodies to give each person. What a blessing these servants are, both by their selfless actions but also by their good example to the rest of us. (See Nov. 10)

Recently, I asked John if he had a special Bible verse that was meaningful to him. He quickly replied, "For me to live is Christ, and to die is gain" (Philippians 1:21). He went on to say that he wanted that verse inscribed on his grave marker. This coming Sunday morning, John will baptize a man and his wife who came to believe in Jesus as their Savior through the kindness and witness of John and Kay. The fact that this couple is African-American is all the more meaningful to us since they are the first of their race to become members. Yahweh used the Rushes to "carry" these new believers to our church and to Himself.

Who do you "carry"? If you are not serving in this manner, ask Yahweh to give you the pleasure of being His hands and feet to bring others to Himself. He will answer your prayer.

Yahweh in Your Worship

Thank You, most merciful Yahweh for reaching me through others. Now help me be a carrier.

December 31

Yahweh Wants Me to Seize Every Day with Him

Yahweh in the Word

> "I will praise Yahweh at all times; His praise will always be on my lips. I will boast in Yahweh; the humble will hear and be glad. Proclaim Yahweh's greatness with me; let us exalt His name together" (Psalm 34:1-3).

These words of praise from David express his commitment to continually boast in Yahweh, proclaim His greatness, and exalt His holy name.

Yahweh in Your Walk

We (Val and Jim) want to thank you for joining us as we have walked together through this past year. The idea of seizing the day with Yahweh has been a growing experience of learning the significance of this very special name and how it applies to our daily living. We trust that you have also made progress in your understanding of Yahweh and how significant is His name.

    Allow us to briefly recap some of the more important truths we have explored this year:

    1. Yahweh first revealed His name to Moses at a burning bush in the desert. He said to him, "Say this to the Israelites: Yahweh, the God of your fathers, the God of Abraham, the God of Isaac, and the God of Jacob, has sent me to you. **This is My name forever; this is how I am to be remembered in every generation**" (Exodus 3:15). Yahweh is God's covenant name.

    2. The name "**Yahweh**" basically means, "I AM." By giving His name to Moses, Yahweh was revealing His eternal nature—"I AM, I always have been and always will be—the only true and eternal God." Moreover Yahweh was giving Moses the assurance that whatever he needed to bring His people out of bondage and into the land of promise—I AM. His name says to us today, "I AM whatever you need to be and do all that pleases Me." Yahweh is our complete sufficiency.

    3. Yahweh has many titles such as Father, Lord, Master, Almighty God, Elohim, Redeemer, Savior, Holy Spirit, but only one name—Yahweh. His Son's name Jesus is **Yeshua** in Hebrew and means "Yahweh is salvation" or "I AM salvation."

    4. We have looked at the many combinations of Yahweh's name, such as Yahweh Yireh, Yahweh Rophe, Yahweh Nissi, Yahweh Shalom, and others. **Each of these reveals more about Yahweh's provision for all our needs. We are complete in Him.**

Yahweh in Your Worship

I seize this opportunity to worship You, Holy Yahweh. Thank You for revealing Yourself to me more fully. This year has been a journey of learning. I look forward to the New Year with You.

Printed in the United States
By Bookmasters